GOON

ESOTERIC OUTLAWISM
&
GUN-SLINGIN' METAPHYSICS

BY

CLAWSON SMITH

ISBN: 978-0-578-70647-4

To he who deals out only in the sunlight and wields iron, who treads the wild paths and answers to only his heart, this work is dedicated to you. May the gods ever remember your name and deeds.

CONTENTS

SIX-SHOOTER PHILOSOPHY

Words should be bullets and books loaded guns.

Shooting and writing anything remotely philosophical should follow the same rules: fire only when you mean it and shoot goddamn straight! Blow your opponent's brains out! Don't pull the trigger if you don't know what will happen. Don't speak about Big Ideas unless you're prepared to live with the consequences. In this decadent age where thoughts or words are violence—and while so many works try so desperately to come off as neutral—this book is a cocked Navy Colt on your nightstand. All books *should* be this way—dangerous, unorthodox, and make you feel the burning sensation on the back of your head in a library. You should be banned from society for reading such things and join all the other idea-pariahs in the wild, you heathen!

Poetry is most eloquently spoken by gunfire.

Did you pick up this venomous piece of literature for entertainment? Did you want to live vicariously through the life of an irredeemable maniac? I hope you're ready for that late-night train ride where an urban youth sees you reading this and bludgeons you for such sin. If not...perhaps you should try reading something safer, like Hemingway or *My Life As An Immigrant Sucks, White People Suck, Weep For Me* by Somalian Woman #196.

Thousands of books of the abstract are published a year on how you should think, speak, and act. They also happen to be published by faggots who jerk off to their own sterile thinking—the equivalent of a dork who walks up to their lane at a shooting range, fumbles with their retard-proof Glock 17, and discharges an entire magazine of blanks.

Call me a bigot if you so prefer, but this truth is unquestionable: philosophy would cease to proliferate in such a terrestrial manner if pretentious academics could be legally drawn and quartered in the public square!

I, the voice of this book, am no such snob. I am the spirit of a burglar stealing into the houses of the genteel, pseudo-crats of Hollywood—replacing all their $1000 designer vodka with plastic Taaka, scrawling dicks on their post-modern 'paintings' in fat sharpie, taking a plasma cutter to the backs of their toilets, and leaving an effigy in Elder Futhark on their walls. You won't find my voice at any conference or expo of babbling sycophants.

I didn't write this tome—it was channeled through my body like the high-pressure ventricular valve spurting the blood of the gods down my throat. The passages within were not concepted in some college dorm room or in some sterile 'designer' office, but in the realm of the insolent: in the beer-soaked shadows of a run-down party house, within the silent slot canyons of the desert, and on the rebellious pages in a seminary president's study. I don't claim to own any of these ideas, only that they are the authentic ways of Man—the steel that shapes the cylinder of the revolver.

It *should* read like sandpaper scrubbed on the eyes of a yuppie hipster who picked this up on your coffee table, admiring my ex-Art School touch on the cover. He'll yowl with IPA in hand, bleeding eye sockets, cursing my name for eternity. Good. This work was designed to stomp on the pretentious paper-thin philosophies catered to soothe the dopamine-rotted minds of our generation.

This book did not come to me with the intention of useless insult or even the subtlest of deception. So I will not mince meaning nor extort sympathy from you in translating its ideas. One of the greatest travesties I experience daily in the modern world is that people are predictably soft on their intentions and rarely convey their bare opinions. Shameful. I will openly mock for what I see fit, nothing more.

In return for these bullets of ideas, you will swear you will not commit the foulest crime of mischaracterization: willfully misunderstanding. I have left no stone unturned in this tome of mine and would prefer you to analyze my life with the sharpest razor of skepticism. Even if you are among the slime-regurgitating race of propagandizing sub-humans known as journalists I demand this: don't paraphrase me. Leave my words whole and untarnished by your ribald trickery. Others can decide for themselves if this is a work worth reading swallowing the fecal slush of some nu-age news site.

If the truth of a man's journey in its raw form is what you came for—to glean from my flesh some understanding—then you came to the right place.

Philosophy of the 21st century is the pastiche of the intellectually-minded and the con artist. It is highly regrettable that the 'art' of philosophy is irradiated with the malaise of pretentiousness. Marcus Aurelius and his *Meditations* is left preserved behind the glass of the past, but we cannot have modern philosophers because the term is worth fuck-all now. Philosophy once meant the aesthetics of one's life, the export of their experiences culminating into a timeless artifact that could be examined later. Not a guide to life but a written *experience* of it. Philosophy was never about verbal gerrymandering and overly-articulate ciphers attempting to sound overly prophetic and intelligent...yet here we are.

The modern world is full of those who declare themselves philosophers and intellectuals. You'll sooner find an egg-headed dork like Vox Day before an enlightening Zarathustra. Sturgeon's Law or no, this is the truth. So many want to be known for how intellectual and refined they are. My first piece of advice in this book is if you meet one of these goofy types who call themselves an 'intellectual' you should immediately spit on their shoes, call them a shrimp-faced bitch with an overinflated sense of superiority and inform them that their glasses make them look like a pedophile. And if you can get away with it, slug 'em in the face.

If I began this book telling you that this was merely a work of '*radical heraldry in the conflict against modernism, esotericism spoken from the mouth of a dissident and barbarian*' it sounds more romantic than spiritualism and philosophy. But I have legitimacy to these things. I have lived through them. And the truth is, I have much to say about ideas and believe strongly in the classic archetypes of philosophy after all this time—of Aurelius, Aristotle, Nietzsche, Thoreau, Heidegger, Evola, Kierkegaard, Cicero, and others. I believe in bludgeoning your enemies and shitting outside. But I also believe there's an invaluable and often unasked question to be asked: what does the average man gain from reading philosophy—even mine?

Animals retain a level of 'self-perpetuation' that they can adapt and survive. We humans have this but also through intuition—the undefined aspect of our soul. Hamsters don't build 5G towers or missile-proof bunkers. We humans have a collective intelligence in this strange post-liberal time, much like the dark recesses of the internet. Endless collective potential and intelligence without wisdom.

Human intuition in the capacity both large and small is not secular but a spiritual channel. Our focus can be one or a thousand bees driving their stingers into a bear's underbelly. A vigorous fountain of raw intelligence we possess that previously could have upset nations, unraveled churches, and altered the course of humanity. That spiritual intelligence cannot be studied under a microscope by some dweeb who likes Big Bang Theory. That soul is best and must be analyzed by philosophy, the most fallen art.

A fatal error that occurs is this concept of what I call 'The Classical Music Conundrum' as it pertains to philosophy: the idea that intelligence and spiritual understanding occur when one listens to classical music or reads philosophy all day. "*Once we listened to Beethoven but now all we have is Snoopdog*", they say. Utter fucking nonsense. That music was reserved for the snobbish elite—none for the rabble! All save for a minuscule fraction of posh humanity was unable to truly feel the effects of classical orchestras, no matter its instrumentality to the mind. Folk music developed, I would argue, the foundation of what would become the music of the everyday man: rock, blues, metal, rap, punk, etc.

Even the immortal Nietzsche fell into this trap of believing that only the high-brow, top-wit types would associate with his ideals. Hundreds of thousands have read his work and gained some inspiration from it. Few understand the Will to Power and his view on morality I would posit, nonetheless Nietzsche is not a rare philosopher. Philosophy is not profane in this way because it is such a common figure. It is profane because it is a tool and often abused for the wrong purposes, otherwise attempted to cater to the masses. Would you let a retard with a jackhammer dig at your house's foundation to pry only a few staples?

Philosophy cannot trump one's intuition—it should be symbiotic, that it does not rob one of their intelligence but that it aids it through wisdom. It should be personal to every man. The reason why so many lobotomites called our 'fellow humans' adopt abstract philosophic ideals, not for their merit or understanding but as a couch-served scape rope—their intuition sucks, so they need to rely on the Mommy Establishment so they can devote time to metaphorically stare into a corner. When they could have figured this out for themselves by action, they would rather be tattooed by the baboons of Authority. Modernity's cruel devices have tricked people who might otherwise be autonomous that they must suckle the tit of toxic waste that is fed to them through every form of media possible.

Many philosophies are utter garbage because they are built by those who are worthless. They are obese trust-fund babies of New York who mentally masturbate. Don't trust any man who spends his entire life in an office or in a lounge contemplating what everyone should believe. His mindset will be one of fast food bags, Xerox sounds, and the hum of his insect dominion. Ideas, by the way, cannot occur or be found via a bubble nor vacuum. Weak people spawn weak ideas for the same reason that planting a coffee bean in irradiated dirt will give you poisoned weeds. Jocko says "GOOD" in the face of adversity because his philosophy revolves around grinning at the idea of conflict like a neo-Stone Age gorilla man and punching it in the mouth.

Authenticity backed by experience is the sharpest of tools.

Philosophy in its abstract form has persisted like a crippled rabbit. Plenty of modern intellectual types spend their entire saga of writing about the 'fall of liberalism', attributing it to any number of factors with the tools of philosophic dissection before preaching—impending doom is coming for the neoliberal world. Even if they are right, what benefit does that bring to the average man? Why tell him his world of luxury and comfort will end in a nation-sundering civil war with his countrymen, his family butchered and fashioned into edgy Fallout-type costumes and neighborhoods sunk beneath lakes of blood because some Frenchman's ideas were warped? Why lie to him rather than the truth: that liberalism fails because it is weak.

While there is truth to it, what is the intention of abstract philosophy and the pursuit of assimilating these bloated concepts of academia?

Fear is the simple answer. Fear controls us, or rather it can. Fear is the eldest and most powerful tool of the thinker. Even if these other philosophers point out that these electric-chairs of emotion are shoved beneath us—to control our actions, how does give man the capacity to free himself

Why do you think that comic-book and action movies from Hollywood are so effective at ensnaring your average media-consuming man? They pander with charismatic celebrities with relatable archetypes, slap them down into a pseudo-realistic setting, squeeze sympathy from the audience, and then pose a fake threat to these hypothetical character's lives with fake 'fear'—drawing upon the protective herd-instincts rooted deep within us. You'll find there's little substance to the 'epic speeches' given by some character and grow bored before he blasts away to the drop of some overplayed, jiving 70's rock tune to smoke some alien scum.

I could simply replicate what the entertainment

industry has done effectively for over a hundred years: coerce people into mindsets by advertising fear, sex, and the promise of 'adventure'. I am no such manipulator. I do not believe in fear, except in the basest of self-preservation. Fear is for cattle and those willing to be cattle. The keyword there is willing, of course. Intuition cannot survive while it is controlled. And that is precisely what the modern world demands: servants yoked by the created fears of coercion.

My conviction is that philosophy is not fallen because it is useless but because it has no practicality. It can only exist in this temporal thinking realm reserved for academics and the word-salad chefs of the world. Otherwise hacks, hucksters, and flabby retards. A man of the 21st century should start studying Kublai Khan rather than Hegel for this reason—the world we inhabit is one of inauthentic abstraction. Ideals are marketed like flash-pan holiday trends.

Some might say I chose the Western theme due to its inherent 'edgy' nature—that this book is performance art for the wannabe criminal. I say because Goonhood is not only born of the West, but it operates under the same framework.

I grew up on Western films and have since realized a critical aspect of their theme—there isn't this overarching good versus bad. There's always an *ugly*, a gray anomaly of morality that strikes a chord in the common man: the dynamic of the sinner. Everyone has wickedness in them, a little bit of anti-hero, and a vice. An unspoken dogma—it is this reason that everybody is strapped with Winchesters and Colts—knowing that a 'friendly face' at poker could unload lead into their face at any moment. Lawmen are easily corrupted, their principles waver at the sight of unclaimed cash. Hookers and barkeeps are capricious. The vacuum of power is tempting to all.

I have gravitated towards the morality of the Western for many reasons. Firstly, I find the spirit of the European explorer in a harsh land—specifically the fur-trapper, mountain men, and outlaws to reflect the same noble virtues seen in Indo-European societies and worthy of adopting. Cowboy or outlaw, prairie wife or cantina whore, The West seems like a recourse of traditional archetypes. Or the raw spirit of the masculine and feminine, raw and untainted by the monotheistic vice of domination, global politics, and so forth.

I returned to this after reading Nietzsche and Voltaire as I explored the barren rim of coyote territory. Such thinkers led me to believe, through hiking meditations, that assimilating truth requires blood and sweat in return for wisdom. We can clean our rooms and speak the truth as Jordan Peterson says—yet what is this 'self-improvement' good for if we dwell in bunkers hidden from the world? If living yearns to be explosive exaltation of passion, how do we commit while squander our years in layers of security and neurotic gymnastics?

In other words, *what the fuck* are all these other books on 'development' if you remain a good little rule follower—afraid of some cactus and sun?

So is Goonhood a philosophy book?

That depends if you can empathize with my tales of the wastes—as a child and man—are worth adopting. If you'll listen to a former Mormon, Boy Scout, and an anti-intellectual.

See, I did not write this for the caste of those flagellating intellects who jealously guard their sub-par knowledge behind vaults of academia and paywalls. Nor to persuade the open-minded. I am what can be closely approximated to the outlaw, clinging to my bandit fort in the hills, offering you what values I have learned in exchange for your money and blood.

Gods willing, I would demand the offering of no less than a dozen scalps in return for this book. A hundred! Sadly, I don't think I would sell very many copies if this were the case. Scalps are not a common currency of this commercialized epoch....*unfortunately*.

WELCOME TO THE NU-AGE

What gods do you pray to?

Are they 'ok' with your punchable lesbian of a sister? Do these deities tolerate your atheist friends who are 'spiritual but not religious' because they wanted to smoke weed and slay some puss in high school—only so they would avoid singing hymns and wearing a goofy suit? Have you sacrificed anything more than a minute naming these gods rather than wincing at the thought of slitting even a chicken's throat and washing the soil with its blood—just for a scrap of divine favor? Are your gods strong, or do they wither in their computer chairs like the pathetic ham planets that make up nearly fifty percent of the First World population? Can your gods even communicate to you through concrete floors and your overpriced hipster furniture?

Have you ever pondered why pagans and Christians wear symbols of historically metal-as-fuck gods whose triumphs are remembered for bludgeoning their enemies with magic and steel—never a virile patron 'god of merchanting' who promises bounteous interest rates to bankers? Does it ever occur to you that those NASA t-shirt wearing fags who worship Big Science and the retarded star-fuck determinism of Neil Degrasse Tysons are just as zealous as the Westboro Baptists?

No god's name dances on your tongue, you say? You claim to have none! I say claim because regardless if your answer is that you have none, this is a lie—*every* man has a god.

If you have a phone currently, drop it. Break it even. You won't find the real gods on the internet, in your curated 'newsfeeds' or in the Tinder bio of a mindless, 20-something female who slothfully fishes for attention from their dozen subhuman beta-male simp goblins—there are gods there, Aphroditean even, but they are not the kind to be worshipped. Better you save yourself and abandon the craven addiction of social media status than to become an effigy to it. Darker gods hide in the walls of unsalvageable Rat Metropolises, on the breath of hookers and the bags of fentanyl. Their corporate logos are scattered by the thousands in apocalyptic piles of plastic we pile into the earth. So many are unwilling clergymen, the subconscious cult of modernity who is oblivious to their carnal sacrifices.

Here is where I slash a rusty razor at your ankles to shame—you, modern man, have been a participant to the experiment of secular religious studies and have perhaps heard of said gods in your revisionist textbooks, under the glow of industrial lighting, in the synthetic cubes of schools. A pathetic method of education, truly. Yet there is a character who wanders outside the Ruins of the West, who spits on your gods, cannibalizes their corpses, and leaves them to bake under the solar glow of the true and immaterial powers!

He is the cultured thug and he's come to piss on the walls of your establishment and slap your girlfriend around...

The Goon!

You probably take strolls through your neutered cities, going out for a bite by the strip malls with your companions, more likely your wife. You've probably observed a group of hoodlum-types, skateboarders, 'urban youth' who collect on the corner of a parking lot. In the hair of a breath you lock eyes with the red-rimmed, bleak gaze of a stoner, floating on his heels through life and you wonder: how do they seem so content? How can an Adderall-gulping loser—filling the air with inane slang derived from a rap-culture you barely grasped yourself in adolescence—seem so carefree of the world? As you stomp ahead, you probably assure yourself it's the drugs—when it wears off, the stoner will be miserable like you.

But that's not the only thought that disrupts your daily motions. As your girlfriend pouts, you bullrush into the chain restaurant, snorting at the menu as the thoughts linger and steep in your brain:

"Was it always this bad? Were there always so many of them? Where do these jobless punks live? Are they committing a crime? Are they going to spray my eyes with acid and rob me goddamn blind? Why hasn't anyone done anything about this? Shit, is this going to get worse?"

By now your girlfriend looks concerned—eyes bulging as her mouth moves but you're belligerently ignoring her, seething as you order your indigestible, gluten-free, vegan, romaine rabbit meal with 'organic' ingredients and a whole encyclopedia of random food items that escape your knowledge. You furiously stuff your debit card into the reader as a Mongol warrior thrust his seed inside every Chinese broad from Tibet to Beijing. Now gravity has taken over—this boulder of thought is rushing down the peaks of intellect into the valley of your conscience.

Surely this cannot go on much longer. Society can

only handle so much dead weight. Is rap music really turning them into these degenerates? Or is it weed? You tried weed once at a party and you came out functional. Is this normal? How does civilization continue when the vulnerable youth leer on the fringes of your centers of commerce—the comfortable fast-n-fresh restaurants and false luxury sold to the middle class—that are your stomping grounds.

It dawns on you like an unsealed carton of eggs left in your storage room: all those history classes mentioning the threat of Barbarians At the Gates™ are occurring before your eyes on a completely ordinary evening. No longer are they a pack of stringy stoners and wayward children but Visigoths and Khans with fluid moral compasses and instinct for self-preservation—complete with their own gang infrastructure, initiation rituals and insular codes of honor. They've run from the cops numerous times, know what gas station worker won't inspect ID for packs of American Spirit, and have a mental map of the local area via skateboard. Their cousins are in jail and they will soon join them. The suburbs may as well be the wild of the West Papua and these hooligan kings the indigenous nomadic tribes of the jungle for their micro-knowledge of the terrain.

You realize that you gobbled the lie of sterility and could pay the ultimate price right here in the parking lot. Even if you have a gun strapped to your waist, a cold sweat creases your brow. Because we've co-existed with this violence hierarchy for documented tens of thousands of years and longer than that: waging spiritual warfare, kin slaying, romantic butchery, and unending gore oceans of genocide. Suddenly it's no longer about the threat they pose to you in the current moment because that history is your reality.

Suddenly you're angry because modernity beguiled you with wordy manipulation, convincing your subservient subconsciousness that this kind of primitive behavior isn't acceptable anymore. That our society doesn't drive on a complex, organic woodchipper of meta-instincts and barbaric compulsions fueled by our worst tendencies. You were told you were advanced beyond the 'bigotry of yesteryear'. You don't need to concern yourself with the restless barbarism that coincides with moral law zero—that every creature and being must persist and will do so along innumerable moral frameworks.

'We're civilized now. Women have rights and we're progressing towards...not a utopia, but maybe a better world...' you blindly mumble as you prepare to head back out to the parking lot:

"People have porn and Netflix now...isn't that enough?"

Is it? The fact that you have even uttered such a question should indicate that the answer is embedded in your insecurity: you knew this all along, brainless. This thug with a sharp-eyed gaze is what you could have been, had you acknowledged the Nietzschean truths. What even was that crazed German talking about? Didn't Hitler praise him? The philosophical rug was ripped out from beneath you moments ago—you just realized that you're in limbo.

You should feel robbed of your identity from the marrow of your upper skeletal frame to the adrenal juices that pump through your veins. Your core purpose as a human, as a vitally competent being whose purpose is to protect and hunt. Not some paper-counting money shrew and limp-wristed 'ally' to perceived slights against 'minorities and women'—a code-writer with manboobs whose job is to maintain some gay and useless application on some spinster's tablet. No, this is not mankind.

As a real man once said: 'I'M AN EXPLORER. I'M A PIONEER! I'M A HUMAN!' You call that man deranged but he'll have more red blood cells as a withered 90-year old worm than your firstborn son in his prime! Are you starting to understand the wisdom of the neo-reactionary gorilla Texan Alex Jones and the vitality of bold, if not insane declarations? Has it dawned on you that this cultured thug—this utter Chad—is radioactive with his confidence and yet you cannot figure out how this helps you?

By now your girlfriend's shrill petitions may as well be a mouse's dying whisper in this scenario, because my knife of artistic clarity just fucking skinned, gutted and scalped you like grass-chewing herd animal modernity has made you into. I'd make a trophy of your corpse but it'd be worthless on a wall—you're one of millions. An unwary, inoffensive, and worst of all manageable types of prey. A docile rule-follower and obedient drone navigating through life on autopilot, clocking in and out of consciousness with utter indifference.

You believed that these monsters didn't exist anymore.

In any time in history, there is but one vice, one currency that man is subject to: power over others. The instinct to lord over others, mold the world-clay with your fingers, and to leave your mark in the annals of history are the strongest drives. Only a liar would say he has not felt the magnetic pull of this temptation. The exchange of this currency is the gasoline that fuels the engines of civilizations. Like water it can never truly be "destroyed" but liquify and disperse. It can shapeshift and alter, but will always return to the hands of Man.

How does one get more of it? War of course, our most natural tendency. Yet soldiers are optional. A uniformed mass can do more harm than good. If one is under heavy scrutiny and must operate "in the shadows" to consolidate power, how does one carry it out?

What do Al Capone, The Taliban, Communists, and the FBI have in common? Using anonymous enforcers to carry out their dirty work and ideological mission. To enact violence against their enemies ambiguously, using the types of criminals and savages who have questionable morality. These organizations employ the type of men who are "allowed" to act primitively in order to conduct activities normally restricted for your average footsoldier. A Nietzschean privilege, you could say.

This is the Goon archetype.

But not all Goons have served as enforcers, nor have they always been useful to society. Outlaws number among this crowd—those who didn't rob banks but merely ignored the civilization that crawled behind them by train. Varangian guard chose to help the Byzantines but could have joined either side. Guns for hire were aplenty fighting communists in the jungles of Africa—even to this day. Men who have no qualms for violence and adhere to a code of meritocracy are the most dangerous and useful to those who clutch for power. Specifically...the esoteric Goon who abides by more ancient codes and rules than the flimsy ones of today. Those who have nothing to lose or everything.

This ideological Goon is something else entirely.

Unlike his compatriots who bag the families of rival cartels, or who set fire to a union building to intimidate them, the ideological Goon is calloused against the World that seeks to use him. He does not play the role of a pawn of any organization or bureaucracy—he sets his mind on breaking bricks of these bloated institutions rather than kneecaps. Using anonymity he can carry out the Will of gods, of ancient values, or of values entirely foreign to the greedy Tyrants of Modernity. And if they are educated? These Goons are imps revolting against the devil's programming—leading other such horned spawn and hallowed souls away from the hellscape that the mindless mob occupies.

Goons are unconcerned with the societal honey-traps of amoral and illegitimate, liberal laws. The cultured thug does not possess a shred of empathy for those who ignore the 'inner morality' of the overman. We understand that there are men like us—these deprived creatures of impulse who cave into their instincts for looting and rape. Yet we are not these mindless hooligans.

Do goons care about living freely in a plastic society? Freedom is possible only to the being who can secure it himself by any means necessary.

I don't have a utopian ideal for you to breathlessly pledge to—that's the job of moronic idealists! Goons are not idealists, such as the circular-thinking, cone-headed Molyneaux types whose mommy issues leave them with liquified frontal lobes and money fetishes. The Goon lambasts the idealist for their inconsequential ideas of materialism, inflated self-worth, or unachievable ideas.

Neither do we wear the badge of milquetoast narcissism, thinking ourselves somehow intellectually superior to such cone-heads. I and my comrades am too cognizant of how petty self-adulation is. We are grounded by experience, leathery palms, and simple understandings. Our hierarchy simply has no room for fucking know-it-alls. We are the clergy of Lord Byron, those who dance under the pale moonlight on the graves of the moral purists and chest-beating humanists. We are the reincarnated ghosts of guile and violence.

And how did we get here? How did I get here? The path to it is natural and it is inherited, yet another you may discover. My own conversion to Goonhood has drawn long but is easily explained—I grew bored of the ineptitude of the modern world, disgusted with its rhetoric, and reviewed my life in its fullest. When I was asked as a child "what do you want to be when you grow up" I never considered being rich or influential. I wanted to explore without aim—flex on the boundaries and to heed authority when I wanted to. Even as a kid I knew materialism was for fags and modern housewives.

Goons need authenticity. Tools and brotherhood. We cannot survive against The Horde without them. These instruments that lead to revelations of the world are not so you have something to whine and kvetch about like the knee-jerking anti-SJW, nerdy YouTuber types—hardly the case at all. Goonhood is utility, the toolbelt at your side, and should not be abused or treated lightly. It is a choice that you willingly make when faced with your reality.

I did not come here to merely preach about what I

think.

I came here to tell you how I discovered this six-shooter of wisdom by what I did.

There is a way out of the nebulous nothing that we drift through—a desperate and bleak future. I believe it is in the hands of Goons. They hold the solution to the madness: authenticity. Death of the ego and the self-actualized spirit. And so my demand is repeated:

What gods *do* you pray to?

Who are *your* prophets?

What spiritual philosophy governs *your* existence?

The psyche of you, the identity-obsessed modern human, might now turn on your narcissistic soul and ask a question: what exact spirit speaks to me? This is your own shadow—the daemon as carefully recognized by the Ancient Greeks.

Sadly we are not sitting on the slopes of untamed lands, cross-legged Bronze Age men in furs before the campfire, chewing on the limbs of rabbits caught by our merit—such as Conan when he so casually inquired of his newfound warrior bro from the perspective of one raised by the harsh and judgmental Crom. We are not afforded such luxuries in the modern world to have the inquisitive mind of a barbarian thrust upon an unfamiliar landscape, eager for adventure. Our world is not so fantastical.

Yet there has and will be awakening.

The youth cannot be kept from the knowledge that their fellow man forever, these 'herd animals' were created by these godless, bureaucratic circumstances. Like the Germans of Weimar, bitterly aware that the world loathed and laughed at them, curb-stomped into an era of destitution and depravity that eventually turned them into madmen in a Mayan-like frenzy of blood and sacrificial darkness—our generation's fate is no less violent.

If you have a pulse and even with that monkey-lizard brain under that skull, at your core you know that for all the jewels of the modern world cannot sparkle or hold luster enough to hide the fetid slime that lies beneath. You know under the layers of commercialization and programming, the true nature of the Leviathan as some have called it, contemporary civilization and its urban jungles are truly wicked. It can change the sex of amphibians and much worse to boot.

The napalm truth is that the sterile, modern man—referred to aptly by BAP as the bugman or the Orwellian slave—has regressed to primate form by the facade of progressivism. They've been sold on the covenant pushed by the prophets of commerce and sworn allegiance to techno-Babylon. That *is* a god with a cult who has initiated a devolution, turning strong forms into grovelers who hoot at holograms of females, rotting their teeth with sugar and injections of daily chemicals. The modern male has been domesticated and 'hollowed', programmed to follow traffic codes with nobody to watch, dressed in a suit and tie in constant fear that Big Mommy Government. Or, if it suits our faceless establishment, that our men are to act as the mass crude tools of violence and depravity—to reduce our lives to rubble.

Women of the modern spirit can only take 3 forms. The first, sour drones who've been programmed to go against their base instinct and pretend to be like men—turned into spinsters with little hope of ever recovering and recognizing their feminine soul. Second, you have the quirky 'New Girl' Zoey Deschanel type who stuffs non-threatening men around her in a cushioned simp-bubble, pretending to be Audrey Hepburn with snappy spunk. The last are simply objects of desire, totems of flesh, and cruel aberrations who have torn at their clothes and demanded to be worshipped as a goddess of lust. All three are depraved and nothing but shadows of the feminine

Venus.

Tell me that this whole event is not a religion of decay and submission and I'd tell you to chew on an icepick.

Indeed, the spirits of man and woman have been corrupted but no less zealous. We have lived through such dark times in ancient days with only our fists and that same monkey-lizard brain ejaculated into the brutal primordial world as infants. We were cast into endless plains and tundra ruled by chainsaw-tooth, SUV-sized bears who fed exclusively on mammoths and sabertooths, capable of sprinting at six times any man's speed and prevented any dwellings from being erected by their sheer tenacity. An era where gods were as dark and cruel as the environment man was forced into. In a twisted way, I believe that if such creatures existed again in our weakened time, our peoples—not to be confused with the finicky creations we call civilizations—would be brought to our collective knees, with all our technologies.

Every time we slam the button to restart society, we rediscover what we are: the transcendent spirits of flesh and soul. For example in times of crisis and hardship, churches see massive boosts to their attendance and sign-ups—the common man will turn to Jesus Drive-Thru 'spirituality' to calm his panicky monkey-self. With every hurricane, plague, or war there is a vindication of the idea of the post-Titanic civilization where trials will peel off the counterfeit layers of a man's soul, reducing him to his basest and raw: a creature controlled by fear. That fear—like the cosmic horror Lovecraft annotated so perfectly—is that man is the ant riding a plastic straw in a typhoon. We return to the Iron Age, the post-Atlantean period as described by Evola, where man will re-learn the Riddle of Steel and fight under the banner of dead gods, wading through seas of blood to erect new monuments, new societies.

This is why I demand to know what gods you pray to!

Are you brave enough to face that inner daemon—that shadow known by every traditional society that Christians mistakenly call the 'holy spirit'—not whether you believe there is something there, but why you haven't pursued it yet? Can you delve into the cavernous crevices on the edge of your dampened sixth sense, the flickering light on the edge of the precipice where the light-drinking void welcomes your entrance?

Nietzsche stared into it long enough to reap that the abyss is us—it is the daemon of our collective consciousness. How long can you surf the Kali Yuga and its swells of cultural feces, seafoam of pedophilic gore, and bleached skull beaches before you realize it isn't just humanity that accidentally surfed here but rather created this decadent world? Will you realize that when you leap to ride the tiger and it bucks beneath you, as you grip its striped hide with your fingernails you can't help but notice that there is a hill of skeletons of tigers and men in heaps around you?

The only salvation in this abhorrent period I can offer you is that there are two kinds of gods: temporal gods who are reincarnated during epochs as psychological band-aids and gods who dwell in oak, ash, and thorn.

Those of the latter dwell in petrified redrock hoodoos, inscribed by animalistic graffiti. Elder gods who have been lost to us cannot be found in the stuffy, pornographic puritanism of an Orthodox church. In the space between time, accessible by sacred mushrooms and evocative rites are mere whispers of the elder kind. I can confirm there are such primordial forces who live in the world, that you can access. I've heard their whispers in the rivers and booming woe from the bones of the mountains. They are not nature itself but live through nature—utilizing the wild as a vassal to man. Leaving bread crumb trails to their forgotten temples, they invite the worthy and initiated to seek out their wisdoms, so that they too might be reincarnated fully and fleshed from their tombs.

As a 21st century punk I have discovered these crumbs amidst the cracked concrete of the urban jungles and gleaned understanding past the decaying fog of the modern world. Through the ideals eschewed by countless others by violence and introspection, I have been able to transcend and offer the same gift.

The name I have given the transcendent and authentic art of my life is Goonhood. To tell you how I got here, I will detail to you my story to its fullest content. Below you will find my own visceral memories in their entirety as proof of my own coming to this Goon philosophy. It may be accurate. It may be entirely fiction. That is up for you to decide.

Let us start at the beginning...

CHILD BANDITRY

Equality is a dirty lie.

The first baby steps to claw your way out of the sticky, ideological spiderweb of democratic equality—this concept that men were 'created equal' like plastic rainbow spheres in a human ball pit—must be done without delay. You're already losing precious breath if you still believe in equality. As the elementary concept it is, drilled into the soft skulls of children's brains at the half rate propaganda daycares of public education, the rot of individualistic mob-rule was cemented into those cavities by our boomer predecessors along with iron studs of so-called equality.

'Equality is righteous', they said. Fuck what the boomers said. They drank the Brian Jonestown kool-aid in the '60s, LARPed as hippies until it wasn't financially feasible, and shaped the world in their shitty image. Globalism didn't happen in a vacuum, by the way. Boomers sold the country for their Sun Valley homes and ESPN packages. The kind of person that preaches 'when you're young, you think with your heart and with your mind when you're old' like some prophetic duality they discerned under the moonlight—instead of stolen lyrics from Pink Floyd—as some bloated, greasy-fingered Oracle is the one who deserves to drown in their own spit.

It's important to understand that this 'democratic' concept of equality that dominated the 20th-century zeitgeist is an invention that robs you of your social instincts, a verbal form of infectious autism that dulls the edge of judgment—our most valuable possession in the jungle of humanity. To speak of the mere word will summon a fervor among the zealots, especially those left-wing and Marx-worshippers. Pushing for ultimate equality is in the same vein as the pathetic attempts by tyrannical mothers vowing to 'eliminate bullying' from every school district, every classroom, exposing their obsession with control-freak nature all because their snot-nosed spawn cannot cope with the banter of their fellow booger-eaters.

I credit my parents for never taking this victimization approach. When other parents shuttled their children between their soccer and piano practices, mine drove me to every duel-like brawl that I was challenged to—of which there were dozens—they felt a sense of pride they derived from when I would fight my bullies, even allowing me to call them 'shit-heads' after I came in with swollen cheekbones and black-eyes. For this reason alone my childhood was incomparable to the cushioned one of my peers.

I firsthand learned that equality was not a force but violence was. It was to act decent to others who've never even given decency a split-hair appraisal.

Heed this here, limp-wristed journalists who might stick their shovel-nosed faces in my work in a shallow, page-flipping way for their 'gotcha moment' too publicly shame me as some kind of supremacist: not only are you a faggot, but you don't even believe in equality yourself. Unlike you, I tested the theory of equality in the wild, believing it fervently once myself.

See, when I speak of equality I do not mean in the context of merely gender, race, age, or so forth. I mean the relatively contemporary idea of viewing our fellow humans on a smooth plane of moral existence—that we as a collective species must not judge our fellows on merit, actions, or any logical premises and treat them completely equally. You can't even repeat that sentence without the nasal condescension of an overpaid third-grade teacher.

Equality isn't just impossible—it's jumping on a

lifeboat bearing a hundred other passengers and the feeble hope it stays afloat so long as others scoop water by hand like you. Except those other passengers don't even consider your efforts to stave off their impending watery doom. They're hungrily eyeing the only poor sop with a gun and a bag of jerky. They're stacked in a sweaty orgy off in the corner and sinking half the damn boat. They're stomping in tantrums and deflating the lifeboat with every footfall. They're pretending that all is well and they're back at their shitty house party, downing bottles of overpriced wheat-piss. They're screeching at you to keep scooping while they lounge behind the protection of a ring of thugs.

In the situation you have a moment of self-awareness: equality isn't a truth. Equality is a mandate—an invisible tool of conformity that allows for simple management of the masses. You can't not believe in equality and heed your internal instincts, you bigot! Now eat our synthetic trash, listen to the professional officials we cherry-pick, and gobble up the laboratory-fabricated horse-cum we force them to shove down your throat so you believe in useful deceits like universal equality!

Nature is inequality and humans are defined by all

nature: both esoteric and exoteric. All you need to do is to look towards children. Towards the complex battlegrounds of recess, a social atmosphere completely untainted by these so-called democratic philosophies.

Leave a group of a hundred children at a playground unsupervised and in less than five minutes you will have a balkanized state complete with boundaries and an ever-changing chain of hierarchy: flower-pickers, wood-chip diggers, monkey bar athletes, video-game lawyers and bully warlords. Gang-like cliques will roam and engage with their rivals who wear the outdated fashions and colored shirts. Hobbyists will trade cards on the fringes so that the bullies might not tear them in bloody pieces. Various slang and vernacular will become isolated to specific regions of the playground like the hundred-thousand variants of Pacific Islander tongues.

There is no equality in this place—not the kind that these democratic demagogues would have you believe. Humans don't deserve equality! The same degenerate liberal-types who deny that instinctive hierarchies trump their bumper-sticker philosophies would simultaneously tell you that we are but several steps removed from monkeys, a few thousand years evolved from a species that brains each other for sex. Boomers are as useless as their milquetoast ideas that they parrot.

I was raised in an atmosphere that should have been more equal than any other: an insulated bubble in the mountains, uber-wealthy, highly liberal, and ethnically diverse. Considered a retreat by the insectoids of Hollywood and the bandwagon cults who ooze behind them, my place of upbringing was 'the dream haven' for the ex-hippie boomer elite. Park City or Granola Land as my friends called it: a land of vegan milk and honey. By all accounts, I should have adopted their braindead ideology by how aggressive their propagandizing efforts were in school.

The ski resorts, Granola Land's main attraction besides the Sundance film festival, were somewhat tolerable if you avoided the crowds—insufferable, beaked-nose tourists who sneered at you after your friendly banter, claiming they were only vacationing there because the 'après-ski in New York wasn't good' and your rural state was savage and zealous. At those times, I was proud to be a Mormon boy of the high mountains, a descendant of fur trappers and pioneers—not some urbanite Jew who despised the nature he was so privileged to visit.

Something to consider is that while Park City/Granola Land is called a 'city' to leech taxes, it is functionally not one. There is a tiny police force whose sole occupation is busting the cocaine-fueled antics of middle-schoolers and cartel activity. If anything ever went bad in Granola Land, these feel-good ex-hippies would be gnawing on their neighbors like the fucking cannibals they are.

One iconic Christmas Eve, a moose was dropped on a powerline after being air-lifted out of a backyard they trashed—my first indication that pagan nature gods are real were the moose guardians who rampaged through our neighborhoods and devoured every transplanted berry bush they found—and shut down the grid for miles. We reveled the entire night by candlelight, my relatives who'd grown up in such poor conditions were unaffected. Meanwhile our neighbors panicked themselves into comas like cats who'd ingested Adderall. They'd never been subject to such torture as a power outage.

Something that the modern working class doesn't understand is how the posh, multimillion-dollar lifestyle really is. The people of Granola Land lived the curse of the Aztec Gold of the Black Pearl: the ambrosia of wealth could not satisfy their thirst, caviar turned to ash in their mouths, nor did the company of their fellow man harmed or slaked their lust. There were no families in Granola Land, only rich progenitors and their feeble, drug-addicted offspring. I still know of one of my former friends who lives with his parents there—divorced, former millionaires—who dwell in the same house after squandering their wealth. He beat his dad into an ER visit for alcohol and the father still allows him to live rent-free, unable to kick him to the curb while the divorced mother claims dominion on the upper floor, howling like a wounded panther at the wealth she squandered! Pathetic.

Granola Land is the horror reflection of the 21st century—the culmination of the American Dream, a generation of self-indulgent sociopaths and their godless society imported from California. If you threw a rock into the general population there, you'd hit a half-dozen goblinoid bankers and their Russian trophy wives. You could tell by their ugly spawn there was no love there, only greed. The divorce rate was astronomical and far higher than the national average, which was to say the least. Alcoholism and drug abuse were merely symptoms of these secular 'aristocrats'.

My first experience of racism that I witnessed unknowingly was visiting the homes of the barons of

Granola Land. I was with one of their children as they parked one of their four Land Rovers, entering with scowls on their spray-tanned faces, screeching into the kitchen about how a 'dirty wetback' cut them off on their 0.5-mile commute from the mountain café. The most racist comments I've heard in my lifetime—including among truckers from backwoods gas stations, Idahoan radicals, and a handful of my abusive Mexican kitchen workers—were by far the hook-nosed bourgeoise on their journey across their kitchen and into their rooms. Often I'd hear their kids repeat their favorite slurs at school between giggles.

Only by my own experience will I never be convinced that the shadowy KKK boogiemen so often referenced in popcorn journalist pieces could ever come close to hating other races like the AWFL and banker types. Or that they aren't secretly run by the CIA, FBI, or so on.

I heard every taboo word within the exclusive sanctity of these baron's art deco homes decorated with obscure Africa-cana rugs, nu-age sculpture bereft of anything European or American for that matter. They would lie to your face that this is not the case, but you can go look up what certain NBA team owners say about their African mistresses...I can assure you that these people were quite the bigots they claim not to be.

After all, I broke bread with them.

History tells us that the Roman patricians grew to despise the Gauls and other slaves they imported to build their infrastructure over time. The slaves who hated the Romans—a timeless lesson of ethics and civilization—were metaphorically flinging their shit towards the aristocracy. To play the devil's advocate, why wouldn't they? As Evola points out, the patricians believed in '*auspicia sunt patrum*'—meaning those of the plebian and imported worker class were without ancestor or proper rites, unable to transcend and speak to the gods. When you reduce any race to an animal bereft of any higher spiritual ideal, expect it to lash out with tenacity in your direction. Those secular barons fell into the same trap as the Roman patricians did—denying vir and replacing it with greed.

Such was the case of Granola Land in my youth, right when the plebeian Latin populations were brought in to rapidly build these developments, mega-houses, and mansions. Just like the Gauls, these Nicaraguans, Guatemalans, and Mexicans abandoned their xenophobia for each other for a common enemy: the elites of our town. In a matter of a decade they formed communal longhalls in a condo complex known as 'Taco Bell Towers', outbreeding the existing population ten-fold, turning into an interconnected Latin syndicate.

When I speak of cartel activities I am not exaggerating—the police were/are overburdened with the rampant crime posed by the Latins. Even in middle school it was frequent, bi-weekly occurrence for the Joses and Juans dragged out of class for drug possession, guns, or other illicit activities while the rest of us played Pokemon. Our undeveloped, overstimulated brains could not grasp the bandito lifestyle nor its fruits—neither did the barons, to their earned misfortune.

The only respite that places like Granola Land boast is that it is surrounded by 'the good folk'. Hearty, rural men and faithful wives who own dozens of wolf-like dogs, arsenals, and maintain a steady watch on their degenerate neighbors.

Childhood is a unique and often underlooked thing—it's always under-analyzed by those who wish to sweep certain demographics and statistics under the rug. A child can develop normally in abnormal conditions, depending on the home, style of parenting, and schooling given to them. Children do not lie about how they feel unless they're taught to or they believe it will allow them to survive. They're innocuous and pleasantly blunt in this way. Equality has to be pounded into them unceasingly at every activity in their childhood—in school, at home, even in their entertainment—otherwise, they'd learn by experience and follow the same instincts that built this civilization in the first place.

I, along with my brother and only a handful of friends there, was perhaps among the few children who developed normally after being raised in Granola Land. Often when I encounter an old acquaintance from my hometown it is in the innocuous circumstances of a mutual's revelries or gas station. Never are they friendly or hospitable—cocaine has that particular vampiric effect on even addicts of a few years, melding its victims into true nocturnal types who shy from the sun. I speak of degenerates and stoners often but the children of Granola Town are among the most pathetic I have encountered, infrequently successful, self-sufficiency a unicorn among their traits. Liberal parenting is the sole cause of their enslavement.

Perhaps you may have noticed this: liberal parenting, the feel-good kind, is formaldehyde to a child's soul. In those chaotic dwellings unworthy of being called a 'household' there is another taboo 'N-word': NO. Peers of mine would brag that no such word was uttered to them and it showed in their childhood. There wasn't a mass rebelliousness spirit in them, despite their Che Guevara t-shirts and Bolshevik phase exhibited in middle school—no organized coup could have sprung from that pitiable populace. Instilled in my peers was this more accurately a cultural rebellion by self-love, a very anti-traditional mindset of masturbatory self-gratification.

I grew up alongside these aggravatingly pretentious 'me' types you see on Instagram or Twitter with hundreds of thousands of followers. All of them sprang up from the wealth-saturated families in Granola Land—raised on the spongy white-bread value of liberal 'principles' that governed the late 90's of hyper diversity and propaganda. Guess how many of them initiated the socialist revolutions these upper middle-class fags started? It's a low number.

You know the type. Looks 'Californian', blondes or the light scruff and dopey look, the same dumb floppy hat, overly filtered photos. I can assure you from over twenty years of these types they are all the same: vain lobotomites with such excessively narcissistic tendencies that their mind has developed a subconscious survival filter for any less-than-positive remarks aimed at them that could threaten their miserable, atomically brittle existence. Without the social media attention and imaginary clout force-fed to them by a food tube of endless nullified yes-men and simp culture, they would shrivel like avocados baking on a roof of their broken-down VW bug in Death Valley.

I fantasize about seeing corpses of Instagram 'Influencers' littering the boiling sands of the Mojave—a boneyard of DSLR cameras and hipster clothes who got lost after trying to find their next 'nature' photo on their wretched collages.

Alas, the one thing boomers have succinctly observed are millennials who even as children were the 'Decay Generation'—bred to instinctually eradicate the Americana of yesteryear by radical narcissism. The only problem is it was their ineptitude to blame for this.

Human children require four things to reach adulthood: food, sunshine, and a tribe to be connected to. I would posit that there is an equally if not dominant factor not included in this list...a frontier to explore.

Historians have held fruitless debates for centuries

on the topic of societies that reach the zenith of civilization—Romans, Persians, Norse, etc. Morons have argued that life under distress and torture this achievement is fulfilled. Bullshit! In California, you have an entire caste of adult-children who are American Gopniks because of the dot.com bubble, LA riots, and hyper-diversity. Is there anything more chaotic for a child to observe than the space-strangled Amazonian environment where dozens of races and their respective tribes fight tooth and claw for the scraps of power and wealth? Can you imagine? The humans who are spawned from these wretched places are hardened and tougher, yes, but will only produce such a chaotic society as they learned.

It is not an insignificant thing that in fantasy books your stereotypical virile protagonist is raised on a quiet farm, picturesque mountains in the background, on the edge of a great Wild where dark and mysterious things lie—later only to explore and discover their kingly lineage on their Heroes Journey to come! It is not Arthurian—it is much older and imbedded in our very blood! This youthful vigor contesting with and against nature is not merely a European ideal, though I suspect it derives from the Proto Indo-Europeans and the eldest peoples as it is prominent in spread-out civilizations as Mongolia, Iran, and Greece.

We had such a mountain we lived on in Granola Land, above a golf course and the highway junction. Behind us was the ridge and behind it an expansive Frontier plentiful of dangers to any child: moose, coyote, hare, deer, and cougars. Sagebrush became scrub oak and steep ravines led to redstone bluffs. Longer than the child's eye could reach did it span beyond in a green ocean. Few of my peers ever ventured over the hill for the simple reason that it was unknown. Their parents reinforced this with folklore about children going missing and so forth.

I never felt afraid wandering up to those heights, overlooking the vast wilds of that Frontier as a child. Partly because of our family dog—a 150-lb Alaskan Malamute—but also instinctual. I had read enough Louis Lamour and Treasure Island, thinking myself some sort of little pirate-outlaw who was capable of whatever I came across. This naivete allowed me to fully entrust my safety with my dog as a partner. I think back fondly to those days, climbing far past where my parents could keep an eye on me with my massive fur-tank by my side, scrambling through the hills that none of my peers ever had seen. Besides the numerous moose or rattlesnakes we ran into, there was never a moment where I denied the Wild from my blood. As a child it grew into my like a tree's creeping roots might, firmly snaring themselves in my blood.

Give a child a camping trip and he'll appreciate nature. But give a child a wilderness to live off of and he'll become one with nature. And eventually he'll become a fascist.

My father was obsessed with involving my brother and I into team sports at a very ripe age: soccer, baseball, basketball, football, even swimming. I had little interest in any of these as an infant warlord, save the incentivization of a Pokemon card pack as a bartering chip that I could pawn to my friends, should I score a goal of any kind. I used to ridicule him for this until I realized that it was a quite clever endeavor on two fronts: socialization and competition.

Without supervision children naturally form dynamic social hierarchies even in their spit-dribble infancy. Given the activity of sports, they develop leadership qualities and learn how to corral one another. Few children wouldn't benefit from being introduced to these principles through Olympian activities and games. In this boiled-down equivalent to ancient games, through football and soccer, Western kids gravitate towards these self-governable instincts that have resided for thousands of civilizations.

While I gained some insight into the value of youth sports and meritocracy myself, it wasn't long until I grew ill of being smacked by a baseball by cross-eyed Derricks and Andrews, outran by spaghetti-bodied Puerto Ricans at soccer. The concept of a 'goal' never impressed upon me as a child, particularly the abstract numbers, and the politics within the team grew stale quickly. In my stereotypical fashion, I tossed by baseball glove into the dust and smirked at my parents, declaring I would no longer play.

Little would I know, without any foresight, that abandoning them was the greatest boon to my childhood. The sport that trumps all others. True meritocracy, the kind rarely manifested to an upper middle-class brat: sanctified, low-stakes warfare.

My eighth birthday brought me a bicycle, the mountain-crossing kind with nice treads and low gears. Living on a steep, short mountain with plenty of dirt and gravel paths that bisected the neighborhood, along with the uncivilized Wilderness above the houses, the gift of this vehicle was no small matter. I developed strong legs after riding 2+ miles each day to my friend's house in the high neighborhood of Crimson Eagle—a hilly, forested part where the elite lived. My parents handed me the keys to my freedom with a helmet and little micromanagement.

It was during these first rangings outside of my street and beyond—to the unfinished lots and ravines full of coyotes, skunks, and strays that I came into contact with my first dungeon: a foundation with a miniature fort erected from plywood on its mount. In a box hidden in the concrete depths of a half-finished housing development, I discovered a plastic Berretta, the kind that lobbed little plastic BBs. Like a rusted sword dredged from an Atlantean tomb as a spry, sharp-eyed youth I was destined for this treasure.

Mind you that I was already well-versed with the lore of the Kommando via endless re-runs of GI Joe, Future Weapons, and a seasoned veteran of long-run plastic army men campaigns fought on the frigid reservoir beach we would go to in summer. I was a regular 9 year-old John S. Mosby, enchanted by strategic theory. Something became much more consequential: a spirit of transcendence through visceral conflict, something I inherited by blood. My brother likewise was granted this genetic archetype.

Some might call it the 'inner viking' or the destiny of a warrior, not be confused with the soldier or law enforcer. This archetype did stir up brief moments of 'patriotism' when I reached the virile peak of my teens when I considered joining the military and seeking my own Lawrence of Arabia moment. This occurred at the backend of the Afghanistan war, and I later discovered that this glorious warrior lifestyle would consist of boiling inside a base in oven temperatures, being the easy target for piss and rocks by belligerent mud children, only to being potentially crippled for life for a mere grocery run.

My rebellious spirit overwhelmed these feelings—reminding me of my issues with authority and discovering my mischievous nature spared me from what would have been a miserable existence within the restrictive regime of the modern military.

More than a decade later I have discerned my pathology from this point: that BB gun and the foundation. In a uniquely Promethean way, it established the same immortal link that young Scandinavians uncovered eons ago when they went foraging through an ancestor's burial site during the rite of Alfablot—the pagan origin for Halloween, indicating the time when the elves or ancestor spirits required communing and sacrifice—finding old tokens and weapons, calling themselves the names of that particular ancestor. Without any prompting or taught principle from my parents, the instinct to hunt out monsters and tyrants was ignited within me as I cradled that plastic pistol.

Only a few years later, I would use it in the sacred art of the Eternal Sport—The Initiation of Manhood—or fisticuffs with my peers.

You can tell a great deal about a young man's upbringing by his interest in weaponry, competition, and relationships with fellow men. It's instinctive for the male spirit to 'seek out' beyond the coziness of his parent's domain like a hunter-gatherer, to test the boundaries that will reciprocate with either punishment or reward. Yet another vindication of my statements of the corrosive, pussyfying liberal parenting style—the loudest, brazenly blaming teachers for their child's bruises from the playground as if their spawn was subject to some kind of inadvertent Mengele-style torture. Bruises and scrapes were worn like badges of honor!

It doesn't take a Big Brain to figure out how a young man treats this sacred initiation into manhood either with sadism or honor. I observed varying levels of both through my own eyes. A reoccurring character of my early years known as the Red-Haired Devilspawn was the prime example of the former, which I will discuss at length.

After gaining my Atlantean Sword of the airsoft gun, dozens followed suit among my peers. Airsoft was relatively new, relatively cheap and protective eyeglasses were abundant. Small skirmishes became a common solution to disputes: lobbing BBs from our bulwarks, those hills, and unfinished housing development trenches. A code was established early on as the Older Kids had access to greater arsenals—bigger guns, automatics, and faster bikes. We would leave them to their brutal devices and avoid their battlefields. Lawns and backyards were considered 'green zones' while the unfinished lots and developments outside were considered a No-Man's land where the Law of the Jungle reigned.

In the beginning it was more akin to the civil, gentlemanly conduct seen in the wars of the 18th century: rules of engagement left room for time-outs, lifting your hand above your head would indicate you were 'killed' and when the massacre was complete or lasted too long, we would adjourn for refreshment. There was a polite camaraderie shared between us like-minded children, conveyed by an unsaid agreement: this was a game and we were here to have unadulterated fun. I'm unsure how long this period lasted, only that the novelty of sanctioned warfare can be contrasted harshly against what came next.

The older kids deigned it timely to remind us that they were in charge. Descending from the hills like phantom raiders, they took our game away from us in that cold, detached manner—no different than the Danes pilfering Wessex.

Overnight our fortresses of plywood had been sundered by bike and boot, ammo cans looted and tossed into the steep gullies, stashes of plastic guns smashed and our fields defiled by their treads. Some kids cried. Some folded—their spirits unable to overcome this act of destruction. Many, if not all of our peers, tossed their hands in the air and declared this was the death knell of our favorite pastime—the older kids had seized uncontested victory in their eyes. For none among us had comparable arsenals, transportation, or knowledge of the landscape.

A handful among us did not see this slight as a triumph but a challenge. Instead of admitting defeat, we observed this as an abstract point against us—bullies: 1, us: 0. I noticed a visible alteration in my friend's expressions when we spoke about the damage—we were going to get these fuckers. Our moment of sorrow was swiftly replaced by the aura of retribution. We began to calculate what could be salvaged and what would be replaced among our weapon stores, inspecting the tread marks where they arrived from, discussing which hills would likely house their bases. No longer were there sophisticated talks of grand strategy—of BB enfilades, trench reenactment, and fabricating medals out of old soda cans.

I could say there as we discussed supplies, mobilization, and reconnaissance, something stirred within my bones. Nothing proposed was anywhere near the modality of true warfare like the death of friends or the dull misery of endless nights on fireguard. Yet there was a virile enchantment—the air of anxiousness and eagerness that surfaced at our war-table.

For all its childish simplicity and naivete, when I think of those early days it truly hearkens to the maxims presented by Ernst Jünger, of his 'anarch': the free warrior who understands his own, deeply embedded draw to warfare. Likewise his disgust for the authority of godless institutions that wage it—acknowledging he must wear his anarchic spirit as a belt, wield it as a blade, and don camouflage so he might participate in The Campaigns. Jünger's introspection in a war that has been otherwise clouded by the re-branding of global peace-thinkers reinforces the continuity that warfare is inherently youthful and entirely necessary.

War is performance, the ultimate sport. Even as a child I understood this grail of vitality, despite our society's best efforts to distract me from ever discovering it.

Nothing curdles my blood to a boiled paste more than how some air-sucking normie misunderstands his own species, comparing himself to everyone around him via some nerdy Comic Book reference. To go further, how these yuppie creatures believe that our kind is peaceful and that violence is the exception, not the norm. I've altogether given up explaining to these mundane worms that the men they cross every day choose the path of least resistance and violence is only subsumed by its consummation of energy and rewards.

Red-Haired Devilspawn is the prime example of a violent actor—one who puts theories of peace as a principle to rest. He was my best friend and closest from my early childhood to teenhood. We were virtually inseparable for a decade and our families grew 'close' as they could for being spiritual opposites. My parents came from rural aristocracy, the noble patriarchy of explorers and ranchers —the opposite of Red-Haired's mulatto berry-picker matriarchal hive, who were constantly at odds with one another in ruthless selfish competition. When my father gained success he stashed his hard-earned dollars into a savings account—which we would later entirely depend on during the Recession of '08—whilst their cannibalistic family chimped out over every Apple tech-gimmick and never had the discipline to save their money. I'd be utterly shocked if they captured even a quarter of their wealth from those profitable years.

The most important factor about Red-Haired Devilspawn that I came to learn was that he was gay. There were a few signs that became more apparent as we reached puberty—he constantly asked if I had fetishes and wanted me to tell him my fantasies on our bike rides home—but I was oblivious to his intentions. My other athletic friends who were naturally competitive and confident of their manhood began to gravitate away from Red-Haired when he wanted to make movies including him singing Rihanna and Britney Spears—his voice was slightly nasal and higher-pitched even when he hit 14. I think my parents noticed it at around 12, but they didn't want to appear bigoted to cleave our friendship pre-emptively. I am grateful they didn't. I learned many valuable lessons from that friendship.

I don't believe being homo is a born trait or spirit, and if it is it is not common. Every single homo I have met, save one, was subjected to inordinate amounts of psychological and physical abuse—it should be obvious that this causes one to adapt and react towards this violence, resulting in a perverse inversion of sexuality.

I witnessed Red-Haired Devilspawn's abuse firsthand by two fronts: a household of fermented chaos, ran by angry women, constantly screeching down the halls and bitterly jabbing each other. The other of course was his father, a tan WASP who had played football and was involved in charter schooling. He was a sociopathic man with a dark glint in his eyes that you could tell held unspoken anger or sorrow—a madness certainly. I later found out that he was a highly functioning paranoid schizophrenic who would purposefully go off his medication and had a history of beating women. Yet his career in the business world was exceptional!

At the beginning of our friendship, Red-Haired Devilspawn and I did great things: we built a fully functioning snow-cone cart with a yoke-bicycle system at age 10, a series of mini-films with green screen effects by 12, and a YouTube music channel with a few thousand views per video by 14. There was always another project we were working on, creating and innovating and building. Our LEGOs were plywood scavenged from the nearby gullies and construction sites; the entire neighborhood we'd patrol for new ideas after a BB-gun skirmish with our rivals. We even built a mounted water-balloon sling onto our snow-cone cart and successfully drenched several bullies with our piss!

It was not to last. The homo, as I stated earlier, is not one who sees violence as a utility or in circumstances demanded, a sacred transgression in a pagan way. Red-Haired Devilspawn felt vindicated during our battles with the neighborhood bullies, a primal satisfaction when his enemies bled from the BB bullets. He admitted to me on one occasion that he'd discovered a dead squirrel on the side of the road and played with its corpse, mocking its state. A memory I'm sure he willfully discarded but it left a seismic impression on me and his natural disposition.

Stereotypically, he became known as the 'cheater' in our BB gun games—often ignoring when he got shot unless it was quite painful where he'd proceed to scream and run towards the enemy, unloading his magazine into some poor child. The first time he did this I thought nothing of it than foolhardy bravery. It dawned on me one afternoon on the hills as I sat cross-legged after being shot through by a shotgun, that Red-Haired Devilspawn wasn't playing our game: war with rules. He didn't care for the sport or the honor within it. He had no qualms with breaking the rules as he saw fit and lashing out with unbridled rage at the innocent near him. It came in handy when we fought the neighborhood bullies who too, didn't follow our rules of engagement. But he became unmanageable in that tear-stricken, feral state. Often these episodes would climax with violence and he'd fall into a heap, sobbing and kicking the dust.

I have later chalked this up to him wanting to impress me and his suppressed anger surfacing through the spirit of faux-combat. I discovered through a mutual friend who had learned in confidence from Red-Haired that he would often write about me in his journal and angrily scrawl that I was 'obstinate and a beautiful idiot' when I overlooked his version of adolescent flirting. But truthfully, I believe that the former was stronger than the latter—homos are all miserable.

It is not sinning but a movement against the grain of humanity, living a LARP lifestyle that ends in death by gay-plague or a hollow existence. This is why gays 'act out' so outwardly—it is absolute and undeniable cope. Violence is a visceral orgasm for them so saturated that they cannot experience through any other mundane means. Is it any wonder to any human with a pulse why the homosexual and transgender suicide rates are so high? They cannot suffer themselves, let alone the world that is their own Narcissus mirror.

Red-Haired may have come from a family of nu-wealth—of white SUVs and a million-dollar home but like many of his counterparts in Granola Land, it was a cushioned hell. A glittering Palace of Versailles where the halls were punji pits, rooms filled with cyclosarin gas, and walls lined with the flayed skins of a hundred thousand refugee children. There is no monetary value that can ever stave away the bleak agony of such a conflicted spirit such as Red-Haired. His father bought him a snowmobile and an Apple desktop that would have been worth $10k nowadays and it may as well have been a letter to a military school and a bullet to eat.

For this reason, I cannot help but sympathize with the spirit of the dreary, weeping homo. I see my friend Red-Haired Devilspawn bent over on the carpet in futile agony, nowhere to hide from his dark-eyed father—leering over him with a closed fist or a belt while his mulatto mother snickers from the background. It is a scene of silent horror and brazen truth.

I would not wish even this fate on my enemies.

Having a vicious homosexual as your childhood friend has some astounding side effects—ones that you simply cannot gain from having merely your bros or buddies. It's the equivalent to sticking a black mamba into your child's room instead of a golden retriever.

Sure the dog will act as dogs will: curl up like a loyal footwarmer with the charm of an innocuous child, a perfect companion to his slobbering human counterpart. A poisonous snake however is no such ally because the child cannot be truly relaxed around one. He must learn to live on the edge of the knife around this snake, dance around the room with a trepid foot, and be it that he earns scars cohabitating with this lethal creature, he will comprehend every twitch of the tail, a coil to make a swift strike. Lest the child is bitten and succumbs to the poison, he will walk away from this encounter observant and keen to behavioral patterns—far more than any of his coddled peers.

While I am no snake-dancer, my friendship with Red-Haired Devilspawn left me with a third eye for depravity and the evils of humanity.

One cannot simply befriend a homosexual with sociopathic tendencies—that is detached equivalent to the pathetic 'Friend' function on social media. One must immerse themselves in the slime of that world, headfirst, and embrace the grim truth that dwells in the under-soul—that graffitied subway tunnel of the fallen spirits of our societies, a concrete sardine can that reeks of fentanyl addicts and hooker corpses. Underneath the rainbow and overzealous smiles, this is the reality for the 21st century homo.

Back when we first hit adolescence, we established a code word "Bottomless Pit", a red flag coming from a closet homosexual. It was used whenever we would talk about women or our deepest desires. I did not find it odd at first that he cared more about what I wanted to 'do to women' than the women I preferred—never offering up his own love interests. Even as a devout Mormon he viewed women no better than animals to be played with, like the corpse of the squirrel. He would remark that I had poor standards yet obsess over my naivete fantasies...this was a mistake. I was foolish to share these private thoughts but I genuinely thought he had my best interests at heart.

They are not like women, nor like men—behind closed doors, any woman with a 'gay friend' will admit that they are entirely lost on advising him. The majority of homos have no rules, nor principles to tether them to the earth. They are driven entirely by the hell in their heart and the whim of their chaotic soul. Homos are the spiritual 'lunar men' who fell to the emasculatory war waged of the 20th century, victims of the bombs of gynocracy and propaganda pamphlets containing their illegitimate claim to dignity—that for women to be more than 'merely women' and the solar patriarchy defeated, homos must join the ranks of the insurrection. Homosexuality was not an accident in a vacuum but the superficial disease, a debt due to the 'liberalization' of women and we're going to pay that price for eternity.

If you are a high-functioning man or woman, you cannot intervene in their life. It is humane and better you leave them like a stray beast than to try and be bitten. Few and far between are the homosexual men that are aware of their own nature.

As for Red-Haired, it was less than two years later that he decided he would suddenly revoke our friendship, turn his back on me and declare me a sexual scoundrel—that I was perverted for my desires to be with women. In that progressive, feel-good school in Granola Land, he wielded the power of shame and slander for no reason other than this: I had begun to openly distrust him. I no longer agreed with him on every matter, arguing when he was out of line and demanded he curtail his abusive nature on myself and other friends.

My mistake was costly—I had trusted him with the endowed privacy of brotherhood and paid the price. It ruined my ability to trust others for years...perhaps even to some degree, my lifetime...

The lessons you learn as a child can end up in the mental trash can as you plod along through pubescence and adulthood. But in those rare moments, reflecting on those innocuous years will grant you clarity in adulthood—obliterating the smog-cloud of social laws that smother your intelligence.

For instance, as a teenager and aspiring artist in college, I believed wholly that equality was how humanity 'moved forward' in some vague, positive timeline of our species. Now in my mid-20s, I have come back to my 8-year old mindset on the topic and will happily ridicule anyone who protests that I'm not 'progressive enough'. What a fucking waste of oxygen...debating whether equality is even a worthwhile endeavor. For hours on end I would talk sideways about whether we could ever make society parallel and all men gain the same fruits. I was retarded for those years.

Children begin in a hypostatic state, aware enough of their existence where their perceived reality is already 'owned' yet they engage with it in a gnostic way—purely like the vital ether known as Mana by the Polynesians—and exert that willpower upon the world. You see, children are unfazed by the psychological exhaustion omnipresent in the normie population that is exhibited after years of domestication. This is because of the law of 'owned space' aptly cemented by Bronze Age Pervert and the timeless, spiritual dimension of the traditionalist mindset posited by Evola come to intersect when it comes to the virile spirit of a child.

In their own bumbling, unfiltered way, children don't

measure each other on the playground with the rosy glasses of liberalism. A kid is absent of ego—a demiurge of the universe and aware of the hyper-present phenomena that present themselves in their own daily lives. Children wander curiously not as Adam or Eve in the Garden but like litters of lion cubs exploring their social environments, ignoring God who is sleeping. They have little care for the snakes or the idea that the Garden is a temporal space—the little lions do not believe in the constructs of outer authority...at least not yet.

That casual, innocent fearlessness is the Hyperborean spirit and without fucking question the epitome of untested hypostasis!

Humanist types like Steven Pinker assert that in a rigid bureaucratic public education workcamp, children will be socialized against violence and bigotry and therefore become less so over time in his delusional utopian fantasy. This is the equivalent of those same lion cubs empathizing consciously with Eden for being a dumb whore for eating the apple: all because out of her slothfulness, she refused to cook lima beans, peacock eggs and, roasted snake for Adam— choosing instead to ruin their 'paradise' because of her gyno-retardation. No, those lions cubs would not give a shit. Why would they? I am rigidly positive that even if lions could conceive of these pedantic, superficial ideas like equality, they'd care even less. Wasting energy on morality arguments is wasted energy that could be utilized for hunting gazelle or precious naptime under the eternal sun.

If we held violence under the same standard of equality as we do for liberties, then Pinker would backpedal faster than some black-bloc rioter caught slinging their limp fists past their intended target and smacking a Samoan beef-monkey by accident. He's never had to experience his ideas in action—whether equality is working in urban Detroit in the squabbling hellhole of their courts or on the opposite end of an AKM on the outskirts of a village in Zimbabwe. Pinker is the type who projects his theories as law because there are no repercussions for error on his part—only half-assed jabs from neoliberal news sites who want to appear more Viva Socialista that take issue that he's not ok with 'punching Nazis' for a means to his utopian end.

Another topical point on equality involving children is the competition native to all animals with a male/female spirit. As stags lock horns over desired mates, bears swing over salmon rushes and tropical birds gloat with their rainbow wings so too are our machinations to move on the hierarchy. Equality could not exist in the wild nature—it would lead to extinction or be reversed to prevent the former. Every set of beings must adhere to that first law of morality: persisting above all else. Children subconsciously act upon this and proceed into life wielding this, even unknowingly. That harsh judgment that occurred between the wealthy spawn of liberal urbanites and the lower class of Latinos in Granola Land would be chalked up to as 'racist' now—that's a shallow interpretation. What was really happening was spiritual warfare, based on caste and tribe culture. Resources always appear finite to the youth and so the competition begins.

'All men were created equal' sounds nice but is fucking retarded when analyzed beside moral law zero and the competition that comes from it. No one starts 'equal' because equality would necessitate standardization of mind, flesh, and resources. All children would be test-tube babies reared in stainless steel kennels, fed the same vitamin-dense gruel, and educated by neutral-voiced and optimized educators from speaker systems wired into their cages. To have true equality you must isolate the variables that would give other children the upper hand and even then you're radically braindead to think that genetics doesn't eliminate the 'progress' you achieve in this scenario.

It should be a crime punishable by death that so many children have not experienced the freedom to reflect inwardly so they might understand their own spiritual governance.

THE ECSTASY OF FOOL'S GOLD

Concept this for a moment: a utopian European-Christian state. Everyone prospers and has healthy relationships with their family and God. Some brazen fellow might call this 'Zion', a holy land dedicated to the perseverance of such a faith. Would this place become an empire of theology and industry? Would every inhabitant be wholesome and virtuous if the drive to build such a state surfaced from merit and love of God? Would it stand for thousands of years?

No. I would call this pure projection. A fantasy world.

Because I was raised in the crumbling ruins of such a place, on the outskirts of Happy Valley—the HQ of Mormons and their supposed 'Zion'—a utopia that many have heard rumor of, entirely populated by white people that were once polygamist explorers. I can tell you, for certain, that Happy Valley is no such utopia and never will be. There is a reason why Mitt Romney is so revered there. It is a land quickly losing its 'traditions' to modern democracy, its people broken by virtuous arrogance, and even the institution of the Church that few even grovel to, is nothing more than a shekel-laundering scheme. The men are rarely manly, their women usually frumpy and their ham sandwich culture has become hated by even their aristocracy.

Given the sudden swan-dive we've taken through the Overton Window and the rapidly immolating moral systems amongst all Millenials, Mormonism is soon destined to become dust in the wind...

Traveling through the heart of America and meeting Christians of every denomination, a phrase often repeated is the idea that 'Mormons aren't Christian'. That somehow the fact that the denomination had its own holy books besides the Holy Bible that reaffirmed its existence outside the stereotypical Evangelical pantheon, a distinct holy capital of Salt Lake City that wasn't located in their indistinct Flyover City, and was wealthier than all of the other denominations combined has grants credence to the logical syllogism: Mormons aren't Christian.

Do other Christians even know what their religions is?

Mormonism is the *pinnacle* of modern Christianity. Like pre-destined apple pie, Mormons were the inevitable force via the Protestant doctrine and the revisionary Americana spirit. If not for the pedophile emperor, Joseph

Smith, his harem of 34 wives and his devout followers—my ancestors no less—who crossed the entire country in a remarkably pyrrhic journey, some other modernist version of Christianity would have come about. Make way European-style Jesus-cult. We're about making money first, cross and that other gobbledygook later.

It should be stated fairly regarding the founding of a religion that Joseph Smith was either a shrewd opportunist or sociopath genius. Though many of my fellow apostates are aware that he was both a Freemason and a treasure hunter—taking a great deal of the etymology of the Book of Mormon from handbooks on Latin dictionaries or island villages where famous pirates had sunk treasure—they overlook the ingenuity of the Mormon campaign. Joseph Smith was able to convince hundreds, even thousands of families to sell their worldly possessions, come across the turbulent Atlantic, and make an often-deadly journey to a land that is desolate as the OG Zion itself. Tell me that is not the modern equivalent of Thulsa Doom, wielding the power of steel with a charismatic, almost sorcerous hand!

No, Mormonism is *quite* Christian.

From the beginning when it was just a weed in the crumbling cement of Roman culture, the Christian cult succeeded to strangle the tradition of the solar state by the Jewish 'virtue' of dual loyalty—that duality of morality that allowed them to deflect blame and yet empowered their radical subversion of authority. Rendering unto Caesar a picnic basket bereft of any fruit or food, the Christian cult did not believe in the power of the other gods or the state it belonged to, abusing their status as a legitimate religious entity so it could weaken its father. Like a reversal of the Greek pantheon, Christianity was a wicked Zeus who was conceived in the dying belly of Cronus, chewing open and suckling on the innards of the Titan so he might spring from the corpse of his father.

Throughout the entirety of the Bible there is a lack of heroism, of glory by virtue by the might of mortal men that one would find in pagan archetypes. Instead, there is the ancient gynecocratic tradition of the virgin birth, the symbol of spiritual power granted via Mary to Jesus. This is taken to the extremes when the martyrdoms occur and each 'victim'—including the Son of God himself—is referenced to as a child of God or the Mother or so on. One could say the spirit of Christianity is rooted in that Semitic spirit of victimization, on the universal 'suffering' that they must endure to transcend.

No other modern denomination has been able to clone that same 'journey of suffering' and transform into a doppelgänger of the Semitic tradition as Mormons. Just like the Jews fleeing Egypt with Moses like Joseph and the journey westward, they likewise captured the spirit of the martyr by self-exiling themselves across the plains. Mormons even went to the length of calling other white people *GENTILES* for not being members of their faith—despite that they were an overwhelming majority Anglo and Scandinavian—LARPing as Semitic Puritans without a drop of Israelite blood among their entire congregation. Furries have more of a claim to their delusional, degenerate fetishization of animals than any Christians do to being 'Jewish'.

Whenever Mormons are challenged on their ancestor's crimes back east, they'll always stretch some yarn about how 'the Missourians wanted us dead without repercussion' and how 'Joseph died because they couldn't tolerate us!'. They will cry bullshit when you point out that the Mormons committed theft and all manner of crimes—even torching a printing press who challenged their rule in Illinois, while still claiming to be the victims of persecution. Or better yet, the relationship between the outlaws and their Mormon neighbors who happily sanctioned their lawless behavior so long as they weren't the victims of the crimes themselves. Cattle rustling and train robbery weren't against the Word of Wisdom so long as it was your neighbor and not you at the end of a revolver.

Despite the exclusionary racial laws, this is why Mormons are so often in league and claim to be the same blood as Zionists. It's their shared contrived sense of victimhood at the hands of the World™, that they are ever fleeing from death, and so they must control it. Perhaps this is why Mormons became the white hybrid-Semites—being only 1.4% of the US population and still being worth billions upon billions, owning millions of acres and Hawaii...

I was never a bad Mormon. Contrary to my rebellious blood, for much of my childhood and into my teens I was a studious and respectable member of the LDS church. I never swore, I shined my Sunday shoes and I never missed a meeting. I was considered one of the most reliable and dutiful boys of our ward, always available to harvest the hard-earned dollars of my neighbors in 'Fast Offerings'—the church's roundabout way of extorting their members like every other Christian denomination. If you were to look outside on Sunday afternoons, you'd catch a glimpse of my chubby assed self in those stereotypically Mormon suits—a poorly fitting, wide-shouldered black blazer.

I can't tell you why I was such a fastidious member. Only in highly introspective moments am I able to 'drift' back into that mindset: the comfortably numb and suppressed male drone, more than eager to oblige and gladly shill for the Church. I suspect you could ask a Ruskie prison guard at one of the Gulags a similar question. They'd shrug and say 'it was just life and it was my job' between mouthfuls of contraband ethanol. After my 're-birth' I've diagnosed my previous state of mind to death of ego that I can only rarely glimpse on equinox moons whilst John Denver plays in the background. It is a strange state of thinking being so fantastical and sentimental.

Though I never reached the prestigious title of 'missionary' and traveled as a naivete 18-year old to tell strangers that they *needed* my message about the international religion founded by the visionary pedophile and charlatan extraordinaire, Joseph Smith, I earned every step along the way towards the highest priesthood. If certain events had not unfolded and the mask of spiritual limbo had not been ripped away from my face, I am not arrogant enough to assume that I would have become a modern goon, a pagan scoundrel. On the other hand, I can say without a drop of insincerity that I do possess the soul of the rebellious type. They say all trauma leaves scars, many that are still raw on your psyche. I don't need a study to believe that to be true.

Some days, I truly believe I would have still been a rebel as a Good Mormon Boy—trapped and silently screaming beneath the meat and skeleton of a drone, unable to comprehend the devices that kept me restrained.

For this reason, I do not hate Mormons, nor their religion. It is no longer part of my spiritual consciousness. No matter how much this work may appear that I am pouring vinegar into the wounds I inflict upon Christian thought, it is not to insult for the pleasure of it.

What is a nerd? How do we define the nerd? Upon what premises can we distinguish a nerd from, say, a hobbyist or enthusiast? My definition of the nerd is such: the intelligent and emasculated male who accepts his place in society—at the bottom, happy to contend with mediocrity and self-induced shame, only imagining exaltation so long as he can wander through life without being harmed or gaining the unwanted attention of others.

The spiritual nerd is the axiom of the modern Mormon man, the emasculated BYU WASP. The average Mormon male is a mentally crippled and dopey thing—an absolute *nerd*! He has no choice in his destiny, regardless of his disposition. Unfortunately by the circumstances that have sprung from the radical decline of femininity of the last century and the Christian tradition of worshipping the lunar spirit, he is shackled by the balls and forced to lick the feet of the oligarchy. From a young age, he is instructed that his entire purpose will be to be a good husband and father—both on their own are positive traits—and never to stray from being decent and generous with his service.

You must understand that for the Mormon nerd, his responsibilities expected of him are nearly innumerable: to administer the sacrament, knock doors for cash, guide his fellow wayward youth, attend and participate in scouting (until recently) live the covenants and rigidly refuse the worldly temptations his peers will indulge, read the Book of Mormon/Bible exclusively, prepare for his 2-year long mission that will come as soon as he graduates high school, and then everything else expected of a boy as far as education and work. Ah but the most important part? He will eagerly await to be married right off a mission to a dutiful virgin who then will help him rear a family from the ripe age of 20.

Some of you must be thinking, with jealousy or ire: *"Mormons are living the bygone American Dream of 1950! Absurd!"* I'm afraid to inform you that this dream has outlived its eligibility.

The rot that has permeated the sanctity of marriage and union of man and woman during the post-modern society—feminism which began as a noble delusion and became the 'YASSSS QUEEN' movement, has crippled the Mormon Nerd. Marriage in the 21st century has been put on indefinite suspension due to hypergamy and the liberalization of women. At least for the average Millennial male, he has an escape from the women that have abandoned him: degenerate vices like liquor, weed, porn, and fast-food slop. Some on the solar side ignore such impulses and turn to the Temple of Iron, homesteading, mountaineering, and so forth. For the Mormon Nerd there is no such escape without sinning. To be independent is to be not fulfilling his oaths to the Proclamation on the Family.

Another fundamental truth is that the Mormon Nerd is exclusively Conservative™, if not further to the right. No matter how gay or modernist the secular Christian wings are, Mormonism has produced the single largest body of meritocratic and self-righteous men on the earth. The bureaucracy of the Church is no different than Nike or Amazon and has slowly but gradually backpedaled on its 'values' as a PR move. The organization does not condemn globo-homo, even endorsing it with 'love and compassion' so long as it doesn't get '*butt-hole sticky-icky fucky-fucky*' between its gay members. How goddamned hypocritical.

But as we know, being a Conservative is being impotent. The most inflammatory thinker I have heard a Mormon Nerd quote to me is Ben Shapiro...

However, even the Mormon Nerd understands the political consequence of shifting morals. I'd often remark with my friends in church that the rare times God ever directly punished humanity, it was Sodom and Gomorrah alone that drove the big man in the sky to drop a fucking laser beam that nuked a civilization and turn some bitch into a pillar of meth for daring to look back. "*That's right*", we would say, "*if you're a Christian, your God hates gays with such utter contempt that he doesn't want you to even so much as glimpse with your beady little gumballs at his absolute annihilation of said degenerates without rendering you into a basic food seasoning*!"

Somehow despite this, a great deal of modern Christians can justify that God didn't hate the homo. These people are delusional and should be institutionalized.

The Mormon Church has politically drifted ahead of its polygamous, rebellious roots—abandoning its male priesthood, slipping further and further down that greasy slope towards the pit of narcissistic progressivism. It does not fare better for the Mormon Nerd from here. The Mormon Church has even gone as far as to disassociate itself from any form of political populism, specifically nationalism, which it vehemently opposes. But what would you expect of the religion of universalism?

As those chaste girls of his hometown ward go to college to lose their virginity and soul, the Mormon Nerd remains stapled by his balls to the foundation of his faith—he is disallowed from abandoning his post. He is the sentry to an empty camp. A guard to an empty prison. While female Mormons decided to 'be more than a mom' and pursue fruitless careers, he is expected to rot and wither, his remaining choices for salvation remain to be dumpy or the reviled women no sane man would take. This is why I do not envy, nor hate the Mormon Nerd. I cannot hate what I pity.

Since my apostasy from the faith, I have met dozens of such nerds who have ultimately reared against Mormonism Inc—feeling betrayed and wounded by this tragedy. At the pagan rites I have hosted, by the roaring fire and between mouthfuls of whiskey, I have silently listened to their confessions. Like all other nerds when confronted with the sobering recognition of their reality, they yowl at the midnight air like a panther coming home to her den and discovers her litter swallowed whole by an anaconda. Betrayal was always in their eyes but they dared not speak it. The Church was their life. How could they blame it for the lesbian-fluoride in the water that turned their women into untenable pythons?

After venting such anger, any man in such a situation should, I recommended them to refrain from abusing the liquor and offered them words from the Havamal. We'd end the night with joyous cheer and reflect on our revelry with grins later. Even for those who remained sober of our revelry, they went on to pursue the Temple of Iron, reading esoteric philosophy, and are pursuing families. I wish them the best of luck.

Nonetheless, the issue of the Mormon Nerd and his suffering plagued me for days to come. The solution I came to after hearing such similar stories was such: *is finding a woman to marry immediately critical to your survival*? Such a blunt question can be disarming but yield surprising success. None of them agreed. I posited that they should seek three things in the immediate future: wealth, knowledge, and vitality.

It is encouraging that many of my fellow Mormon Nerds have since begun to understand the 'self-imposed prison' that locked their soul out of their conditioned mind. Most began to adopt a Gnostic approach to their faith and have expanded their lists of reading. Through rigorous physical activity, they have already discarded their pseudo-intellectual shell and embraced the barbaric intelligence—discussing symbolism and nature in intensive detail, spotting wild game off the trail and enjoying the simplicity of each other's company. Many I believe have converted to the pagan ideal already…they simply lack the urgency or gusto to axe the flimsy threads holding them to Mormonism.

The problem with women and marriage remains, but there is yet hope for the Mormon Nerd. Should they begin to mass challenge their wrinkled Elders of Zion, rise against their rule as Caesar did of the inept Republic and demand reformation, there will be hell to pay...

Chivalry is dead but it might have had its true revival birthed from the Mormons during its sapling days, had the hyper-feminine lunar power of Emma Smith not been so prominent. I'm not sure why so many idolized her like some feminist icon—despite her treason to the cause, abandoning the cult that moved Westwards with Brigham Young, electing her children as receivers of God's revelations—throughout my youth. I think some wanted her to transcend through the Mormon mythos into a modern Mary Magdalene type.

Insufferable.

How different the spirit of the pioneers would have been, their religion and civilization had there been a cultural shift to idolize the noble thugs like Butch Cassidy and Porter Rockwell, both Mormons but men of action and honor instead of pacifist martyrs like Joseph Smith! A reversal of the tides would have occurred. Rather than molding the proud explorer European stock into WASP crypto-Jews running multi-level marketing companies selling snake oil, this return to the Indo-European caste system would have revitalized an aspect of Mithras.

Imagine! A reality of the Wild West for 100 years, a war waged by a sovereign nation of neo-crusader outlaws plundering the banks and railroad companies who were still staggering in the ashes of the Civil War—paintings of the holy conflict displayed in every Mormon home. The very word 'Mormon' would be equivalent to the honorary title of a knight, granted only to a man worthy of the title. This is what could have been!

Chivalry and action are lacking from the modern Christian heart. No, I am not speaking of the fedora-tipping lobotomize who props a door open for a boomer couple and

I speak of the barbaric element that flooded into the Middle Ages during the metamorphosis of the Christianization of Europe—the original Aryan, Scythian, and Celtic spirit that was so intensively virile and stoic compared to the Machiavellian mask of deceit and shrewdness. This bold aura of action and self-determination that was distinctly pagan enforced a meritocracy of honor that is revered to this day as the height of Christendom. I heard their echoes in the architecture of the fearsome armored warriors posted on the corners of Lucerne, spearing demonic and draconic foes. Nowhere seen was even a hint of a painting of meek and mild Christ, leading a crowd of obsequious sheep to graze in eternal mindlessness.

Virility and the youthful 'pursuit of exploration' has been absent from the rotting corpse of modern Christianity for ages. The outcome of this dark harvest is that we have thus to view Christianity through the lens of concentric Televangelism: the hegemony of the toothy TV pastor and megachurch that demand rivers of tribute. Nothing is more cowardly and subversive than the claim to convert hundreds of thousands for a monetary exchange—and far apart from the 'Imperial Ideal' of the crusader.

I won't be a petty cocksucker and say that Christianity doesn't possess even a ghost of chivalry anymore—quite the opposite. I've met more than a handful of courageous, bloodthirsty Christian men who I'd gladly trek over mountains, share a drink and fight with. But it is the rare *exception*, not the rule. No orthodox or sect is governed by men of pure action and intellect—only those who covet their mandates and petty tax laws.

It is known, alleged but hardly disproven, that the Templars had secret initiation rituals that involved spitting on the cross, denying Christ in a form of repudiation—even accused of engaging in homosexuality and admitting to worshipping Baphomet. While I think the latter two could have been slander to justify the torture and heretical hysteria, there is validity to this ritual. The Templars were the pinnacle of the solar principle, aspiring to heroism and courage over the Islamic threat to their perceived Holy Land. They deeply believed in the ethos of freedom, faith, and duty. Why would it be so difficult to believe that the Templars themselves rejected the soft, unaffirmed character of abstract 'salvation' that encompassed the Big Church?

The real dig at Christianity is self-inflicted. Christians are their own worst enemy. It is that you can never *not* be blasphemous to question the ideals, even from within. It's a neurotic game of running inside a revolving door, divided into a thousand different spaces housing each denomination and non-denomination—but you can never fully enter into the lobby of God's Kingdom beyond. You can step back outside and reassess if you'd like to re-enter and step inside a new space, but you can never be considered equal by your peers—Mormons, Baptists, Protestants, Catholics, and the rest. They'll keep the revolving door permanently moving. Round and round they'll all go, playing the game they build themselves, pushing faster at the hope they'll find themselves inside the glass and marble glory of Paradise.

You might think this game ends until another group of incorrigibles discovers a 'contradictory scripture' and then another group of nerds will split to make their own denomination off an entirely insignificant error. A pathetic waste of life and energy dedicated now to a 'glaring' error in the ever-changing Bible that somehow was previously ignored. Every hundred years, another Nicene Creed.

To anybody with a stubbornly free spirit, this puritanical arrogance is a futile pursuit of hellish fervor.

One redeeming quality the Mormons and their institution—besides the foundation of the family structure—is their endowment of scouting, previously the Boy Scouts before the church divorced itself over the homo scandal. I've heard many of my peers complain about the outdated methods of the Boy Scouts regarding the antiquated uniforms and goofy rituals. These same urbanite peers also couldn't fell a tree, ignite a fire with their hands alone, or feel at home in the wild if a revolver was pressed into their feeble necks. I would argue that scouting and its principles were the only *true* education I received as a youth.

The modernist pathologies of education, especially in private and charter schooling, consider themselves supreme by the way they organize themselves as complex, up-to-fashion with soft pastel splashes of 'design' and cloak themselves with slogans full of convoluted verbiage like "creating dynamic environments that engage students to be world citizens tomorrow with open minds and open hearts". These programs boast exemplary 'testing scores', pad their staff with counselors, and market their crab cake brainwashing by promising your children will be on the fast-track to successful careers. Make your child intelligent in just a few years...all for a modest price of course.

What wealthy parents like those of Granola Land fail to understand when offloading their brats into these institutions, is they cannot cheat 'the system' of the highest order of meritocracy. Their money cannot simply buy their children out of the most primordial and precious tool we have—that what separates the wheat from the chaff—deprivation. It is the art of presenting a task to a child with finite resources and limited experience. Survivalism. Within the cultured confines of a 'field trip' or group activities, a private school can introduce the children of the elite to learn the Latin names of plants and 'analyze them' but never truly *learn* the environment around them. Everything is skin deep.

Some being, whether it was a God or a cow licking primordial ice, gave Man a brain but also claws and a tongue. Children have the instinct to explore their habitat with these because each bug bite or found treasure of a mushroom, a young human will understand the boundaries of nature. This is something that no science or math can teach you.

Boy Scouts was the actualization of Transcendentalism. What else could you expect from the likes of Lord Baden Powell and Frederick Russell Burnham, veterans of the African Boer Wars? Bushcraft masters, military junkies, and men of grit. Hitler himself was so envious of the Scouting Program that he banned it and recreated one in his image.

The Scout's core goal is that through 'deprivation within nature', a child is given a framework of psychological and mental tools to handle his environment. While the consequences of nature are less severe than a 13-day slug through the grizzly-dominated Bob Marshall wilderness, risks are nonetheless present.

Stray too far from your campsite and you would be as good as stranded from civilization. Eat the wrong berry and expect to paint your tent with puke. Piss off the wrong peer and he'll smear his feces on your rain fly.

My first foray into Boy Scout Camp was at a place called Camp Indian Axe. Going there it was utterly devoid of this feel-good advertising I was given in my education in Granola Land—we were told to bring nothing but our uniforms, tents, hatchets, fire-starting tools, swim shorts and a flashlight. Game boys were confiscated and candy rationed. While at night we reveled and hooted playing night-games, our entire days were spent in the dirt, whether it was learning practical first aid, wilderness survival, or practicing our swimming—all essential skills needed in the wilderness.

Yet there is another more poignant lesson in scouting that I encountered: mentorship. A woefully accurate statement is that celebrities are made role models in this banal, culturally defunct world because fathers aren't around or have a weak impact on their son's lives. Scouting remains one of the few places where this mentorship can still guide boys towards successful paths even for the mere two weeks they might be together. I met some scoutmasters in my time, some ex-military, others just engineers and businessmen who cared enough to dole wisdom to us in our early teens. Some of those lessons were eternal—such as learning how to control my mood by simply going taking strolls through nature and learning to control my breathing.

I am compelled to state that none of these scoutmasters were bodybuilders, millionaires, or any of the 'highest' forms of successful men. I doubt those kinds of men would have any interest in participating in scouting or a similar outfit. This is what is so detrimental to our case: finding male tutors in the highest levels of competency for our next generations. Greed is a powerful shadow in this regard. There is no monetary benefit to passing on such valuable wisdoms to youth. Even for a rich man, he would likely feel little compulsion to share the secrets of his trade to his firstborn son.

Is it any wonder that in a time when masculinity is held in such contempt—fabricated into some parody of its actual self for the sake of cultural mockery by the hollow-eyed vultures that run this marionette show—that Scouting and camaraderie among young men are also villainized?

My fondest and perhaps the most impressionable memory I have of scouting is of conquering Bonesaw—a rumor we'd been told of since our first day. On the shallow lake of Indian Axe, the organizers of the camp had constructed a gigantic craft, a fighting platform with dozens of canoes lashed together to form this behemoth barge manned by a score of the teenage and adult camp guides. To that date, Bonesaw had never lost. On the second to last day, we were given the opportunity to do what previous scouts were unable to: sink it to the mud. The rules of the naval battle were simple: scouts could team up in small canoes and attack Bonesaw in any way they saw fit, so long as our canoes remained afloat. Myself and Red-Haired Devilspawn were among the first wave to assault Bonesaw.

It was a massacre.

While our strategy was to slingshot around the small island before both abandoning our craft to board Bonesaw, the other scouts had long been sunk and defeated, floating in their orange jackets and crying for the safety of the shore. We expertly—because we'd spent all week preparing our canoe handling—used the island in the center to slingshot around and caught Bonesaw by surprise. My chubby ass was able to knock off a few counselors before I was kicked into the water. Red-Haired was not so lucky, catching a few fists in the mouth before landing in the reeds. It was against the rules to punch but a feisty, opulent 17 year-old whale had decided she was above the rules.

I'll never forget Red-Haired in his homosexual fury, grabbing fistfuls of mud by the reeds and lobbing them at the unprotected eyes of the gibbering counselors on their barge. Utter chaos, that lad. By the time the second wave of canoes had slammed into Bonesaw, it was over—the older scouts piledrove the mud-blinded counselors into the bilgewater and reeds while the rest of us commandeered Bonesaw, sending it to the bubbling 'deep'. With mud in our eyes and water in our noses, we cheered as the barge disappeared beneath the surface. We were the first scouts to ever sink it, thanks to Red-Haired and his rule-breaking.

The lesson learned? The world is a place of rules it sets but does not follow itself.

So *always* fight fucking dirty.

Inevitably and soon, the Mormons will come to a crossroads of culture. The world is swiftly moving towards a period where every institution must retain a Diversity Commissar and a People's Militia of enforcers. While I don't believe the Church has lasted so long without bribery and their connections to New York, an unforeseen split in their seams has occurred at the university level—including at their prestigious BYU. It is filled with anemic, buzzcut troglodytes who slaver at the mouth at their 'white heritage', demanding the eradication of 'all oppression'. Those Mormon Nerds I spoke of are largely single—I know and speak to many of them—who grow nauseous at the thought of marrying such wenches. I do not blame them. But they have no say in this—the die has been cast!

What will remain of the Church when their centrifugal force of the traditional family unit is no longer self-sustaining? There will be a call to arms for children but the birthrates will remain pitiful. The Mexican migrant will fill the urban neighborhoods and the fragmented 'Sons of Zion' will be nothing less than a diaspora of bees, bereft of their hive and a purpose, cursed to float through life and pollinate merely for the pleasure. If there was any vitality in this exodus to Zion in the 19th century, it has long been sapped by their elders.

Will the Mormons revolt? Only time will tell. There are a few bold nationalists who propagate among their ranks among the hordes of Randians and Romneyites. But my money is that it will take Avant Guard rule-breakers, the punks and Goons, not the straight collared rule-followers to claim the future of the Western World.

BLOOD AND GRANOLA

Violence is a lost currency. The subconscious lust of every man's ego, his desire to inflict mortal judgment. In many ways, it is the keystone of humanity.

But nobody can ever tell you what it is *like*.

It can be penned in visceral brutality in the clash of iron like a medieval saga by Cornwell, or romantic Shakespeare. You could spend your entire life watching martial arts films, studying the speed and kinetic force a fighter wields, his foot movement and technique, so on. A world of literature exists for man's favorite pastime—the art of war—and is readily accessible for anyone to delve into. The training in a safe, sweat-stained environment, be it karate, krav maga, or jiu-jitsu will toughen a man. And after all of that, none of that will prepare you for the mindless bedlam that is *fighting*.

I spent my childhood and teenage years brawling, wrestling, smacking, beating, tussling, rustling, and warring with my peers. I can instantly tell when somebody has never thrown fists or been the recipient of an actual pounding—it's always in their eyes when they speak of these things. Opposite of this is the glazed-over, dark glint of acknowledgment that comes from somebody who has been engaged in a brawl or worse.

Recently a photographer released documentation of soldier's facial features before, during, and after their deployment to combat-active bases in Syria and Iraq—you will see what I mean when you see it, their hardened, sullen expressions are so starkly opposed to the common man's. No, I don't mean that fighting alone is the same as modern warfare but there is a similarity to the two: people can be distinctly separated by their gaze, simply whether or not they have dealt lasting damage to another human.

A singleness of soul is forged instantly when Man is made to inflict his ultimate will—the mortal gravity of violence—upon another and knows when it will be reciprocated. An apathetic focus makes one seem like a pickaxe designed to obliterate stone without a qualm.

My theory on why men envy the fighter and lust after the military man is that they wish for two things: escape from their overworked existence and to indulge in our basest instinct. Warfare is in our blood. Even if we aren't related to them, the reason many believe we came from apes is due to the chimp's insatiable aggressiveness, its hooting cannibalistic self. Why else do you think that women have fetishes of pirates, bandits, and warlords on their cheesy romance novels? For the same reason why pudgy neocon American men buy themselves into debt to prepare themselves for the 'boogaloo' and even the most staunchly Marxist woman will admit to fantasizing about being tied up in a rapey manner and choked by a powerful man.

The book-inspired movie of Fight Club appealed to so many men of the turn of the millennia specifically because of its contextual dissection of the modern urbanite: yearning for an unsanctioned contest in an emasculated society, not the sterilized achievement system that replaced the meritocracy of yore. While the movie took a strange, hyperbolic direction into unfathomable chaos and schizophrenia, the movie itself broke free of what you might consider the careful programming of Hollywood. 'Fight' was no longer a dirty word—it became a symbol of pride among the subterranean pariah society of Fight Club. So many men I know who watched that film have become demystified of the shrouding and exoteric modern world. Whether it was the catalyst or a side effect, a mere splinter in their consciousness, the outcome has been the same.

During a bar-crawl for a mutual's 21st birthday, I

tagged along with their group in the urban capital of my youth. A random man who lurked among us joined me at the third or fourth bar where I was nursing one of those shitty, overpriced IPAs. Without warning, he began quoting Tyler Durden, about how ugly the city was and its soulless spaghetti artwork wrought in plastic and steel. I thought he was joking at first, realizing that he began to tear up. I think the alcohol and my carefree presence allowed him to confide his secret hatred for the society he found himself in. I had not watched the movie at the time so I simply nodded to his rambling. A common and myopic review of the film from many normies is that 'men deeply desiring to fight' is a pathological coping mechanism for fatherlessness.

Is it? Do men *only* fight to vent their buried sorrows onto the world through vicious fist-slinging? Or is there something more...perhaps a divine anger that men discover...a pure kerosene fury like the blood of Tyr running white-hot in their veins which distills even time itself in the act of war?

Early on I was a participant to mostly puppy fights and roughhousing with my friends, my brother, and a few rivals. None were serious or resulted in less than a bruise and wounded ego. It wasn't until I hit 5th grade before I got myself in a real fight.

Movies always make the mistake of presenting physical conflict in a way that seems too predictable—everyone is broadcasting their next move, their feelings worn like a coat, the dialogue crafted in a way to grant a character *control* of the situation. These 'realistic dramas' are all written by women whose apartments reek of cat piss. Fights rarely have a prelude. You could be standing in the same classroom and not know the brawl occurred until it's over and the horde is gathered around. The majority of the dozens of fights I was a participant in were in ordinary environments during innocuous times, walking down a hallway or off a bus, with no warning except the blunt force of knuckles rapping on your skull. And they're over in seconds.

To be frank I remember little of that first brawl I had with a far larger opponent. He reeked of burrito, his ham-like hands throttled my throat. I can remember laughing and crying at the same time, dangling from his grip. It must have lasted only a dozen or so seconds.

Hours later and I was nursing my throat with an icepack in the principal's office. She was a middle manager dike, a true suburban Karen who laughably wore pantsuits at an elementary school and had little understanding of the male nature she so fervently emulated. Her opening statements were abstract regarding 'learning environments' and how I was as to blame as the 200 lb, 6' foot tall supersized gordito who tried to wring me like a chicken. Outrage filled my midget child form but I had no alternative but to sit and pout. My folks came, debated with her, and took me home.

That was only the first time of many.

Say you encounter another goon outside the bar. You caught him glancing at your girlfriend while you ordered spiked lemonade or some other fruity nonsense. In a lapse of judgment, you called him an abrasive slur. Before you can escape into your Uber, this guido lumbers towards you—all two hundred and thirty pounds prepared to sling you into a hospital bed. Suddenly your survival instincts are challenged in your mundane, urbanite life. Do you run? What do you do when he gets to you and pummels your smart-ass mouth?

Fighting is eighty percent breathing, ten percent technique, and the rest ego. By learning how to focus with a cool head when fists fly, you can predict and react to your foe quicker. This is the lesson you'll never learn in a martial arts studio. Forget the 'rushing bull', hatchet kick, or whatever other judo move to use his weight against him. You forget everything that isn't muscle memory.

Cut your ego. Looking cool is a side-effect. Focus on breathing, like meditation. In and out. When you get hit—and no doubt, your gums will turn to hamburger after a few rounds of pummeling—keep your tongue in your mouth. Keep your eyes open and when he moves, move with him. Fighting is a dance for chimps and gorillas. You'll survive almost every encounter by holding your ground and breathing. That tunnel vision I speak of is the raw fact—if a train was blaring into your right ear, you'd hardly notice. Most brawls are blind.

The second rule is the easiest: conserve your energy. In Thailand, there's a bar with an MMA ring built inside so you can fight an amateur Muy Thai fighter for free drinks. Rarely, if ever, the scrappy Thai man loses—even against a string of American Thads. Why? Because the Thai man is a master of energy conservation. He wastes less than a breath waiting for his foe to tire their bludgeoning fists against his tanned hide. He'll counter-attack and knock men twice his size to the mat like a jungle cat with ease. I knew someone who fought one of these Thai tigers and was amazed at the sheer endurance and confidence they possessed.

Harness only a scrap of this skill—turtling down, retaliating only when necessary, will grant you an intense advantage.

Ignore the guido's grunting and his impulse to whale on you, the fear that this mass will drive you to the concrete. He'll exhaust himself if he doesn't maintain breathing, which is likely. Making him move unnecessarily and without notice will set him off-balance—good. He might trip up or otherwise take your steps as a kind of retreat.

Last is the most important rule: *you didn't back down like a pussy.*

I didn't write this little guide on how to win to fight but what to do when you're in one. Just like how when you pick up a gun and you're a shit shot, so are you a poor fighter. The difference is that fists are bullets and you'll end up with sore cheekbones and a bruised ego afterward. But there's more, of course. If you actually fought this knockoff Jersey Shore co-star, then you're probably sitting in a squad car, your wrists already slapped in irons, mentally awaiting the jail cell. Teenagers are hardly allowed to do this kind of thing anymore, let alone 'adults' who are supposed to be courteous and all the other nonsense rules that we Europeans make and nobody in our diverse society follows.

What you just did in this hypothetical scenario fulfilled a primordial rite that so few men in this age dream of—earning yourself a badge that cannot be faked or reproduced. A saying goes that "a man is only judged by the weight of his actions" or so on.

If you did not cower and responded to the physical Will of another man, fist to fist, you now understand that the gravity of your soul is not confined *merely* to words or abstract thoughts but extrapolated in its explosive entirety. The power of Thor in your bones, metaphorical might behind every swing.

You're now a *man* in reality...

As per my childhood in the Diverse States Inc. I fought my fair share of Europeans, Mexicans, Half-Halfs, and Africans. You can learn a lot about race by how people fight. It's not a matter of whether you're an 'evil racist' or you're a hall monitor egalitarian with an agenda or chip on your shoulder. By pure observation, you can determine significant cultural differences between races and understand your place in the food chain. Survival always trumps appearing nice. Cultures and their forms of fighting are in fact, quite 'diverse'.

European or white kids haven't changed since the Viking Golden Age. They scream *'FORM THE SQUARE'* as they chant for one on one champion duels. Winner takes all, honor is everything for them. Mexicans or other Latinos like tag-team, maybe their Mayan ancestors formed hunting pairs. I always brought a buddy—willing or otherwise—to help when a one-man fight became a three-man. But in my experience Blacks or Africans have a total disregard for these codes entirely. Africans fight no different than the communist warbands and profiteers during the Rhodesian conflict: a mass horde clusterfuck of flesh and senseless violence.

I got in trouble with the only black kids in one school—all adopted by upper middle-class white families, yet somehow ended up acting like an inner-city gang. One of them, a 5'4 Kevin Hart-wannabe and accused rapist yelled that I called his mother a 'n*gger-chimp' when he forced himself on a lap of a friend of mine. After the whole event, I wish I had. Another lesson from this was to *never apologize to appease a mob, especially for a social crime you didn't commit.* I went on the bus and apologized dozens of times, pleading to not be called a racist.

You see, it doesn't matter with them—they wanted to

justify the fight they were looking for.

I was ambushed during lunch by no less than a dozen of these mongrels, who had no desire to allow me to defend myself or my words. It was chaos. While I was chewing on my food, they surrounded me and slammed me into the table. I remember distinctly coughgin up my food in chunks on the table, throwing fists in every direction, hoping I'd catch one or two, thinking I might die. All I remember is the jocks—who I had no relations with as a punk and druggie—reaching in and pulling me out of Gorilla Town, defending my beaten hide as the horde only hooted for blood. The cops soon came after and made arrests, pulling tasers out and corralling all the students out.

In the aftermath of the fight, there were 3 permanent expulsions, 7 suspensions, and a month-long ordeal of negotiations with various parents. When the dust settled it was made known to me that several of the ringleaders of the ambush were already on probation for innumerable conflicts and violations. I had to stay inside the school counselor's room for the rest of the week with a friend in case there was another ambush. Parents of the black hooligans called it a 'racial attack' and threatened lawsuits because their Bible-named Chicago adoptees would be barred from athletic scholarships for being charged with aggravated assault. They never denied that their black 'sons' had committed a hate crime, nor that they wanted to fight. One parent even dared to tell the school that I 'might get shot' if I wasn't careful about what I said.

A friend of mine posted a story of a man who survived a gruesome mauling by a Yukon bear with a face that looked like it'd been kissed by a woodchipper, killing the bear with a string of life left and his face hanging off his bones. It went quite viral and he was shocked that he could categorize the responses in a file cabinet just purely based on the race of the persons commenting: Europeans replied that the man was the echelon of masculinity, Arabs thought he should have died, Asians were more interested in the bear's disposition, and Africans believed he had 'lost' because he was wounded at all.

I was not as shocked as he was, given my experiences.

I would prefer it if all cultures and people had such a dedication to the idea of honor and noble contest. The reality of course is not as utopian or egalitarian as it might seem and explains why in the 21st century, Scandinavian girls get their heads lopped off by Moroccan men. German girls are drugged and molested by Somalian 'migrants' who lurk in the urban shadows. Rape gangs in the UK are sheltered by NGOs and various 'activist' groups. Such barbarism in ancient times would have resulted in a furious swell of longships destined to sunder the North African coastline and salt the earth for generations.

But it is utterly beyond the pale of the dogmatic liberal society to highlight these differences in how diverse war is. We do not live in a time where making such statements, no matter how truthful, will make you appear as a student of the world but the opposite. Bugmen and other such loathsome characters would rather their fellow whites kiss the feet of Wakanda militias dressed and beg to have their pudgy wives be raped in retribution for slavery.

This firmly reinforces my previous mantra and adds a new one: *never apologize for social crimes and always know your opponents.*

Have you ever considered if a Pashtun freedom fighter in Korangal valley has ever had a stress-induced coma over being called a bitch? It's a fruitless exercise. He'd just level his 50 year-old AKM and unload into his accuser. Or laugh full-bellied with crooked teeth. That's what thousands of years of warfare will do to a tribe: it will fortify them against pitiful anxieties that cripple the West.

We were once a psychologically hardy people. Mountain men and explorers used to tread the same soil of the Rockies, leaving the skulls of Indian assassins and log cabins built by their bare hands in the vast wilderness. But the comforts of modernity have rotted our collective gums and made us toothless against The Wild. You can't walk into a decent neighborhood without seeing the dark lenses of a hundred surveillance systems—and for what? If I was a true bandit or robber, I'd merely knock out your power box behind your house, dress like a repairman, and come in broad daylight. And I have little doubt those homeowners sit in their office cubes in a cold sweat, fastidiously checking their security app and over-analyzing every flicker of movement on the street. How have we become so soft?

We have villainized ordinary violence, declared it obsolete and buried it in a shallow grave.

On the other hand, the fetishization of state-sanctioned violence through the military is something glaring in the early 21st century among Millenials. Not just the first-person shooter video games, camouflage fashions or hyper-fascination with gun collections but with another credence—having a friend whose been to Iraq, reading books on ISIS or being an 'expert' on foreign policy. Being a veteran in any capacity is no longer a career choice but is a medal in itself—granting one immunity in conversations and privileges of 15% discounts at select retail stores.

It is surreal to see my fellow American citizens grovel and slobber 'thank you for your service' to the feet of soldiers who, at the behest of the Military-Industrial Complex gangsters like Raytheon and Northrop Grumman, fought an illegal war so Israeli-Spook operations could survey 'Strategic Resources' for later mining. They'll beg for expert advice on how to shoot their rifles and talk about how they 'wanted to join the military'. This sort of odd pseudo-patriotism is extremely common but makes complete sense.

The First World has declared that the only way for a man to heed his internal governances and employ his ultimate will of violence must be licensed and highly regulated—in doing so, he simultaneously enforces *their* Will by default. A protocol is placed on all Violence™ and can only be accessed by a mountain of bureaucracy. This creates a social uniform that can be displayed outwardly like a camouflage BDU—available only by he who is allowed to wield this sacred power. It drives a natural wedge between the few who follow their instincts and those who wish to appease the state, the unwashed masses. Criminals will still exist but man will doubt whether or not he is *allowed* to use violence.

Is it any wonder why so many envy the military man for owning the privilege to wield Violence™? The Taliban for freely retaliating against invasion? Colombian cartels for seizing power? But it must be this way.

Violence cannot be merely barbarism. Violence is social upheaval and redefining the boundaries that man dwells within. By and large, it is the blood that pumps within our collective consciousness and keeps us feeling alive. The only difference between the pacifistic period of the 21st century and before was that the winners of the last true wars understood that unregulated Violence™ meant an end to indefinite economic prosperity. They'd rather culture and society grow stagnant by the artificial ceasefire than to see the rivers of milk and honey fail to flow.

I don't write this with any level of satisfaction but the opposite. A world of men who cannot act violently—justly or otherwise—will only produce rainbow celibates like

Duncan Trussells who mentally masturbate about 'existentialism' on ketamine and not semi-mythological characters like Fredrick Selous whose names would inspire the likes of Rhodesian warbands immortalized as some of the fiercest fighting elite since the Spartans and Ulfhednar.

However, this tranquility dart of synthetic pacifism has an expiration date. Even in our most static, docile state, men can be so...unpredictable.

I always hear about how people are 'stressed'. Stressed about life, their spouse's health care, or if their TV show will get another season. Assuming they are telling the truth, I always ask why they go to a shrink and not diagnose themselves—asking the deep root of *why* they are stressed so easily. The typical response is a feral snarl—especially from women—who have no comprehension of this invisible puppet-master that yanks their heart every which way.

Yet I do not understand why stress has become such a dirty term.

Stress, this ghost of panic that elevates our emotions to form artificial conflict within our psyche is not a purely negative thing. Anxiety is expressed in someone who is conflicted—I have found generally in people who have trouble confronting their thoughts. Young women, for instance, are highly susceptible to anxiety. The feminine spirit is not one that adapts well to the high-stress corporate environment, the shark-tooth meat grinder that demands flesh for a reward. The 20-something female graduate cannot compete with the soulless psychopath salesman who is bereft of the capacity of human interaction beyond negotiation. Not all women are fragile eggshells but do you *want* a mother to be a corporate drone? Do you think the feminine ego needs to be hardened like reinforced iron, indifferent to children who need her embrace?

Stress should be vindicated—it is a power to use, a trainable skill you can develop to maximize your potential! Modern men hate it because they *waste it* on video games and women in their idle boyfriend shopping on Tinder. How egregious that such a valuable tool is discarded in the name of comfort. The lie that stress is something to be 'overcome' by exoteric means has been expertly marketed and sold in the West. Nobody ever questions this.

Sprint into the nearest mall and hurl a javelin into the stomach of the nearest powdered up wench. You have a

20% chance that it will impale a woman who's prescribed to antidepressant pills. ONE IN FIVE! This is not a joke! From a society that cannot decide whether the animals we've lived off of for thousands of years are edible, are the very same that mindlessly medicate themselves into hormonal oblivion with alien names like Zoloft and Prozac based on the professional advice of physicians. Do the pills make them happy? These are the same childless women who are constantly swirling deeply down a drain of psychosis ranting daily on Twitter, calling everyone right of the hyper-neutral liberalist perspective a '*fucking Nazi*' and demanding the death of all men.

This is your brain on drugs.

Picture the lab-grown horror our future will be where that number of pill-popping women will climb to *fifty* percent. Children won't even be a dream for our young couples. Neither will couples. Or any relationships between men and women. You'll have pay-to-play online dating for incels while the Millennials adopt Generation Hermione so they can LARP as parents to their mulatto cyborgs for the rest of their miserable, sedentary lives. Cat ladies will be considered legal guardians and granted tax breaks for each litter box in their cubby-apartments. The most sterile Kali Yuga imaginable.

Apocalypse aside, how many humans will it take to be sacrificed in the name of psychiatric greed—the white-coat Moloch—before we understand that anxiety is not a pernicious demon?

Evangelical philosopher types who cloak themselves in the civility of facts and logic are nothing more than idealist charlatans who deny the existence of the violent world. I fell for this honey trap after discovering Jordan Peterson—magnetized by the Canadian icon and his witty Kermit the Frog tone speaking the mind of Alan Watts. Overnight I became a 'rationalist' and dedicated my soul to this Rawlsian liberalism—the secular ethics and dedication to moralism in a decaying world.

Another figure I found myself fascinated by was the egghead Molyneux and his NAP, or the Non-Aggression Principle. Besides his scant bits about humans being tax-cattle and the elementary arguments on communism, I soon found that his search for truth types was not as investigative and curious as presumed. The idea of Universally Preferable Behavior or 'Universal Ethics' that is grounded atop the platform of Logic became absurd the longer I dwelled upon it. Consider this for a moment: what is logic but a derivative tool to analyze a subject?

How can this omnipotent LOGIC be anything more than a microscope—infinitely useful but limited to its ability to produce meaning beyond the original subject? What difference is there that the notion that all humans are linked together by this universal aura and Christian ethics?

The last is rhetorical, of course.

This agreement Molyneux poses, this NAP, that underlines that all social contracts and agreements *must* be non-violent so our world becomes symbiotic? It's belligerently retarded. If adopted, the Africans wouldn't see it as spurious but as an opportunity to prey upon pacified 'Western' civilization—they would send fleets of Somalis on zodiacs to pillage the coasts of the sterile Europeans. Chinese would blockade the United States, rape it of its earthly resources, and subjugate it under a plastic dynasty for a hundred thousand years. I would not even suspect much would change from the Invisible Empire of global financiers who already rules the West, save their glee that their work is done.

Libertarian ideals like the NAP are a luxury enjoyed only by the Anglo. Homogeneity has made them naivete, painted dumb smiles on their face while they believe in the 'moral corporation'. This is why you only see white men who endorse this philosophy, their circles absent of the 'diversity' they desperately pledge their movement will attract. Sharks of the leftist school of thought will ruthlessly declare this collection of white men as 'supremacy', circle around the life-raft ideology of libertarianism while the survivors cry out that 'they aren't the racists'. The sharks don't care—they're out for blood. Libertarians will sink to hell like the rest of us, albeit more gracefully.

The claims that LOGIC is the journey to truth and that by adopting these abstract principles rooted in Jewish and Christian law, we will somehow liberate ourselves from the grisly reality of mass-abortion, factory farming. and a drone-strike-happy authoritarian government?

Inevitably the true intention of these so-called 'great thinkers' from the secular liberal sphere such as Jordan Peterson, Molyneux, Shapiro, and the mass of these Intellectual Dark Weenies is to remove the balls from the European thought. It is purely an astroturf movement—multi-faceted but all marketing the same mentality: turning as many heterosexual European men into toothless, neurotic individuals who consciously try to disassociate themselves from their natural tribal tendencies so they don't form a coherent group. The

Intellectual Dark Web and their pathology are no less than a lame Diogenetic attempt to eradicate whatever remains of the founding spirit that settled America, except they're bereft of the Alpha Indifference that is so idealized from the Greek anarchic spirit and left only with the gay 'citizen of the world' tenet.

Yes, violence is a choice. But war is the jungle we dwell in. Peace was never an option but dignified suicide—to lay in the fetal position on the earthen floor and wail to be robbed of your autonomy. Man cannot persist as a species without aggression. He lives freely with a knife fashioned from a sharpened femur clamped in his teeth, his hands taking him up a mossy cliffside—prepared to hunt or be hunted as he ascends every upward...

Fighting as a solution to conspire against the modern world seems counter-productive and insane. I understand this. Soaking yourself in the inescapable fear that you must hunt or be hunted—the possibility that a single blow could crush the wrong part of your eggshell skull and end your existence all because some weird backpacker pagan man told you to...seems absurd.

But it's not.

What are you living for as a man or a woman? Is your penultimate destiny to make spreadsheets for an apathetic sociopath who'd happily use your eyeballs for golf balls—all so he can buy a nicer BMW and drop his brat mulatto children off at a more pretentious academy? Is the sum of your actions as a human to vacation after years of debt slavery—to enjoy life in retirement with overpriced margaritas at Turtle Bay as a vampire Boomer, speculating with half-zonked waitresses at the wet bar if you would have gone spearfishing if your spine hadn't been wrecked from that office chair.

In antiquity, not every noble nation had a professional army but it did have a caste of males who were warriors. Hoplites were also patriarchs who could vote as they had skin in the game. War was not just a hobby or the 'only solution' to solve issues—it was a blunt, metaphysical force. Priests received elemental ambrosia from the gods through initiatory practices and rites. Warriors could also be gifted such transcendent knowledge through warfare—such as the Mithras cults who went into caves and offered the future blood and spoils to their bloodthirsty deity. All physical conflict had a unifying principle: it psychologically and spiritually separated men from human cattle.

A recent bit of banter I posed to a group of tech-thirsty programmers was that their career—their very lives were 'designed for them' down to their squared glasses, fetishization of Science and the virtual programs they designed. Some recoiled and hissed, but a few admitted that this cleaved straight to the marrow: they knew it to be true. The Gods of the Modern World had sewn their life-thread to endless lines of letters, hyphens and frustration at Indian cohorts. Their destiny was made for them, down to their Grubhub orders and choice of gaming chair their spine slumped into. One even asked 'how can I free myself of this life'?

Easier asked than done.

Life is a struggle against nature and that is our destiny. Too many understand that to resist the struggle is the pathos of modernity—placing yourself in a padded collar and walking willingly in the cell—yet their resistance is words online and an eternal fist shaken at the Invisible Masters. Or better yet, adopting failed ideologies that are universally hated in order to spiritually rebel. This is no more useful than the cowardly AntiFa-gs who walk in black bloc and LARP in the streets, chanting *Viva La Resistance*.

Rioting and impulsive anarchy are self-immolating,

literally and metaphysically. When you merge with the crowd—the mindless mob to loot NIKE shoes, rip ATMs from sidewalks, and curb-stomp post office drivers because of a shared ambiguous hatred for the Establishment, you become part of the flame. Soon you'll be a pathetic pile ash and a scapegoat for an insurance claim. Those who chant for 'equality' will put their homes to the torch and soon equally be homeless on a pile of ash. Polite society that pretended to be egalitarian led to this. A society that has grown too complacent and has forgotten that life *is* fighting.

"Adversity is the first path to truth" is the commandment of Lord Byron as is, "Man, being reasonable, must get drunk; the best of life is but intoxication". Undeniable. Reading books is only equal to breaking fists upon another's skull. A man cannot be intelligent by intellectual debates alone, nor can he write about courage without ever having to exude it. Ernst Jünger and Yukio Mishima were only masters of poetry in the raw form because they understood the *beauty occurring through violence.*

If we are to be beings of wit, we must know what bull-headed foolishness is. Fighting is not the destination to taking the higher path but the path itself. And with a bleeding abrasion and a missing tooth, we will learn the secrets to divinity.

WILD THING

Frigid pyramids of immortal glacier and ridges ascend over painted grasses and minuscule needles of pine forest. The frost jotun Denali looms over the tundra, King of the Alaskan Boreal—breathtaking in the brief moment of unshrouded solar magnificence. The mountain range demands the respect of all spectators in that rare image—captured in less than a heartbeat—of the raw world so hidden from so many. Millions have seen this photo by Ansel Adams and unapologetically misunderstand why it commands their undivided attention, their yearning to see it firsthand.

Why is this?

Only the illusion of nature can be captured by a camera.

Fingers always point to nature as this primitive place as a way for their wielders to distinguish themselves apart from it—not unlike how a Western teenage girl aggressively rebels against the 'iron fist' of her father or the nearest patriarch. Urbanites tend to refer to their concrete tuna can apartments as 'their woods' offhandedly—there is a cope here because synthetic sprawls are always attempting to imitate nature. This is why so many 24 year-old Jessicas have Urban Planning degrees and snivel about "like, we need to turn [INSERT CITY NAME] green". As if shoving hedges into an intersection and planting invasive elms into the sidewalk will hide the heroin needles, the Chinese takeout boxes and the pulverizing weight of unceasing decadence.

I'll never forget the blunt and apt words of one of my Scoutmasters who defined nature as: *"a world in a constant state of decay and death that somehow achieves moments of ecstasy and unparalleled splendor. We as idiot humans try to replicate it without the icky parts but somehow manage to insert our own evils. The only truth about nature is that we can never escape it."*

To the most ardent, Subaru-driving, fleece-vest wearing, gray-haired granola this is the reality. Nature attains its beauty beside its mass of ugly, rotting, or barren self. The rainbow hills of the Four Corners region rest on a graveyard of silt and mud, shaped by a hollow wind. The majority of America is not gorgeous Yellowstone or stunning Escalante but of thousands of miles of flat, virtually indistinguishable grassland that was once a floodplain. Drive across the majority of it—

you will wish you scraped your skull on the asphalt and be done with it all.

The spectacle of nature cannot be surgically examined without the entirety of itself. To truly grow close to it, you must accept not just the distilled images of serene meadows but the maggot cities that worm through ribcages of moose carcasses, the putrid gasses of geysers that soak the ground in chemicals and the mummified horrors of the creatures who stray too close to the petrified lake in Tanzania and its toxic waters. That 24 year-old urban planner, Jessica, would have her stomach's contents emptied in her cheap apartment floor if she was able to conceive of how many baby moose skulls ferment inside the gut of a Kodiak bear.

Nature is as much the blonde bombshell Ukrainian housewife as it is the super rapist Ted Bundy.

Man creates the reality he dwells in because his survival-oriented brain tells him that resources, shelter, and safety are good. His brain is not lying to him—a brain does not know how to lie, that is an act of the soul. The lizard brain is a petulant child, a needy muscle. It will demand and cry for attention to which the soul will either comply or ignore. Think of it as being offered a doughnut

or another highly satisfying but guilty treat.
Your *brain* salivates at the idea of sinking your teeth into the soft sugary dough, not in a malicious way but because you're hungry and want energy. Coach yourself long enough and you will free yourself of this animalistic impulse. Same for porn. It is just one way your brain holds your body at ransom.

If there was a metaphysical lens to view the mind, you would discover that under our skull that our true Self is in a schizophrenic gulag—held hostage by our external self that is governed by a chaotic web of thousands of various such impulses for material need. Philosophers have talked about this for millennia because it's obvious that no soul, divine spirit or ethereal force could exist in this volatile realm.

This is why man builds civilization against nature. It is not because man must conquer nature or that the advance of technology will lead us towards utopia. Or better yet, the atheist neckbeard's desire for convergence with AI. Neither will occur. Man does not build the tools of civilization so he might become a robot or some other bullshit. The rivalry between nature and civilization is entirely amoral—not out of wickedness but earnest warfare.

Take the merciless desert like the flesh-boiling waste of the Atacama. Mankind could not thrive or even exist natively in such an environment alone due to the hyper-aridity and lack of even the most basic materials such as wood or food. Civilization could not survive there...but men could, given the right tools and proper experience. We would commend these men for dwelling in such a place, even primitively. Compare this to say, Zimbabwe—long live Rhodesia—a lush region where its warful civilization is present but the law is obsolete. So many humans living in a land prosperous and abundant in resources. We degrade these humans that dwell in paradise. Why?

It is not the civilization that is revered and valued but *the dogged effort to sustain life* that is so admirable. The act when tested against the brutalities of nature.

I have been a skier since I was 4 years old, an explorer at 8, and a backpacker at 11. Not once in my memories did I go out in the wilderness and regret it. If anything, now in my mid-20s I yearn to be far away from warehouses and busy thoroughfares, speed-demon sons-of-bitches in their overpriced German coupes. My heart beats to the tread of gravel and hard-packed earth beneath my feet, the ghostly quakes of aspen trees in fall, colored like a dragon's gold hoard. Constantly I wonder and hope if each time I go on a trip, a journey or a jaunt into the wild, with every droplet of blood that soaks the earthen floor my metaphysical self is siphoned away in some benevolent nature-vampirism. My soul will be eternalized in some distant meadow or mossy redrock crag when my body is dust—carved into a trunk or chunk of rock where my whisper can be heard in the breeze by another young explorer who might cross my sanctified soil and feel the glimmer of transcendence.

Traversing through America both East and West, I have visited nearly every biome I have heard of and feel different in each one. A nerd might go on about how each provides different resources and utilities—bah! I might have repeated these at an earlier age but now all I feel is the spirits of each piece of land, every environment. Swamps and marshes always have inspired a melancholy gloom, especially in the Pacific Northwest where rotted stumps of great trees are laden with moss tarps—concealing the dark depths of warrens where goblins might spy from within. Burned rock outcroppings of the Western deserts where all is laid bare under a merciless sun have planted the seeds of meditative peace.

The pagan in me finds resonance with the Native American ideal of the 'sacred sites' and how each is marked by attributes and vivid history. To be fair while I don't wholly endorse the Noble Savage ideal, there is a solar quality to tenets of Native American culture and it would be disingenuous for me to avoid this confession. If as a pagan I endorse the concept of the ancestral Indo-European burial grounds, I must do the same for the 'indigenous' peoples.

Man can buy land as a commodity but he can never 'own it'. A caretaker and steward we humans can be certainly, yet to own the environment due to a set of abstract numbers of a fiat currency is a negligent fallacy. Mastering land means to master over life—to have a deified reign over the powers of reproduction, decomposition, and vitalization of every grain of existence within that 'land'. We can and have been stewards but are utterly powerless against our environment—we can never be owners. I'm not here to make the argument that *no man* should be able to have property rights, homesteading should be punishable by death, and that we should dwell as anarcho-primitivists who share every chunk of fruit we find and live in harmonic stupidity.

Rather we misunderstand our relationship with nature.

Back when I associated with ilk such as tankies and all manner of Marx-worshippers, my fertile mind was introduced to the nature-socialist Rosseau and his 'state of nature', a very romantic philosophy for the time. I had just started backpacking and spending more time in the Wild than I had for the majority of my high school. I'd been witness to the worst sides of man and resonated with the idea that modernity and even property rights were to blame. Inequality was only manifest in a world that was not entirely natural. Being that my morality was capricious and not based on anything solid, I assumed the tenets of Rosseau's anarcho-primitivism were sanguinary.

But Rosseau is fundamentally wrong: humans when born are not inherently 'good'. Nor does he even believe in his own advice. "Make the citizen good by training" is his next nugget of wisdom, which would beg anyone with a pulse to question his logic. If Man is naturally born good and society corrupts him, you are left with two inadequate options: *train society or isolate man*. Rosseau is a massive retard—and a hag-humping, child-abandoning faggot, as Voltaire astutely pointed out—

because he draws a border around man and society as if they are mutually exclusive and not tied at the waist. As if society is *not* man's nature.

Liberalism has been the petri dish for the first of Rosseau's options of training society and we've discussed this at length. Democracy by mafia rule, education by state-enforced sodomy, and the plasticization of everything that makes us culturally unique is the result of attempting to 'train society'. Which leaves us with the second option of solitude.

I would love to air-drop communists into a secluded region of Patagonia. Can you imagine? They'd sooner harvest each other's kidneys for sustenance than make a perfectly-functioning democratic society. They'd cannibalize each other and forget all but a hollow memory of ethics. Drone footage would pick up effigies of Karl Marx made out of the petrified intestines of the unlucky martyrs, hammer and sickles made out of baby skeletons, and communal villages of such horror Hollywood would not dare reproduce.

Isolation in nature is utterly impossible. Man is not a creature without his tribe and would rot faster as a hermit than with any disease. There is firm reasoning behind the trope of the maddened loner in the wilderness, 'The Wizard in The Hills'. Sorceries and mysteries might be made known to him but at the heavy penalty to his social wellbeing and mental state. Rosseau would have you believe that this character should become the standard for *all* men—to live out their days away from one another like monks to avoid creating unequal hierarchies that exclude him.

It's a shame that the retarded Rosseau excluded himself from participating his own theories. But as I've pointed out before, most philosophers are cowards.

Years of backpacking from a young age taught me a valuable lesson: don't heed the advice of fat people.

Do you know what it's like—trekking over 50+ miles with a heavy backpack, over hills and dales, through desert and mountain with only the calories you can carry and the determination to press forward? If you're in shape you'll sweat. If you're unhealthy you'll slug your way along. But if you're a fatty, you won't just lack the physical capabilities to pull your weight but you'll act as a parasite to your company: weight everybody else down by your engorged, red-faced self. And remember that fat people can't hike alone—either they get hurt, turn around out of cowardice or they continue and cease to be fat.

Camping with fatties means more resources for them to consume. You will have a harder time waking them up, getting them to start the journey and you'll never hear the end of their complaints. Fatties are like children but worse—a child is compact and manageable. Out in the wild fatties are cognizant of their inabilities and will yet *persist* to brazenly whine about their struggles, how heavy their pack weighs, how long the journey is, and so forth. This is why the ham planets of people can thrive and dare to call themselves 'normal' in the modern world—in every sense they are the average modern creature: a slothful, indecent being who demands others orbit around their needs and not vice versa.

I am repulsed by such creatures of such fragile spirit.

If the sum of a man is his actions and deeds then the obese slugs of our world are worth zero. Fatties are consumed by their corporeal self and cannot surpass the physical will of another man. Why are there so many fat incels, or formerly known as virgins? The answer is imbedded in the query. At no point in time will we see a fat philosopher arise whose ideas are worthy of praise or rival another great thinker.

If you ever spend a great deal of time around the willfully fat and ugly, you realize something spiritually broken within them. Virtually all of them have surrendered to their shadow, to the dark and negative voice in every soul. Instead of utilizing that spirit, they believe their physical self is incompatible and unworthy with a metaphysical one. You see this with fat comedians or these chubby online personalities. Refusing to walk through the flaming gate of ego-death and self-actualization, they create an alternate self they can vicariously interact through—a sub-persona that is usually sarcastic, self-denying, and at times comical. Behind that veneer of their alternate self you will catch glimpses of that oppressed spirit, caged behind a bastion of putrid flesh.

It is truly sobering to try to empathize with this kind of person and their state of existence. Forever they will deflect and deny that this inner self exists, pointing towards their folds of fat crying "this is me!". Being fat is not metaphysical. Neither is it a destiny, just as the rack or guillotine are not personalities.

Hope exists for them in a phenomenal ego death—the likes of which few experience. Likewise to their conflict, we must recognize that our carnal flaws must not hinder our path and strive for transcendence!

One climb in the mountains that stood out to me was with a friend of mine, perhaps a year ago. He'd long spoken of moving out to the Alaskan Wilderness and starting a community homestead. I'd previously assumed he was a man accustomed to the wilderness and was versed in the art of bushcraft and survival. We decided to camp when snow still coated many high valleys and clefts near to us. I thought little of his somber demeanor as we began our ascent under the shadow of peaks in the late afternoon sun. As dusk fell and our boots took us beyond the sight of the car, he began to slow and gazed more worried as time progressed. I asked him what was bothering him.

In a spluttering way, he replied: *"there's an evil air here, it's too quiet. It's demonic. I don't think we should be here. We should probably turn back."*

Now I am not one to disregard the currents of emotion in any area, specifically the wilderness but I had not felt anything of the sort. I often grow meditative when hiking and am quite attentive to the 'spirit' of the land I'm traveling on. So I began to ask him a few questions. His disposition quickly became defensive when it became clear that his feelings were based in the observation that 'Satan' residing in the darkness of the mountains and that he himself had done little to no camping in the region alone. For the entirety of the trip, he became worse, almost incoherent as dusk became stark moonlight above and he transformed into a trembling rabbit in the woods.

A curious, uninformed bystander might ask: *"what was it that bothered him?"*

Mentorship of the Mountains.

What truly unraveled him is that he was confronted directly by the void of the mountains: the residing spirit imbedded in the high angled cliffs and residing glaciers that are superimposed on the comparatively fragile human soul. He could not *simply will himself away* but was faced with the reality of the mountain's mirror—forcing him to swallow his insecurities buried by the day to day videogame play. At the time he was struggling with his spiritual identity and going into the mountains only incited his unresolved conflict to extrapolate into his present disposition. His extreme discomfort under the shadow and moon only heightened the longer we remained. I think this negative transcendence in the wilderness could have turned him into a wild animal, given only a few more days.

How can simply visiting the mountains have such a mythological impact on one's soul?

Journeying to a place like a mountain is inherently atavistic. The significance of the climb is representative not just of the mountain's history but of the individual who climbs it—specifically to ascend into a higher plane of spiritual enlightenment. Both Noah of the Bible and Frodo of the Lord of the Rings share a similarity: sacrifice, fire, and power granted by the mountain itself. Despite both mythologies invoking the idea of high beings like God and Sauron, the mountain itself is given a distinct character that is mutually exclusive from that of any deity.

The mystery within mountains is one that was once viewed as a pathway to immortality, to ascend into them would grant an 'invincibility' to the mundane world until they descended once more. Enigmatic and supreme in their glory, it was the mountain that would grant prophetic wisdoms to who was capable of accepting them—evermore enlightening the higher the peak, the harder the climb and more sacrifice involved to rise to its crown. In antiquity, mountains were pagan gods of their own, vassals of other gods or pantheons of their own that would reward ascetics and adventure-seekers with enlightenment impossible within the modal reality.

Further back in my life when I was indecisive of my

destiny—right on the cusp of entering higher education, I took a trip to the hardest mountain I have known: King's Peak. While it only boasts to stand at 13,000 feet, it was a penultimate feat of endurance for me to reach its apex. A joke I heard that became evident is that the mountain itself is but a pile of rocks—a cairn of Giants piled high to mark their favorite watering hole. Ascending the bare mount over slabs of rock, there is no earth to pad your feet as you find your way to the first few false summits. Many turn back after realizing that they're well below the peak. I would say more than half of the fellow mountaineers we saw would stop or turn back at this point.

The peak of King's was worth it, of course: a ladder into the heavens, bared against the elements and defying its rivals in grandeur. But this was a side effect of our journey.

On our slide back down into the valley of King's, beneath the red-rimmed walls of the massive cirque of her sister mountains, suddenly my perception of how saturated and preserved her upper region was. It was as if the valley had been gray until our descent. Before me was a hyper-colored gateway into Hyperborea, abundant of alpine flowers, amethyst lakes, and her caretakers—

pairs of moose casually crossing our path with no fear of our invasion. The aura of this place right at the boundary of timberline was truly higher, a current of metaphysical *victory* trickling from King's Peak that was only accessible because we had sacrificed to reach the glorious mount.

King's was not *just* representative of my impending career and life choices—it was manifested before me that the eternal rewards of Hyperborea are possible only through such pure sacrifice and a mentor so wise as a mountain.

If mountains and forests represent the highest form of man's attunement to his environment, then deserts are the antithesis. Where the alpine cliffs have 'faces' because they have mysterious but human features, fauna like hairlines and waterfalls like tear ducts, the deserts are the opposite. A desert is faceless and ultimately devoid of such gifts of nature. We associate the desert with death, "*going into the desert to die*" as they say, to remove one's humanity from the equation. Ruined civilizations and the bones of humanity rest solely in the desert. Into our modern age, we even associate aliens or otherwise inhuman forms of life capable of dwelling in the sandstone.

But are deserts *purely* death?

I have visited several deserts in my lifetime—badlands, mesas, reefs of rock, cold deserts, tropical deserts, wastelands, and high deserts to name a few. The energy of *sóh-wl̥* or sun in the Indo-European tongue is omnipresent in these biomes and the fundamental reason deserts are considered 'evil' in some respects. Bleached bones and half-shattered cities in Syria, yes? *Within the desert, the primordial solar energy is inescapable if not utterly tyrannical.* Similar to an immensely authoritarian pharaoh of old, the sun is a punitive and merciless god of death—unchallenged in his reign over blistering grains of sand. This does not mean that I believe the sun is incapable of reward or enlightenment.

In my each of my treks down in the southern deserts of my homeland I have felt impressed by this dormant, ancient god-king of the Desert and recognized it as a volatile force of nature—albeit, one that grants great boons to those who suffer in its realm. When I have navigated forests of prickly cactus and sagebrush, across rattlesnakes sunbathing, down the tricky pitfalls of slot canyons and hug the crimson walls at the bottom in case of flash flood—each of these an easy death in such a remote and harsh land—I am the recipient of incomparable experiences. Have you ever smelled the desert after a rain? I cannot put that fresh, perfect smell to words. That rain could swallow you in a slot canyon but its smell is exotic—it could probably trigger an orgasm in the right circumstances!

Even with the Nile, the Egyptian chapter in history is one that is considered hyper-spiritual, of Egyptian culture's firm grasp of metaphysics. Would have this civilization and its cultural breakthroughs—due directly to their extreme esotericism—been possible in a perennial environment like the Boreal? Fat chance. Were the enlightened Egyptians so advanced because they stood on the brink of the virile Nile and the wasteland around them. Standing on the needle-sharp fence between vibrant life and blistering death? It appears this way.

Yes, the desert will devour babies for breakfast and spit their scorched little bones out without hesitation but also confide in you the greatest gems of all. I think this is the reason that the desert is also mythologically critical—man's trek across the wasteland is meant to excise the weakness from us. Lawrence of Arabia is an example of the bronze age vitality through his endurance of the desert and its fruits. The Indo European civilizations that I reference so often made one of the greatest migrations across dry steppes—even to fight Darius and the Persians, willingly confronting the desert with their teeth bared. I don't think the pagan spirit would be what it is without this testament of survival.

Last but not least the Outlaw is only so remarkable because he makes his banditry in the desert. His posse and forts may make their home in the mountains but his routes, his career is made solely in the desert. He is the product of it as much the Native Americans, an archetype of man's necessity to lose their humanity in the barren land. So long as there are deserts—whether, of nature or modernity, the Outlaw will be there as the arbiter of the Wastes.

My conclusion on this chapter on nature and my experiences there throughout my life thus far have been formative for the moral precipice that humanity is standing upon.

We live in an age of rapid technology advancement with the looming, if not impending outcome of AI and the potential of a transhuman future. Without jumping the Ted Kaczynski gun and soliciting others to start mailbombing campaigns, let me pose the end-all question to all those who have not yet considered it:

Man eventually and must decide if we are to cultivate ourselves through nature or become interchangeable through industrialization.

I am not being facetious. This is a moral question for every man and woman to ask themselves and their involvement in this scheme we call civilization. Technology is no longer a tool that reduces menial labor and offers exoteric comforts but is rapidly redefining how mankind functions in his environment. Jobs, while they won't all be replaced, are systematically being reduced to customer service and tech positions. Robotics may not replace all blue-collar and labor force occupations but by the laws of capitalism, their *inherent value to the consumer and the merchant will inevitably eliminate a significant portion of the human element.* AI may be a distant future in America for its capacity to subjugate but in the apathetic, technocratic human-locust syndicate of China, there are no such sentiments. It's in their best interest to develop super-machines to subdue their competition, as it is to lie, cheat, and steal as they have done for centuries.

If China or any other futurist state can develop AI

then Man will be forced to adapt or suffer the immediate and likely deadly consequences of an uber-human intelligence. I don't pretend to know the stratagem of the Asian peoples regarding AI or hyper-intelligent computers, only that their history is informative enough. No doubt Israel will be on that bandwagon—always wanting to be on the cutting edge of arsenal and technology—with their improved version of Chinese tech. If it is then in this hypothetical scenario that man is forced to make this moral choice, we already know the outcome will be anything but a revolution against digital overlords.

So is anarcho-primitivism the next best choice to avoid this hellish Matrix scenario? I do not think so. I fundamentally disagree that man can live in a perpetual state of anarchy—we will always have tribes and clans who wield the same pie of power, only the slice size changes. Nor do I think the libertarian 'solution' of self-neutering through the Non-Aggression Principle will result in anything better than one-player Russian Roulette. If living without technology and being entirely natural was the solution, how come the Amish aren't running the show instead of AIPAC?

We men are never satisfied to be complacent with

power. There will always be wars, exchanges, and power plays in which it shifts hands, whether we condemn or condone it. One thing that remains constant is that nature is the only conflict that we can never win. If we try to merge with AI to live completely carefree Virtual Reality, our brains will melt and reduce us to flesh-slag—fertilizer for the tuna and trees. By uploading our consciousness to a computer I'm confident that our 'nervous' system will detect that we are no longer bound to flesh and the laws of nature and summarily seize. We are not immortal and never will be—no matter how badly the Millennial celibate wants to evade living in their reality. Apple has no interest in caretaking a server room full of vats of brains—only the free labor or monetary value those brains might produce.

Goonhood is not any -ism but learning how exploring and becoming so familiar with nature encapsulate this concept: instead of revolting against our nature, we must *become* it. Embrace it and call it our own. Become utterly lost in the woods, wander the wastes and stumble over mountains. In ecstasy, our kind can swallow whole the floods, lay with the beasts, and let our exoteric skin become one with the winds of change.

By transmuting transcendentalism, becoming uber-competent in survival, and harnessing its secrets, we will discover *why we feel such a connection to nature* in the first place.

THE RITE REVIVAL

While visiting Europe last summer, I was walking down a country path on the way to a Bronze Age graveyard. On a narrow unpaved path that wound through a rolling field on the edge of a Neolithic forest, I found a great and elder oak tree. It was nestled at the flat belly of the field that may have been toiled once in times before steel and Charlemagne. Along the path was an old man reclining in the shade on a bench, overlooking this tree. I had not yet approached the bench when I noticed the birds that besieged the elder oak—a score of ravens stood under its boughs like black apples. Suddenly two dark forms sprung up from the canopy and circled once before beelining to the tree that shaded the bench. My eyes tracked these ravens to the bench—the old man was gone.

Vanished like smoke against a moonless night.

Was it my imagination? Was he even there to begin with? I *swore* I saw him there like any of the other folk on that early summer day, nodding to me as I forged my way behind the Central European hills behind Zurich. Was he ever there? Auspiciously the ravens hadn't even landed on the tree ahead of me before darting back to the elder oak tree. Without parade or declaration, then every raven on the ground sprung up and flew to the nearly-petrified forest I was heading to. It was likely I was hallucinating due to jetlag and caffeine overdrive. The old man may never have been sitting in the shade to begin with.

Within an hour, I was standing beside the unmarked burial ground of a primordial people—forgotten by the metropolis they founded. A sacred site to even the Catholic woman who had led us there, her understanding of the historical potency. But even her reverence would have paled to my sudden sense awareness born from what I had seen before entering: the ravens, the oak, and the old man.

To this day I have tried to doubt this memory of Wotan—willingly disbelieve it as a fantasy, that no man had been there. I have found since my initiation into paganism that I cannot lie to myself.

Christianity I always compare to a boat I was born upon. It wasn't sinking to my awareness, nor causing me any afflictions but neither did I have a choice of my circumstance being birthed on the foredeck of the HMS Mormonism. Would that boat of Joseph Smith and his treasure hunting galleon have arrived on the glimmering shores of an ethereal haven if I had stayed upon it? I'll never know. Such is the capricious nature of being born with an open mind and a wary heart. All I know is I could not stay on that ship—it wasn't my choice and I was never meant to be on it longer than my childhood.

Diving off the vessel of religion is truly a swan dive into unknown seas, murky depths without bottom, and shadows of formless shapes visible in the fog that clouds around our third eye. Atheism and agnosticism are but driftwood floating on the currents, pretending to be an option and sometimes progressing towards a direction but never driven by anything more than whims and the wind. The seas are mortality—death to the spirit and a gloomy chasm when treading for too long. We don't have the luxury of waiting to be sucked down into the abyss and whatever horrors await that nothingness.

In this analogy, there is an island—rather a chain of connected but independent landmasses that have been there. Age is deceiving for they are *timeless*. Unaffected. These islands are not fabricated by the materials of man because their essence is as old as the sea itself. Perhaps even older. This island is paganism, polytheism, shamanism, whatever it was called in the time. Before humanization, the winds of change and volatility of the seas that consume the other vessels dependent on the constant reaffirmation of fear—the islands are ever-present. A vision of the islands appears in the dreams of Man due to their idyllic, mysterious quality. The ships of Christianity, Judaism, nu-age Yoga-ism and so many others have kidnapped those from the sands or on the brink of their shores, yet never have the islands been destroyed.

This analogy is not intended as a condescending one aimed at those who have decided to stay on their ships. I don't pretend to be arrogant enough to know *what faith is for you*, only that I can't ignore the design of centralized religion or ignore my constant amazement when I research the elder worship. It's a matter of self-understanding and the framework of asceticism. Does a Buddhist need the confirmation from a rabbi whether his meditation practices abate his temptation to indulge his vices? Does a Brahmin need permission from a caliph on how he should devote energy to Saraswati so he might become a better student?

Ask yourself this if you are stubbornly anti-pagan: if your religion's procedure in the past was to destroy pagan sites, artifacts, or otherwise attack the primordial ways to claim virtuous dominance, then is your religion truly about control over a nation or about enlightenment of the self? It's a rhetorical question. Religion isn't about belief—it's about war. Governments did not become theocracies post-Rome simply because they became more faithful but to seal the Christian faith in the cement of law, institutionalizing the state with absolute divine authority. Worship could no longer be personalized or varied—how could you mobilize a hundred thousand Franks with a hundred different deities? God became the king, no longer the wise instructor.

Zealots claim that by sinking your teeth into sin, you cannot taste that which is good and wholesome. Though I typically ignore the advice of those whose organizations are riddled with pedophiles, I agree with this principle wholeheartedly.

My early twenties until only recently were filled with debauchery of all flavors: whoring with random girls at parties, drowning myself in cheap booze, and associating with a whole cast of degenerates. I used to spend my weekends in a refurbished meth house in a run-down urban suburb, cozying up to anti-fascists and art school dropouts. My antidote to a night of mindless drunken behavior would always involve more poison—washed down liquor and a trip to a greasy breakfast diner that was known for its outdated, hellish 70's décor. I've found it an apt hell for my condition on my last night there: the ragged, middle-aged waitress beyond attempting to work for tips, her compatriot server who hadn't bothered to button up his shirt, the walls of mirrors and felt ceiling.

You can't find God in your omelet in that rueful place, let alone a natural world of mystic metaphysics. Perhaps that was why it was so crowded on Sunday mornings with miserably, bleary-eyed human automatons. Drowning yourself in syrup is an easier alternative to enlightenment—to stare at the mirror walls is to recognize how pathetic you are, sitting there at 11 am with a migraine, clutching your beer-gut, your equally pathetic peers who are lost as you are. The pancakes are merely a side effect. I shudder to think what kind of wretched potbellied vampire I would have become if I had not vomited out of sheer disgust with myself and adopted solar truths.

For years, I was adrift and dog-paddling in the waters as a dubious atheist for years, wandering with my eyes half-open and tongue quick to debate on why 'all religion was false'. Don't forget that Atheism is a God in itself, being 'scientific' the token virtue. My comfort was other's pain, relishing the moments where I had stumped a Christian on the 7,000-year dilemma or a Muslim on why he didn't partake of pork. It was petty and I enjoyed it with bitter satisfaction.

Rather by accident than choice in this destructive phase of my life where I was content to be a menace, the isles of paganism *found me*. Although being a descendent of Anglo and Germanic explorers and being acquainted with their history from genealogy is no small thing, what happened I still had no part to play. Perhaps the 'gods' or a mischievous spirit was tired of competing with my insufferable campaigns or it was destiny that I would stumble blindly into the Old Ways. Either way, I was unprepared and left feeling humbled.

On a cold, sandy beach of a lake in the mountains, an acquaintance of mine asked if I knew about 'Norse paganism' and what a rite was. Knowing nothing of it, I was dismissive but curious, participating with a detached interest. Under the stars and with Jack Daniels in hand, she performed the blot and invited Freya, Frey, Odin, and her ancestors to join us. I did not expect the sudden gusts of wind that blew in and formed a bubble around the sand, how bright the starlight became against the dark canvas of night, or the ember that formed in my stomach. My friend cast runes spoke reverently about how her rites had gone well that summer and we ended once we had asked our questions.

Not in any dramatic sense, but afterward I did feel this esoteric *impression* that there was something deeper to the ritual, that I'd only viewed the top layer and still felt this timelessness to the simple symbolism. I struggled to understand *why* I'd felt this way when my spiritual upbringing had stressed that only malevolent powers were so strong outside churches and temples, seeking to deceive and turn me away from Glory™.

On that beach I got my taste of that sacrifice by token of 'sacred evil'— submitting our ego into the coals of our fire, pouring libations for ancestral spirits we did not know, we were heightening our power by acknowledging how *free and wild* this 'other' world that we barely understand.

Online it is frequent you will see criticisms of 'Hollywood Paganism' that it is unbridled passion, the faith of eating cake all day. The drunk 'biker Viking' with axes and unbelievably busty women on their arms that you've seen so common in video games and TV shows.

This is the deception but so many fall for it. I have debated such 'biker heathens' who believe that paganism is some subjective fetishization of bearded warriors, calling themselves 'Ulfhedin' or other such crusted-brain bullshit.

Countless resources are available to even the mentally retarded on traditional paganism such as the temple of Upsalla: dedicated to sacrifice in Sweden, livestock, and willing men dedicated to appease Odin. To reach Hyperborea you had to achieve untold honor and glory to even understand how to get there—no ship or landmass could allow mundane mortals to travel there. You could call it Faustian. See, sacrifice is not just a suggestion but the damned requirement! This is why so many puritans struggle to understand paganism. It is the idea that to break free of the profane you must conduct rituals with sacred evil, certain taboos allow one to achieve this comprehension of the mystic world! The very thought that paganism and the ancient ideals of spirituality were that the gods, the spirits, fate were on your side *because you simply imagined it so* is fucking foolish. There is no passive ritual, as it is to walk into a congregation and float along with the other sheep.

Screaming like a lunatic on and offline, I still have had

countless friends and acquaintances ask me how to conduct themselves as a pagan. I've never spoken to my relatives about it simply because they have never asked nor would they gain any usefulness out of my spiritual journey—similar as if a mountain lion divulged its predatory habits to a gopher. Some of them merely exist as the water of the shallow end of the WASP breeding pool, designed purely to consume and never ask the big '*why*'.

History is the greatest tool in understanding paganism, not for its context but in the pathos of the historian. See, when a scholar of history is exploring an event in time, it is not unreasonable for him to assume that event might have multiple interpretations—various perspectives on the parties who documented said event. A credible historian rejects a single 'valid' version of history because he knows that the factors at play, biases of humanity and the ways events play out are often inadequately documented. Now imagine if there existed a historian vehemently denying every other perspective of a historical event save his own—which occurred in a minute fraction of time compared to the whole of the history—not for the context of said historical event but for the eventuality of a destination his perspective reaches.

The pagan history treats mythology quite differently than the dogmatic interpretation of celibate monks. Gods could be considered to be literal beings or the source of a value within a legend. Unlike the monotheistic, linear perspective, even the calendar was affected by spiritual practices, known also as 'sacred time'.

One of the most striking differences between Christianity and paganism is how the latter treats the negative value of life: the unaesthetic, dishonorable, and shameful. Instead of 'sin' and the idea that dualism controls every aspect of ethics and life, the pagan perspective denies it altogether and demands beauty out of the bloody world. Purity isn't possible if there is far more than just 'good vs evil'—it is the harsh reality that the sacred isn't liberalized but accessible by worthy sacrifice.

Like how a morbid fat woman protests outside a gym, handing out pamphlets reading 'Obesity Cures You of AIDS!', this is the modern world on our pagan history.

In a secular Judeo-Christian frame of mind, this linear perspective we must reject, how do we 'accept' the old gods?

Heidegger speaks that *"if one accepts the greatness of something, then the* beginning *of that great thing remains what is greatest about it"*. If we are to take that to our hearts, it is then natural to assume our ancestors—who were nothing like that pussy Abraham—did not worship Woden/Odin as the value itself but rather as a *fountain of values* that emanated from them. What good are the gods and their days of the week if Ragnarok wipes them and their lessons out? The same goes for Mithras, Jupiter, Vishnu, etc.

A man who discovers the rich and complex ontology of the mythological world by paganism also realizes his direct relationship with the world, his spirit tied to it, and he must re-learn how it operates. This view is what fundamentally differentiates the pagan mindset from the Cross Cult that establishes that everything under the sun, even the sun itself, is God. In this reality, Jesus is the obnoxious middle-man that rents you Divinity in small payments of $19.99, threatening to ever take it away from you.

By understanding *why* our ancestors worshipped the perennial powers and the exact *intentions* of the various rituals they participated in, we begin to piece together the 'macro' of ancient societies. It's critical here to understand where worshipping the dust of the past can grant insight—but rather than obsessing and fetishizing Tradition, we take the lessons of the old gods and utilize them. Turn them into tools in our belt.

Supernatural experiences I never pass off as coincidences any longer. I hike alone and see two burly, pale-coated goats watch me from the high crimson cliffsides as a pair of ravens encircle my path of ascension. Perhaps in previous days of my atheist history, I'd call it a 'cool experience'. But my animistic instincts tell me that these animals are not merely denizens but chained to the same cycle as I am—manifested as archetypes in the wild. The mountain goats represent the body, of iron thews that do not fear the adversity of sheer cliff faces or the battering winds. Likewise, the ravens represent the shrewd mind that perceives and analyzes, the assessment from 'a distance'.

A man on a mountain watched over by goats and ravens, all subject to the volatile elements of the dry alpine cirque. The longer one might analyze this particular event, the less it makes sense that it is all random chance. It would take a conscious suspension of disbelief that this is this event is *not* that the anima of nature—the psyche of the *other* seems to thread the three beings together. Where a Catholic might scour for signs of The Devil in the rocks, the pagan hypostatizes this virile encounter with passionate fervor! In other words, the pagan takes these to heart with not just hope that it is the metaphysical world acting through the animals, the setting, and particular time *as an archetypal means in itself* we can understand through without deduction or logic. It is pure symbiosis, not in the survivalist way but in the sense that all three creatures are connected by rich and complex factors that seem too uncanny to be written off.

I am not a Kantian but as a pagan, I do not see the gods as a slavemaster, that I am a means to their end, nor a rival to my existence. I don't condemn myself and remove my liberties out of an abstract and convergent obsession with 'returning' to a Yahweh from a desert I've never been to, seen with my own eyes, or felt distinctly his presence. If anything my experiences in Mormon temples were as abstract and confusing to label or identify *which power* I was communicating with when compared to my transcendent experiences in the wild.

For instance, if tomorrow when I hike into the high desert canyons and Jesus were to appear beside the granite-studded streams and demand I listen to his wisdom, I would ask why? What are your intentions, sky rabbi? For what reasons should I—a man who is aware of his spiritual freedoms, unyoked by the conformist dictations of any organized religion and a practitioner of the ancestral worship—submit to him and become subservient to *his* will? To his global church? If he said that the world was his, I would laugh. I've already seen enough of the 'other world' to know that there is far more to it than a 2000 year-old cult from Israel.

I am not arrogant to assume that any one man is wrong to find paganism a strange spiritual lifestyle. My only advice to folk who are wary of all faiths is that they *continue to be so*. Be dubious in all but your own experience. Do not take other's lives as gospel, their trials and tribulations like a fast-food order, a one size fits all. Know that the folk religions like paganism are not about following a priest because of the trout they caught, but to observe the priest and learn how to craft a pole like theirs so you might catch your own.

Psychedelics are not for everyone, nor are they always required to dip your toes into the spirit world. Life and its mysteries cannot be solved easily with peyote or

DMT—that is the same line of thinking as pill-popping and other feel-good solutions. That said, my most powerful single pagan rite was with psilocybin. It does not surprise me after using it that the Beaker culture of the Indo-Europeans mixed it with their mead, or that other shamanic practices lead to visceral visions. I don't often share my more intimate spiritual experiences...however, I promised several anonymous creatures and friends that I would speak of this particular rite.

Let me take you through it.

A former roommate of mine that I refer to as The Wizard, a Jungian at heart and pagan by everything but title, was the instigator. The plan was to go up a remote, narrow canyon in the late spring and take only an average dose. I had reservations about the experience going into it—I was always the one to avoid putting toxins in my body, even marijuana throughout most of high school. The Wizard assured me that it would be highly beneficial and he knew that I would take to them well.

Under a flat gray sky, we initiated our entrance at the bottom of the river where the trail snuck in serpentine fissures through rock and moss. Chewing on the stems of the mushrooms we hiked quickly to our spot. The further we climbed, the fewer people we began to see until our destination—until there were none but the two of us. Our place was supposed to be a great boulder that stood where the sky touched the treeline. Rain and nausea began to settle in and we swiftly found a lower, shaded area under the canopy of trees.

Then the vibrant dream began.

Green like a rainforest after rain, I can't describe the color I saw but intensely garden-like. Next came the round of giggling where we tore at some strange, alien fruit and began to chuck the hairy shells down at the stream below where the cliff hung over a flat pool. Like primordial monkeys we hooted and relished in chaos until it was time to descend once more. We found ourselves at the wide, slow-moving pool that acted as a buffer between waterfalls, the overhang beside us like a cavern into the earth's core.

At this point, the fog settled to the point where neither of us could see beyond the pool as if our ritual was *confined* to this small area by ethereal boundaries. I remarked multiple times how strange it was, how perfect this spot was in this forest that began to deepen the longer I stared at its edges, it darkened and became indiscernible. Time began to slow and it finally dawned on me that I had slipped into 'the realm between realms' when even the rain had begun to slow down.

I must pause at this moment and give some context about The Wizard. He and I are close friends now, but there was a time we were rivals—enemies even. Our mutual acquaintance was no less than Red-Haired Devilspawn and at the time of our first meeting, the Wizard and I were at each other's throats. Years later we reconnected and found camaraderie where there'd been none, becoming fast friends and eventually roommates where we'd cook steaks, play Magic The Gathering and speak about Egyptian mythology. Another thing about The Wizard is his luck. I've never met a man who is so inconceivably fortunate with whatever game he touches: cards, video games, guessing games, anything. If there's any kind of chance involved, he will always win by some near-magical stroke with a trickster glint in his eye.

A transfixing moment occurred between the two of us as we began to speak about our childhood, how coincidental that we'd become friends, then onto relationships. The Wizard began to speak about his current girlfriend, a red-headed devil and suddenly everything stopped making sense. My body stood before the rock, he beside me crouched on the gravel in his poncho—I lost sight of what we were…only for new forms to reappear. His face was turned into a shadowy mask and my jacket a burly coat of fur. Like a trickster magician, The Wizard's voice became distorted like an echo. For no reason I felt compelled to say: "*you've always been a trickster since I've known you Wizard*" to which quickly he said I was "*a dumb wolf*". I laughed gustily at that.

More and more images of us appeared at the pool as the out of body experienced continued. Like companions over time, our archetypal spirits were intertwined to, reborn again only to connect once more. Thor and Loki. A raven and a wolf. A cunning trickster and a loyal brute. There was something so true about what I experienced I couldn't help but feel wetness around my eyes—something so beyond what I had thought the experience on mushrooms would bring. Melancholy but also resonance, like an unasked question of my very destiny in life was made known to me without ever having to ask.

The Wizard then sprung to his feet and began to dash up the trail—the continuation past the waterfall. I followed him as closely as I could but it seemed by sorcery he was faster than I, his bounds worth two of my strides. For a moment he was a raven hopping delicately upon the stones and I was scrambling like a four-legged canine, splashing behind him. My feet were suddenly wet. When did the trail become a river? At that moment, a song began to play from the mountains, the tolling booms from the inside of the mountains as if trolls were trying to break free of their stone prisons.

The Wizard was waiting for me at the top where the stream split from the gushing waters. He was grinning and pointed at the water. When I stopped I understood why: the river was singing to us. I know it was because I could hear the waters' ambiance beside it. The voice was neither male nor female. It was something entirely else that I have never heard since. God, spirit, or a ghost, I'll never forget that I was privileged to hear its wordless poem.

When we descended the fog lifted and our journey was over. We came off our high at that exact moment—as if the waterfall was the gateway back from the Magic Forest and there, a group of hikers appeared at the mount of the pool. The gods had decided it was time that we return to the mortal realm. When we were packing out our things, the hikers turned to us and remarked that they hadn't seen us until we were almost upon them. Everything was strange until the moment we left the mountains.

Since that day, I am certain and absolute that the metaphysical realm is the source of us, whatever we Men *are*. Is it heaven? Hyperborea? I am not privy to those answers. It is the land of our ancestors and in some way, it told me what I needed to know.

My only regret is I didn't spend enough time in this realm—this Forest beyond mortality but I have some small comfort knowing that when I die, I will visit this place.

To repeat a pagan historian I admire, Thomas Rowsell or known better by his video persona, Survive The Jive, the keystone of living as a pagan is not just to discover your soul through individual worship and sacrifice but also to create a *hof* with your friends and family—a local cult. Like a neighborhood ward or a gang of priests, the goal is to establish a social pagan circle that you celebrate solstices, participate in rites, and share fellowship with. No ancient faith or religion ever had any impact from the individual worshipper. Love it or hate it, the rarest men are the ones who don't require a group or affiliation to feel a connection to the metaphysical—to a god or God. Prophets are worshipped because through them, a channel of esoteric energy is carried downstream to their tribe.

The reason why such customs and celebrations are so necessary for a religion is for it to build the structure of reciprocity around the abstract and esoteric. Man needs this framework to settle his spiritual roots down so he might absorb and attune. And due to his nature, he wants to be lead to some degree. Without either he will drift.

Paganism struggles in the modern sense that it is decentralized and therefore without an overarching hierarchy with apostles, magistrates, and law to enforce it, pagans must take it upon themselves to establish these communities. This could be as simple as conducting a backyard shrine with totems and runestones carved into wood to host a blot with some neighbors. It can be done in urban environments of course, but as I have stressed before, raw nature is the fertile soil for spiritual seeds. Planting them in aluminum and plastic with your fellow tuna-can dwellers will only make you yearn for the real thing.

I once attended a 'Viking party' back a few years ago before I established my local hof. It was a backyard BYOB type of deal. I wasn't sure what to expect, only knowing it was hosted by pagans. Little did I know how ridiculous it would be. Every man there was fat, a twink and wearing absurd outfits: kilts with fur, half-naked, Scottish facepaint and mead horns. The women were equally disgusting—leftwing nutjobs, lesbian hookers, and honking like geese. Between the fake sword-fighting, animated movies, and the odor of unwashed bodies I was near to the point of murder. I considered it when one rainbow-haired troglodyte screeched that 'Odin was with her' out in the grass. I wanted to behead her with a pie-knife. Thoughts of mutilation fermented in my mind when some of the tranny AntiFa types started chittering about how they beat up Neo-Nazi Odinists at their local fag rally between fondling each other's junk.

Sure, one could say that it was a fruitless but harmless festival. I don't think the gods would feel disrespected by such an opulent display of degeneracy—rather they wouldn't pay any mind to it. The real crime committed is that there was no real passion to anything, no sacrifice or effort besides the money to pay for the fattening foods. It was a slothful, loathsome occasion. There was no pagan spirit there, as I have felt at other rituals near rivers. They were pretending, LARPing as 'vikings' because their ordinary lives were mundane and pathetic.

What neo-pagans, traditionalists and all others of likeminded spirit is the path opposite of these feel-good parties. Atop the mythological ontology of our pagan past, we must achieve glory, dynasty, and community. To live a pagan life is to establish a spiritual village and leave a worthy life to celebrate. To celebrate is to honor the gods and the mysterious ways of the world through nature we live within. To live close to nature and nurture a village is to have a place for children to develop without the poison of modernity. And in that place, the mythological perspective will return to us!

Many orthodox Christians online believe that in the 21st century they will see cathedrals in the West, cowboy-monk hybrids herding cattle, and other such absurdities. This kind of thinking is detached utterly from reality of what trends have shifted spiritualism in the last 100 years.

Have you noticed how many European 'Buddhists' there have been in the last decade? It is almost a generational religion. And it is not a coincidence.

The contemplative asceticism of Buddhism is the natural progression for a collapse of the monotheistic Cathedral. The self-initiation as seen synonymous with 'waking up', 'self-enlightenment', and nirvana is a stoic, if not noble pursuit. Due to the poignant statement that Abrahamic faith has the impression on the individual as 'compensation of the feeling of inferiority' according to Nietszche, God's greatness bestowed on Man is the justification of his own existence. Aka self-perpetuated spiritual slavery, but with extra steps.

This 'Eastern' thinking—that shares the ancient roots of paganism—recognizes the Neoplatonic element of removing this dogmatic condemnation of the self by a benevolent tyranny and participating in a reality that is driven by serving oneself. By unnaming a foreign rabbi deity and taking transcendence in their own hands, these modern Buddhists recognize the internalization of divine qualities—instead of worshipping another divine but trying to purify ones own life to *become* divine by esoteric training. Now take this and blend it with the vigor of life and understanding of the natural and metaphysical realm as being both intertwined, not being good or evil, but something in between that our ancestors participated in! That is paganism!

In the age of the internet, it is impossible to gatekeep information. The determined will find a way. Unlike heretics of old, the common man can discover how 'pure and wholesome' the Catholic church truly is, how its rites, symbolism, even its architecture is just a fast-food replica of ancient pagan Rome. While it is a tool that can be abused or cloud ones ability to discern useful truths, this virtual Library of Alexandria will open more doors to potential pagans than ever before. As the Catholic Church concedes to The Mob of Egalitarianism™ with every year, it will become clear that there will never be a hegemony of '*epic catholic crusader space marines*' without a total collapse of all systems save religion—The Vatican will not survive such apocalypse.

Freedom of information will always lead to the freedom of soul.

The asceticism and self-spirituality of Buddhism that overtook America, along with the microscope of the internet that we are just learning *how* to use is paving the way for a neo-pagan future—especially once it is recognized that paganism is the eventual 'free' society, the pathway away from the herd.

Towards the latter end of my high school, my friends and I found a secluded forest above a little-known canyon, wedged between a high alpine basin and an isolated mountain. A perfect spot surrounded by granite slabs, pine and aspen trees, under a small peak. We gave it the name, The Hamongog, after a trail not too distant and for its unique name. The Hamongog became our place of meeting, to bring worthy girls up to join us in our feasting and debauchery. At one point we even built a small hearth with limestone chunks and gravel from the nearby glacial flows. The Hamongog because notorious, as our little clique was often called 'vikings' after forged our jewelry, wrestled and boasted that we were like Northman reborn.

Few knew its location, but nearly everybody who heard of it wanted to visit. It became grandiose, our high school peers speculated The Hamongog was a real hall with moose skulls adorning its frame—a place of undead Dane spirits and ghosts. The rumors of The Hamongog became so inflated and ridiculous because of our reverence for it and never disclosing its location to the public. It was a place beyond the reach of the nosy journalist caste of the school newspaper, the block-headed jocks, the obnoxious stoners, and the sweaty wimps. The Hamongog was a place you had to be invited to, selected by those who carved its bones with its blood.

When we were supposed to be busy doing the standardized brain-melting sessions of 'homework' we would fantasize about how we'd build The Hamongog up into an actual hall, a cabin we could visit during winter and ski down. We constructed plans, pooled cash to buy cement but summer would soon take many of us to our jobs. It was always a pipedream that we'd quit our lifeguard and food industry jobs to trek with packs full of building materials and assemble this homestead in the wilderness. While these plans never materialized because of our responsibilities, preparing for college—something about The Hamongog never left us.

Eventually, this place will be built, be it in a remote location in the High Uintah wilderness or on a property where only the select can find it. I know of some other pagans who have erected such places for their tribes, their own cults, and conduct their rituals there. With my same *hof*—friends who are also pagan by blood, highly-skilled craftsmen and those who dwell beside nature—will complete The Hamongog in its entirety so others can be inspired of its promise.

The spirit of The Hamongog shall return again.

I've had many dreams but only truly *lived* through few. None of them were overly romanticized in their imagery, but those powerful and gripping ones seem as though my life was tethered to their outcome—that I might not awake afterward. One such powerful, subconscious experience came to me around the time I was resolved to live as a pagan on this world and accepted this philosophy with open arms.

I must share it.

The dream began in a location not dissimilar from the high desert region of my home: dry mountains of gravel and slate, bereft of any foliage save the sagebrush and lone trees, pools of icy water decorating her floor. A thick fog carpeted the land, obscuring the earth beneath, the sky gray—making the time of day undiscernible. Together on the flattened peak of such a mountain, along with my friend the Wizard in his tattered Mexican poncho, we sat cross-legged around a simple campfire. I have never seen a brighter fire—sparkling like amethyst and ruby as if the splendor of truth itself was cradled in iridescent illumination.

Spread around the camp were a number of blankets with rope woven through their edges as if they were makeshift suitcases. On these blankets were stacks of tomes—books, journals, novels, and scrolls. There must have been dozens of such bundles scattered about—in my dream mind, I knew these were the last records of mankind. I had to protect them. We had dragged it all the way to that remote, sacred location in the hills—the flame, knowing that they would come for these priceless artifacts.

The Wizard across from me nodded knowingly, to which I then realized he had a number of explosives and a staff across his lap. I too had a weapon—my AK-47, with magazines scattered along with the tomes besides my legs. A mirror was propped up next to the fire in my dream that caught my attention: I was bearded and gray, unlike the coal-black agelessness of Wizard next to me, a man who'd was ready for his final days.

Nearby screams chilled my blood.

Climbing the hillside around us were a horde of hostiles: rainbow-haired urbanites, the slavering hounds of Marxism, jackasses phonies with their suits, and past friends who were fallen into decay. With firearms and munitions, they assailed us from every angle, their ugly faces rearing behind twisted boughs of dead trees—their trunks blackened from an unknown wildfire. The Wizard throwing sparkling grenades and I leveling my rifle, together we defended that hillside like guerilla masters. Skulls popped, brains flew, and it seemed that blood began to run in rivers.

The violence was endless. Not once did the enemy relent or retreat. I knew in my dream that I must die—not even between my ferocious and Wizard's trickster ways could we repel them from our prize forever. Each bullet seemed closer to nail me in the chest, every thrown axe, or their own grenades to end my life without warning. Fiercely, we were pushed to our heels—to the ethereal fire. It seemed that all would be over.

And suddenly it ended with the glimmer of a golden dawn on our peripheral, barely piercing that shrouded haze that made our mountain of gore seem the lonely one. A single bird as dark as the night sky crossed my view and landed by the fire, croaking at me like a horn to signal the battle's end. I recall glancing at myself in the mirror near the fire and finding myself unrecognizable—a figure darkened by the blood, tar-black as a house fire, a shadow of a man.

The symbolism and context of this pagan dream I will study for the remainder of my life, I am sure. Drunk I was on the intense passion granting me the perspective that this dream was *no* circumstance. This anarchic era is my destiny. Since then I have visited this place in dreams—the belly of this lifeless, metaphysical land like a frozen Afghanistan, on the border of somewhere *golden and great.* Each time I have searched for this mount, but somewhere in my subconscious self knows I won't find it before I am gray.

I was born a pagan and will die as one.

MERITOCRATIC LAWLESSNESS

Rust consumes the strongest of iron, states a Scythian proverb. Man is defined by the scars of his skin, not the smooth and unrefined flesh—his 'little bitch' moments, if he can walk away from them, and what he learns by failure. No athlete was made without broken bones, nor can any of us aspire to glory without stepping foot in the killing fields.

I often shock people when I admit to them now that I was a Bernie bro for several years, a stage of my life where I reached the dredges of potential—that my physiognomy sagged, my shorts went up almost to a size 40, and I was an unconscious and domesticated soul. That I desperately yearned to be a piece of the urban puzzle, walk the streets to get a café coffee, and socialize with my fellow apartment slaves. My ultimate desire was to leave the earth and drift endlessly to explore stars beyond my awareness, to live the sci-fi fetishist life. And for a time, I did indeed dwell in this frame of mind—it was not glamorous but hollowing. I feel no shame admitting when I was truly lost, not because I am better now but because I am able to expound *why* I was lost, how simple my plummet to platonic existence was. By my rogueish childhood you may think this is impossible but let me assure you that the soul of *anyone*, no matter how prestigious or noble, can regress.

It is disgustingly easy to be weak.

To say that it began in college would be disingenuous at best—my divorce from the Mormon tribe was certainly a catalyst, where I began to put my faith into nebulous Science and Progress and called myself an "atheist". Surely, I did not believe in atheism but I believed that I was an atheist and therefore I thought as one. My willpower—which never waned—firmly rooted me alongside the 21st Century Atheists of Hitchens, Harris, and so on. My world began to resemble a shell of its former self: mountains no longer had character but numbers to associate their size, my palate adopted the sour taste of hipster brews, and I found that people who sounded "smart" took a higher priority than family. I certainly thought myself as a revolutionary with my dopey stickers on my Subaru, using a complex vernacular around friends, and felt elated to be called a "self-righteous bastard". My identity revolved around skiing, soft punk rock, and the amount of drained Americano cups littered my trunk.

Girls make it worse. I was caught in the wheelspokes

of cuckery, too afraid to be direct with them, and preferred to make passing remarks when one was within distance. I never committed fully to the person I wanted to be because, in my grand stupidity, I wasn't able to establish an objective foundation of what I was as a man. With countless women my only aim was to indulge my basest desires and I constantly wandered away from admitting my greatest *primal* instinct: to continue my lineage. By straying from this objective reality, I wasn't tethered to my male identity and rather was abstract in love life.

Nobody in this catatonic hive-state ever asks each other *why* they think this way. I believe this is tied to shame—shame of one's body and overall spiritual wellness. Everybody is a habitual smoker but nobody wants to admit it. Your fellow drones inept as you funnel this self-loathing like a Syrian teenager does explosive shells into a mortar, yawing that they are more than a cog in the wheel because they simply want to believe it. But there is no willpower involved. None. When you are a spiritual insect on the floor you do not allow others to enact their Will and fly to freedom—you lock your bug-jaws on their legs and rip them down back to your subservient factory floor.

As have so many men of the epoch, my identity of my actions became irrelevant to my egalitarian future—nothing I had done until my early adulthood had contributed to "progressing" or so my compatriots told me. I couldn't define my mythological story of where I came from, so my arc of what I was to become was defined entirely by a faceless ideal.

I lost that...and much more...

Men rely on their awareness on the food chain and therein where they sit in the sexual pecking order. In all the castes being poor or rich, white collar or blue collar, men are constantly moving up and down the hierarchy to see whose genes are the most reproductive. Despite their bitter resentment for denying this fundamental role they play in the woods of human society, not even the titty-toting nu-males of today can abandon the hierarchical frame when they talk about "the 0.1%, male toxicity, becoming any ally" or any of their fecal terminology referring to their soulless ideology. Everything they define to be villainous—the upper crust of the male food chain who has access to the most beautiful, the most fertile of women—is fundamentally anti-democratic, anti-egalitarian. They cannot escape the rules of the game and cannot help but highlight its existence with their wordplay, despite their voracious hatred for it!

I am not intending to preach to the choir, but meaning to restate a well-known concept here: what happens when you take this very anti-progressive truth to society as a whole?

To put a nail in it, what do we call this blistering realization—this unique peeing of the soul that awakens within the animalistic you—that *you* cannot level the playing field, that nature's laws define our lives as individuals and tribe, and that no amount of human effort can reverse what is in our blood? Some have called this "the red pill" of self-politics, the antithesis of liberal thought and its eventuality, Marxism. I'm not trying to steal the terminology of who coined it, but it is an asset to the conversation. Some call it a mindset that has its roots in ancient civilizations of heightened spiritual awareness, a dharma with the intensity of a blistering oilfire that burns eternally in one's soul. If you have lived through this experience, you may have your own analogy or explanation for this.

Verily it becomes a spiritual statement that is so certain of itself against this alien concept of "equality" that it can often have an anesthetizing effect on one's soul. A friend once told me that he didn't want to be red-pilled, not because he believed in Marx but because he knew that the truth would cripple him and all his passions. I respected his candor and honesty. How many of us would choose the blissful existence over the one that discovers the "hidden agenda" that seems so innocuous and humanitarian? I would have, more than once. Once the box has been opened, there's no hope of returning anything into it.

I had such a moment traveling overseas on an airplane where I became hyper-aware of the plastic reality I was trapped in: hundreds of chubby test subjects all making their pre-determined "choices" of Hollywood propaganda, snacking on seed-oil poison, and belted down in the crammed tuna-can of a plane. Like a test capuchin behind invisible glass, I broke free of the ketamine dream as I recognized this and screamed for release. I balked at the thought that my fellow humans paid a fortune to be shuttled like cattle to an tourist paradise—a land sterile to any real danger or adventure, where they'd engorge themselves on the same fattening food as they abused back home, and have a pretty backdrop to make love to their monstrously disgusting spouse. I considered stealing one of the parachute/boats and sending it 30,000 feet to a possible death simply so I could depart from this hell.

This form of hyperawareness becomes visceral reality when you are awakened. Every moment feels like you're breathing in air for the first time, your momentary interactions with your average "normie" are like a mirror to remind you that *you're not like them*. Better days it can be a transcendent experience where the colors of the trees are vivid, the taste of steak wondrous and juicy. On worse days, you feel as though you're the only man alive, wading through a filthy swell of rats who look vaguely human and will never feel. Your pineal glands will scream and thrash against your psyche, reminding you that you are quite alive physically and spiritually. You will also want to stomp those rats into drainpipes.

So when did I have my true "moment" of clarity?

Spring of my last year of college—before I unceremoniously dropped out of my art program—I was working for a startup, a company who produced look-alike Vans shoes. My resume is notoriously stacked full of small companies like this, most that ran themselves screaming into the ground like a downed B-52 before they'd reached a full financial year. As a hatchling entrepreneur myself I found it invigorating to be a part of somebody's dream project—this quickly turned into nihilistic pessimism when I discovered most small businesses fail because their owners are slush-brained retards who don't take criticism or advice. This particular company was one such failure: owned by a wannabe Tom Cruise, a trust-fund kid who strayed too far from the Iron Rod and got yanked back to his Mormon pedigree by his father who founded the company—a former college football legend who never actually made it to the turf, known as "The Dreamweaver" for having fanciful ideas on how to run his company in the ground. He also managed to be completely unaware of the internet even by 2015. Branded as a pseudo-skate company, run by posers and genetic lottery winners, I spent most of my time working on the printing process and the front store. It was a disaster from the start.

At the time I was working on a Graphic Design degree, having already worked with Adobe software, and having some experience working a job doing exactly that. Working for the shoe company, I hoped to land a position doing illustration or design work for them once I got my degree—their lead design guy was a former snowboard icon from the Old Days, before Burton or Rome, a real fucking knuckle-dragger who spray-painted Misfits t-shirts as a teenager and sold them for cigarettes at their concerts back before "merch". We'd take our lunches at this local deli and trade stories about fights we'd gotten into—guy had too much yellow chew-bottles rolling around in his truck, but he was alright. I was eager to apprentice under him.

Part of my secondary education was getting bombastically shit-faced at parties in the city with my other degenerate friends. I've spoken a bit on those before. That summer was hot, so naturally we drank out on the porch and cooled down with iced coffee. Alcohol and caffeine fueled our rants on the street, audible only to the methheads and homeless who claimed that rank suburb, a fallen place where my friends could afford. Several events transpired at that house that slugged me out of my slumber. The first was a former friend—a fake punk who claimed to be the descendant of reformed Nazi sympathizers, whose family owned a vegan restaurant downtown—is now a tranny officer in the local AntiFAg branch. He told me that, in no uncertain terms that he'd gotten notice from some "friends" that lived across the country that political revolution was underway and needed to know if I was reliable, that I could be trusted with sensitive info. I balked at the question, asking what he meant exactly. His answer was to look around the room and simply state: *"some people here won't be allowed to live here...or at all"*. Mind you that this was a full year before AntiFa or Marxist legions in the country were active or causing any major destruction. I didn't talk to him again after that.

The next occurrence at the house was roughly a few months later, the last party I attended. Things had been rough at the shoe factory, some of my friends there had been axed, as was the snowboard guru who clashed with the Dreamweaver. My drinking turned from harmless revelry into self-medication to alleviate me from misery. I had recently spoken with some of my old buddies about Bernie and socialism—I decided I no longer wanted to vote for him, or anybody really, my mind was focused on figuring out what my next career move was. During some point in the party I wandered drunkenly to the room of one of the inhabitants, who happened to be a computer programmer and an absolute lobotomite. Standing around the room were a number of his "buddies", categorical degenerates complete with SLC Punk paraphernalia, dreadlocks, and "FUCK FASCISM" patches on their jackets. One of them remarked that he'd overheard my admittance that I didn't want to vote for Bernie while another literally smoked a crack pipe—no hyperbole here. The programmer in his infinite wisdom, demanded I apologize for "giving a vote" to the racist, naughty white men who ran the country. I refused in a joking kind of way.

Suddenly comments about how I looked like a "hippie frat-boy" and "FUCK YOU" started to be thrown across the room. Somebody pulled a knife. I wasn't sure how long we stood in awkward limbo before violence may have broken out, but I remember grabbing my own knife—a tiny, survival one—and running out the door. I sure as hell wasn't about to get stabbed. An eyeblink later and I was walking down the street, aimlessly but in any direction besides the house. My mind was reeling. I didn't know how to process the threats, only that the hostility derived from a modest disagreement.

The next Monday, still hungover, I mulled over this event at my desk in the back of the renovated warehouse. To be quite truthful I felt guilty—frantically thinking up ways to make amends, I was still very much a drone of equality: a libertarian who leaned towards the side of free thinking, guns, and weed *MAAANNNNN*. Yet the experience had rocked me to my core—cracking my resolve that if I cared about their right to vote and whom to vote for, that feeling would be reciprocated. Anarchy danced on the edge of my tongue while my confidence in my fellow man waned, threatening to pitch itself into the negative. Political uncertainty that a future where I could be friends with people on "both sides"—a merit I had beaten my chest over as being a neutral, anti-establishment type—ballooned in my chest and at some point in the days later, I grew far less optimistic of the "progress" I thought society was destined to achieve. And a shadow of doubt lingered on whether I needed to beg forgiveness from the degenerates in the room—to admit fault and truly adapt to their cause.

This tumultuous shift set in motion things to come, my transformation of mind and spirit...without it, my words would not have echoed across the chasm of time to you on these pages.

Lie to a girl. Tell her that life begins and ends with her happiness, regardless of the cost. Bestow upon her the vile candy that she is the center of everybody's lives, that they lust for *her* happiness, and this will reciprocate for them. Lead her with the notion that her sarcastic charisma, no matter how rude, is the personality that will gain smiles and favor. Show her that the System is tolerant of her behavior, like a parent to a rebellious rugrat, who will not only tolerate her misbehavior but enable her worst characteristics like a child's harmless pranks. And last but not least, make sure she understands that the men who do not shower her with affection for this behavior are of the worst type—miserable scoundrels and undeserving thugs.

Inundate this girl through electronic programming by television that is designed to entrench and harvest her most human, most basic human impulses to socialize and feel included in "something". Not at all coincidental that her parents are likely working or unavailable during these types of programming. Don't forget to adorn this expansive lie with girls who are relatable and barely older than her, who will act out these lies and be rewarded for doing so. Fill the stage of this propaganda with colorful scenery, catchy dialogue, and an idyllic "soft" reality that a young girl would feel comfortable in.

Does this sound remotely like Chinese mind-torture techniques used on American soldiers—convincing them deeply to accept communism?

Try Disney Channel for *twenty years,* one of the most watched TV channels of our generation.

Do you think this was all unintentional, every step of this perverted scheme to dupe girls and imprint on their blank consciousness a tattoo of un-nature that would turn them into the modern equivalent of Medusa? Consider that after this in an epoch of degeneracy after the sexual liberation—that these women are supplemented with hitpieces by "journalists" throughout their teens and college that are essentially thinly veiled male hate-porn? Or now, where these childless women with no family or ties to their country are found so numerous among supporters of global revolutionary fronts—characteristically towing their emasculated eunuchs of boyfriends to rally against the imagined enemy of "fascism".

Sam-hell! A thousand pounds of dynamite lain between freshman dorms of opposite sexes could not create such a crevasse in the sexual environment as this!

Imagine after all of this attempting to "redpill" such a girl. You might as well ask her to deglove herself with a cheese grater. Breaking the social-political conditioning of such a creature is attempting to reverse this tainted sentiment of their childhood by replacing it with your mere assurance—no amount of charm is capable of this. If even accomplished, it is a damaging process and will leave psychological scars no opium can heal. Spiritual recourse and walks through nature can help, as well as a firm foundation she can plant her roots in.

Women are plants: they don't invent the rock-studded soil that we men offer to them. Nor should we expect them to be fully-grown by the time we meet them on this strange ecological journey. It is as much of our burden of blame to carry for the Derailing of the Female Psyche and their aversion to family, kin, and tradition. Both matriarchs and patriarchs are found guilty for surrendering their roles over the past centuries—trading luxury and synthetic promises of grandeur for their spiritual duties as leaders. You see this with the Gen Xers, Boomers, Greatest Gen, Silent Gen, and so on. Categorically since the liberalization of women and the integration of them into the workplace. A cycle of instability and darkness triggered by the failure of inept elders...not different at all from the Iron Age before the magnificent Bronze Age.

Mark my words, today or tomorrow, the fall of Man leads to the decay of civilization. But the fall of Woman leads to the death of it.

On the topic of cycles, another Scythian, Anacharsis writes: *"A vine bears three grapes, the first of pleasure, the second of drunkenness, and the third of repentance."*

The hardest rock you swallow during this process is that your fellow normie, the average heartlander, silent majority, whatever you'd like to call them are simply unable to grasp the concept that this war of politicking is a spiritual conflict. I believe it is antithetical to their persistence—not because it is beyond their potential because of IQ or any such bullshit—for this to resonate with them.

In the same way that paganism was natural to man but understood by this slumbering mass in a shallow way, fast food is also rotting their bodies, and they don't think but *act* unconsciously. Our brain is not "spiritually-facing" because it is consumed by our most base and necessary instincts: eat, sleep, reproduce, and breathe as long as possible. Nowhere in that fleshy mass is a primal desire to speak to Yahweh—it simply doesn't exist. It takes trauma and powerful substances to rip us free from our ego and allow us to transcend, even momentarily, beyond mortal coils and to view the unseen. For this very reason I believe the priestly caste existed, the caste that dwelled in the profane reality was incapable of achieving this level of super-reality.

And yet, to win this spiritual conflict? We must *live our own reality* apart from the modern one. Spiritually divorce ourselves in this age and prepare ourselves for the next, darker one. To remain in the labor camps of corporations is self-induced madness.

Is this accomplished with doom cults, as the Christians have done with their Second Coming?

I could never fully indulge my fantasies to believe that I will simply be snatched up into the heavens by God's hands in the nick of time as the earth around me is lain to waste and swallowed by apocalyptic tides. Neither do I think the right thing to do is become a Thoreau or Linkola and escape into the wild entirely. What *good* did either of them do? To *merely* be a spiritualist zealot in the modern age isn't enough to wage spiritual war, to be a fascist is to preserve traditions just so the next tyrant sells them for gold-plated AKs, and to be a Hard Green naturalist is to desire earthen floors and mandate unnatural birth laws. None of these ideals are complete or will endure.

"Be prepared"

A simple but acute statement. What is "being prepared"? I was a boy scout for years, learned how to adapt to the wilderness during them, and earned my Eagle long before Boy Scouts thrashed in decadence and became unrecognizable. When I've reflected on these experiences and where my political compass alters, that motto struck me like a cast iron pan against a midnight sky—be prepared. Prepared for what? The longer it simmered in my brain, it occurred to be just how prolific this statement becomes.

Being prepared for a spiritual conflict means anarchy of spirit, to create an authority from autonomy. Equally demanded is the discipline to rein in these liberties and use them to thrive in a hostile world. Think of this as an unworked alloy of iron, raw potential that must be crafted with the shrewd hammer born of wisdom.

I finally realized in those years around the election that libertarianism was an Anglo-Saxon demanding his lord requisition more raw iron to forge to fight the invading Danes, instead of honing the rusted and corrupted swords he already had. By simply demanding more liberties, we do not become more free—we become fat and lazy. Wasting the potential from generations of warriors and smiths, this merchant frame of mind will ultimately crumble under a stronger Will. The downfall of the libertarian ideal is its strength—individualism, the marketplace of ideas, and the pro-capitalist sentiment imagined as the building blocks of America have been abused by those who do not respect the blood that earned such freedom, like welfare these values have been inverted and exploited. Corporate hegemony and a dollar-slave market is the destination.

Jordan Peterson says: "*do not let your children do anything that makes you dislike them*" but does not take that further to the next step—not allowing your family, your friends, and your countrymen shoot themselves in the foot with .40 hollowpoints by capitulating to the mob of democracy. I don't think that our Canadian psychologist is ignorant that over time, even the most meritocratic person feels obligation as a member of a tribe, be it family or nation—such admittance would have just obliterated the efforts of the Internet Dork Web to castrate the growing reactionary men of the 21st century. I *had* to experience this harsh reality that libertarianism and hyper-individualism were sugar pills to the real problems—to understand my flawed conception of what my efforts should have been in were largely due to empathizing with Peterson's life, which I do not discredit to this day. But psychologists are not going to save us from the dark maw of a hostile cycle, of a future American

Apartheid state—the Kali Yuga will not be survived via therapy and petting cats.

That is not being prepared. What is?

This was the code I developed:

Train as if I'm a bandit in the woods being tracked by authorities. Shoot in the hottest, worst conditions possible with iron sights. Eat as if it could be my last meal, starve myself of food and water to prepare for an eventual starvation. Enhance the friendships I have with men I trust, eliminate the ones with those who wouldn't commit a crime with me. Learn my local environment of its natural resources, how to interact with fauna and not be eaten by a cougar while I sleep. Read everything that challenges me, ideological or by pure difficulty of prose. Only date somebody if I can see myself having children with them. Test my spiritual resolve by submitting it to vigorous, ego-killing experiences. Speak and act when I mean it, otherwise stand back and learn if there's nothing to be said or done.

And lastly to immerse myself in a spiritual, meritocratic lawlessness. In the words of one of the founders of the Boy Scouts, a hard-ass and man of his time, Frederick Russell Burnham noted: "*there is nothing that sharpens a man's senses so acutely as to know that bitter and determined enemies are in pursuit of him night and day."*

Goonhood grew from this sapling of an idea because being the silent, competent goon who is spiritually virile and self-sufficient in any environment hard to kill by any measure—spirit, mind, or body—is what the modern world *desperately seeks to eliminate.*

And why should we give it what it wants?

SUNSET IN THE WEST

All gunfights have their end in Westerns. No good tale lasts forever. I have spoken my piece and must return to the wild again. Too much time in the city makes me anxious. Just like the Mongols when they sacked China and left immediately when the illness of the urban world soured in their bellies.

I do still have a few final thoughts I would like to leave before concluding this tome. By now you should know what gods I pray to. But you might ask *what* I believe we should do? What have the gods whispered in my ear? How do we pursue a future here in the West when it is so emasculated—so inauthentic and drab? I have a few ideas I would posit to my fellow Goons...

You are what you listen to like a chameleon is to the tropical fauna and branches. Man adapts to the 'spirit' of what he absorbs. You don't need studies to figure out that eating food in plastic is bad or if a Double India Pale Ale will make your balls shrink. Look at the 'men' who drink such things. I know—I was one of them, on a rainy day in a sushi bar with my hyper-liberal, art student girlfriend, sipping on that sour shit and talking about how Bernie needed to win. I don't need some graph to show me that I was a fucktard hippie burnout at the time. I was *there,* I *know* that what I put into my body affected my disposition, how the beer and fattening food casted a fog over my wit. Just like how I dumped her on the brink of my 'awakening', so should you abandon bad habits.

Early on, one of my mentors said: '*music will affect your mood, whether you want it to or not—there's a time and place for it*'. This principle applies to all media. How can you become a Goon if you're sipping that gutter-oil called soda every meal, if you never go outside, or if you *think* like a docile little hamster? Apply this to what you watch.

Go to a sports bar, grab yourself a basket of wings, and just wait patiently until the advertisements start to flash on the wall of TVs. Notice something? Sports bars are catered to the tired contractor and truck driver. So why are all the ESPN channels featuring chubby, incompetent losers in interracial marriages? Wait, why is a men's razor company featuring a tranny painting his face like a clown and groping another man? The basket of overcooked buffalo wings is merely a compliment to what you really paid for: to sit and be propagandized—to be mocked and made to submit. If you have even a ghost of a sperm inside your balls, you should want to vomit and throw your plate into the nearest screen.

Instead, you should be making actual edible wings at your home, invite your friends over, and build something. Make it into a weekly or bi-monthly occurrence. A fence, or a treehouse for those little rascals you suddenly feel the urge to produce. By being productive in this way and forging these bonds, you'll forget altogether what the alien experience of 'going to the sports bar' is even like...

Get a gun. Practice with it. Make it your lover.

I shouldn't have to state this but you are your own defender. Communists are liars—we still live in the Wild West. The rules have merely changed. Outlaw justice has been traded—a poor one at that—for safety. Chaos is inevitable in our near future and we should expect it. No, we should wear it like a damn cloak. Ride it like that damned feline that weird Italian baron Julius Evola kept talking about.

Don't become paranoid or playing pretend Army like these boogaloo dweebs. All you need to do is practice. Get comfortable with it. If you have friends who are veterans, offer to buy them food and have them teach you the ropes. It's really damn simple.

If you can't legally possess one, or don't have the stones to 3D print one—find an alternative. A crossbow. A prison shank. Your fists and teeth. I don't care. Invest in your own defense, just like you'd invest in your education. Even if that means weightlifting, cardio, and fight nights in your basement. Always become harder to kill. Not only will you inflate your own confidence by becoming your own meaty, sharp-eyed commando, but you will find a lust for the Eternal Sport. You'll welcome the race war, riots, or whatever the hell comes to us.

Stop putting so much energy into politics, specifically parties and movements. No matter their merit or promise, they are temporal and capricious. Principles will always be preyed upon by the charismatic charlatans of Washington.

Politicians and their mottos are nothing less than cargo cults with the thin veneer of moral marketing campaigns. I saw this, perhaps the most truly, in the 2012 presidential election of Barack Obama. He was thrust onto a mile-high pedestal by every corner of the media—ejaculated by the masses as a Jesus-Mugabe hybrid, complete with biblical slogans to accompany his presidency. I knew apolitical numbrained stoners who would, at any given scenario, defend the institution of Barack Obama breathlessly. It was utterly bizarre to observe how they swore with a dagger poised at their veins that Obama would save the United States from a bitter decline, bringing sunshine back to 'The West' with the sweeping globo-liberal scepter of promise. So many were polarized into casting their lot with Mitt Romney: a known crook and McCain type.

People say Trump is different and perhaps he will stand to be. I would not bank on it with your soul. The spirit of the rebellious president and the shenanigans of past days will soon be regulated by the managerial Two-Sided Coin parties. Instead, recognize what someone like Trump can do, who he appeals to, and learn from his talents. Rome didn't fall in a day and even if you are an accelerationist, you must understand that politics happens *after* the bills are paid and stomachs are full. Focus on what *you* can accomplish.

Do you want to know why such a vast country that boasts 'democracy' and 'freedom' only has a sub-majority percentage of the population vote in any given presidential election, yet it widens the crevice between the perceived idea of ideology? Because the game of politics was fabricated on the fulcrum of human's greatest vice and civilization's strongest asset: the undeserved allegiance we give to these gods of politics. This fear I spoke of at the beginning of this tome is such a device used in political rhetoric.

Like the underdeveloped indigenous countries who laid out runways for cargo planes to land from the 'big man' of the modern West—to bring them jeeps, guns, and cigarettes as the Melanesians of WWII—politicians and their fundies play on the fears of even the skeptical intellectuals. Media pundits 'manufacture' or otherwise enhance any given crises to heighten the public's general awareness of said issue. Politicians are painted by their simple Wonderbread solutions, usually in-line with synonym-issues that got them previously in office or are part of their ideological 'tribe' and then begin the process. Their organizations and non-profits act as the villagers, weaponizing their campaigns by raking the dirt outside the town square, creating airstrips from the urban jungle, donations and fundraisers as flares and adornment to 'prepare' for the incoming deliverance.

You hear from the village square, as the politician speaks: *"I am the plane bearing the fruit of unattainable prosperity! Take your ten minute-democracy out of the calendar year to ensure I can deliver said supplies*!"

The election of 2020 will come and go. Very little will change. Posturing will persist skirmishes will continue between the two sides of the same coin—globalist conservatives and liberals alike—and everything will seem to be tipping one way or another. Don't kid yourself. The money makers won't leave it up to chance. Unless you're a sociopath billionaire with the funds to make Change™, investing in a political institution is masochism—it'll leave your soul to hang and dry.

Play the trickster. Poke fun at the institutions and guide them to self-immolation. Don't get caught up in the fire. It will only leave those around you burned.

America will end one day, just as Constantinople, Rome, and Atlantis.

A materialist pursuit is equally as destructive. Nobody goes into a sales job for the cash alone—money is meaningless in its symbolic, paper form. The context of money, the high value placed on somebody who can provide luxury for themselves and all around them is fundamental. Money itself isn't status but the freedom it gives. This is why capitalists are hypocrites when they argue for the existence for their system; out of one side of the mouth they chant about the unregulated system whilst they whisper out the other—don't allow robbery or the great 'equalizer' of violence to reign free, lest they'll lose their precious vaults.

It's also self-explanatory why most of the top-earners and capitalists of this world are weak-bodied, spiritually vacuous, hollow-eyed sociopaths—they're insulated in their deluded fantasies that, at no point, are they ever threatened by the mortal world. They constructed a LEGO castle safe-space system of monetary gain that cannot be touched by your greasy paws—you savage! Don't you dare topple that! Wait until they call you a Marxist despite your undying hatred for pointing out the gaps in their plastic brick foundations—it's a trick that's lost its edge throughout the last generation. Philosophical gas-lighting can only work when your victim buys your bullshit.

'Violence is for the lesser intelligent', they prattle off as they write checks to the Military-Industrial Complex to usurp the authority of a third world country. 'War is always trumped by the peace of finance', they proclaim as the stock market tanks by their hand, causing mass unemployment and starvation. A market, by the way, that's run entirely by robots. 'Let us decide your fate, we're the experts', they tell you while they lobby and plug in some equation to their money-making machine to create endless wealth while your children are pummeled through a sausage-link factory of brainwashing conveyor belts called the Public Education System.

Every wondered why their arguments sound nice at face value but lack any validity? Same reason why the summer salesman going door-to-door selling security systems to the unwashed masses in Michigan sounds sincere. He's a master manipulator. I've sat in numerous, entry-level sales training and every single one of them outlines the same message in bold, Comic Sans font: *you need to trick people into believing what you're selling by distracting them, shooting the shit for hours until you charm them into buying into you*. That's it. Like magic, old people melt before you!

Capitalism is a trust-fund kid's game, run by experts and designed by the banker caste to make everything in the world appear like a video-game with values attached to the mundane and the spiritual—which the caste has virtually no knowledge of. The term 'fiat currency' is so profound in its derogatory way of describing why not only the money but its inherent value is meaningless.

Money is still something you need, especially if you

like land and living comfortably. Greed is just the easiest drug to become addicted to, besides laziness. Remember that you can play their game but still maintain a soul if it does not replace your drive for glory!

Dating and the pursuit of a rewarding relationship is a goal will yield a priceless reward: a legacy. However, don't fall into the trap of desiring to be married—even if the person of your desire has the potential to become a tyrant. It is far better to be alone and satisfied with life than to be married and miserable. You will become like a Mormon nerd or worse.

I lock horns with women constantly. It's not my fault that the atypical, modern female has been so conditioned—bred into the harsh creatures they are by manipulating weak-minded men into a corrupted framework. I've turned it into performance art for the world to see: shedding female tyrant's egos with my Blade of Bluntness, slicing away layers of liberal dogma that suckled them through the socialized education system, and the lacy PINK lingerie that the media bound over their eyes. Peeling away the false skin so it might be seen in the bald sunlight is a fun game to play, I'll admit. After years of practice by dating, speaking to, and observing them, I have developed the skill at revealing what the modern woman truly is: a shallow and depraved creature. As entertaining as it is, my dating has only suffered since I started playing this destructive game.

Sure I have stories about how terrible modern women are, especially the college-aged, Ramona Flower-worshipping, Tinder-obsessed brand. They are utterly defunct humans save for their 'spontaneous quirkiness'—a byproduct of the Disney Princess Effect™ that strangled their true nature and replaced it with a vacuous fleshsuit that can utter sidekick punch-lines and safe sarcasm with bizarre 'weirdo voices'. My friend coined it perfectly that these girls grew up with Disney Channel and become consummated by it, their souls died at age 8 and were replaced by one of these teenage celebrities who themselves were manufactured in a factory.

I worked with a girl in her early 20's who was the perfect specimen of this phenomena. Her work ethic was abysmal, obnoxious with her constant 'Black Girl' voice, and lived at home with mom and dad. She wore a jean jacket with the most egregiously normie pre-sewn Star Wars patches on it, a fanny pack and California t-shirts that are supposed to look 'vintage'. I once asked her—when she proclaimed to love classic rock and punk music, listening only to the atrociously bland Def Leppard on repeat—who the Clash were, as is the necessary procedure for gatekeeping a tribal identity. She knew not even a single song by the band as you might expect. She had zero concept of punk rock meant, what the zeitgeist of the anti-authority and anarchic punk movement was. She'd never been to a punk concert, or any concert that wasn't sterilized and family-friendly.

Famously she filed a complaint against me with the HR of our company when she asked me why I didn't like her blaring Mamma Mia every day of the workweek, as I had also explained that it was a film about a middle-aged failure of a woman who was living as if she were 20. I guarantee that she will never be married and if she does, her husband will be a man of the lowest self-esteem.

But if you can meet a quality woman if you're a man and vice versa, this is what few achieve but all strive for. It's in your blood, the duality of the masculine and the feminine. To avoid it is just foolish and pig-headed, but like everything else—don't let The Hunt control you. If women continue in this trend like Mamma Mia girl, they will become their own caste of spinsters and drive younger women to avoid such despair in their own lives.

Marriage and the union of families is a far stronger

bond than any company or political organization.

Lastly, I will speak on my predictions of the future and how Goonhood can affect it.

Modernity has been disastrous to the plebeian condition, not the human one. Yes, the modern world is still the 1st World sweatshop run by goblinoid gangsters corralling the masses with their eternal administration of urban tyranny while the LCD screens feed sterilizing messages to the masses. It is the dimension of the over-saturation of goods with human life as the lowest common denominator, a shared observation by groups as polarized as tankies and Nazis. You may even catch earnest admissions of this from the Establishment itself in rare moments of transparency.

But this is what is observed from the plebian perspective because that is the ant farm—the perspective of the horrified specimen on the concrete, crawling on the prison floor with the sudden awareness that it is the product, not the smartphone or the trash-bag from McDonalds. This condition of depressive cognition is called 'the black pill' on obscure, anonymous internet forums, a play on the Matrix dichotomy of ingesting the 'red pill' will grant one awareness of the sinister simulation, inferring that there is only one path forward: doom and gloom. The black pill is what the blood-sucking hidden masters want their subjects to ingest, or otherwise remain oblivious. Why?

Because the depressed drone, stripped of his romantic illusions, will clock in every day like all the other good little drones. Each night he can stumble into his urban, sardine-can apartment, wade through a sea of Coors and watch Fight Club—yammering to himself about how he'll start their own fight club under the dive bars. This being has not escaped the modern prison he vilifies—he is merely an unhappy worker bee. His hard-earned cash is no different than vegetable-brained Clara next door, making 'donations' from her e-pornography videos, spending it on crystal lamps for 'healing'. The unifying factor of these two and millions of others is that they have accepted this lifestyle—a disposable one. Neither Clara or unhappy drone will leave anything behind of value, that will be remembered or can be utilized for the children they'll never have. This disposable life won't even be given the honor of being recycled—it will be abandoned to the landfills.

You cannot obtain clairvoyance when you believe your future is enslaved. Plebeians cannot revolt against the modern world until they accept the perennial lifestyle and free themselves of the padded cuffs. This is what is understood by patricians of the 'soul'. They leave behind a legacy worth honoring!

Why do you think a mafia enforcer's shit-tier .357 revolver with scratch marks engraved into its cylinder to mark each hit has more perceived value to the everyday man, than say some highly futuristic AR-15 with every gimmick, flashy tech and sight on sale at a gun show? The mafia revolver has inherited the soul of its user—a cold, apathetic murderer capable of both evil and the carefree impulse of every man in existence: the ultimate Will over life and death. No matter how many hands the mafia's revolver passes through, there is immutable energy it will forever retain. It is the vagabond's blade given a name and spirit! AWFL types will loathe Christopher Columbus for his colonialism, even tear down his statues, but will never eradicate the colorful threads of his discoveries.

Civilization is the whim of circumstance specifically because it is temporal. Societies are soluble. No civilization can withstand the sands of time, yet the barbaric spirit does, reincarnated indefinitely in stoic stubbornness. This makes all the more sense when you compare the ideas of Robert E. Howard and Conan—

civilization will always be at odds because it strives to overcome barbarism, not the reverse. It is a tree that tries to strangle a monolith, even as it produces fruits that will tumble and rot at its roots, attracting termites and other pests. Other trees will come but none will succeed in toppling the monolith of barbarism.

Be a Goon. Lift weights. Eat healthy. Hike mountains. Start reading books by racist old men and whatever else you want. Get your friends together and host fight nights. Build undetectable woodland forts. Learn how to garden and hunt for your own food. Stop paying for services that hate you and your people. Don't apologize for being a "fascist" or whatever these clowns think that means.

Start a family or strengthen your own. If there's one thing I've learned from my Mormon upbringing, it is the concrete union of families. The way to preserve culture and our way of life is by the bonds of families—not in a political club with strangers who have similar interests.

Little by little, when you look around you, those Marvel shirts and potgut physique will disappear. You'll go shooting with some random people and hear one guy quoting Mishima between hitting a gong at 300m with his lever action. You'll tell women you're an organic-based, free-roam, and cageless fascist. She'll arch her brow but ask to know more. You'll hear about a Wells Fargo burned down to rubble just down the street after a mob of Black Panthers started realizing that 'white people' don't own banks.

Cities will be put to the torch, whether we like it or not. I do not endorse this mass hysteric racial rioting but it's not in our power to stop it either. The tiger will eventually exhaust itself. I swear, if I hear another pagan lament about the burning of cities I will fucking convert to Egalitarianism—don't make me do it! Death and destruction is part of the perennial cycle, you Neanderthal monkeys! There *cannot* be spring without a winter! The most beautiful of groves are birthed from the ash of a wildfire. When you watch the concrete jungles fall, remember this.

It is within the Goon's power to *not* merely destroy life and to carry the hatchet for the shadow but equally to create homes, families, and live by nature. You will cause ripples with this—other Goons or those who value your value in the hierarchy of violence will follow. They'll pick up shop and move beside you. Yours and their kids will create alliances. Modernity will take its course and the tiger will eventually tire. It's the state of mind to understand this and simultaneously stake your claim in the wilderness, to stand up for your principles, and create something that lasts forever. You don't need to be a pagan or live a life as I do. I merely use my own life stories to explain how I came to this point, to better analyze my philosophy so others might be so introspective.

I hope one day to meet the hypothetical Goon who was afraid of the stoner in the chain restaurant parking lot in the old bandit nests of Escalante. He and his brood of eight kids, all named after famous outlaws and pirates, will be having a pow-wow on the cliffs. By the campfire, he'll ruminate about Butch Cassidy and his legendary exploits in the West. He'll talk about how proud he is of his kids for their exploits, how they'll all grow to run a hundred-acre pagan homestead before going off on their own adventures where the modern world is on its last breath.

This reality can happen! I hope it will! A day where a philosopher is only as worthy as his ideas in action, where journalists will flee in fear where their lies result in their demise, where the bureaucrat banker fear the barbarian in the woods they so despise, and the day that the world is the free and wild place it yearns to be!

Until then I will remain in my high desert fort in the redrock...

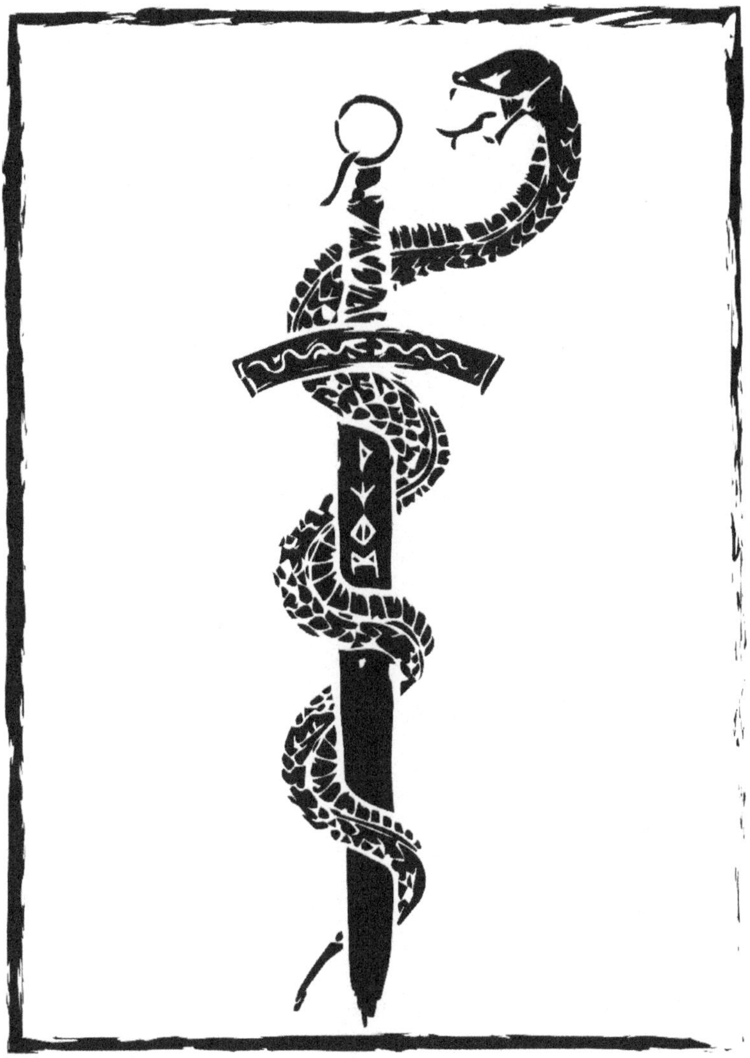

Made in the USA
Monee, IL
12 October 2020

44803701R00132

Blackberries in the Summer

–

The Story of Eulalie Salley and the Aiken Winter Colony

by

DON BOZEMAN

Blackberries in the Summer

Comments: aikenauthor@gforcecable.com
Author's website: AikenAuthor.com

ISBN: 978-1-941069-04-2

Prose Press
Pawleys Island, South Carolina
www.ProsePress.biz

DEDICATION

This book is dedicated to the memory of Eulalie Salley, legendary for her work in the suffragist movement and for her crucial role in the development of Aiken and the Winter Colony.

Eulalie famously said, "We folks in Aiken live off the Yankees in the winter and ***Blackberries in the Summer***." The unique community that she and those Yankees created lives on in the hearts and lives of those who remember and treasure their legacy.

Eulalie Sally

CONTENTS

CONTENTS continued

Author's Note

The author has endeavored to portray the events and personalities described in this book as accurately as possible. Where inaccuracies may occur, he begs your indulgence and welcomes corrections for inclusion in later editions. He has taken literary license to create dialogue and scenes where it is felt they may provide continuity, add dramatic impact, or clarify the underlying narrative.

Prologue

She was alone with her thoughts, surrounded by the very men who had fought her for over fifty years. Her son Julian, the rock that she could always cling to in times like this, was by her side. He nudged her gently from her reverie.

"They're calling for you, Mother."

She caught the last few words of introduction from her old friend, Senator Gilbert McMillan.

"...the lady most responsible for the legislation that was passed here today, Miss Eulalie Salley."

It was the first day of July, 1969. The legislature of the sovereign state of South Carolina had finally approved a bill ratifying the Nineteenth Amendment to the Constitution of the United States of America. The bill had languished in the musty archives of the state capitol for almost fifty years since its original introduction in 1920. This act, passed that day by both houses of the legislature, was the symbolic fulfillment of the lifelong pursuit of the 85 year old woman—to bring equal rights to the women of her state.

She rose slowly to her feet, leaning on the cane that she had stubbornly resisted for so many years. Julian helped her to the aisle where the Speaker of the House and the President of the Senate waited to escort her to the well of the chamber. Members of the assembly rose — along with the packed galleries—to pay homage to the frail, gray-haired, woman as she made her way to the front. With obvious difficulty she negotiated the steps to the podium. She leaned her cane against its base and surveyed the audience over the top of her rimless glasses. Many of the women who had fought alongside her through those long ago years were there. Sadly, she thought of the many others who had not survived to witness this final triumph. There was a lump in her throat as she reflected on the long struggle and the many hardships they had endured together. She was overwhelmed that so many had come—come not only to support her but to bask in the reflected glory of this historical moment. She cleared her throat.

"My dear friend," she said, nodding to Senator McMillan who had been her lone champion in the legislature, "I thank you for faithfully supporting our cause for the nearly fifty years that have passed since you first introduced this amendment in 1920. Yours was the lone vote for its passage each time it was resurrected. It took great courage for you to stand with us. Finally, the wisdom of your stand has been confirmed by this body. To the rest of you I say,

'Shame on you! Why did it take you so long?'

As a lifelong Democrat, why did I have to turn to Senator McMillan, a Republican, to champion our cause?" She paused to let her words sink in. "Now, however, I thank you for finally coming to your senses. The nineteenth amendment to the Constitution became the law of the land in 1920, following its ratification by the 36th state, Tennessee. Therefore, I have enjoyed the right, and the privilege, of voting through all these intervening years. Now, thanks to you and your vote here today, I will be able to do so with the full blessing of my own state of South Carolina. It is a glorious day, and I am thankful to Almighty God that in my eighty-fifth year I am still alive to witness it."

When she had finished her remarks, she retrieved her cane and made her way back down the aisle. Julian embraced her and led her out of the chamber. The assembly stood applauding until she disappeared through the entry doors. Her crusade was finally over. She could now go home to her beloved Aiken and "Edgewood," her home atop Kalmia Hill.

1

Marguerite Eulalie Chafee II

The cry came loud and insistent from the second-floor window of the stately Victorian townhouse on Greene Street in downtown Augusta. It was December 11, 1883, and the weather had turned blustery with gray, scudding, clouds hinting of an early snow. The doctor bent over the mother and placed his stethoscope on her heaving chest. Her auburn tresses lay tangled around her neck, snarled and sweaty. The small girl cradled in the arms of the midwife was the firstborn child of Kinloch and Eulalie Chafee.

"It was a bit of a struggle, Eulalie, but you have given birth to a healthy little girl with golden hair. I gave you a wee bit of laudanum for the pain. It'll take a little while for it to wear off. In the meantime, I've given instructions to Della as to the child's care for the next couple of days. Your milk should start soon. If not, Della knows how to prepare a nursing bottle for her. I'll drop by in a couple of days to see how you are doing."

Dr. Guthrie descended the spiral staircase and stepped across the hall to the library where Kinloch Chafee was puffing on a pipe and absentmindedly riffling through papers on his desk. When he heard the doctor's footsteps he spun around and bolted from his chair to greet him.

"How is she Doc? Is she all right? Did the baby come?"

"Calm down Mr. Chafee. Eulalie's doing fine. There were a few minor complications. I gave her some laudanum to ease the pain and calm her down a little. She'll be drowsy and will probably sleep for a few hours."

"What about the baby? Is it all right?"

"You have a beautiful little girl. She's going to be very tall and thin. She has blonde hair and a healthy pair of lungs. You can go up and see them now, but don't tire them out. Della is going to stay on for a couple of days, and I'll drop back by to check on them soon. I believe Eulalie said her mother was coming up from Louisville to lend a hand for a few weeks."

"Yes, I sent Luther this morning to get her. I told him to take that new surrey with the pair of matched bays that I gave Eulalie for her birthday last summer. She *never* takes them out," he said peevishly.

Kinloch Chafee was an avid sportsman. He relished the outdoors and the companionship of other men who shared his interests. Eulalie on the other hand was afraid of horses and guns and tended to remain secluded at home most of the time. She enjoyed the arts and was an accomplished pianist, having studied at a prestigious girls school in Baltimore. From her grand piano in the parlor she often entertained the passersby on Greene Street with works from the great composers; Bach, Strauss and Mozart. Over the years, an estrangement had developed between the couple owing to their differing interests and the Victorian influences of the era. Their marriage had settled into one of quiet convenience where they each lived happy but compatibly separate lives. Observing the plight of most of the women of her era, Eulalie Chafee was heard to remark that, "Men build for their wives very pretty prisons."

Mr. Chafee was careful to make as little noise as possible, but the creaking board at the top of the stairs undid his efforts.

"Is that you, Kinloch?" Eulalie said weakly.

"Yes, dear, Dr. Guthrie told me we have a beautiful little baby girl and that you are doing just fine. That's wonderful news." He bent over the bed to kiss his wife on her moist forehead before turning to address the midwife.

"Della, can I see my daughter now?"

"You sho' can Mr. Chafee. Now hold her head so it don't flop over. She don't have much strength in her neck yet."

Kinloch cradled the small infant in his arms and pulled the blanket back so that he could see her face.

"She's beautiful Eulalie. It's a little early to tell, but I think she's going to look just like you."

"What shall we name her?" she asked.

"Why, she looks so much like you that we have no choice but to name her Marguerite Eulalie Chafee as well." Eulalie's father had named his daughter for the beautiful young girl portrayed in Edgar Allan Poe's poem, Eulalie. Roger Lawson Gamble loved that poem and was fond of reciting it to his young daughter.

The Gambles were wealthy planters with two large plantations near Louisville, Georgia that were legacies from the King's grants given to his ancestors before the Revolution. Now, nearly twenty years after the Civil War, the Gamble fortunes were in decline. Hundreds of the slaves he owned before the war had fled. Those few who remained with him, either as hired-hands or share-croppers, couldn't possibly cultivate all of the 40,000 acres that he owned. Much of the land lay fallow. At the same time, a precipitous drop in cotton prices, to five cents a pound had devastated the general economy of the area. Roger Gamble decided to sell his townhouse on Greene Street and move back to Louisville.

Kinloch Chafee oversaw his mining interests from the Gamble mansion. Kaolin deposits had been discovered in large quantities around the Augusta area. The fine, chalky, clay was in high demand for industrial uses in products such as china, paper and paint. He had prospered as long as the demand held. Now his mining business was hard hit by the failing economy. When the house was sold, he and Eulalie decided to follow his in-laws to Louisville. Marguerite Eulalie Chafee II would spend her formative years there, under the watchful eyes of her mother and grandmother. The lessons she learned at their feet would guide her to a vision for the role of women in society that was very different from her contemporaries.

"Grand Mamá, why do you talk like that?" the young Eulalie asked one day. She was sitting with her grandmother Gamble in the swing on the front verandah of their columned mansion, perched high on a bluff overlooking the dark, swirling, waters of the Ogeechee River. Eulalie's mother interrupted before the older woman could answer.

"Eulalie! That's very impolite! One should never ask people questions like that. You might embarrass them."

"It's all right Marguerite," her mother said. "She has a right to know these things. It's just childish curiosity and, after all, it's part of her heritage."

"You see, Eulalie, before I married your grandfather my last name was Gobert. My grandfather, Benjamin Gobert, was a very important man in France. He served as an attorney to King Louis XVI. Well, one day he got himself into trouble when he wrote something that upset the king. He was called before the king's court, and he was sentenced to die on the guillotine for treason. Somehow, through the intercession of some powerful friends, he managed to escape and fled to the island of Martinique in the Caribbean. After the French Revolution, he moved his family to Charleston, South Carolina where he became France's representative to the southern part of the United States. My father—your grandfather—Jacques Gobert, was born there shortly after they arrived. So I was raised in a French speaking household, and that's the language I learned as a child. And that's why my English sounds strange to you."

Mrs. Gobert's attention was distracted by a man emerging from the nearby stables. Her husband, Roger Gamble, sprinted across the lawn. The rain was coming down in torrents now. He removed his wide-brimmed, straw hat and slammed it against his leg to knock off the water.

"God damned Yankees," he muttered. "I know some way or t'other they're to blame for this infernal rain, just as I'm certain they caused the drought last summer and the extremely cold winters we've been having. All the cotton seeds we planted last week are washing into the river. Now we'll have to start all over. That is if the fields ever dry out enough. Nothing has gone right ever since that devil Sherman came through here in '64. Twenty years of Yankees, carpetbaggers, and scalawags have ruined our way of life. I don't think we'll ever get back to the way it was before the war." He sank wearily into a rocking chair near the swing.

"Roger, you shouldn't use such language around the child," his wife said.

"I'm sorry, Martha. I just get so despondent every time I think about how those heathen Yankees have ruined us."

Eulalie rested her head on her grandmother's lap. Despite the chill in the air from the rain, her face was flushed and her hair was wet with perspiration. Martha Gamble placed a hand on the girl's forehead.

"Eulalie, this child is burning up with a fever. We'd better get her inside."

Eulalie lifted the little girl from the swing and carried her into the small bedroom off the parlor. She placed her on the bed and covered her with the crocheted spread that was draped across the foot.

"You must be careful, dear," her mother said. "In your condition you shouldn't be lifting her like that."

"Oh, it's all right Mamá. She's not that heavy." The Chafee's second child was but four months away. "I knew I shouldn't have allowed her to play in the rain," Eulalie said. "Now she's caught a terrible cold. I just hope it doesn't develop into anything more serious."

The young Eulalie remained in bed for the rest of the afternoon, lapsing into fitful bursts of sleep. After supper Nancy brought a bowl of chicken soup in to her. The mulatto maid had moved with the Chafees from Augusta to Louisville. Eulalie took a little of the soup and promptly threw up on the bed. Nancy called for her mother.

"Miss Eulalie, this chile sho is sick. She ain't drunk more'n a spoonful of this soup fo' she vomited it back up. She hotter now than she was fo' she went to bed. I think she gots more'n a plain old spring cold."

"You may be right Nancy. If she's not better by morning we'll send for Dr. Morgan. Oh how I wish Kinloch were here. He won't be back from Charleston for another week."

2

The Fever

The sandy drive that arced in front of the Gamble house was a sea of mud. Doctor Morgan reined in the soaked mare as he drove the small, black, carriage under the *porte cochere*. He returned the whip to its stand and hopped down. A young groom ran over to take the reins. The sides of the exhausted horse heaved from the long run out from Louisville. White foam oozed from around the mare's bit and splattered onto the bare feet of the small boy. The doctor retrieved his bag from the back seat and dashed up the steps, stamping the mud from his feet as he went. Martha Gamble and Eulalie Chafee were waiting for him there on the verandah.

"Ladies, please forgive me. I would have been here sooner, but we had an emergency in town. The Reverend Everett didn't hear the train whistle in the driving rain and drove onto the tracks. The train's cowcatcher struck the back wheels of his buggy and turned it over. He was thrown out. Thank goodness he didn't fall onto the tracks, or he'd be dead for sure. The horse bolted and drug the buggy over the top of him and broke his leg. One of the spokes punctured a lung. Me and Dr. Purdue patched him up as best we could. Dr. Purdue took him to the hospital in Augusta. They've got better facilities there to treat him. The old horse didn't fare so well. They had to put it down."

"Oh my goodness!" Martha said. "Do you think the preacher will be all right?"

"I don't think the leg will be a big problem, but I'm worried about his lung. If it gets infected he could be in for a lot of trouble." He pulled his watch from his vest pocket and flipped it open. It was past three. He looked at Eulalie. "Now, tell me about the girl."

"It came on all of a sudden yesterday. One minute she seemed fine and the next she was burning up with fever. I'm afraid she got soaked in the rain and came down with the chills. She didn't sleep at all last night, and she can't keep a thing on her stomach. We kept her down here in the parlor bedroom. Come this way." She led Dr. Morgan past the stairs. Nancy was sitting on the edge of the bed applying cold cloths to little Eulalie's burning forehead.

"Eulalie, I'm going to look you over and see if we can figure out what's ailing you," the doctor said. "I won't hurt you, but I'm going to need you to help me a little bit. Okay?"

"Yes, sir," she said raspily.

"First, I need to take your temperature. Now, I want you to open your mouth and I'm going to put this thermometer under your tongue. Okay?"

"Yes, sir."

After a couple of minutes he took the thermometer from her mouth and held it up to the light. The thin red line of mercury stood half-way between 102 and 103 degrees.

"Her temperature is pretty high. Have you given her anything to bring it down?"

"No," Martha said. "We thought you would be here earlier, so we waited. We wanted you to see her true condition."

"I see. I'll give her something when I finish my examination."

He opened the worn leather bag and took out his stethoscope. He placed the bell on the girl's chest. She shuddered from the shock of cold metal.

"I'm sorry. I guess it was colder in that buggy than I thought." He took the bell and held it in his fist until it absorbed his warmth. He then resumed the examination, listening to her breathing and her heart. He pulled the device from his ears and draped it around his neck.

"Her heart is strong, but she's got some infection in her lungs. Now I need to look at her throat." He took a small wooden paddle and depressed her tongue. "Say ahh."

"Aaaaaahhhhh."

"I don't like the looks of that," he said.

"What is it, doctor?" her mother asked with concern evident in her tone.

"Look at her tongue. It's as red as a strawberry, and there's a white patch at the base. I think I know what this is, but let me check one more thing. Will you pull up her gown so that I can check her torso?" Eulalie slipped the ribboned nightgown over her daughter's head. The girl whimpered in pain as the doctor ran his hand across her chest "That's what I was afraid of," he said. "See this pebbly rash and the dark bands in the creases under her armpits. I'm afraid that confirms it. Little Eulalie has scarlet fever." He pressed his finger into her flesh. When he removed it he left a perfect impression in white. "That's another thing you see with scarlet fever," he said.

Martha Gamble was dumbstruck. She called the doctor aside and in a whisper she asked, "Doctor Morgan, is it very serious? Several years ago I had a cousin who had scarlet fever. She died in great agony. You don't think this is that serious, do you?"

"Mrs. Gamble, at this stage it is impossible to tell. Sometimes the disease can be quite mild, and the patient suffers nothing more than a sore throat, swollen tonsils, and a rash. In others, complications that are more serious can develop, even rheumatic fever. When that happens there can be damage to the eyes, the joints, and even to the heart. We'll just have to wait and see. In the meantime there are certain precautions we can take that should lessen the chances of that." He returned to the bedside where Eulalie's mother was stroking the girl's face as tears rolled down her cheeks. She looked up at the doctor with imploring eyes. She wanted him to tell her that her little angel was going to be all right.

"You must keep the child in bed for at least two weeks," he said. "She must not be allowed to get chilled, or it could lead to the dropsy. That could kill her if it gets into her chest. In two or three days the areas where she has the rash will start to peel like she had been sunburned. That's a normal progression of the disease. Don't give her any solid foods until I see her next week. I'm leaving some Epsom salts, saltpeter and potassium. Mix them with clean water per these instructions, and give them to her three times a day. I think she'll be all right, but send for me immediately if her temperature shoots up."

The two women saw the doctor to the door while Nancy continued to apply cold cloths to Eulalie's head, all the while humming old Negro spirituals to her until she finally fell asleep. Eulalie's fever fell to 100 degrees on the fourth day. The women thought she was out of the woods.

"Mama, can't I please get up now. I'm feeling much better and I'm tired of lying in this old bed."

Contrary to the doctor's instructions, she was allowed to go to the table for supper. She ate her soup and a little of the boiled chicken before complaining of the chill in the air. She was sent straight back to her bed.

"Miss Eulalie, Miss Martha, come quick!" Nancy was standing at the bottom of the stairs in the early morning light, shouting up to their bedrooms.

"What is it Nancy?" Eulalie was the first down the stairs.

"She done took a turn for the worse. Her fever is gone sky high, and I can't get it down."

Eulalie felt her daughter's head and reached for the thermometer on the bedside table. Her temperature had spiked to 104 degrees.

"Quick! Send Mose for Doctor Morgan. Mother and I will try to get her fever down."

Two hours later Mose and the doctor returned to find the girl little changed.

"When did you first notice her fever going up?" Doctor Morgan asked after taking a quick look at Eulalie.

"Nancy came in to check on her about five in the morning and she said she was crying and talking crazy. She called me and I came straight down. When I took her temperature, I knew she was worse, and I immediately sent Mose for you."

"I'm afraid complications have set in. I'm not sure how serious they are until I do a more thorough examination."

"Eulalie, do you hurt anywhere?" he asked.

"All over," she responded. He lifted the covers and felt the girl's knees. She winced in pain.

"I don't like this. Her joints are swollen and feverish. This may have turned into rheumatic fever." He listened again to her heart and lungs.

"I don't detect any increased congestion and her heart seems all right. I'm more worried about this high temperature. The first order of business is to get it down. Please bring me two cups of cool clean water."

While Nancy went for the water the doctor took two vials of powder from his bag and measured out a small amount of each. When the water arrived he dissolved the powders in the glass.

"Now, I want you to sit her up and hold her while we get this down." He raised the liquid to her mouth.

"Eulalie, it's very important that you drink this. It'll help you to get better." It took several minutes, but she finally finished the medicine.

"Ladies, if you don't mind, I'd like a good strong cup of coffee while we wait for the medicine to take effect."

"Certainly, doctor. Come out to the kitchen. Nancy, you stay with Eulalie. Call us right away if she gets worse."

"Yes'm."

The doctor stirred his coffee. Eulalie looked worried and frightened.

"Doctor Morgan. I know you said to keep her in bed and not give her any solid food, but she seemed so much better, and she begged me to let her come to the table. She wasn't up more than twenty minutes. She had some soup and a little boiled chicken. You don't think that could have caused the setback, do you?" A pained expression came across the doctor's face and Eulalie knew the answer to her question. He sipped his coffee before responding.

"We'll probably never know, my dear, but it couldn't have done her any good."

Eulalie began to cry again.

"Oh, what have I done to my baby?"

"Don't be too hard on yourself. This might have happened no matter what precautions we took. You can't ever tell about these things. The important thing now is to get her well as soon as possible."

They returned to the bedroom. Eulalie had fallen back to sleep. The doctor felt her head.

"The fever's coming down now. I think we're out of the woods. I'll stick around for another hour or two just to make sure. She may complain of pain in her joints and she'll probably be a little weak." He fixed his gaze on the mother and said, "I'll be back on Friday. Make sure she stays in bed. I recommend you change all the linens and her clothes every day and boil them. Sterilize her dishes immediately and have everyone wash their hands with soap after they've been with her. Try not to get too close to her. She may still be contagious."

Martha, Eulalie, and Nancy began a twenty-four hour vigil. Eulalie was never alone for a second over the next several days. When the doctor returned on Friday, she was much improved but still complaining of soreness in her legs. Her temperature had returned to normal.

"Eulalie, I want you to try something for me," Doctor Morgan said. "I want you to sit up and swing your legs over the side of the bed."

She struggled to sit up, and her mother helped her. She finally got her legs over the side.

"Now, I want you to try to stand up."

Nancy held her arm on one side and her mother on the other, and she slowly stood, wincing as her feet hit the floor.

"Now, I want you to turn her loose and see if she can stand on her own."

The women released their hold and the girl crumpled to the floor. Her mother screamed.

"Oh my precious baby, what have I done?"

"It's all right Eulalie. This is normal with rheumatic fever. She'll probably grow out of it, over time. Meanwhile, she may need some assistance in getting about. As her legs strengthen you may think about getting her some crutches. Thank goodness I don't see any damage to her eyes or her hearing, and her heartbeat is very sound. If her ailment is confined to her legs we'll be very lucky. Keep her in for another week and then you can start exercising her legs.

3
The Long Road Back

Kinloch Chafee received the telegram from his father-in-law, Roger Gamble, at noon. It broke his heart. The message was very simple and cryptic.

"Return home as soon as possible-STOP-Eulalie II seriously ill-STOP-Rheumatic Fever-STOP"

He feared that his only child might die before he could get home. He hurried back from Charleston as fast as he could. The train got him to Hamburg, on the South Carolina side of the Savannah River, early the next afternoon. Old Mose was waiting for him there. He jumped down from the rear platform and grabbed the graying man by both arms.

"Mose! How is she? How is my little Eulalie?"

"She be a heap better now, boss. Doctor Morgan, he broke her fever, and she's a mite perkier now. She still in bed and her legs ain't working so good, but the doctor say she gone be all right in the by-and-by."

"Thank the Lord. All the way back from Charleston I was afraid she might be dead. Get me home as fast as you can without killing my wife's horses. I want to see my little girl."

"Yassuh, Mr. Chafee! You jest hang on tight."

It was after six when the carriage pulled under the *porte cochere* of the plantation house. The horses were lathered and spent.

"Mose you take good care of them now. Soap'em down

good and give them an extra ration of corn. They've served us well today."

His wife heard the carriage pull up. She stood on the verandah holding a lamp.

"Thank goodness you're home. We almost lost our little angel. Doctor Morgan thinks she'll be all right, eventually, but right now she's having great difficulty walking." She broke into tears. Kinloch embraced his wife before running through the house to Eulalie's bedside. She was asleep, her golden curls spilling across her pillow, her thumb securely in her mouth.

"My God, she's so pale and thin. Has she been eating at all?"

"Only the last two or three days. Her strength is coming back slowly."

"If only I had been here. I could have done something."

"Don't be so hard on yourself. The doctor said she probably caught it from one of the children she was playing with at church school. He's seen two or three other cases of scarlet fever lately. It wasn't anyone's fault. It's just one of those things that happen. The main thing is she's going to be all right. We can deal with the rest of it."

He looked at his wife. He saw the deep circles under her eyes. He knew he had to be strong for both of them now. He stood erect, smiled wanly.

"You're right, dearest. I'm dog tired. If you'll get me a glass of milk, I think I'll turn in. I want to be up early before she wakes." Kinloch tossed and turned until the morning sun began to filter into the room. Fitful images of his precious Eulalie drifted through his dream filled night.

The path back to wellness for Eulalie was painfully slow. She was confined to her bed for long periods. She walked with great difficulty, always requiring support. Four months had passed when young Mattie joined the family and Eulalie began to move about on crutches. They were fashioned for her in the wood shop Roger Gamble built after sending several of his workers to England to study cabinetmaking. They had returned to completely refurnish the plantation house with reproductions of the finest English furniture.

Kinloch ached for Eulalie. Her illness isolated her from most of the normal joys of childhood. She could not take part in the games with young Mattie and her visiting cousins as they tore about the property. She delighted in feeding their flock of geese, and Nancy would take her down to the pond almost every day. Still, her father longed to make her life better. He struck upon the idea of building a cart for her and bought two beautiful, white, angora goats to pull it. Eulalie quickly learned to command the goats and was flitting about the property to the envy of her cousins. Occasionally, if they were nice to her, she would allow them to ride. As her strength returned, she would unhitch the goats and ride them like ponies.

"Papa, look. I'm riding my goat," she would shout. Kinloch was pleased. Unlike her mother, he entertained visions of Eulalie becoming an accomplished rider and joining him on hunts.

"You be careful now, honey, you're still not well. I don't want you falling off and breaking a leg."

"Don't worry, Papa, I'm a big girl now."

Life on the plantation could be difficult at times. Upheavals in the economic and political life wrought by Reconstruction were immediate and devastating. Attitudes and prejudices that had been created over generations of slave owner privilege, however, were slower to change than molasses in winter.

Martha Gamble was a fusion of aristocratic France and genteel Old South. Slavery had been the norm for her life and, truth be known, she longed for its return. She was never comfortable with the idea that the slaves had been freed. Outwardly, little changed in her treatment of those who remained to work the fields and serve in the house. On one occasion, she witnessed Nancy disciplining Eulalie with a switch she had cut from a peach tree. She flew into a rage.

"It is not your place to switch that child. If she misbehaves you should bring her to me or to her mother. I won't stand for one of the help raising their hand to a white child. Your services will no longer be needed in the house. Monday morning you will return to the fields. You will report to the overseer, Mr.

Overton. He will tell you what your new duties are to be."

Thanksgiving came shortly after that incident. While everyone was distracted by the festivities, Nancy slipped into the attic, doused it with oil, and set the house afire. By the time the blaze was discovered it was too late, the roof was already collapsing.

"Roger, I want that woman arrested and thrown into jail," Martha Gamble said. "She set my house on fire out of pure spite because I sent her back to the fields."

"I'm not going to do that, Martha. This is a plantation matter, and I'll handle it my own way, in my own good time."

Roger Gamble was the autocratic master of his plantation domain and he ruled it with an iron fist. However, his failure to deal immediately with Nancy proved to be a fatal mistake. A few days later, the deranged woman stabbed her husband and then decapitated him. There was no way for Gamble to keep the law out of this mess. Nancy was arrested, tried, and sentenced to death. She became the first woman ever to be hanged in the state of Georgia.

The family moved into temporary quarters on another plantation while the house was being rebuilt and refurnished to Martha's exacting specifications. Eulalie helped her with the plans thereby displaying a real talent for house design and decorating that she would put to use later in life.

4
Aiken

Eulalie was nearly nine before she could throw away her crutches and bid goodbye to her goat cart. With an improving economic climate, her father decided to move his family to Aiken, South Carolina, the town where he was born. Kinloch's father, Otis Chafee, came from a wealthy Rhode Island family. As a young man Otis was told that the illness he had contracted would eventually kill him. Thinking that a southern climate might help his son, the father sent him to Charleston where he met and married Mary Kinloch. Friends in Charleston, aware of his illness, told him of people they knew who had gone to Aiken for their health and had miraculously recovered. The young Chafee moved his bride to Aiken and began a long but successful recuperation.

Mr. William Gregg, founder of the Graniteville Mills, was a close friend of the family, and he took the couple under his wing. He gave Otis Chafee fifty acres of land on Kalmia Hill, west of town. Gregg himself lived nearby, as did several wealthy planters and businessmen who came in the summers to escape the stifling heat and pestilence of Charleston. Reinvigorated and encouraged by the community, Kinloch's father became a successful businessman in his own right, living to the ripe old age of sixty-nine and fathering nine children.

"Eulalie, you can open your eyes now," Kinloch said. They

were seated in a hansom carriage in front of a white, shingled, Victorian house on North Laurens Street in Aiken.

"What is it, dear? What are you showing me?"

"Your new home. I've bought it for us. We're moving here to Aiken. The business is doing well. It's closer to Augusta, and I can ride the train over there. Most of my family is here. Besides, we've overstayed our welcome in Louisville. I truly appreciate what your father did for us, but it's time for us to be on our own."

"Why, George Kinloch Chafee, when did you learn to keep a secret? How long have you been planning this?"

"Ever since the fire. I knew it was time. I just needed to find the right house. What do you think?"

"I don't know what to say. It's such a shock. I need a few minutes to absorb it all. I know it will be good for the girls to be in a town with other children, and they'll have plenty of their Chafee cousins here. I hate to leave Mamá and Papá, but you're right. We need to stand on our own two feet. Now, take me inside and show me my new home."

North Laurens was a wide boulevard, one of many such streets included in the original plans for Aiken when it was laid out as a railroad terminus in 1834. The north-south streets were named for South Carolina counties, the east-west ones for towns. Grassy medians filled with trees and ornamental shrubs divided the driving lanes. Eulalie put her talents to work immediately, drawing up plans for major renovations to the two-story Victorian. She added a shingle-covered turret fronting on Laurens Street, with floor to ceiling windows. She installed the first indoor bath in Aiken. Young Eulalie relished splashing in the large, tin-lined, tub with her friends on hot summer afternoons.

Life in Aiken, now a thriving city of 2,500, was vastly different from that on the isolated plantation near Louisville. With her renewed strength and her natural exuberance, Eulalie made friends easily with the other young girls in town. Now that Eulalie's health was not their major concern, the Chafee's thoughts turned to the education of their two daughters.

South Carolina had no state sponsored school system; nor did most of its cities. Only the well-to-do could afford an education for their children. Most of the local citizenry saw no need for it. Farmers and laborers needed all their boys to help them eke out a living. Girls were expected to get married, keep house, and raise children. The wealthy northerners, who came to Aiken in growing numbers for its healthy climate and horse-friendly soil, wanted good schools for their offspring to match the ones back home. They built their own.

Eulalie and Mattie learned their three R's from their governesses. Both parents had received good educations, and now they wanted the girls to be equally well prepared to take their places in polite society. They enrolled the girls in a small private school. It proved inferior to the ones established for the children of the Winter Colony.

Increasingly, working-class families were moving to Aiken to provide the goods and services demanded by the burgeoning Winter Colony—wealthy families who were willing and able to pay handsomely. The merchants and professionals also wanted good schools for their children. These conflicting educational needs were reflected in the evolving class structure of the community.

Atop the social hierarchy were the wealthy seasonal visitors who moved in their own circles as defined by their private passions; polo, steeplechase, foxhunting, golf or any of the other seemingly endless pursuits that money could buy. The second tier was occupied by the professionals and merchants, many wealthy in their own right but seldom invited into the inner sanctums of the Colony. Third in line were the tradesmen and the laborers. Their fleeting glimpses into the lives of this imported nobility came in their roles as gardeners and craftsmen. At the bottom were the Negro families, living on the fringes of town and at the fringes of its society, in their small but neatly maintained cottages. They occupied the lowest rung on the social ladder, yet ironically, in their role as servants, they were the only ones privy to the innermost secrets of Aiken's winter aristocracy. The information they gleaned in the confines of the wealthy was a valuable commodity. They guarded it carefully and used it discreetly. It was an underground currency; useful in their dealings at all levels of the hierarchy. Information was gold. In another strange twist of fate, it was this group, relegated to the lowest and meanest of positions, that was given the first opportunity to receive an education.

5

Martha Schofield

Shortly after the end of the Civil War, Martha Schofield, a Quaker missionary from Bucks County, Pennsylvania, moved to the sea islands of South Carolina to minister to the children of the freed slaves. There she contracted tuberculosis. On the recommendation of friends she moved from the island of St. Helena to Aiken in 1868 to recuperate. That move was one in an amazing series of coincidences that combined to promote the development of the town —and the Aiken Winter Colony.

When she arrived, Miss Schofield had every intention of returning to St. Helena Island after her recuperation in order to continue her teaching. She soon discovered, however, that the need for someone to minister to the freed blacks in Aiken was every bit as urgent as it was in coastal Carolina. She took part of the $468 dollars she had saved and purchased a parcel of land on the northeast corner of town, adjacent to the properties of the black community. She set about raising funds to construct and operate the Aiken Normal and Industrial School for Negroes. Her arrival in Aiken was not without controversy. Her predecessor in ministering to the black children was run out of town by unreconstructed segregationists. The same people who forced that teacher to flee now set their sights on the same fate for Martha Schofield.

Martha Schofield

The Original Schofield School – circa 1875

Wilbur Driggers stormed into the office of Mayor E. H. Oakley, tracking mud and manure across the floor with his cracked and battered brogans. Driggers was a dairy farmer northeast of town. He was waving a document in the air.

"Have you seen this?" he demanded. "This paper says that some woman named Martha Schofield has bought all the property between me and the nigger community and she plans on building a school for all the little darkies. I want to know what you are gonna do about it? Why, the boys in gray buried over by St. Thaddeus church must be spinning in their graves. They didn't die in the War so that some nigger-loving Yankee could come down here and stir things up."

"Calm down, Wilbur. Miss Schofield has complied with every law on the books. She even got Mr. Croft's law firm to file all the papers. Every 'i' is dotted and every 't' is crossed. Whether I agree with you or not, there ain't a danged thing either one of us can do about it. Everything is perfectly legal. Now you go on home and simmer down."

Cooler heads prevailed. The school's doors opened in 1870 with 68 students and a staff of three. Miss Schofield made many treks back to Pennsylvania and across the east soliciting funds for her school. The majority of her support came from the Society of Friends (Quaker) community, but small donations from Aiken's black community and larger ones, given surreptitiously by her Winter Colony sympathizers, fueled its expansion. Miss Schofield's efforts even caught the eye of Susan B. Anthony, founder of the suffragist movement in America, who donated a considerable sum to the school.

Initially, all the students lived nearby and walked to classes. Later, residence halls were built to accommodate the students who lived outside the community. By 1900, over 6000 students had passed through the school. Many went on to occupy prominent positions in law, medicine and academia. One graduate, Matilda Evans, became the first African-American woman doctor in South Carolina. Classes in the three R's were combined with practical courses in weaving, woodworking, carpentry, farming and many other skilled disciplines, all designed to produce graduates ready to pursue a trade or profession.

Despite the initial opposition to the founding of the school, it soon became recognized as a major asset to the city, the county, and the state. Less than ten years after the school opened a local official, during a major public speech, paid honor to Miss Schofield.

"You have done more for the black community than all the politicians in Washington combined," he said.

In 1916, 300 former students gathered in Aiken to honor Miss Schofield on her seventy-seventh birthday. On the day appointed for the festivities, she was discovered dead in her room. Three days later, those former students, the faculty, and the staff, along with many citizens of Aiken, gathered at the train depot to pay tribute to her and witness her departure for Pennsylvania and burial alongside her parents. As the train pulled slowly out of the station, the crowd began singing her favorite spiritual, "Steal Away Home."

6

Reconstruction

The antebellum era of the Old South died forever in 1865. Lee's surrender at Appomattox and Lincoln's assassination in Ford's Theater ushered in one of the darkest periods in history for the South in general and for South Carolina in particular. As the first state to secede from the Union, and for having fired the first shot of the war at Fort Sumter, South Carolina was singled out for harsher punishments and more severe privations than any other secessionist state. During the ensuing ten years, Yankee carpetbaggers and their Southern scalawag collaborators made life intolerable for the survivors. The shattered vestiges of a once vibrant agrarian culture were gone with the wind. Two hundred years of southern aristocracy were ground under the heel of a cruel Reconstruction. Federal troops—a galling majority of them black—were quartered throughout the state. The Republican governors, appointed from Washington and ruling under martial law, ran roughshod over the defeated population. Unelected black politicians, most unable to read or write, sat in the state legislature. The top positions in government were held by freed slaves, appointed despite their lack of even a rudimentary education. Laws were passed with many signatures represented by a scrawled *X*.

Hamburg, the railroad terminus on the Savannah River just 15 miles west of Aiken, was seething with corruption. Whites seeking to pass through to Augusta were harassed and subjected to insolence and abuse. Public discontent in South Carolina boiled beneath the surface. Finally, in the summer of 1876, it erupted.

Mr. Thomas Butler of Edgefield, returning from a trip to Augusta, sought to pass through Hamburg, but was barred by the black militia. He brought suit against the militia and its white officer for illegally blocking passage on a public highway. At the trial on July 8, 1876, several hundred men, many wearing red shirts, poured into Hamburg. The trial quickly turned into a legal impasse, tempers flared, and the resultant courtroom scuffle overflowed into the streets. Shots were fired. A pitched battle ensued wherein several black militia and at least three whites were killed. Sixty-one white men were accused of murder. Rather than submit to a "kangaroo court" in Hamburg, they surrendered to the Aiken County sheriff where they could tell their side of the story in an Aiken County courtroom. They were released on $1,000 bail each.

The outgrowth of this battle and other confrontations prompted the formation of a band of vigilantes. Their unofficial uniform became a red shirt, and soon after they became commonly known as "The Redshirts." They sought to protect their women and businesses from rampaging bands of freed slaves. General Wade Hampton, South Carolina's foremost hero of the war, was recruited to be their leader. Sporadic battles erupted between the Redshirts and roving blacks. Several farmers were killed and many businesses burned; some with the owners trapped inside. Governor Chamberlain placed Aiken and several other counties under renewed martial law. The uproar convinced the state's Democratic Party to adopt the "Mississippi Strategy"—Mississippi was the first southern state to regain control of its own affairs—and put forth a slate of candidates for state office.

The election was held on the seventh of November. Hampton received a majority of the popular vote but was denied office when the votes of Edgefield and Laurens Counties were declared invalid. The Democrats protested. As a result, two governments were installed in Columbia in 1877. For Republican Governor Chamberlain the futility of the situation was soon to be underscored by President Rutherford B. Hayes's April decision to remove U. S. troops from the state. Shortly thereafter Chamberlain left, and Reconstruction was officially over. Now it was time to try to forge a society in which blacks and whites could peaceably co-exist. What ultimately evolved was a society wherein the blacks would be free, but in name only. Lincoln had freed the slaves, but he had not set them free.

7
Education

The Aiken Institute, an elementary school for white children, was officially organized in 1888. Public subscriptions were offered for $25. When sufficient monies were pledged, the board of trustees selected a site at the southeast corner of Colleton and Chesterfield, hired an architect, and began construction. Principal J. F. McKinnon opened the doors of the two-story, red brick, building with its prominent white cupola in 1891. Students were charged a modest tuition that was affordable by most of the families in Aiken. The school year was eight months long.

"Hurry, Eulalie," Mrs. Chafee said, "you don't want to be late for your first day at the Institute."

The Chafee's arrival in Aiken coincided with the second year for the Institute, and Mrs. Chafee was anxious for her two girls to enroll. Eulalie was not so enthusiastic. Having become accustomed to the freedom in her new home, she resented being cooped up in the classroom. She stared out the second floor window at the budding trees of spring and longed to be romping through the woods with Mattie and her cousins.

"Mamá, do I have to go? I'd much rather study here at home with Marie (her governess). Besides, my eyes get so tired, and there won't be time to rest them between classes."

"Eulalie, stop it! You're going to school and that's that. You cannot get a proper education at home. You need to interact with other students in a formal setting in order to develop proper social skills. Now go up and see what's keeping Mattie."

Eulalie's interest in learning was piqued when a new teacher from the Low Country joined the staff. The sensitive young man came from the Carolina coast and he told stories that mesmerized Eulalie—stories of rivers, and marshes, and beaches. Years later, those stories would figure prominently in her real estate career.

Notwithstanding Eulalie's dislike for school, she applied herself and completed the required course of study. She was turning sixteen, and it was time to introduce her to the social life of Aiken.

Mrs. Chafee was seated in the first floor nook created by the turret addition to their home on Laurens Street. She was reviewing sketches for a house she was planning. She was also watching for her girls to come home from school. Mattie appeared first, impishly running circles around Eulalie who was trying desperately to concentrate on the paper in her hand—they had stopped at the post office on their way home. Eulalie smiled and broke into a run, her feet scattering the scalloped, saffron-colored, leaves of the Gingko tree that her mother had planted that first spring in Aiken. It was early December of Eulalie's last year at the Institute, and the spirit of Christmas was in the air. The corn shocks and pumpkins of Thanksgiving had disappeared from the front porches. The first garlands of green spiraled around the light standards along the medians of Laurens and Richland.

Electric power from the hydroelectric generators on Horse Creek in Graniteville had been extended into town. William Gregg had installed the generators to provide lighting for his textile mills. Through his generosity and vision, electric power was brought to Aiken. The city was among the first in South Carolina to boast of electric street lamps.

"Mamá, Mamá," Eulalie shouted as she came charging through the front door, "look what I just received. The Cochrans are giving a party for their daughter Mary. She's asked Joanne Barnes, Margaret Fulford and me to join her. We all have birthdays in December. It's going to be like a debutante ball with an orchestra and everything. Isn't it exciting?"

"That's wonderful, darling. Your father and I were just saying that it was about time you were formally introduced. I think it's fantastic that the Cochrans have decided to do it. I must call on Jo Beth to see what we can do to help. When is it?"

"December 10th. Isn't it perfect? A birthday ball and Christmas, all in the same month. I can hardly wait."

"Is Mattie invited?"

"Yes, but she's been so snotty to me lately that I'm not sure I want her to go."

"Eulalie! Don't be so petty. Of course your sister will go. I assume the parents will go as well."

"Yes ma'am. I understand from Mary that there are over fifty names on the guest list, including some from the Colony."

A door opened behind the stairs. Martha Gobert Gamble emerged from her bedroom, dressed from head to toe in black. She leaned heavily on a cane. Roger Lawson Gamble had died a few years after the Chafees moved to Aiken. Martha had a stroke that same year, and she was partially paralyzed on her left side. Following the stroke, she moved from Louisville to Augusta to live with her daughter, Mary. Despite her infirmities she was a frequent visitor in the Chafee's Aiken household.

"Eulalie, I need some more of the medicine that Dr. Warren prescribed. Do you think Henry can get it for me? I'll give him the money. I know exactly what it costs."

"Don't worry about it Mamá. He'll just pay for it and you can repay me later."

Martha Gobert had ruled her home on the plantation with an iron fist. She doled out the ingredients for each meal and would brook no waste. She didn't understand her daughter's *laissez-faire* attitude toward the servants.

"Eulalie, I don't understand how you can let the help have such a free hand in the running of this household. If you're not careful, they'll rob you blind."

"I don't believe that, Mamá. At some point you must trust the people you employ. If they know you trust them, they will be responsible. They know if they are not they will be found out, and they will lose their jobs. And they know without proper references no one else in Aiken will hire them. Besides, it's so much easier if I don't have to worry about every little thing." Eulalie was notorious for not participating in the running of her household. She was fond of saying, "If you don't know how to do something, then you won't have to do it." It was a trait she passed on to her daughters.

"Mamá, Eulalie has some exciting news. Tell her Eulalie."

"Nana, Mary Cochran's parents are giving a party for her sixteenth birthday, and they've invited me and two other classmates to join her. We all turn sixteen in December, so it'll be kind of like a small debutante ball. There'll be an orchestra and everything. I understand they've invited over 50 guests. I wish you could be here to enjoy it with me."

"Thank you, my dear, but I have to return to Augusta next week. Mary is expecting several guests and family for Christmas. I promised I would help her with the arrangements. It sounds like a wonderful party, and I'm sure you'll meet some very nice young men there."

"Mamá, if you don't mind, I'd like to take Eulalie and Mattie to Augusta with you when you go home. We can have lunch with Mary and then go shopping. Both Eulalie and Mattie will need new gowns and accessories for the ball. I've heard nothing but good things about Ruben's, that new department store on Broad Street. We'll make a day of it."

"That's a wonderful idea, Eulalie. I wish I were able to go shopping with you, but I just can't get around like I used to. I'm sure Mary would enjoy it."

"Wonderful. We'll take the train on Wednesday. It'll get us into Augusta by ten, and we'll have the entire afternoon to shop."

The death in 1861 of Prince Albert—consort to Queen Victoria of England—had plunged the British Empire, and much of the civilized world, into mourning. For the queen the mourning would continue for her lifetime. Thankfully, for the world of fashion, the mourning ended by the1870's and new *haute couturiers* began to move away from the dour styles favored by Her Majesty. Dark colors gave way to vivid reds, yellows, and greens. The crinolines and cages of the immediate postwar era morphed into corsets, *bustiers* and bustles. The voluminous hoopskirts were replaced with flat-front, pleated garments whose crinoline underpinnings were gathered behind to form an exaggerated bustle. To offset the protruding *derriére* and create a wasp-like waist, young girls clung to bedposts while their maids pulled on the corset strings, squeezing the breath out of them. Whale-boned corsets and *bustiers* pushed upward, forming proscenium stages on which to display a lady's cleavage. No aspiring debutante was considered properly dressed without these latest *vogues*. However, by the turn of the century, the whalebone reinforced armor gave way to more delicate shapes with long bodices tapering into fitted, flowing skirts. Jackets and puffed sleeves were ready-made platforms for ornamentation.

These were the Gay Nineties. Fortunes amassed in steel, railroads, real estate and finance fueled an explosion of conspicuous consumption. Those fortunes followed their owners—the Astors, Vanderbilts, Mellons, Hitchcocks, Carnegies, Iselins, *et al*—to the Winter Colony in Aiken. Supply followed demand. Soon, the latest designs from Paris, London, and Milan made their way to Augusta by boat from Savannah and by rail from Charleston. The shelves of Rubens, and similar high fashion shops along Broad Street, were overflowing with the finest styles available.

Union station was a splendid Spanish Renaissance building on Barrett Square in downtown Augusta. Liveried hacks lined up to receive the shoppers as they alighted from their Pullman cars. Mary Gamble's driver pulled his carriage into the lane in front of the hacks. The Chafee family, along with the matriarch Martha Gamble, climbed aboard and proceeded to Mary's home on Greene Street. Following a light lunch of chicken and a green salad, Mary joined the Chafees for their afternoon of shopping. Martha stayed behind to rest.

The girls were positively giddy with anticipation as the carriage dropped them at the doors of Rubens. The store—newly opened in 1898—covered most of the 900 block of Broad Street. Well-dressed clients arrived in a steady stream from the depot and from Augusta's upscale Summerville neighborhood, located on the western heights of the city. The girls and their mother shuttled back and forth from the lady's fashion floor to the fitting rooms. Four hours later, the Gamble carriage was piled high with shopping bags and hat boxes. Mary dropped the Chafees off to catch the five o'clock train back to Aiken. She stood at the rear of the depot platform to avoid the explosion of steam and cinders as the spinning wheels of the locomotive sought traction to carry the weary shoppers home with their treasures. She waved until the caboose disappeared into the covered bridge over the Savannah River.

Eulalie was resplendent in a pink satin gown that displayed her five-foot eight figure to maximum advantage. Ribbons in a darker pink were laced through eyelets in the bodice. A grosgrain ribbon of the same color circled her neck. It was held in place by a gold, cameo brooch at the throat. The skirt was gathered and held so that it trailed behind her in a graceful flow. The jacket had flounced sleeves with epaulets of the same color as the ribbons. Her hair was upswept and fastened by a broad comb of tortoise shell. Kinloch Chafee stood in the hallway and marveled at the vision in pink descending the stairs.

"Eulalie, what a beautiful gown. You are positively radiant. I don't want to see the bill from Ruben's, but whatever your mother paid for that gown it was worth every penny. Who would have thought that the little girl in the goat cart would turn out to be such a ravishing beauty?"

"Papá, you're embarrassing me. I know I'm still that same old "ugly duckling," but I do thank you for the compliments. Wait until you see Mattie."

On cue, her sister floated down the stairs in a cloud of green silk organza with a contrasting wrap around her shoulders that crossed and tied in front. Mattie was several inches shorter than Eulalie but her body had matured more rapidly. She was broader at the hips with a pinched waist—Gibson Girl figures came to mind— and she definitely needed less padding than most girls her age. Her coquettish behavior had drawn stern warnings from Kinloch. Young men flocked to her side like bees to honey. Tonight would prove interesting.

The three girls were to arrive a half-hour early to plan their debuts. A four-piece string quartet was setting up in the alcove beneath the curving staircase when Eulalie and Mattie arrived. The girls went immediately upstairs where the three other debs were applying the finishing touches to their makeup. Eulalie eschewed lipstick. She applied only a smidgen of rouge to her high cheekbones. Mattie was made up in a similar fashion although she longed to effect the Gibson Girl look she so admired.

"Oh, Mary, can I try some of that lip rouge?" she said. "It's such a beautiful color."

"Mattie, you know Papá will disapprove," Eulalie said.

"Fiddle-dee-dee, it's not going to hurt anything." She took the brush and applied a thin layer of red to her lips. She added a bit more rouge to her cheeks then stood back to admire herself in the full length mirror. "I think that looks positively stunning," she said. "I don't see how anyone could object to that." The grandfather clock in the Cochran's parlor below struck eight. Mary looked out the window.

"The first guests are arriving. Mattie, please go downstairs and tell my mother that we are ready."

The Cochrans lived on Colleton Avenue in a stately, white-columned, mansion. A number of their neighbors were Winter Colony residents. Mr. Cochran's business brought him into contact with many of them, and they became close acquaintances, if not fast friends. Several had accepted invitations to Mary's party. She saw the Corbetts crossing the street. Other guests were alighting from their liveried carriages. The strains of waltz music drifted up the stairwell. The anticipated moment was at hand.

The fathers of the four honorees gathered on the upstairs landing, waiting for their daughters to emerge. When the

 Debussy

bedroom door opened, Mr. Cochran signaled to his wife downstairs. The quartet began playing de Bussy's "Girl with the Flaxen Hair" as each father escorted his daughter down the stairs. It was not lost on the musically literate in the audience that all four girls were blond.

The reception line wound through the spacious parlor of the house. It took over a half-hour for all the formal introductions and congratulations. There were several unattached men there, but try as she would Eulalie could not remember all the names. Never mind. She would inquire later. Finally, the inquisition was over, and she could steal away for a moment. She crossed to the dining room where she took a seat along the wall behind the serving tables. She was all but hidden from view by the punch bowls and the mounds of finger sandwiches and *petits-fours*. From her vantage point she could survey the room at leisure without being seen. She saw one very tall man in a tan jacket with leather elbow patches. Hardly the attire one would expect at a formal party such as this. There were three other men gathered in a knot around Mattie, who was furiously scribbling. As usual, her dance card filled up much faster than Eulalie's, but she didn't mind. She still needed time to recover between exertions. Besides, it gave her a chance to become better acquainted with her dance partners. Mary Cochran approached the table to refill her punch cup.

"Pssst! Mary! Over here!"

"Eulalie, what are you doing hiding out in here?"

"I just wanted a few minutes to get my bearings and rest my feet. I thought we'd be standing in that line forever. Mary, who is that man in the brown coat? He certainly looks out of place here."

"That's Julian Salley. He came to town a few weeks ago. He's a lawyer. He just joined one of the local firms. He did some work for my father. Father asked me to invite him. He seems nice enough. Kinda cute, in a country sort of way."

"Well you can have him. He's not my type. He looks like a real country bumpkin. What about those three men hovering around Mattie? I don't think I've ever seen them before."

"They're from Dr. McGahan's sanitarium out on Richland, near the Park in the Pines hotel. The one on the far left is Mr. Wright. The one in the middle is Mr. McLean, and the one on the right is Mr. Ashmore. Mother met them at a function last month and thought I should invite them. They're all from New York."

"Mr. Ashmore is quite handsome," Eulalie said. "Do you think if I just casually walk by that you might pull me aside and introduce me to him?"

"Surely. Just give me a minute to get back over there." Mary refilled her cup, grabbed a finger sandwich and wandered back into the parlor. Eulalie circumnavigated the room, approaching Mary from behind. She bumped into Mary's elbow.

"Oh, I'm terribly sorry, Mary. How clumsy of me. Did I spill any punch on you?"

"No, but I think Mr. Ashmore may have some on his shoe. Here. Hold my cup. I'll be right back." Mary ran off to get a cloth.

"I'm terribly sorry, Mr. Ashmore," Eulalie said. "I hope I didn't splash any of the punch on your clothes."

"I don't believe so but little matter if you did. It affords me the perfect opportunity to meet you."

Charles Ashmore was in his mid-to-late twenties. His dark brown hair was slicked back and parted down the middle. He sported a thin mustache. There was a twinkle in his deep blue eyes. Eulalie was struck dumb. She couldn't believe this handsome young man was paying court to her. It was Mattie that usually had the men wrapped around her finger. As if on cue, the other two men rushed to assist Mattie as she began removing her cape. Eulalie gasped. Now she understood why Mattie had insisted on wearing it. The low cut dress from Ruben's was supposed to have a lace insert at the neck. It didn't. There was a startling amount of cleavage for a fourteen year old. Eulalie was sure that Charles, like the others, would begin fawning over Mattie as well. She was surprised when he continued their conversation, completely ignoring her sister. This act alone would have been sufficient to capture her affection, but there was more. Charles reached for her hand.

"Would it be all right if I called on you tomorrow evening?"

Her heart skipped a beat.

"Oh, I'm sorry. Tomorrow is my birthday and my family has plans." She saw the disappointment in his eyes and quickly added, "But next Friday we're all going caroling if you'd like to join us."

"I can think of nothing I would rather do. What time should I call?"

"Come at six. We'll have mulled cider and sandwiches before we go and dessert when we return. It should be a lot of fun. There will be ten or twelve of us."

"I will count the hours." The overture to a Strauss waltz filtered from beneath the stairs as Charles asked, "May I have this dance?"

"You certainly may, Mr. Ashmore." She lifted the train of her dress and placed a hand on his shoulder.

"Please. Call me Charles. I hope to see a lot of you, and Mr. Ashmore is much too formal."

Eulalie glided around the room on a cloud of happiness. Never had she felt like this. The evening flew by and the grandfather clock in the entry struck eleven. The carriage that had brought the men from McGahan's pulled under the portico.

"Goodnight, Miss Chafee," Charles said. "I look forward to seeing you next Friday. It has been a wonderful evening. Happy birthday."

Eulalie watched as the three paid their respects to the hosts and then departed. She wished the night would never end. The other guests began to drift out into the cool, crisp, evening air. The twinkling stars seemed so close she felt she could reach up and touch them. When she re-entered the parlor, she noticed the tall bumpkin in the brown coat. He hung back until most of the guests had gone and then walked over to her.

"Miss Chafee, please forgive me for approaching you unannounced. My name is Julian Salley. I've recently moved to Aiken and begun to practice law here. I couldn't help noticing that your father, Mr. Kinloch Chafee, is one of our firm's clients. When he introduced you this evening, I put two and two together. I'll be doing some work for him, and I wondered if it might be all right for me to call on you sometime."

"I am sincerely flattered Mr. Salley, but it is an extremely busy season, and I don't think it would be wise for me to take on any more personal engagements."

"Perhaps after the holidays then?"

"Perhaps, Mr. Salley. We'll see what the New Year brings."

"Then I bid you good evening, Miss Chafee. I pray that you will have a wonderful and happy holiday season. I will be in touch." With that Julian Salley retrieved his coat and hat, leaving Eulalie to wonder how she could avoid seeing him again. Mary Cochran came into the room as he left.

"My! My!" Mary said, "Two beaus in one night. Aren't you the busy little bee?"

"Hush up, Mary. I told you I can't abide the man. Now he wants to come calling on me. I put him off until after the New Year, but I don't know what I'll do then. Why don't you take him off my hands? You said you think he is cute."

"No you don't little Miss Chafee. I do think he's kind of cute, but I'm not going to bail you out of this situation. I'm just going to sit back and watch you stew. It ought to be great fun."

"That's downright mean," Eulalie said with a twinkle. "And I thought you were my best friend."

"I am, you ninny, but this is just too delicious to pass up."

Eulalie playfully punched Mary on the arm. "All right, but be careful—and keep looking over your shoulder."

It was a bittersweet moment for the four young girls. As the festivities drew to a close, their rite of passage into womanhood was ending. Soon they would finish their studies and take their places in the adult world. Eulalie warmly embraced each of her friends. Then she stepped back and turned slowly in a circle seeking to absorb every detail of the room. She closed her eyes as she imprinted the evening in her memory. She wanted to preserve the exact moment when she had first met Charles Ashmore, the man that she knew would become her soul-mate for the rest of her life. With a smile on her lips, she followed her family into the chill of the evening.

8

Birth of the Winter Colony

The sirocco winds from North Africa blew through Celestine Eustis' hair as she walked along the beach. The parasol that protected her delicate skin from the harsh Mediterranean sun billowed with each gust. She watched in amusement as her niece, Louise, frolicked in the surf, racing forward as the waters receded then scampering back to avoid the waves lapping at the hem of her dress. The stately *Villa Louisiana* on the hillside above the beach belonged to Celestine's brother, George Eustis. She had traveled to Cannes on the French Riviera with his family from their mansion on the *Ile de France*, one of the most stylish neighborhoods of Paris. The Eustis home was frequently the setting for elaborate gatherings of the elite in French society.

George Eustis was the scion of a wealthy New Orleans family. He served two terms in the United States Congress just prior to the Civil War. By the time the shells rained down on Fort Sumter, he was ensconced in Paris with his family and his sister, Celestine. Following the outbreak of hostilities, Jefferson Davis appointed him secretary of the commission of the Confederate States of America in France, a position he held for the duration of the war. The French were openly sympathetic to the cause of the South.

Louise Corcoran Eustis, wife of George Eustis and mother to William, George, and Louise, was herself heir to the Corcoran banking fortune of Washington D.C. She died in Paris in 1867 of tuberculosis. Now her husband George had succumbed to the disease as well.

Celestine and Louise were dressed in mourning black as they strolled along the beach. The funeral services were concluded and her brother's remains shipped back to America for burial in Washington's Oak Hill cemetery. His will had been probated naming Celestine and Grandfather Corcoran joint guardians of the three Eustis children. The Corcoran family decided that the children's best interests would be served if they lived with their aunt Celestine. Now she had to make the difficult decision—where?

"Lulie, what would you think if we moved to New Orleans?"

Harriet Louise Eustis had been affectionately called "Lulie" since she was a small girl. She and her two brothers were born in Paris and had spent little time in America. While they had learned English in the Eustis household, their *lingua franca* was French.

"*Tante* Celestine," the precocious five year-old asked, "will Willie and George go with us?"

"Of course they will, darling. I promised your father that I would take care of the three of you as long as I live. I can't think of ever separating you."

"Then if you think it best, we should go to New Orleans."

With the settling of her brother's estate in France completed, Celestine Eustis returned to her ancestral home in New Orleans, Louisiana, her three young charges in tow. She quickly re-established herself at the apex of Creole society in her native state and began renewing ties with friends and acquaintances around the country. It was on her return from a visit to a friend in the small town of Aiken, South Carolina that she discovered her dear Lulie was stricken with the same dread disease that had killed her parents—tuberculosis.

The stifling heat and humidity of New Orleans made it doubly hard for the sickly young girl. She would come in from play with her young friends, wheezing and gasping for breath. The doctors recommended that Louise be moved to a drier climate, one free of the miasma of the bayou. Celestine wrote to her friend in Aiken.

"Zoe, could I possibly presume on your friendship to bring my little niece Louise to Aiken for a few weeks. She is suffering terribly here in New Orleans and the doctors have prescribed some time in a more healthful climate. I noticed there were several clinics in Aiken for the treatment of various lung diseases when I visited you last month. Perhaps I can enroll her in one for a few weeks."

"Of course you can, my dear," her friend replied. "I will be delighted to have you, and you can stay as long as necessary." Now Miss Eustis had the unpleasant task of telling Lulie that she would be uprooted once again.

"Lulie dear, the doctors have said we must get you out of the New Orleans climate for the sake of your health. A dear friend has agreed for us to stay with her for a few weeks while you receive treatment. Will it upset you terribly to go away for a while?"

"*Tante,* will George and Willie be going with us?"

"Yes, dear."

Then I guess it's all right, but that means I'll be leaving my new friends here. Will there be young people for me to meet there?"

"Aiken is a very nice little town in the sand hills of South Carolina. There are many families with children there. I know you'll love it. Why there's even a forest right in the middle of town where people ride, and hunt, and go for long walks in the woods, and the air is so clean and pure that it takes your breath away."

After just three months of breathing that healthful, pine-scented, air, Louise showed remarkable improvement. Her chronic cough was reduced significantly. She no longer wheezed and gasped for breath. Her ashen pallor disappeared and a rosy glow returned to her cheeks for the first time since she left France. Celestine had kept the Corcorans current with her progress, and in consultation with them it was decided that for the sake of Louise's health she should make the move to Aiken permanent.

Celestine found rooms for the family at the Phoenix boarding house. She returned to New Orleans to prepare for the move to Aiken. A month later, following a sea voyage around Florida to the port of Charleston, the little band descended on Aiken by train. Two carriages and several drays were required to move all the servants and baggage from the railway station on Union Street to the Phoenix. After a few weeks it became obvious that the rooming house arrangement was not satisfactory, so Miss Eustis bought the house from the Legare family and set about remodeling it to her liking. When she had finished, she christened the house *Mon Repos.* In addition to *Mon Repos,* Miss Eustis maintained a home in Boston, however, she would spend the majority of her time in sleepy little Aiken looking after her three charges.

Louise continued to prosper in Aiken. When she turned seventeen she was presented at a debutante's ball in New York. The ball included practically every family in Lady Astor's "Blue Book" registry of the most prominent members of society. The young beauty immediately caught the eye of several prospective suitors. None were a match for Thomas Hitchcock's attentions. The eligible bachelor, heir to newspaper and financial fortunes, wooed and wed Lulie Eustis. They were married in 1891 when she was twenty-four and he was thirty-one. Tommy Hitchcock moved his new bride into his north shore Long Island home.

Louise Hitchcock became an immediate fixture within the high-society crowd of New York, but she dearly missed her romps in the Aiken woods. It was not long before she convinced Tommy to visit Aiken with her. He discovered a thriving horse community with polo fields, fox hunts and steeplechases and felt right at home among the sandy hills of Lulie's hometown. Soon the Hitchcocks joined Celestine as homeowners. They bought the old Phoenix boarding house from Celestine, modifying and enlarging it over the years to accommodate their growing family. Both Celestine and the Hitchcocks acquired much of the property in the neighborhood of *Mon Repos,* adding many houses for leasing and for the use of their guests. Ultimately, they owned 8,000 acres. Much of that property was later transferred to The Hitchcock Woods Foundation and preserved for future generations of Aikenites. Although many wealthy people were already coming to Aiken from Charleston and other population centers, the imprimatur of Tommy Hitchcock was the key to Aiken becoming the Newport of the South—the Aiken Winter Colony was born.

9

The Yankees are Coming

Aiken was pelted with a devastating ice storm in early December of 1896. Trees were downed all over the county. Men labored to clear them from the roads, turning them into firewood for the winter. Thankfully, only two casualties were reported in the Journal and Review that week. Attorney D. S. Henderson slipped on his way to the courthouse and suffered a sprained wrist. Young Miss Eulalie Chafee fell on the ice near her home on Laurens Street, breaking her arm.

However, the storm did not prevent the arrival of trains from the north. Mr. and Mrs. Thomas Hitchcock and her aunt, Miss Celestine Eustis, arrived at *Mon Repos* for their winter sojourn in Aiken. Mr. Charles F. Havemeyer and his wife Camilla arrived on the same train from New York. They moved into Dr. B. H. Teague's home, "Pebble Ledge," which they had leased for the winter.

Charles Havemeyer's father owned the American Sugar Refining Company (later Domino Sugar). Havemeyer's parents felt that his marriage to Camilla Moss was beneath his social station. The marriage proved to be tempestuous and resulted in at least one separation. The winter in Aiken was to give their union a chance to heal, away from the glaring spotlight of family and friends. Two years later, on May 9, 1898, "Carley", as Charles was known, would be found dead of a gunshot wound to the head. The coroner ruled the death an accident.

Common wisdom was that it was a suicide. That speculation was heightened when his estate was probated and found to be worth only $300,000, small by comparison to others in his social strata. Tragically, two years later, his sister Natalie Mayer would die of a self-inflicted gunshot to the heart. Same story, same speculation.

Once again Aiken was to play a role in another of fate's ironic twists. "Carley" Havemeyer's widow Camilla would marry Frederick O. Beach in November, 1899. William K. Vanderbilt acted as best man and Winthrop Rutherfurd was an usher. Beach was a handsome, wealthy, playboy and a gadabout on the New York social scene. The couple later purchased a cottage in Aiken from George Croft, Julian Salley's cousin and confidant. Subsequently, the couple traveled to Aiken for most winter seasons. The Beaches later became the focus of one of the most notorious criminal trials ever to take place in Aiken.

Less noticed by the casual reader that day, was the story on page three of the Aiken Journal Review about the lynching of Calvin Kennedy, a black man accused of "outraging" the fifteen-year-old daughter of a prominent farmer in Williston. The forty-year-old man had been captured and taken to the home of the girl's parents where he "confessed" his part in the rape while also implicating another black man as the chief perpetrator of the crime. Kennedy was placed in the custody of two men to be taken to Aiken for arraignment. The train from Williston was flagged down in Windsor by an armed gang of ten men. The prisoner was bound, tied to a tree, and shot multiple times. His head was torn apart by a shotgun blast from close range. The second accused man remained at large. No one ever identified the men who lynched Kennedy.

"Lulie, did you see this piece in the paper about that poor man who was killed out in Windsor," Celestine said to her niece. "I don't understand why there are so many killings and lynchings down here these days. I know we certainly had our share in New Orleans after the war and during reconstruction, but I thought by now we'd gotten past that. I guess not."

"I don't know," Louise Hitchcock said, "Let me see that."

She read the article and shook her head. "*Tante* Celestine, I just don't know how there can be so much hatred this long after the war. It's been over thirty years. That girl must have known she was signing that poor man's death warrant when she said he attacked her. No black man in his right mind would ever even talk to a white woman on the street in this area, much less assault her. It would be plain suicide. Why, I can remember when you first brought me here how the Negroes would cross the street just to avoid the possibility of offending white people. You'd never see them out after dark. If they worked late at an event or at a party, they'd ask to be driven home."

"Martha Schofield is certainly doing her part to educate them for a better life," Celestine said. "The bigger problem is educating the poor whites who feel threatened by the black people and the un-reconstructed rebels who keep terrorizing them. They're the ones that need educating the most." The door to the kitchen opened and Thomas Hitchcock came in.

"Just put that trunk over here, George. I want to go through it before you take it upstairs. There are a few things that I want in the office. You can take all the other bags up to my bedroom."

"Yes sir, Mr. Tom. You just let me know when to take it on up," the black retainer said. George was one of several servants the Hitchcock's brought with them from New York each winter. Many others were hired locally, just for the season, to replace those left behind to maintain the Hitchcock homes on Long Island and in Manhattan.

"Louise," Tommy said, "Have you seen the letter I got from Bill before we left New York?"

Bill referred to William Collins Whitney, former Secretary of the Navy under President Grover Cleveland and creator of a family fortune in rails, steel and oil. Bill and Flora Whitney were notorious for the lavish parties they threw while in Washington. It is estimated that in his four years as Navy Secretary, he and Flora entertained over 60,000 people. Whitney, though several years Hitchcock's senior, was a close friend, confidant, and sporting companion from New York.

W.C., as his friends called him, parlayed the fortune of his wife into a fortune of his own. He became heavily involved in New York politics but never ran for office himself. He was the power behind the throne—kingmaker. Unlike the more staid, older money, families, W.C. was the most ostentatious member of the upper class. He owned three mansions on Fifth Avenue in New York as well as several palatial estates around the country.

In 1896, after the socially required three-year mourning period following his wife Flora's death, William Whitney married Mrs. Edith Randolph, widow of a British army officer. There was speculation that both Whitney and J.P. Morgan had earlier shared the favors of the beautiful and vivacious widow Randolph—before Flora put an end to the affair. After Flora died in 1894, Whitney resumed his liaison with Edith, creating a major rift with Flora's brother, Oliver Hazard Payne. A rift that would continue until Whitney's death.

Payne had never married. Rumors abounded that he had an unrequited, romantic obsession for his brother-in-law—Payne and Whitney were roommates at Yale. Payne had introduced his sister Flora to Bill. Flora was not a raving beauty, and there was speculation that Whitney coveted the Payne fortune. The relationship between the two men remained solid until the Randolph affair. Payne was devoted to Flora and considered Bill's marriage to Edith to be disrespectful of his sister's memory.

William Collins Whitney

Flora Payne Whitney

Edith Randolph Whitney

Payne's fortune from Standard Oil and other investments rivaled the fortune that Whitney amassed, and he offered to leave it to the Whitney children if they would denounce their father. This proposal succeeded in dividing the family. William and Pauline sided with their uncle. Harry and Dorothy stayed with their father. William went so far as to drop his given name; thereafter he went by his second name, Payne.

"No dear. It should be in that trunk with all your other correspondence."

Tommy Hitchcock flipped open the trunk and began to rummage through the pile of papers.

"Here it is. I just wanted to make sure I had the right date. Yes. Bill and Edith will arrive on December 20 and plan to stay through the week of New Year's. Harry and Gertrude are coming with them. I asked Corny and Alice to come—if they can get away. Bill is sending his Pullman up to Newport to get the children. I urged him to bring his ponies. I'm anxious to show him our polo field. If I know him, he'll be as taken with Aiken's potential as I am. Mark my word, by this time next year two things will have happened; Bill will own a place here in Aiken, and Harry and Gertrude will be married."

Harry Payne Whitney was William Whitney's oldest son, and Gertrude Vanderbilt, Harry's girlfriend, was the daughter of Cornelius and Alice Vanderbilt. Her great-grandfather was the founder of the Vanderbilt dynasty. The Vanderbilt's were in residence at their recently completed cottage, "The Breakers," in Newport, Rhode Island. The "cottage" contained 70 rooms and 65,000 square feet of living space. It was the most opulent house ever built in the greater New York area. Built today it would cost over $300,000,000. It replaced the former Lorillard home on that site, which had burned. Vanderbilt wanted to preclude another fire, so the new house was constructed of all fireproof materials. Even the furnace was located away from the house. It was situated under the street in front of the driveways. From that day forward, snow and ice never accumulated on that stretch of roadway.

Thomas Hitchcock knew his friend Bill Whitney very well. The following year Whitney purchased the former Joye boarding house. The property covered the entire city block bounded by Whiskey Road, Easy Street, Newberry Street and South Boundary. It was a stone's throw from the Hitchcock's *Mon Repos* residence. In a move consistent with his brash nature, Whitney hired a prominent New York architect and directed him to fashion a four thousand square foot addition to the house—and he wanted it completed in time for Christmas, which was less than six months away. Money talks. One year after having spent Christmas with the Hitchcock's, William and Edith Whitney hosted their own grand celebration at Joye Cottage.

Joye Cottage

Two years later, in February 1898, Edith Whitney suffered a massive injury when riding in Hitchcock Woods. She was riding on a taller horse than her usual mount and her head hit the roof of a covered bridge at Robinson's Pond. She fractured several cervical vertebrae and was paralyzed in both arms. She was in a coma for several days. Two months after the accident, she was sufficiently recovered to be moved to the Whitney's

New York home. Bill Whitney had a special carriage equipped with rubber wheels to smooth her ride to the train for her trip to New York. Eulalie Salley recalled seeing the carriage as it passed the Aiken Institute on the way to the station on Union Street. Edith Whitney recovered sufficiently to attend the local steeplechase races but she soon slipped back into a coma. She died on May 6, 1899. William Whitney never fully recovered from the death of Edith. He died in 1904.

Prior to the arrival of the Hitchcock's and Whitney's, several wealthy families from Charleston came to Aiken in the summers and a smattering of Yankees came in the winters. Most of them did not move in the same circles as the Hitchcock's. Those who didn't purchase or build their own homes were usually found at the elegant Highland Park Hotel, located at the foot of Railroad Avenue (Park Avenue). The four floor, Second Empire, structure could accommodate 300 guests in grand style. Rooms were hard to come by from October through March. Mr. B. P. Chatfield opened the hotel in 1870. It sat on a fifty acre tract which was in turn part of a 350 acre farm with walking paths and riding trails. It had the most modern plumbing system of any hotel in the world. Effluent from the hotel was carried almost two miles away and then sanitarily treated before being used as fertilizer on the Chatfield farm. The sixty Holstein-Friesian dairy cows he kept there were sleek and healthy.

Tommy and Louise Hitchcock

"I'm looking forward to having our friends and family here for the holidays," Tommy said. "Do you think we can put together a hunt for Christmas Day, and maybe have a picnic in the woods? Henry has finished the new pavilion at the bottom of

"The Devil's Backbone." We could end up there after the hunt. Even if the weather turns bad we'll have shelter."

"I'll get Dora and have George drive us up to Mr. Hahn's," Louise said. "I'm sure he'll have plenty of provisions coming in for the holidays. I've already sent him our order for Christmas and New Year's. We'll just get what we need to make up the picnic and add a few bottles of champagne." Dora had overseen the Hitchcock's kitchen since their wedding in 1891 and had served *Tante* Celestine before that. George had been Tommy's valet for ten years and, by now, was practically a member of the family.

Hahn's grocery occupied the southwest corner of Laurens at Richland. Mr. Hahn's residence was at 707 Hayne Avenue, just a short five-block walk from his business. Hahn was one of many German immigrants who exploited the opportunities presented by the wealthy winter residents of Aiken. His grocery catered to their every whim: prime cuts of meat, fresh produce, gourmet items from around the world, wines and spirits. On occasion Hahn could be found sitting by the phone late in the evening, awaiting a call from a prominent hostess. The phone would ring when she was ready to serve dessert and he would deliver fresh ice cream—she had not installed freezers in her own kitchen. It was this attention to detail that afforded him the handsome house on Hayne Avenue.

Louise Hitchcock held a bottle of Dom Perignon. She was checking its vintage when she noticed the tall, statuesque woman with dark, black hair at the rear of the Hahn store. The girl standing beside her turned so that Louise could see her right arm. It was in a cast and was supported by a sling around her neck. The girl walked toward her, idly checking the merchandise displayed along the aisle.

"You must be Eulalie Chafee," Louise said. "I saw the article about your fall in the paper. I'm so sorry. That was such a terrible storm, so unexpected. Are you going to be all right?"

"Oh, yes ma'am. It's just a hair-line fracture. The bone

didn't separate. The doctor said I'll be as good as new in a few weeks." Eulalie stared up at the young woman's face, paused, then hesitantly asked,

"Do you ride in the woods off South Laurens?"

"Yes, I do. Quite often as a matter of fact. Why do you ask?"

"I ride there sometimes too. I think I saw you last week, down near the track. My mother said the people who own the woods don't mind. It's so beautiful, so quiet, so peaceful. When I'm way back in the woods, the only sounds are the birds and the falling water. I love that place."

"I'm glad that you do, Eulalie. I tell you what. When you are all well and ready to ride again, just knock on the door of the house on Laurens near the entrance to the woods and I'll go with you."

Eulalie blushed then stammered a response.

"Are you Mrs. Hitchcock? Does your family own the woods?"

"Yes, my dear," Louise smiled. "And your mother is quite right. You're welcome to ride there anytime."

"Mrs. Hitchcock, it's so good to see you," Eulalie, Sr. said as she joined the conversation. "I read in the paper that you and Mr. Hitchcock and your Aunt Celestine had arrived last week. Welcome back."

"Thank you, Mrs. Chafee. I was just telling your daughter that she's welcome to ride on our place at anytime. I hope to see the two of you there soon."

"I'm sure you'll see Eulalie," her mother said laughingly, "but I'm not much of a horsewoman, so I'll leave the riding to her. Thank you so much for your hospitality. It's good to see you and Miss Eustis back in Aiken."

"You're entirely welcome," the young bride responded. "I look forward to a visit from young Eulalie and I hope to see you again soon Mrs. Chafee." Louise strolled toward the butcher shop where Dora was inspecting a rack of lamb chops.

"Isn't she beautiful, Mamà? And she's so *nice*."

"Yes, she is, dear. But, you must know that the Hitchcock's are very wealthy people and they tend to associate mostly with their own kind. So don't be too disappointed if she doesn't choose to ride with you."

It would be many years before the innocent young Eulalie fully understood her mother's admonition. After all, the Chafee's were not poor. However, the chasm between the Chafee's "well-off" and the Hitchcock's "filthy-rich" was a divide that most Aikenites would never successfully cross.

10
Coming of Age

"Good evening, Charles," Eulalie said as she answered the door. "I'm so glad you could come."

Charles Ashmore wore a light blue, cardigan sweater over a plaid, wool shirt. He was hatless, but he had a fringed, black, muffler wound about his neck. The temperature was in the 40's.

"I wouldn't have missed it for the world. The other folks at McGahan's are sick of me counting the hours until tonight. I'm afraid I've been a terrible bore all week."

"I'm sure that's not true, Charles, but I appreciate the compliment. Come on in. Most of the others are already here." She led her young suitor into the parlor where the others were gathered around a display of sandwiches and mulled cider.

"I believe most of you met Mr. Ashmore at the Cochran's party last week. Charles, I'd like you to meet my friends." She led him around the room, re-acquainting him with the party guests and introducing those who were new. There were five other couples. Her mother and Mattie moved about the room making sure that everyone had sandwiches and cider.

By six it was becoming dark outside. The carolers donned their coats, gathered their sheet music and candle holders, and trooped out into the night. The fanciful, wrought iron, lamp posts wore garlands of pine and holly. The troupe made its way down Laurens, serenading the homes as they went. They turned onto Curve Street and then Hayne Avenue which was lined with grand winter homes, most occupied for the season since early November. Several blocks later they took Fauburg north and doubled back along Richland, stopping at St. Thaddeus to admire the nativity scene on the lawn out front. Eulalie and Charles drifted toward the rear as the group covered the short distance back to Laurens and headed for the Chafee house. Charles reached for her hand. He held it firmly in his until they turned up the walk.

It was near ten before the last of the apple pie was gone. The carolers began to bid their goodbyes. Charles was the last to leave. Eulalie stepped onto the front porch and closed the door behind her. Charles bent forward and bussed her on the cheek.

"I hope you don't mind," he said. "I'm not in the habit of kissing young women so soon after we've met, but I just couldn't resist."

"It's all right, Charles. It's not as if I've never been kissed."

"I'm sure that's true of someone so beautiful and poised as you. I'm just jealous that I wasn't the first. It's been a wonderful evening. I look forward to spending many more with you in the future. Good night."

"Good night, Charles. I too had a wonderful evening."

She walked back into the house on a cloud. Charles was everything she had imagined him to be; handsome, charming, chivalrous and funny. He had a quirky wittiness that endeared him to everyone he met. Yes, she was sure he was the one.

Eulalie may have been sure, but her mother wasn't. Eulalie, Sr. had seen too many families crushed by the death of a loved one from tuberculosis. In the previous two centuries the insidious disease had killed a billion people around the world, especially ravaging the poverty stricken populations of Asia and Africa. Over a hundred thousand were dying each year in the United States. An estimated eighty percent of the population carried the TB bacteria in their systems even though less than10 percent manifested the severe effects of consumption. It was a scourge that ignored social boundaries. While a preponderance of the deaths was among the poor, social status was not a barrier to contagion.

"I'm worried about Eulalie," Mrs. Chafee said to her husband at breakfast. The girls had already left for school.

"Why?"

"It's obvious that she is smitten with Charles. I can understand how an impressionable seventeen year-old would be. He comes from a good family, is well mannered and handsome, but he also has active tuberculosis for which he is being treated year round, either here or at Dr. McGahan's clinic in New York. I just don't want to see her get hurt if his condition worsens."

"Oh, I don't think you need to worry," Mr. Chafee said. "It's just a schoolgirl crush. It'll play itself out in time."

"I certainly hope you are right. The look on her face this morning argues otherwise. But, I'll wait to see what develops."

The following weeks saw a steady parade of visitors through the Chafee household. Chief among them was Charles Ashmore. Each weekend and often during the week he came to see Eulalie. Despite Kinloch's opinion to the contrary, there was no diminution in Eulalie and Charles' ardor. If anything there was an increase. Spring came, and Eulalie Chafee felt compelled to take action.

"Kinloch, I am still worried about Eulalie. I think she's spending way too much time with Charles. He's almost ten years her senior and it doesn't set right with me. And then there's the tuberculosis. I've seen too many families devastated by that disease. I don't want her to pin all her hopes on him and then have something terrible happen to him."

"What do you propose to do? She seems to genuinely care for Charles. You can't just up and forbid her to see him."

"As soon as school is out, I want to send her and Mattie to Mrs. Teague's Boarding School in Saluda. It will give things a chance to cool down and for them to decide if they really love each other enough to commit the rest of their lives together. If they still feel the same at the end of the summer I won't stand in their way. Will you consent to that?"

"Yes, Eulalie. I still believe that what she has is a schoolgirl's crush. Three months apart should cool their ardor."

"But Mamá, why do I have to go," Eulalie said. "None of the other girls are going away for the summer. It's not fair."

"It may not seem fair to you, darling, but it is in the best interest of both you and Charles to be apart for a while. It'll let you decide if you really love each other and are willing to commit to the rest of your lives together. If you still feel the same when you come home in September, then Kinloch and I will not stand in your way." Eulalie saw the steely determination in her mother's eyes and knew further argument would be fruitless.

The remainder of the school year sped by, and soon graduation was upon them. Eulalie had picked out a beautiful white satin dress from Rubens. The puffy sleeves and long white gloves lent an air of elegance to her statuesque frame as she crossed the stage to receive her diploma. The Chafees came from all over. Mrs. Gobert rallied from her sickbed following her most recent seizure, and attended. Everyone gathered at the Chafee's home for refreshments afterward. Charles was invited. Eulalie was surprised that Julian Salley was there as well.

"Mamá, why is Mr. Salley here?"

"Your father asked him to come. He's doing more and more work for Kinloch's company and they've become quite good friends."

Julian sat on a bench well away from the mingling guests. Mr. Theo Croft, one of the Chafee cousins and also a member of the law firm, sat beside him. Between bites of cake, Julian told him how much he admired Eulalie.

"Theo, I'm going to marry that girl!" he suddenly proclaimed.

"But, Julian. She's already spoken for. It's common knowledge that she plans to marry Charles Ashmore. She can't marry you." Julian calmly put his fork down and looked Croft in the eyes.

"We'll see, Mr. Croft. We'll see."

The summer dragged by. In Eulalie's absence Charles had decided to take a mining job in South America. The lovers corresponded almost daily by mail, but that was little balm to their aching hearts. September rolled around and their ardent reunion belied the Chafee's belief that it was all a temporary fling. Eulalie pressed her parents again to consent to the engagement.

"On one condition," her mother said. "That you will wait until you are twenty-one to marry."

"But, mother, that's such a long time."

"Those are my terms, young lady. Take it or leave it." Eulalie knew when she had pushed as far as she could. She accepted the decree and the Ashmore/Chafee engagement was announced in the *Aiken Journal and Review.*

The Chafees went to great lengths to distract the couple. Eulalie was enrolled in Mary Baldwin College in Virginia for a while. Her parents thought exposure to girls from across the country might broaden her horizons beyond the parochial boundaries of Aiken. It didn't work. She hated school and longed to return home—and to Charles.

Finally it was 1904. She would turn twenty-one in December. She could hardly contain her excitement. But even then storm clouds were gathering. The consumption eating at Charles' lungs suddenly became virulent and he needed almost constant attention. Eulalie felt in her heart that once they were married she would be able to nurse him back to health. She did not understand the corrosive nature of the disease that was ravaging Charles' body. All the skills she had, or could obtain, would not change the course of events. Charles succumbed to the disease before Christmas. Eulalie's world crumbled. She was numb and in abject mourning.

The Chafees tried to lift her from her despondency. They enrolled her in Converse College in Spartanburg. Dr. Pell, an old friend of the family and President of Converse, opened his arms to her. It didn't help. She hated school. She hated seeing all the suitors descend on the campus each weekend. She found no solace there. Then tragedy reared its head again.

George Kinloch Chafee died within a year of Charles' death. Eulalie returned to Aiken. She would never leave again. The double loss affected her deeply. She and the family were in mourning for six months. Then, slowly but surely, life started to return to normal. There was laughter again in the Chafee house on Laurens Street. Old friends came calling. Among the callers was Julian Salley.

Julian Salley was executor of Kinloch Chafee's will. As if needed, this gave the young, newly elected, mayor of Aiken a ready excuse to call on the Chafees. It was amazing how many minute details required the attention of the widow Chafee. During this period, Eulalie warmed to the rawboned lawyer, finally consenting to go on a date with him.

Julian hitched his finest horse to a sparkling new phaeton carriage. He arrived at the Chafee home shortly after noon on a Sunday and the two set out on a trip into the country. Mattie and her mother watched with interest from the verandah as the carriage drove away.

"I think it's a good thing she's getting out of the house," Mattie said. "She's been so sad for over a year. She's starting to get a little color back in her cheeks. Where do you think Julian will take her?"

"I heard Eulalie say they were going to Henry Dibble's place in Montmorenci."

The Vale of Montmorenci lay six miles east and south on the post road toward Charleston. Dibble had established a country estate there where he ran a dairy farm. Courting couples turning up there on Sunday afternoons were always treated to fresh-churned ice cream. Dibble was also president of the Bank of Aiken and commuted to town via South Boundary Street. It was a beautiful street where many of the wealthy northerners were building their winter homes.

"Julian," Henry Dibble said as he handed the mayor a dish of ice cream, "I wonder if I could persuade you to get the city to help me with a little project I have in mind?"

"I'll certainly try, if it's within my authority to do so. What is it?"

"You know that I drive into Aiken every morning down South Boundary with all its beautiful homes. Well, I was thinking how nice it would be if we could plant trees on either side of that boulevard from the city limits down to Whiskey Road. Most of those parcels were reclaimed from open farmland, and there are not a lot of trees along there. What do you think?"

"I think that's a great idea, Mr. Dibble, and I may be able to help you. Just the other day, I discovered some money left over from the previous administration. It was from another parkways tree-planting project. The city used most of the money. We planted over 500 trees in the medians of the parkways. If you can come up with matching funds, I'll try to get the council to allocate that money, and I'll see if we can get the work done by the city streets department."

"It's a marvelous idea Mr. Dibble," Eulalie said. "I've always loved planting things."

The sun was setting when the couple got back to town. Julian helped Eulalie down from the buggy and escorted her up the walk.

"Miss Eulalie it was a delightful afternoon. I trust you enjoyed yourself. I'd like the opportunity to see you again soon, if you don't mind."

"Why, I guess that would be all right," she said. Julian broke into a broad grin.

"Thank you, Miss Eulalie. You've made me very happy."

She was hardly in the door before Mattie had pinned Eulalie's arms to her side and demanded to know all the details of the afternoon.

"He's the darndest country bumpkin I ever saw. Why he didn't even put his arm around me," she said.

Julian's courtship of Eulalie intensified. Soon he was there almost every night. For her part, she exposed him to Aiken society in the hopes it would smooth off some of the rough edges. She invited him on hunts, but he didn't like all the pomp and pageantry. Nevertheless, he pursued her hand relentlessly. Her mother was a big Julian Salley fan and unlike with Charles, she encouraged the relationship. Eulalie's resistance began to wear down. She finally relented and after several months of courtship she agreed to marry him. Years later, after Julian was gone, she would remark to friends that she married him in a moment of weakness just to get rid of his constant badgering.

Wistfully, she added, "Women with talent should never marry. I married in a moment of temporary insanity."

As a young woman in her twenties at the turn of the century, Eulalie was simply submitting to the norms of post-Victorian society. Young women had limited opportunities. They became teachers, they became nurses, or they got married. There were no models for Eulalie in the business world. She had no father to guide her and her mother was pushing her into a union with Julian Salley. In the deepest recesses of her heart Eulalie knew there was something more for her in the world, but she had neither the experience nor the guidance to find it. The wise and independent Eulalie Salley of later years would have made a very different decision.

11
The Wedding

It was the most horrible day of my life," Eulalie would say of her wedding to Julian Booth Salley on December 20th, 1906. Her mother came down with pneumonia, Grandmother Gamble suffered another stroke, and one of the bridesmaids contracted typhoid fever. Despite these calamities—and after six months of planning and preparation—the family was loath to postpone the ceremony.

"Mamá," Eulalie said, rousing her mother from a fever induced sleep, "have you looked outside?"

Eulalie, Sr. sat up in bed and struggled to rise. She reached for her *pince-nez* glasses on the bedside table. Aiken was waking to a cold, drizzling, rain.

"Oh, Eulalie, I'm so sorry. It looks as if your wedding day is cursed. First all the illnesses and now this. Are you sure you don't want to postpone it?"

"How can we? All the out-of-town guests are here, all the flowers are at the church, and Mr. Willcox has prepared everything for the reception. We can't afford to start over. We'll just have to muddle through."

"Very well. I'll be down directly. Make sure Mattie is ready, and please check on your grandmother."

Mrs. Gamble was confined to the guest room on the first floor. She would miss the wedding. An hour later, Mrs. Chafee slowly descended the stairs. She was dressed in a pearl encrusted,

Empire style, white dress of *peau de soie.* The bodice was accented with a blue satin, velvet, ribbon. Lacy, puffed, sleeves gave the outfit a demure look. A small lace cap completed the ensemble.

"Oh, don't you look beautiful," Mattie said. "Why, you could be the bride." Eulalie Salley, Sr., despite this traumatic period in her life, still maintained her youthful figure and delicate good looks.

"Thank you, darling. I certainly don't feel beautiful. My face is flushed and I'm still running a little fever. I just hope I can get through the day in one piece. I can return the compliment. You are positively radiant in that bridesmaid's dress. Where is Eulalie? We must leave for St. Thaddeus soon."

"She's almost ready," Mattie said. "She had to re-box the wedding gown. She's going to take it over in the carriage and put it on in the church vestment room. This rain would ruin it. Do you think Bernard can bring the carriage around back so that we don't get wet?"

"I will ask him to," her mother said. "Now, you get Eulalie and I'll meet you at the back door." She watched Mattie disappear up the stairs before going to her mother's room.

Martha Gamble was propped-up in her bed. Her left side was totally immobilized from the stroke. Minnie Hanscomb sat by the bed coaxing the woman to take a few more spoonfuls of the chicken broth she had prepared for her. Minnie came to work for the Chafee's shortly before Mr. Chafee's death and had remained to care for Martha Gamble after her first stroke. Martha struggled to speak. The left side of her mouth drooped and her words were almost unintelligible. She began to cry.

"It's all right, Mamá. Eulalie knows you wanted more than anything to be at her wedding. She asked if it would be all right to wear one of your garters. I said you would be honored. Mr. Toombs will take lots of pictures. We'll have a big album to show you next week. Eat your soup and rest. I'll be back for the reception. We've only invited family and close friends. If you're a good girl, I'll bring you and Minnie a piece of the wedding cake."

Eulalie and Mattie were on the back porch. Bernard steered the team around the fountain in the backyard and pulled the carriage under the portico. The Chafee wedding party climbed aboard. As the team clattered onto Laurens the rain suddenly stopped and huge clumps of wet snow fell from the leaden skies. Eulalie laughed.

"You know how we're always hoping for a white Christmas in Aiken. How about a white wedding? I'll bet none of us will ever forget this day."

The carriage dropped the Chafee women at the rear entrance of St. Thaddeus. Eulalie and Mattie headed for the dressing room, and their mother went into the sanctuary. There was a flurry of activity as the flowers were being rearranged. A priest smoothed the vestments on the altar and checked that the sacraments for the Holy Eucharist were in order. Assured that everything out front was under control, she returned to the dressing room.

Mattie was helping Eulalie slip the wedding dress over her head, careful not to undo the hours of work performed by Hazel Bishop on her upswept hairdo. The white, silk chiffon, dress draped casually in front and cascaded into a four-foot train behind. Long sleeves, full at the shoulder, tapered to the wrist and were adorned with a vertical row of five pearls. A lace-edged mantilla veil hung to her waist and was secured to her hair with a gem encrusted tiara. Three strands of pearls circled her neck. Her mother dabbed at tears with a lace handkerchief.

"Your father would be so proud of you," she said. "You're so beautiful. He always dreamed of walking you down the aisle and …" Emotions overcame her. She could not continue.

"Thank you, Mamá," Eulalie said, putting her arms around her mother. "I'm sure he's up there keeping an eye on all of us."

"Okay, enough of the tears," said Mattie, the most composed member of the family. "It's time to go."

Vivaldi's Spring drifted across the hall from the sanctuary. Julian Booth Salley and his groomsmen made their way to the altar. Julian had relented and finally agreed to wear a tuxedo. He adamantly refused to wear the more formal cutaway with a black waistcoat that Eulalie had lobbied for.

"I look like enough of a dandy in that dang fool, monkey suit," he said. "I don't need to be puttin' on airs any more than this. Nobody in Salley would recognize me in that thing." Eulalie was satisfied that she had won the small battle.

The Reverend Theodore Wood Clift stood behind the pulpit, towering above the men. All was in readiness. The bridal party made its way to the vestibule of the church. They waited as Mrs. Chafee was escorted to her seat. The last strains of Handel's Air faded and Dr. Clift lifted his hand to signal the organist to begin the processional. The measured cadence of Wagner's wedding march from *Lohengrin* echoed through the chamber as Eulalie took the arm of her uncle and started down the aisle. A strange sense of finality washed over her.

"Was this to be the rest of her life—keeping house and raising children for the mayor of Aiken, South Carolina?" She raised her head and smiled. "No! It would not! It would be the beginning of the rest of her life, but it would be a life to be lived on her own terms."

Now she was ready. *Now* she could say "I will" to her wedding vows, but she could also say "I will" to being her own independent woman.

12
The Honeymoon

If Eulalie Chafee Salley's wedding, and the events leading up to it, was a trial by fire, her honeymoon was a fit episode for description in Dante's inferno. When all the photographer's flashes had faded and the happy couple had combed the rice from their hair, they joined the invited guests for the reception at the Chafee home. By all accounts, it was a celebration marked by much joy and frivolity. Eulalie, her mother, and Mattie, having suffered through the rigors of preparing for the wedding, could finally let their hair down and enjoy the moment. The celebration lasted well into the afternoon. The groomsmen made frequent trips to the carriages parked out front, since Mrs. Chafee did not approve of hard liquor in her home. With each return the men became more boisterous and the party became louder. About four in the afternoon Mattie and three groomsmen sneaked out the rear door and disappeared for a long period of time. The party continued without them, and no one questioned their absence. The appointed hour for Julian and Eulalie to leave for their New York honeymoon approached. Her trousseau and their other luggage were piled into Julian's brand new carriage and, in a final hail of rice, the couple took off for the depot on Union Street.

In addition to being Aiken's mayor, Julian was a prominent attorney for the railroad and the company insisted on providing a private rail car to take the couple to Augusta. They were to spend the first night at a hotel there and catch the morning train for New York. When they rounded the corner from Railroad Street, Eulalie screamed. Their private car had been decorated by Mattie and the groomsmen. It was festooned with cow bells, just married placards and other embarrassing slogans befitting the occasion. Julian stared in bemusement. Eulalie was horrified.

"I refuse to set foot in that car," she said. "I'd rather walk to Augusta than suffer the indignity of the spectacle we would create."

"What shall we do?" an amused Julian asked.

"Just let our Augusta guests take it back while we decide what to do."

They rode back to the house, announced they were not taking the private car, invited their Augusta guests to ride it back to Augusta, and then without further ado, they drove off. They rode around for a while before Julian came up with the idea to hitch a ride on a freight train, get off at the transfer station in Blackville, and catch the New York train when it came through there. So they did, only to discover that the last passenger train through to New York had left and the next one would not be along until morning.

Blackville was created for the express purpose of providing a switch point for trains from Charleston to either Hamburg or Columbia. In its brief existence the town had not acquired many amenities for the travelers that found themselves marooned there. A small, dingy, badly lit, hotel was just across the street from the depot. It was now past midnight.

"Let's take a room and catch the morning train," Julian said.

"I don't know Julian. That's such a dumpy looking place. I'd rather just wait here in the station for the train. It's only a few hours," Eulalie responded.

"You'll catch pneumonia and get a terrible crick in your neck if you spend the night on those hard benches. Come on. We're getting a room."

Eulalie didn't understand why he was so insistent, but she relented. They followed the lone porter on duty across the street and checked in. Fear and trepidation set in for Eulalie as they climbed the stairs to their room.

There's a reason that era was referred to as "Victorian." The sexual repression epitomized by the British regent was alive and well in turn-of-the-century America. Eulalie's mother not only had not prepared her daughter for her wedding night, she had prohibited any discussion of the subject of sex within earshot of her daughters. To say that Eulalie was naive about such matters would be a gross understatement. She now understood why Julian had insisted on taking the room. Carnal lust was a foreign concept to her but one she experienced that night as her older and more experienced husband took her to the wedding bed. She thought the night would never end.

Morning finally did arrive. The rain and snow were gone, replaced by a brilliant morning sun. One could not describe Eulalie's disposition in equally sunny words. On what should have been the happiest night of her life, she had experienced what she would later describe as the worst day of her life. She swore that for years afterward, every December 20th brought rain and snow just to remind her of that horrifying night.

She trudged to the station, dutifully following behind Julian and the porter. She walked in a fog, not fully able to comprehend what had just happened to her and stunned by Julian's detached air of indifference. She didn't remember boarding the train. Within hours she developed a raging fever. The couple disembarked in Washington and Julian checked into a hotel between Union Station and the Capitol building. Within hours she lapsed into pneumonia. Their stay in Washington stretched into two weeks, at which time Eulalie insisted they cancel the rest of the trip and head back to Aiken.

Eulalie's friends were stunned by her physical appearance. She was gaunt and gray. The vivacious young girl that hopped that freight on her wedding night had been replaced by a wan wraith of a girl whose inner light had been extinguished.

"Eulalie, you look like you've been pulled through a keyhole," one of her friends remarked upon seeing her condition.

"Yes," she replied, "and I'll never get married again."

When she had recovered sufficiently, she confronted her

mother at a time when she knew they would be alone.

"How could you do that to me?" she asked her.

"Do what, my child?"

"Let me get married without telling me what went on between a man and his wife?"

"You were very modest, and I knew, if you knew, you would never marry. I thought you would be happier married."

Eulalie never fully forgave her mother for failing to prepare her for the physical demands of marriage. The experience of her honeymoon scarred her for life. She would occasionally submit to the conjugal bed out of duty and later she and Julian would have two children, a daughter, Eulalie, and a son, Julian. Shortly after Julian's birth, the flame of physical love would flicker out completely. The Salley marriage devolved into a mostly platonic one. She still loved Julian, but the physical part of their relationship was essentially over.

The Salley's moved into the spacious Chafee house on Laurens and added a couple of servants to accommodate the increased work load. The home continued to be a hub of activity and entertaining in the community as friends gathered for dances, weddings, birthdays and other occasions calling for celebration.

Mattie was the only member of the household that registered discontentment over the newlyweds living there. She was jealous of Eulalie's new position of prominence in the family and demoralized that she was still single. She continued to be courted by many suitors but refused to make a choice among them. She even asked Julian to pick a husband for her, which he wisely refused to do. Finally, she solved her own problem in 1907 by marrying Dudley Hall, the son of a Winter Colony family whose fortune was derived from Old Medford Rum and a tea importation business in Boston. Mattie moved with Dudley to Boston where she learned of his fondness for drink. She returned to Aiken during the winters. When Dudley died in 1922, apparently from his excesses, she returned to Aiken for good and entered into the real estate business with her sister where she described herself as the "and Company" in "Eulalie Salley and Company." Mattie ultimately left Eulalie and formed her own real estate company. She was the driving force in the development of Kalmia Hill. She purchased an old dairy farm at the bottom of the hill and converted the smaller building into her real estate office and an antiques showroom. She turned the larger building into a tea room on the first floor and a ballroom on the second. It became a popular spot for gatherings by members of the Winter Colony. One hundred members of Aiken society celebrated the city's 1935 centennial there with a costume ball.

Eulalie discovered that Julian also suffered from an addiction. He was a workaholic who often returned to his office after dinner.

"You courted me every night for a year, and now that we are married you go to the office to work," she said.

"That was before we were married. Now I have to support you," he responded. "Why don't you play cards with the ladies or plan the next day's meals in the evenings?"

"I could have done that without being married," she said coolly.

Slowly, but surely, Eulalie's views on marriage, relationships, and a woman's role in society underwent a major transformation. The independent woman that said "I will" at St. Thaddeus' altar, increasingly began to say "I won't" to the demeaning slights that she and other women suffered and to their relegation to a subservient role in society. This transformation slowly evolved into Eulalie's life-long passion, the struggle for women's rights. She only needed a spark to ignite that passion.

That "spark" and the passion it would engender had to wait. Less than two years after their marriage Eulalie became pregnant. She began to experience another in the long list of indignities that a capricious God had visited on women. Her discomfort grew along with her bulging abdomen. Confined to home by the norms of Victoriana, she busied herself with sewing and knitting so that when the baby arrived it had a full wardrobe. Eulalie's crowning achievement during this period was the flowing white dress she made for the christening of young Eulalie III.

Pregnant became a four-letter word for Eulalie. When the baby finally came she cursed Julian and her mother anew for not preparing her for the agony of childbirth. Even the chloroform couldn't completely dull the excruciating pain. The little girl arrived healthy but frail. She weighed a mere four pounds at birth and was carried around on a pillow for the first month of her life. Julian sat on the edge of the bed and patted Eulalie on the head. He had difficulty hiding his disappointment that his firstborn was not a son.

"Never mind," he said, "the next time we'll have a boy."

Eulalie fixed him with a defiant stare and through clinched teeth said, "There isn't going to be a next time!"

She had had all she wanted of pregnancy and childbirth. During her doctor ordered, one month, confinement she exchanged the parlor furniture with her bedroom furniture. The entire household rejoiced when she was finally able to leave the house. Her demands for things to occupy her time had driven everyone to distraction. As soon as she was able, she visited all the shops in town and bought fabric to be made into new dresses for her. She bought so many new hats that Julian protested.

"You have several perfectly good hats already, why do you need to buy more?" he asked.

"I've bought at least one new hat every year, all of my life. Why would you think marrying you would change that?" she said.

"Well, at least you can give me a monthly accounting of your expenses," he pleaded. Eulalie complied, but the reports were so incomplete and incomprehensible that Julian finally threw up his hands and admitted defeat. She just smiled.

"Women make such a mistake letting their husbands think they're smart," she said. "If they think you're senseless they'll take care of you."

Eulalie reentered her life with a vengeance. She began to ride, and to dance, and to do all the other things she had been denied during her confinement. She also maintained her separate bedroom. Coyly she told Julian he could visit her on occasion.

That proved her undoing. Within a year she was pregnant for the second time, and just as miserable as she had been the first.

Julian was concerned for his wife's health. Her bouts of nausea and long nights in agonizing distress worried him. He decided that when the time came he would take her to a clinic in North Augusta that was better prepared to handle difficult pregnancies like hers. The only trouble was that the twenty-mile distance required an automobile; something he didn't have. There were only two cars in Aiken in 1910, so Julian arranged to rent one of them at the appointed hour—for the substantial sum of $25.

Eulalie was apprehensive about the ride to North Augusta, fearing that it would be too jarring and painful over the rutted dirt roads of rural Aiken County. She was right to be anxious. The ride was an hour of unrelenting, excruciating, pain. She almost welcomed the idea of the coming delivery. She rationalized that it couldn't be any worse than the brutalizing trip over to North Augusta. She was wrong. After an interminable night and day of labor, Julian Booth Salley was finally delivered—all *sixteen* pounds of him.

Julian had been so concerned for her health that he promised Eulalie a "grand gift" when the child was born. He did not fail to deliver on his promise. There was a small box wrapped with a red bow waiting on her bedside table when she returned home. She wasn't sure the gold and pearl necklace was sufficient compensation for her pain and suffering, but she wore it proudly. She considered it a talisman, one that would prevent any more pregnancies. Whether it was the necklace, divine intervention, abstinence, or some other unknown factor, she never had to endure another.

Eulalie had been a lifelong member of St. Thaddeus and adored the pastor, Reverend Clift. The reverend called on her shortly before Julian's birth to say that he was being reassigned to a church in Beaufort, near the coast.

"Oh, Father Clift, I was so looking forward to having you baptize my child."

"Don't worry, Eulalie. When you are ready, just contact me in Beaufort and I'll be happy to come up for the baptism."

At the appointed time, Eulalie contacted Rev. Clift and asked him to come, but the new rector at St. Thaddeus had other ideas. He informed her that she was now his parishioner and he would preside over the baptism.

"Like hell you will," she said vehemently. She promptly bundled up Julian and caught the train to Beaufort where the Reverend Clift performed the baptismal ceremony. She moved her membership to his parish, St. Helena's, and returned often to worship there, each time leaving a large anonymous contribution for the parish. Over the years, in times of great sorrow, Eulalie would return to St. Helena's and wander among the tombstones of her friends for solace. When the bishop of the diocese learned of Reverend Jeter's treatment of Reverend Clift, he ordered him to write a formal letter of apology.

With Julian healthy and growing and his wife back to full health, Julian persuaded a reluctant Eulalie to try for a second honeymoon in New York. Eulalie reluctantly agreed. This time around it was Julian that became ill. No sooner had their ship passed Sullivan's Island in Charleston harbor than he became violently nauseated. The storm that sprang up kept Julian firmly in his berth for much of the trip. Eulalie escaped occasionally to enjoy the bracing sea air on the open decks. Julian got his sea legs back as soon as the *terra firma* of Manhattan was securely beneath his feet. They made the rounds of all the Broadway shows, visited Lady Liberty, rode the subway, indulged in Eulalie's favorite hobby—shopping—in other words did New York. After two weeks, spent both financially and physically, they boarded the steamship "Old Comanche" for the return to Charleston. Their original itinerary was to take them home by rail, but Eulalie, believing that they couldn't possibly encounter two storms on the same trip, convinced Julian to return by boat. Wrong!

The ship left New York harbor under pink skies and calm winds. Within hours those calm conditions gave way to a raging gale and gray/green skies, a suitable color to match Julian's gills. "Old Comanche" was blown out to sea and presumed lost for five long days before she limped into Charleston harbor. The storm had ripped out all the docks along Bay Street, forcing the passengers to be taken ashore in lifeboats. Charleston's streets were impassable. All communications leaving the city were destroyed. Eulalie couldn't even let her family know they were safe. That was the Salley's last honeymoon.

13

The Tillman Affair

Julian Salley's life was delineated by his own self-imposed regimens. He arose at dawn, had breakfast while consuming the local news, and left for his office by nine. He came home for lunch at one and was back in his office by two. At five he would have supper, returning to his office by eight. He would arrive back home again by ten and promptly retire.

During her long confinement with Julian, Eulalie embraced her husband's routine of reading the newspaper every morning. In December 1909, while browsing through the legal section, she was drawn to an article that made her blood run cold. It described the heart-wrenching saga of a young woman fighting for the return of her children. The two children had been taken from her and given to her husband's parents. That evening, when Julian came home for supper, Eulalie thrust the story of Lucy Tillman in his face and asked heatedly,

"Did you see this article this morning?"

Julian took the paper and scanned the article briefly.

"Why yeah, I saw it. What about it?"

Eulalie's voice rose an octave or two in her response.

"Julian Salley, you mean to say you think it's all right for a woman's children to be taken away from her?"

Julian's response was a clinically legal view—not exactly the one that Eulalie was expecting.

"If a law is on the books, it should be enforced. Woman is

subject to man."

The steam coming from Eulalie's ears was almost visible. She couldn't believe the man she married was such a Neanderthal when it came to women. Their heated back and forth was interrupted by a knock at the kitchen door. It was the maid from the neighboring family.

"Come in Vidalia. What can I do for you?" Eulalie said in a calmer voice.

"Miss Alice, she say dat ever since yore banty rooster's been coming over into our yard, all the eggs done got smaller. She say y'all needs to keep that rooster to home."

Eulalie listened intently. When Vidalia finished she said,

"Vidalia, you go tell your mistress that those eggs belong to me, and she must send them to me at once."

Julian, jaw agape, stared at his wife.

"Whatever are you talking about?" he asked.

"I'll tell you what I'm talking about. If Lucy Tillman's children belong solely to the father, then the eggs laid by those hens belong to the rooster."

"Well, I'll be damned," Julian grinned. The rooster had won the case for her.

Lucy Dugas was the granddaughter of Francis and Lucy Pickens of Edgefield. Pickens was governor of South Carolina during the Civil War. Prior to that, he was ambassador to Russia where his wife became the darling of the Czar's court. The Czar showered her with gifts of jewelry and insisted that he and the Czarina become godparents to her daughter, who was affectionately called Douschka (Russian for darling). The Pickens returned to America when war became imminent. Francis was elected governor. They were witness to the shelling of Fort Sumter from the balcony of a home on The Battery in Charleston. Lucy was his beautiful and prominent first lady. She was lionized by the southern press for her efforts in support of the war. Hers was the only female likeness to ever grace a confederate bank note.

In the waning years of the old century, the governor's granddaughter, Lucy Dugas, married the son of United States

Senator Benjamin R. Tillman of Edgefield, South Carolina. B. R. Tillman, Jr. was reputed to be an alcoholic, a womanizer, and abusive to his wife. Tillman, Sr. arranged a patronage job for his son, and the family moved to Washington. The change of scenery did not bring a corresponding change in the character of young Tillman.

Both the Pickens and the Tillmans were prominent families in Edgefield. Each had generous land holdings and each was politically powerful. The Pickens were viewed as educated and cultured members of the highest level of southern society. The Tillmans on the other hand were seen by the gentry as boorish, redneck, holdovers from the pre-war era. The senator's reputation as a "woolhat" during Reconstruction gave him political credibility among the common people of the state. He supported General Wade Hampton's "Redshirts" and was present at the Hamburg riots where he vowed to kill as many blacks as possible. He became a demagogue of the first order and earned his nickname, Pitchfork Ben Tillman, by promising to go to Washington and stick a pitchfork into the rump of President Grover Cleveland.

A strong undercurrent of animosity ran between the families. When Lucy announced her intention to marry B. R., that seething resentment rose to the surface. Lucy's parents made every effort to dissuade her from marrying into the Tillman family, but to no avail. The wedding took place, and the feared marital difficulties began almost immediately. The Tillman enmity toward the Pickens surfaced. The senior Tillmans were dismissive of Lucy. They thought she brought the Pickens family prejudices to the marriage. The easily swayed B. R., Jr. soon came to view his wife in the same manner. It was a witch's brew that, together with B. R.'s character flaws, would bubble until it erupted and destroyed the young family.

Shortly after the family moved to Washington, Lucy became pregnant with their third child, which she lost in a miscarriage. She was hospitalized and then bedridden for several weeks. Upon returning home, she asked for her girls, Douschka and Sarah.

"They ain't here," B. R. said. "They went home to Edgefield with Ma."

"B. R., why? You knew I was coming home today. Why aren't they here?"

Douschka and Sarah Tillman

"They won't be coming home again, Lucy. They've been given to my folks by the court."

Lucy slumped back in her bed, dumbfounded.

"What do you mean?" she demanded.

"They ain't here," B. R. said. "They went home to Edgefield with Ma."

"B. R., why? You knew I was coming home today. Why aren't they here?"

"They won't be coming home again, Lucy. They've been given to my folks by the court."

Lucy slumped back in her bed, dumbfounded.

"What do you mean?" she demanded.

"The courts have ruled you unfit to be their mother and have given custody to my parents." Lucy fought back the rage and the tears. She wanted to remain calm and in control.

"No! That's not possible! I'm their mother! They belong to me! They can't do that!"

"I'm afraid they can Lucy. And they have," he said. "South Carolina law gives the husband total and complete control of his family. I could have taken them myself, but I thought Ma and Pa were in better shape to raise them."

As her husband left the room Lucy fell into a fit of uncontrolled sobbing. The next day she moved to the home of a cousin in Washington. She needed time to think and to seek advice on what course of action to take.

Senator Ben Tillman retained lawyers who interpreted the South Carolina statutes to his benefit, and his powerful allies on the state court upheld him. Alva Depass, representing Lucy Tillman, argued that the intent of the legislation creating the law was limited to the father's right only in determining the custody of his children in the event of his death. On the court's interpretation of this point hung the fate of Dousckha and Sarah Tillman. Lucy moved to Columbia and lived with a relative, Dr. Francis Pickens Carter, throughout the trial proceedings.

For three years the debate raged back and forth—from Edgefield, to Washington, to Columbia—and then back again, as the children remained with their grandmother. Senator Tillman, as the respondent to Lucy Tillman's petition for redress by the South Carolina Supreme Court, brought to bear all his powers as a political force. His lawyers maintained that Lucy would likely remarry and take the children away, thereby depriving the Tillmans of their parental rights. His son, having deeded the children to his parents, took a passive role in the proceedings. On February 13, 1910, the court rendered its decision—the children must be returned to their mother. This was a bold move by a court beholden to the Democratic Party in South Carolina, especially in light of Ben Tillman's status in the party. On the other hand, it was a legal recognition of the age-old right of a mother when it came to her children.

One other factor weighing heavily on the minds of those black-robed justices must have been the hornet's nest of opposition created by the brazenness of the Tillmans. From Kankakee to Key West there was near universal condemnation of the Tillmans. Newspaper editorials and opinion pieces across the nation were scathing in their denunciation of the Tillman's actions.

A second but more far reaching outcome of the case was its profound influence on the suffrage movement in the United States. It is no coincidence that just ten short years after Lucy Tillman won her children back, American women won the right to vote. The nineteenth amendment to the constitution was ratified in 1920. It is also no coincidence that a major force in the drive to suffrage was Aiken's own Eulalie Salley who had been so moved by the plight of her neighbor from Edgefield. The seeds of indignation and outrage sown by the Tillman episode took root in her conscience. In time they would blossom into a passion for justice that knew few bounds.

Eulalie and Friends

Eulalie vowed that she would not stand idly by and see women's rights trampled anymore. She saw an advertisement in the Columbia, S.C. paper.

"Membership in the Equal Suffrage League. One dollar."

She sent her dollar in for membership. She would later say that, "it was the best dollar I ever spent." She immediately became involved in local efforts to enroll women in the movement and to petition the state legislature to approve an amendment to the U.S. Constitution allowing women to vote. Her involvement included raising funds for the various campaigns, funds she could ill afford from her own pocket. She joined in bake sales and other functions to raise money, but there still was not enough. If she was going to play a major role in the movement she would need to earn her own money.

Eulalie cajoled Julian into bringing law books home for her to read. Her ulterior motive was to find something in South

Carolina law that would prevent more Tillman sagas. She began to think she might try to become a lawyer herself but gave up that idea as unworkable. She couldn't stand the idea of wading through those musty old tomes for the rest of her life. But she had to do something to earn money.

14

Into the Fray

Eulalie, frustrated by Julian's preoccupation with his law business and unwilling to enter it herself, began to consider other avenues to expand her own personal horizons and to earn money for the suffrage movement. The pointless social activities engaged in by most of her contemporaries held no appeal for her. Through Julian's business affairs, she began to interact with many of the winter visitors to Aiken. She realized that most of his clients had neither the inclination nor the time required to navigate through the multitude of details required to purchase or build a home—especially from hundreds of miles away. She began to formulate a plan.

"Julian, what do you think about me starting a business of my own?"

Julian dropped the paper he was reading onto the breakfast table and stared at his wife in amazement.

"I think it's the most darn fool idea I've ever heard. What kind of business do you think you can get into? The only women I know who work are teachers, nurses, secretaries or maids. I don't reckon you qualify for the first three and I don't expect you want to take on that last one. Don't you have enough going on here at home with your mother and sister and the children to keep you busy. If you're bored I'm sure the folks over at St. Thaddeus could use some help with their charity work."

"You don't understand a thing about me and how I feel, do

you Julian Salley? How would you like to sit here every day listening to the idle chatter of women who have no concept of life outside the four walls of their homes? I imagine it would drive you insane. Well I'm no different. There's only so much I can stand of it, and I aim to do something about it."

Julian had been married to Eulalie long enough to recognize when discretion was the better part of valor. He wasn't about to pick a battle with her over something he knew would blow over in a few days anyway. He decided to hear her out and bide his time.

"Exactly what kind of business do you have in mind?" he asked, being careful to take the condescending edge off his voice.

"I'm not sure," she said. "I've been looking into the possibility of getting into real estate or insurance or something like that. I've noticed that you are getting more involved with people from up north coming here to buy property. I think I could help with that."

"Eulalie, there are half-a-dozen very capable men who seem to be handling the real estate business in town quite well. I don't think they would take kindly to your trying to horn in on their business."

That last statement really got Eulalie's dander up. She fixed Julian with a penetrating stare that said, "*Don't mess with me, Julian Salley. I'm going to do what I want to do.*"

"I don't give a fig what those men think," she shot back, coming as close to swearing as she was capable. "It's women who make the final decisions on most house purchases anyway. Who's out there that understands the women's side of things. I can tell you. No one. Do you think George Mathers has any idea what a woman looks for in a house? No! She wants to know where it's located; where the schools are; what the neighbors are like; the style of the house; what kind of furniture goes well in it. Why, there are a hundred things they'd like to know that old George never thinks about, and I know I'm better suited to give it to them than he is."

Julian raised his palms toward Eulalie in surrender, signaling defeat.

"Very well, my dear. I will not stand in your way. But don't come back to me in a few days complaining about the cruel world out there."

At eight o'clock on Monday morning, Eulalie Salley walked through the door of the licensing office in the Aiken municipal building, after having to maneuver around the portly chief of police who was leaning against the doorframe.

"Mrs. Busch," she said, "I want you to read me a list of all the licenses that are available."

The clerk looked at the thirty-one year old wife of the mayor in puzzlement but did as she was asked.

"Attorney, barber, general merchandise, insurance, physician, real estate…"

"Stop right there," Eulalie said. "I'll take a real estate license and an insurance license."

"For you?" Sarah Busch asked.

"Yes. I can do twice as well as the people that have been showing me houses. It's a woman's job to sell women houses. How much will that be?"

"Twenty-five dollars," Mrs. Busch said.

Meanwhile, the police chief was taking this improbable little vignette in with a broad grin on his face.

"It's nothing but a joke—let's just give them to her," he said. Eulalie left the office a licensed real estate agent and a licensed insurance agent and with all her money intact.

"Well Julian, I did it," she announced when he came home for lunch.

"What did you do?" he asked.

"I went down and got my licenses for real estate and insurance this morning."

"I'll be damned," he said. "I didn't think you'd go through with it. I tell you what. I'll bet you a hundred dollars that you can't earn a hundred dollars in commissions during the first six months."

"You're on," she said.

Eulalie marched back down Laurens Street to the selfsame

building housing Julian's law offices and rented one for herself. She installed a telephone, hired a secretary and bought furniture on credit. She was in business, owed money, and didn't have any customers.

"Everyone in town thinks I have lost my mind," she said. "One of my cousins said, 'Julian knows he can't stop her, so he's just giving her her head.' They all think I will fail. But I'll show them."

15

Suffrage and Success

Eulalie saw herself as a champion of the underclass. She saw suffrage as the first step to independence for women. She worked tirelessly within the South Carolina suffrage movement, but she never joined the National League of Women Voters.

"The typical League of Women Voters woman is highly educated and sensitive," she said. Sensitive was her euphemism for elitist. "They are way above the rabble and can't even see them from the ballot box. On the other hand, I can get down on the level of the common voter on a non-partisan basis. I think partisanship will destroy the efficiency of the League."

Harriet Lynch of Cheraw, was instrumental in the official founding of the Suffrage League in South Carolina. She had many strong political contacts both nationally and locally. It was on May 15, 1914 that the state charter was granted at a convention in Spartanburg, S. C. The league began with 450 enrolled members. Among those charter members was Eulalie Chafee Salley. Eulalie's activities on behalf of the league had been ongoing since the Lucy Dugas Tillman affair. They accelerated as her children got older so that by 1913 she was campaigning almost full time for the league. She was named county chairman that year. She and her aides canvassed the entire county seeking signatures for the suffrage petition.

"Miss Lola Trax was sent down from Washington to help organize in South Carolina," Eulalie said. "She spent a week in Columbia, where we received instructions on starting local chapters and on gaining publicity for the movement."

That same year the League held a national convention in Chicago, and the officers begged for Eulalie to attend. Annie Wright from Augusta was going and she pleaded with Eulalie to join her.

"If you go and you meet Mrs. Catt and Maude Wood Park and Anna Howard Shaw and all those wonderful women, you'll be inspired, and you'll come back home, and you'll help with this organization. We'll go places. I want you to go."

"Annie, I don't have the clothes, and I don't have the money."

"There'll be a way. Now you put your mind to it."

"Julian, I want to go to the suffragist convention in Chicago," Eulalie announced over breakfast one morning. Julian peered over the edge of the paper.

"No. You can't go."

Waving a red flag in front of a charging bull could not have been more effective. Eulalie was now resolved to go to Chicago. The only question was—how? She had no money and no clothes. Luckily, Mattie was visiting from Boston and she and Eulalie wore the same size. Clothing problem solved. Now, for the money.

Eulalie rationalized that one-third of Julian's money was rightfully hers. Julian stated at the time of their marriage that he was endowing her with one-third of his estate. She reasoned that he wasn't about to hand it over in one lump sum, especially since she was lobbying for Chicago, so she devised a scheme to collect it in installments.

"Every morning for several weeks I would rise before my husband. Julian always carried a lot of money in his pocketbook. Every morning I would take a certain amount until I had accumulated enough for the trip. He never missed it." She placed a call to Annie Wright in Augusta.

"Annie, I've got the money, and I've got the clothes. I'm going to Chicago."

The convention introduced Eulalie to all the movers and

shakers in the suffrage movement. She was both awed and inspired by the women she met during her four days in Chicago. One in particular, Jeanette Rankin from Wyoming, who would become the first female member of Congress, impressed her immensely. Their lives would intersect again, many years later, in Aiken.

In those days, Eulalie was known to smoke. She hesitated to smoke in the Chicago hotel room for fear of upsetting her roommate. When the other lady was out of the room, Eulalie would lock herself in the bathroom, open the window, and light up, fanning the smoke outside. This went on for two days before Eulalie discovered that the other woman was doing the same thing. From that point on, they enjoyed their cigarettes in their bedroom. The convention was a huge success in uniting the suffrage workers from all over the country. They left Chicago re-invigorated and ready to do battle with Congress to pass the nineteenth amendment.

"Those early days were very trying," Eulalie said. "Some of my friends turned against me. I had to choose between them and the movement. I felt strongly about what we were doing, so I just had to let them go. There were men who thought that if you were a suffragist you were indecent. One man went so far as to say, 'How can you even sit at the table with a suffragist. Why, she's no better than a prostitute.'"

The Tillman case proved to be the major catalyst for the movement in South Carolina. No single event since '*The War*' had so galvanized the women of the state. Despite warnings from their husbands to stay away from the meetings, the women would slip away and attend anyway.

"One man told his wife, 'Now, I'll kill you if you join the suffragists.' So she slipped off one day and said, 'I'm going to join anyhow. I don't trust that husband of mine. He might take my children away any day.' "

"I told her that under South Carolina law, as it now stood, he could do just that. One day she came in and her eyes were all red, and her face was bruised up.

I said, "What's the matter with you?"

'Well,' she said, 'after the last meeting I went home and my husband beat me up. Now what would you advise me to do?'

"Well", I said, "it's plain enough if he was my husband I would either shoot him or poison him"

"She says, 'Thank you, Mrs. Salley', and walked out of the office. I didn't think any more about it. The next day I picked up the paper and I was just horrified. I saw where her husband had gone out on a business trip. When he came back in he was overheated and she gave him a glass of buttermilk. He keeled over and died. Well, it served him right. She came in two days afterwards wearing a long black veil.

"She said, 'Have you heard of my bereavement?'

"I said, 'Your bereavement! I heard of your good fortune.'

"She said, 'Now what would you advise me to do?'

"I said. 'Just between you and me, I advise you to leave town just as quick as you can.' She left, and I haven't seen her since. She killed that man as sure as day. Julian was horrified."

"He said," 'Well, I'm your husband and I'm an attorney, but I'm going to refuse to defend you because you're going to be tried as an accessory after the fact.'"

"Well," I said, "if I am tried and convicted, and serve a sentence, that will attract every woman to my cause all the more because I'm sacrificed for a noble cause."

Julian's reaction: 'I'll be God Damned.'

Recruiting was difficult. Nearly all the men were adamantly opposed to giving women the vote. Eulalie knocked on a thousand doors. When a man answered she met everything from a curt but polite refusal to cursing and dire threats on her life. If a woman answered, her first response was to look over her shoulder to see where her man was. Her second was, "You'd better leave, ma'am. If he finds me talking to you he'll skin me alive."

Chastened, but not deterred, Eulalie and her co-conspirators trudged on. They clattered over the unpaved, washboard, back roads of Aiken County, dropping a few gear boxes and collecting a few signatures as they went. At home the money doled out by Mrs. Trax and the national organization was soon depleted. The committee needed funds and few of the husbands were inclined to subsidize a campaign they saw as foolish at best and downright treasonous at worst, so the ladies resorted to some very unique fund-raisers.

Interspersed with the almost weekly bake sales, ice cream socials, and taffy pulls, the ladies attempted to stage several major events during the year. Eulalie, as the president of the chapter, could always be found smack-dab in the middle of everything.

One such event was the staging of a play called The Microbe of Love. A climactic scene in the play features a prize fight between two characters called "The Gold Dust Twins." Try as she might, Eulalie could get no volunteers for the roles—male or female—so she enlisted her cousin, Rena Chafee, as ardent a suffragist as Eulalie, to join her. They rehearsed for days and even went to Augusta for boxing lessons—where Eulalie was knocked cold.

Both women were nervous that they would be recognized by their friends and family. They donned kinky wigs, blackened their faces and wore black tights and tutus. It was unseemly that any proper lady would subject herself to ridicule like this. Julian must not know.

The curtain went up and the actors went through their routines leading up to the climactic fight scene. Secure in the knowledge that her disguise was impervious, Eulalie tore into Rena with gusto. Ten seconds later, a tiny voice from the third row said, "Mother?" There was no disguise that could not be penetrated by young Julian Salley. Eulalie had been outed. Julian did not speak to his wife for a week. Her mother was so mortified that she threatened to crawl under her seat, if only she hadn't been so old, and she refused to leave the house for a long time after the episode.

The next fund raiser promised several daring performances by the women. One was to be a woman diving into a tank of water from the balcony of the opera house. Naturally Eulalie was appointed. Word soon got back to Julian who confronted her with the rumor.

"Are you going to disgrace me again?" he said.

"Yes," she replied, even though she had no intention of going through with the stunt. It was basically a ruse to get people to sign up for the entire show. No one was too disappointed that Eulalie didn't break her neck. And, the committee raised the requisite funds to carry on.

The league sponsored almost weekly parades through downtown to advertise their cause and to raise funds. They all wore white dresses and white capes lined with yellow, the suffragette's color. Eulalie usually road her docile mare. On one occasion she wanted a more spirited steed and rented a fractious, side-stepping, black, horse from Tom McGlover's livery stable. She followed a highly decorated car through town and all went well until an over-exuberant band member blew an oom-pah-pah into the horse's ear. The animal reared, breaking the reins and took off at break-neck speed with Eulalie hanging on for dear life. She had elected a side-saddle for the ride and was able to reach the horses bit rein to guide him to a stop. The next week she received a hand-written note from Lulie Hitchcock admonishing her on her riding technique and disapproving of the risky ride. As impressive as these escapades were, the next stunt Eulalie pulled became the stuff of legend for generations of Aikenites.

Manned flight was only a few years removed from Wilbur and Orville Wright's first fifty-nine second glide over Kill Devil Hill in North Carolina. A young barnstormer came to Aiken to hawk rides on his new bi-plane. He advertised a three minute ride for $25, a princely sum when the average worker didn't earn that amount in a month. It was not surprising that he had no takers. He ran into Eulalie and asked if she knew anyone that might be interested in a flight. He reasoned that if he got just one taker then others would follow.

"Would you take a woman?" she asked.

"Oh, I'd take a woman for free!" he said

"Well I'm your girl. I've always wanted to fly high. When do we go?"

"Let's go right now," he said. "Do you have any bloomers? You'd better wear something like that."

An hour later, clad in black sateen bloomers and a shirtwaist, Eulalie pedaled her bicycle toward Whitney Field and her rendezvous with destiny. She was stopped along the way by and old friend who wanted to know what she was up to. When she related her plans to him he asked,

"Do you have Julian's permission?"

"No."

"You go ahead then and I'll run downtown and ask him for you."

When the old gentleman got back to Whitney Field the plane was touching down. Eulalie told him of her adventure.

"There was very little room for a passenger, so I had to kind of sit on the wing and hang onto the wires. I took along some of our brochures, and when we flew over downtown I dropped them out. The pilot got scared that I might fall out and grabbed me. He was upset that I was using him to advertise the league. I said, 'You were using me for advertisement, so I thought it was only fair that I use you for advertisement.'"

Eulalie pedaled back downtown to find Julian standing in the middle of the street brandishing one of her yellow pamphlets. He gave her a forceful lecture on the foolishness of a grown mother of two risking her life in such a foolhardy way. He then gave her the silent treatment for the rest of the week.

Despite the success of the various fundraising events, league expenses were still exceeding income and donations. It became obvious to Eulalie that she and the other members would have to personally subsidize the effort. She knew that Julian was staunchly opposed to supporting the suffrage movement and could expect no help from that quarter. He was still smarting from her underhanded method of funding the Chicago trip.

For her to provide financial support meant succeeding at her new business. She redoubled her efforts and began to enlist realty clients through her friends and Julian's associates. Within a month, she sold a large house on Hayne Avenue collecting a thousand dollar commission in the process. She was giddy with the success. It was the most money she had ever held in her hand. With that commission and the hundred dollars from Julian's bet, Eulalie called Mattie in Boston. She was exhausted from the children, the campaign, and her work. She needed a break.

"Meet me in New York, Mattie, I've got eleven-hundred dollars and I'm going shopping."

The two stayed at the Waldorf-Astoria and went on an unfettered shopping spree up and down Fifth Avenue. She discovered that the Waldorf gave credit vouchers to their patrons that allowed them to charge purchases to their account at the hotel. Eulalie and Mattie took full advantage of this unexpected amenity. When they checked out, Eulalie discovered that she had run up a bill of $1500—$400 more than she had in her purse. She was terribly embarrassed, but she recovered quickly enough and wrote a draft on Julian's account, a fact he didn't discover until her return.

Julian, her mother, and the children met Eulalie at the train. She alighted from the car dressed as regally as any fashionable doyenne of Fifth Avenue. She was rested and ready to go.

"Eulalie, I didn't recognize you," Julian sputtered. "What have you done to yourself?"

"Mother you're beautiful," Eulalie III said

It was 1915 and Eulalie's first encounter with independence. She loved it. She wanted all women to have the same opportunity to achieve their own. Eulalie would spend the next five years building her real estate business and continuing her campaign for women's rights.

"Now I'm ready to set Aiken on its ear," she said.

16

Northern Invasion

It didn't take long for New York society to recognize and embrace the emergence of Aiken as a new winter destination. Each fall, periodicals and newspapers vied to scoop each other as each train pulled out of Pennsylvania Station headed for Aiken. Who was the next horseman or playboy to dispatch his ponies, racers, and jumpers to Aiken? *Harper's Weekly* ran entire sections dedicated to Aiken, this newfound Southern playground of the rich and famous. It was being referred to by many as "The Newport of the South." As each autumn approached, and the annual migration to Aiken began, the *New York Times* society columns were filled with the comings and goings of the Astors, the Vanderbilts, the Carnegies, the Mellons and other luminaries of Lady Astor's Blue Book. The importance of the tiny, pastoral, community, lost in the remote sand hills of South Carolina, was further cemented when Fred Post moved his polo pony business to Aiken in 1912. Later, in 1941, Post, together with his son William, would build the Aiken Training Track that endures as the home of the Aiken Trials. Aiken had definitely become a major equine destination.

As a youth, Thomas Hitchcock was sent abroad to study at Oxford University in England. It was there that he acquired his love of polo. Polo was a sport that originated on the dusty plains of Afghanistan, India, and other far-flung Asian outposts of the

British Empire. The British soldiers and diplomats fell in love with the game and during the mid-nineteenth century brought it back to England. Tommy Hitchcock competed on the fields of Eton and Devon and developed a similar passion for it. When he returned to New York, he imported the sport to America. At one point, he was considered the foremost polo player in the country. His imprimatur on Aiken as the new epicenter of the sport carried added weight with his wealthy friends in New York. Beginning in late October each year, the rail sidings along Aiken's Union Street near the train station began to fill with Pullman coaches and horse cars. An article from the *New York Times* in 1913 epitomized the thrall that Aiken held for its winter guests:

****

"Mr. Julian Peabody, along with his lovely wife Celestine—daughter of Mr. and Mrs. Thomas Hitchcock—left this afternoon for Westbury on a private car attached to the Palmetto Limited. Before their departure, they attended a farewell luncheon given in their honor at *Villa Mon Repos* by Mr. and Mrs. Thomas Hitchcock, Jr. Mr. Peabody is returning to supervise several of his architectural projects underway in Manhattan.

****

The Minister from the Netherlands and Madame Loudon left yesterday afternoon for Washington.

****

Mrs. Thomas Hitchcock, Sr., who has been very ill at Sheffield Cottage, is slightly better today.

****

Everyone in the Winter Colony went out to the Whitney Polo Field for the annual games yesterday afternoon. The same crowd appeared at the Palmetto Golf Club during the tea hour when Mrs. W. Duncan McKim, who was hostess, was assisted by Miss Looran of Boston, who poured. In the throng were

Mrs. William Goddard, Mr. and Mrs. C. Oliver Iselin, Mrs. Joseph Harriman, Mr. and Mrs. Joseph Stevens, Mrs. Edward Livingston Smith, Miss Celestine Eustis, Henry B. DeForest, and Mr. and Mrs. Gouverneur Morris.

****

A number of people motored over from Augusta in time for luncheon at Willcox's and later went to the polo field.

****

Joseph Harriman, who has been in Newport for the past fortnight with W. Earl Dodge, returned here this evening with his two young sons who will spend the Easter vacation with their parents at Elm Court, the W. K. Vanderbilt's cottage on Colleton Avenue.

****

Mrs. William Goddard will be the hostess at tea tomorrow afternoon at the Palmetto Golf Club. On Tuesday and Wednesday Mrs. Thomas Hitchcock and Mrs. Joseph Harriman will entertain.

****

C. Oliver Iselin has offered a handsome silver cup at the Palmetto Golf Club for a handicap match play for men, and Mrs. Iselin has offered a cup for women.

****

If the Willcox Hotel had become the nexus for social entertaining among the moneyed set in Aiken, then the Palmetto Golf Club had similarly evolved as the center of non-equine related sports activities among the colonists. Thomas Hitchcock laid out the first four holes in 1892, making Palmetto the second oldest, continuously active, golf course in the country and the oldest in the Southeastern United States. Those first four holes featured rolled sand greens.

Original Palmetto Clubhouse – Circa 1895

Palmetto Clubhouse 1902-2012

The course and the property were deeded to the Whitney Trust in 1901 to assure its preservation for future generations. The trust continues to lease the facility to the members of Palmetto. A new 75 year lease was signed in 2005. It expires in

2080. One can assume that the Whitney heirs and trustees will continue their support when that lease expires.

Whitney expanded the course to a full eighteen holes in 1895, and then in 1928, James Mackrell, the club's first golf professional, obtained the services of Donald Ross to improve the course and to install an irrigation system. Four years later, Alister McKenzie was retained by several prominent Winter Colony residents. They were investors who had also underwritten McKenzie's design and development of Bobby Jones' iconic Augusta National Golf Club. McKenzie redesigned and lengthened the course while replacing the sand greens with grass surfaces. Thus, in the short span of four years, Palmetto benefited from the services of the two most celebrated golf course architects in American history, Donald Ross and Alister McKenzie. In its 120 years, the club has had only eight golf professionals.

The 110-year-old Palmetto clubhouse was built in 1902 to the architectural specifications of Stanford White who was also responsible for the design of Shinnecock Hill's clubhouse on Long Island. An examination of the memberships of the two clubs in 1900 would reveal many of the same names. White designed many homes in Aiken. He also was the architect for many famous public and commercial buildings around the country. His firm, McKim, Mead and White, was the pre-eminent architectural firm in the United States at the turn of the century.

Stanford White met his unfortunate end when he was murdered by Henry Kendall Thaw. Thaw was a prominent and wealthy member of Pittsburg society and known to be mentally unstable. Thaw accused White of having an affair with his wife, Evelyn Nesbitt. Ironically, White was shot to death in the rooftop theater atop Madison Square Garden, a building White had designed. Evelyn Nesbitt was fictionalized in the movie Girl in the Red Velvet Swing.

New York American

HARRY THAW KILLS STANFORD WHITE ON ROOF GARDEN!

GAS TRUST ACCEPTS 80-CENT RATE.

GIRL SLAIN IN ROWBOAT BY HER SUITOR.

FIVE ICE TRUST HEADS SENT TO JAIL FOR YEAR.

SHOOTS ARCHITECT IN BACK AS HE SITS TALKING TO WOMA

Slayer, Captured, Gives Police Fals Name, but Is Immediately Recognized.

A TRAGIC OPENING NIGH

Bing Crosby
Bobby Knowles
Dorothy Rogers

Fred Astaire
Sam Snead

The names of those who have stood on the first tee of Palmetto and looked out across the valley to the tiny green at the crest of the hill are legion. The buildings of the Fermata School in the background framed the hole, creating an unforgettable image. Presidents Taft and Eisenhower; Princes Edward and Andrew; Entertainers Crosby, Astaire, Harris, Williams; all the golfing greats . . . and the list goes on.

Professional and amateur golfers across the years have made their pilgrimage to Palmetto. Many of the legendary players of the mid-twentieth century used the challenging course as a tune-up for the Masters. From 1945 to 1953, Devereux Milburn hosted a pro-am tournament the week before the Masters. Winners included Ben Hogan, Byron Nelson and George Fazio. Robert "Bobby" Knowles was a member of Palmetto and a major amateur champion of the era. His wife Barbara's parents were Winthrop and Lucy Mercer Rutherfurd. The Knowles daughters, Alice and Lucy, remain prominent members of the Aiken community. Knowles became a scorekeeper at Augusta National for the Master's tournament. While in that position he devised a system for showing scores in relation to par—red numbers indicated strokes below par and green numbers strokes over par. That system remains in use at all PGA tournaments today.

Palmetto Golf Club, as in its earlier halcyon days, remains an iconic symbol for those in the golfing community who revere its history and its heritage. It forms an unbroken bond between a glorious past and a promising future.

Such was the privileged life of the moneyed class that came to Aiken for the winter season. The idle rich found much to like about the tiny hamlet. It was the conspicuous place to be for those in the upper reaches of high society. The weather was mostly kind and there was always something to do. The compactness of the community meant that everyone knew everyone else and therefore everyone knew everything that was happening. Animosities that existed in New York or other social hotspots migrated with their owners to Aiken. There was always the right crowd and the wrong crowd, and someone's nose was always out of joint. Petty jealousies abounded, especially among the women, and slights quickly escalated into subtle but spiteful warfare. Long velvet evening gloves might well conceal the finely honed talons of a social adversary. Eulalie Salley was witness to one particularly lurid episode. It began in February, 1913.

Camilla Havemeyer, whose husband "Carley" shot himself in 1898, married Frederick O. Beach in November, 1899. She was still a ravishing beauty, long limbed and athletic, even after having borne two children. Mr. Beach was a handsome playboy, teasingly called "Beauty Beach" by his crowd. The couple honeymooned in Europe on William K. Vanderbilt's yacht. Vanderbilt and Beach were close friends, and Beach often traveled in Vanderbilt's company.

The Vanderbilts owned "Elm Court" on Colleton Avenue in Aiken. They invited the Beaches to visit them. Camilla was familiar with Aiken, having gone there with her first husband—in an attempt at reconciliation—just before his death. She persuaded her new husband, Mr. Beach, to purchase a home in Aiken.

"I believe you will be very happy with your choice of this house," Eulalie Salley told the beaming couple. They were standing on the sidewalk in front of a strikingly beautiful home on Newberry Street. It sat diagonally across the railroad cut from the Willcox Hotel and across Hood Lane from Deodar, another famous Aiken residence, built in 1863.

Deodar served briefly as a USO facility during WWII. Famous among its visitors was the actor Jimmy Stewart, who trained at the Aiken Air Force facility nearby. A watercolor painting he did of one of Deodar's fireplaces still hangs there. Deodar later became home to George Funeral Home. Ironically, it was at that same field that young pilots were trained to fly the P-51—the plane that took Tommy Hitchcock's life.

"It's perfect, Mrs. Salley," Camilla Beach said. "We're only two blocks from downtown, near the Willcox, and just a few short blocks from our dear friends the Vanderbilts. It also is convenient to the Hitchcock woods for riding and hunting. You couldn't have found a better place for us. I'm anxious to get back here now that my life has finally settled down. These last two years have been very trying, but now that I have Fred we can put all that behind us." She squeezed Mr. Beach's arm and guided him toward the house.

"If you don't mind Mrs. Salley, I'd like to take another look around. I've already got some ideas for decorating."

"Not at all, Mrs. Beach," she said. "Here's the key. Just lock up when you're done and drop the key by the office. By the way, if you need some help decorating, we offer complete design services and I can recommend others in the area."

"Thank you, I'm sure I'll be calling on you for help," Mrs. Beach said as she reached for the key. Eulalie turned and headed up Newberry toward her office on Park.

Well over a year passed. The phone on the wall in the Salley's front hall rang. Julian, who was on his way out the door for his evening office hours, answered.

"This is the Salley residence, how may I help you?"

He recognized the voice immediately. It was his law partner Daniel Henderson. Dan Henderson was known to most people in Aiken by his honorific, "Colonel."

"Julian, you'd better get over here to Fred Beach's house on Newberry Street. We've got a real mess here, and I need you to help me with the police."

"The police!" Julian almost shouted into the mouthpiece protruding from the phone's wooden housing. "What the hell is going on, Colonel?"

"There's been a stabbing of some sort, and it don't look good for Fred. We've got to try to put a lid on this thing until we can sort out what happened. Just get on over here as quick as you can."

"I'll be right there."

Julian ran the six blocks to the Beach home. Henderson was standing on the front porch talking to Chief of Police, H. M. Howard.

"What's going on, Dan?" Julian asked between gasps for breath.

"Well, it looks like Mrs. Beach was hit in the head and stabbed in the throat by a Negro man in the front yard. We're still trying to put the pieces together. She's upstairs with Doc Wyman. He's attending to her wounds. As you can imagine, the poor woman is in a state of shock."

Camilla Beach

"I need to talk to her Colonel," Howard said. "I can't do a proper investigation until I do."

"I understand that Mr. Howard, but in her present state of mind, I don't think you can expect to get much sense out of her. Why don't we just look around out here and let the poor woman rest. You can question her in the morning." The front door opened. Mr. Beach stepped onto the porch.

"How's she doing, Fred?" Mr. Henderson asked.

"As you can imagine she's in a lot of pain from the cut on the neck. The doctor gave her a sedative, and he's sewing up the wound."

Did she get a chance to say what happened?" asked Howard.

"She said she was walking across the yard from the laundry house, after putting the dogs away, when someone called her to the side gate. It was getting dark and she couldn't make out who it was until she got real close. She said it was a black man in a gray suit with a hat on. He said he had something for her and when she reached across for it he hit her with a stick or something and then stabbed her in the neck. She fell back into the yard and he followed her. That's all she remembers. She did say he grabbed at her earrings as she was falling."

"Did she say she knew the man or what he was after?"

"She said she didn't recognize him, but she thought he was after her earrings. They were very valuable, maybe $5,000 or $6,000. He could have seen them on her earlier in the day."

"Thank you, Mr. Beach. Why don't you go on back inside and we'll have a look around."

Howard walked back to the gate. He shined his light on the ground where there was a small pool of blood. Droplets of blood trailed across the lawn to the corner of the house. The light revealed a larger pool of blood just off the porch. There was also a narrow strip of wood shaped like a fence picket lying nearby.

"Looks like he hit her with this stick and she ran across the yard where he caught up with her and cut her on the neck."

Howard held the lantern he was carrying over his head to expand the circle of light. Something sparkled in the grass. He bent to pick up the object.

"If he was after her earrings he only got one of them," he said, holding the gleaming bauble closer to the lantern.

"I ain't no expert," he said, "but I sure wouldn't pay that kind of money for these things. They don't look much better than what you can get at Woolworth's."

"Can I see that?" Colonel Henderson said.

"No sir," Howard said. "This here is evidence. I'm gonna take it and the stick with me to the station."

By now several neighbors had gathered outside the fence

in front of the house, including several members of Dr. Wyman's family. Dr. Wyman lived across Newberry from the Beach's house. The policeman walked over to them and leaned against the fence. He sat his lantern on the ground.

"Howdy folks. Did any of you happen to see what went on here tonight?"

"We were sitting at the kitchen table when we heard a woman yelling," the Wyman's daughter said. "We jumped up and ran to the front porch and looked across the street. A man was banging on the door and yelling, 'Let me in, it's Beach.' Daddy then ran across the street and Mr. Beach let him in. We could hear him saying that a Negro had attacked his wife and run off down Hood's Lane." A black man standing on the fringe of the crowd spoke up.

"I came by here 'bout that time to pick up my wife. She works for Miss Beach. It was light enough and I sho didn't see nobody running down Hood's Lane."

"And who might you be?" Mr. Howard asked.

"I am Charles Woodridge. I'm a valet for Mr. Dolan."

"Are you certain of the time?"

"Yes sir. I had just looked at my new, two dollar, Ingersoll watch when I came up. They was a bright moon coming up. I would'a seen anyone running."

The investigation continued, but no one was charged with the crime. Gossip and innuendo ran wild. There were many raised eyebrows, not only among the townsfolk but among some of the gentry as well. The Beach's hurriedly left town for New York, before sailing on to Europe. They took Pearl Hampton their Aiken maid with them. She became a key witness, having stated that she too was struck in the head by the assailant. Her rambling and conflicting testimony rendered her unreliable as a defense witness. There was plenty of time on that voyage to convince Mrs. Hampton of what she saw that fateful night.

C. Oliver Iselin, husband of Hope Iselin, who, along with Mr. Denny Lyon, was among Camilla's most ardent admirers, was publicly incensed over the rumors that Beach himself had attacked his wife. He dashed off a letter to Mayor Gyles,

"It would give me much pleasure to participate in the lynching of the person or persons who are responsible for these slanderous accusations."

Iselin also offered a personal reward of $500, plus $1,000 through the city government, for the arrest of the person responsible for the assault on Camilla Beach. He also offered $2,000 for proof of attempted rape, another of the rampant rumors flying about town. Some thought that the gentleman, as Shakespeare suggested, protested too much. One police inspector termed the rewards being offered as extra inducements to pin the crime on a Negro. The police chief was prompted to offer this opinion after seeing the crime scene.

"If you put Mr. Beach on the stand, ask him how he sat in his room, 32 feet away from where his wife was attacked, and while she was talking to someone and them scuffling and fighting, and he did not hear her? Also ask him how his footprints got in the flower bed and how a paling from the fence got to the scene of the big pool of blood, as the wife claimed the Negro had nothing in his hand but the note, and as to why he had a portion of that fence repaired right away?"

Two months later Beach was indicted and the governor was petitioned to implement extradition papers to bring him back for trial. Bail was set at $1,000. In Beach's absence, it was paid by Mr. Tommy Hitchcock. The wheels of justice ground slowly. The trial started in February, 1913.

All of Aiken turned out for it. The back benches became filled early every morning by the locals. They knew that when the proceedings got underway they could sell their seats to the Winter Colony curious for two dollars. Local journalists were inundated with calls from New York papers for all the latest "gossipy stuff."

Prosecutor Gunter offered into evidence the earring, the paling, and the little gold and diamond encrusted penknife belonging to Fred Beach, on which a large amount of human blood was found. He also presented incriminating conversations between the couple that had been covertly overheard by his investigators. He ridiculed Beach's story as made-up and his wife's corroborations as an effort to prevent scandal. The defense offered a "witness" who testified that he saw someone talking to Mrs. Beach across the fence, despite the fact that no one else in the area at the time saw anything.

Julian Salley, representing Beach, put his client, his wife Camilla, their servants, and Dr. Wyman on the stand. The line-up of character witnesses for Fred Beach read like the guest list for the annual Christmas Ball at the Willcox.

The jury retired after two days of arguments. It took less than two hours to declare Fred Beach innocent. The jury foreman said, "There's absolutely nothing against you Mr. Beach." Once again, it appeared that money and power had bought "justice." No one was ever subsequently arrested for the crime. The statue of Lady Justice in front of the courthouse was said to have shed a tear from beneath her blindfold.

17
Horse Play

Eulalie found herself becoming increasingly involved in the life of the Winter Colony. Most of her clients came from those associations and produced many of her most lucrative real estate transactions. On occasion, however, the advantages of access to this wealthy and profitable market came with certain hazards. Julian's role in the Beach affair accrued to Eulalie's benefit since his wealthy and influential client was acquitted of the charges. She basked in the glow of Julian's success. In another major trial, however, the outcome cast Julian in a less favorable light. He took on a case involving litigation between two of the most prominent families of the Colony. It's not known how much Julian was held accountable for representing the plaintiffs in the case, but it certainly did not endear him to the families supporting the defendants.

The clamor set off in the highest levels of society by the eastern nobility as they occupied Aiken, could be heard all the way to Chicago. Wealthy families along Lake Michigan's Gold Coast wanted to know what all the fuss was about. The Swifts (meatpacking), the Armours, (meat packing), the Fields (Sun-Times and Marshall Field), the Pullmans (railroad rolling stock), Sears and Roebuck, (mail order), and hordes of the cream of Chicago society dipped their toes into the water of Aiken. Many of the curious came to visit. Many stayed.

The curiosity aroused by the stories brought back to Chicago from Aiken piqued the interest of one Amy McCormick. She implored her husband, Richard R. McCormick, to take her to this little town in South Carolina that had become the rage of eastern society. McCormick was the publisher of the *Chicago Tribune*, the *New York Daily News* and *Liberty* magazine. His publishing empire gave him tremendous political clout. McCormick was heir to the legacy of Horace Greeley—*Go west young man, go west*—an early publisher of the *Tribune*. He was following in the footsteps of the paper's legendary giants. His wife's family owned International Harvester.

Eulalie Salley met the McCormicks at the train station on Union Street. It was a blustery morning in late November. The wind was whipping the last stubborn leaves from the oaks and sycamores along Park Avenue. The "Red Cap" chosen by Eulalie to recover the McCormick's baggage was Russell "Pete" Watson. Watson was a celebrated character around Aiken who worked at the depot for over fifty years. When the winter season was over, Red would go on tour with his magic act. After retirement he became a personal assistant to many of Aiken's prominent families. He could be seen around town in his ubiquitous white linen coat, its pockets stuffed with candy for the kids.

"Welcome to Aiken Mr. and Mrs. McCormick. I trust your ride up from Charleston was without event."

"Why, yes it was Mrs. Salley. I must say though that all our friends in Chicago are always bragging on the mild weather here in South Carolina. I hope this is not typical."

"I assure you it is not. And please call me Eulalie. We're a little less formal down here in the South. I have reserved a suite for you at the Highland Park Hotel. It's only a few blocks from here. The location is ideal for seeing the town. I've also taken the opportunity to speak to Mr. Thomas Hitchcock and tell him of your interest in Aiken. Mr. and Mrs. Hitchcock are the unofficial ambassadors of the Winter Colony. Mrs. Hitchcock came here in 1872 with her aunt, Miss Celestine Eustis, from New Orleans. Mrs. Hitchcock, Louise, had respiratory complications and the climate here was very beneficial to her recovery. Miss Celestine stayed on, and young Louise grew up here. She stayed during the winters and convinced her husband to join her. Mr. Hitchcock has issued an invitation for you to join them for a hunt this afternoon in their woods. He has also offered to host a dinner for you in the evening at their cottage, *Mon Repos*. He would like to introduce you to some other members of the community. I hope you don't think I was too presumptuous."

"Not at all, Eulalie, that was very gracious of you. I look forward to seeing some of my friends from Chicago while we're here. I understand the Marshall Fields are in town, as well as the Joseph Leiters. They've been so vocal in their praise of Aiken that Amy insisted we come down and check it out."

"Wonderful! Mr. Hitchcock will have someone pick you up at two."

Red Watson followed the trio down the platform and deposited their bags in Eulalie's Chrysler. She reached in her purse and pulled out a dollar bill which she handed to the porter.

"Why thank you, Miss Salley. That's mighty generous of you," Red said as he doffed his red cap and ambled away.

The Highland Park Hotel sat majestically on a bluff between Highland Park Road and Hayne Avenue, at the foot of Park Avenue. The hotel burned in 1898 and was rebuilt in 1914. The Spanish Colonial building of 125 rooms replaced the French Empire structure that had burned and which had accommodated up to 300 guests. The imposing new building was constructed of materials less susceptible to fire. The exterior was covered with stucco. Two campaniles rose above the front façade, giving new arrivals the impression of a Spanish cathedral. Sweeping lawns sloped down the hill toward the railroad and the hotel's new golf course which was designed by the famous golf architect Donald Ross. The vistas were breathtaking. The hotel was the centerpiece of the Colony.

"I must say I didn't expect such a fine hotel here in Aiken," Mr. McCormick exclaimed, as the boxy, black, Chrysler touring car pulled underneath the columned *port cochere* of the hotel. Eulalie had learned through experience that her cosseted clients expected only the best. She didn't consider her Chrysler town car an ostentatious luxury. It was just part of the cost of doing business in Aiken real estate.

"I can assure you, Mr. McCormick, that you will not find more luxurious accommodations anywhere than here at the Highland Park. The staff are topnotch and they'll take care of you in royal style." She walked with her guests into the hotel and saw to their registration and luggage.

"If you aren't too exhausted from your journey, I'd like to take a few minutes to map out your itinerary for the next few days. I have some lovely properties lined up for your inspection. Perhaps you will join me in the lounge for a beverage."

An hour, and two glasses of Chassagne-Montrachet, later she was back behind the wheel of her limousine heading up Laurens. She felt certain that she would soon have another large commission check to wave under Julian's nose.

"I trust the hunt went well and that you were able to meet your old friends—and also to make some new ones—last night at *Mon Repos,*" Eulalie said as she met the McCormicks in the Highland Park lobby the next morning

"We had a wonderful time, and I can't thank you enough for making the arrangements. Indeed we did see the Fields and the Leiters. We also met the Whitneys and the Milburns. I never knew some men could be so passionate about polo. I was about ready to grab a mallet and head for Whitney Field myself," Mr. McCormick chuckled.

"I'm so glad your introduction to Aiken got off to such a good start. Now, as I said earlier, there are three properties in particular I would like to show you today. Two are existing homes and one is a property in the horse district that you might like. I know you said that you might also be interested in building a new cottage."

The home on Hayne, backing up to the Highland Park golf course, did not have sufficient acreage to satisfy Mr. McCormick. Mrs. McCormick thought the house on Colleton was too hemmed in by its neighbors and was not convenient to the riding trails. Mid-afternoon found Eulalie's car idling as a group of horsemen crossed Whiskey Road near the Fermata School for Girls. When they cleared, she turned left onto an unpaved street, as most in the horse district were. Two blocks later the road intersected Magnolia at the former Barnard estate. Only the brick foundations remained from the inferno that had claimed the mansion a few years earlier. Half-hearted attempts at maintaining the property had left large clumps of brush scattered about. Weeds grew threw the bricks of the old foundation.

"I know it's not much to look at right now, but this was a grand estate a few years ago, before it burned," Eulalie said. "It was a plantation before it became the Barnard's villa. "There is twenty acres altogether, and it would be ideal for a magnificent cottage with stables. There's probably room even for your own polo field. As you can see, it's right across Whiskey Road from the Hitchcock Woods. The Whitney polo field is almost in your back yard and the Palmetto Golf Club is across Whiskey as well, just off Berrie Road. I think it is an ideal location." She paused to let the information sink in.

"I believe I'll get out and walk around the place," McCormick said. "Do you want to join me, Amy? It's a little muddy, but the valet at the hotel can clean your shoes."

The couple wandered about the property for a half-hour. Eulalie dutifully kept her distance—far enough away to allow the couple privacy but close enough to quickly respond to their questions.

"Well Eulalie, I think I've seen enough," said Mr. McCormick, as he turned to head back to the car. Eulalie looked crestfallen. His diffident attitude told her he was not interested in this parcel.

"Why the glum face, Eulalie. You look like you've lost your last friend. Cheer up. We'll take it. You're right, it's perfect.

Let's head back to your office and draw up the contract."

Not only did the McCormicks buy the land, they also asked Eulalie to find the best architect in the area to help them with the plans. They were to leave in three days, so she had to hurry. She knew immediately whom she would call.

Two days later, she sat across from the McCormicks at the conference table in her office. Seated at the end of the table was Willis Irvin. Irvin was a resident of Aiken, though his architectural offices were in Augusta. Irvin had photographs and bound plans of many of his projects. His architectural training came at the Georgia Institute of Technology and his skills were attested to by the many plaques and awards hanging on the walls of his Augusta office. Two hours later he walked out of Eulalie's office with a rolled up paper under his arm. It contained preliminary sketches of the ideas he had gleaned from the McCormicks as they described what they were looking for in their new residence. He also had a check for $2,500 to bind his services. He was to submit preliminary plans within six weeks, along with a quote for his design services. If the McCormicks approved of his plans, he would be asked to complete the final drawings and to oversee the construction of "Whitehall" as they had chosen to name their cottage. In an earlier incarnation, the property had been known as Whitehall Plantation.

Fifteen months later, the McCormicks moved into "Whitehall", Willis Irvin's Colonial Revival masterpiece that would garner for him yet another major design award. Richard McCormick arrived in Aiken with an entourage from Chicago that included Count Ilia Tolstoy, grandson of the famous Russian author Leo Tolstoy, and Michael Ivanenko, husband of a Russian royal. Both men were known for their judgment of fine horseflesh. McCormick needed to purchase a quality jumper for Amy, and he commissioned the two Russians to find one.

At the behest of their patron, the two horse traders went first to Tommy Hitchcock. Mr. Hitchcock, however, believed that such base affairs as horse trading were beneath his dignity. He suggested they contact his friend S. Charles Baltazzi, another

Winter Colony resident who maintained a large stable of horses at his estate "Nandina" on Magnolia Street. It was only a quarter mile down the street from McCormick's palatial new mansion, "Whitehall."

Baltazzi was descended from a wealthy Turkish banking family. One of Baltazzi's forebears figured prominently in the "Mayerling" affair. Eleni Baltazzi's daughter, Baroness Marie Vetsera, was the secret lover of Crown Prince Rudolf, heir apparent to the Habsburg Empire (Austro-Hungarian). Rudolph, 30, was married to Princess Stephanie of Belgium but was madly in love with Marie Vetsera, who was only 18. In January 1889, the two lovers died at his royal country estate "Mayerling" outside Vienna, in what was controversially ruled a murder-suicide. Rudolph's death threw the succession to the throne of the Austro-Hungarian Empire into tumult. Emperor Franz-Joseph now had no male heir to the throne. Upon his death, it would fall to his brother Ludwig and upon Ludwig's death, his son Franz Ferdinand would accede to the throne. The assassination of Archduke Ferdinand in Sarajevo, Serbia, in June 1914, precipitated the First World War. Thus Rudolf's clandestine affair with Warner Baltazzi's cousin irrevocably altered the course of human history, as well as the lives of countless residents of Aiken and the Winter Colony.

Crown prince Rudolph and Princess Stephanie

Baltazzi searched far and wide for just the right horse for Amy McCormick. He ultimately found the stallion Bacchus II in Paris, France and had the animal shipped to Aiken. The McCormicks inspected the horse and wrote a check to Baltazzi for $3,500—payment in full. A few days later, Amy rode Bacchus II in a hunt. Upon returning to "Whitehall," the horse developed a noticeable limp. The veterinarian she called inspected the horse and declared it was lame and wasn't likely to recover.

"Baltazzi," Richard McCormick thundered into the telephone, "the horse you pawned off on me for $3,500 is lame. I want my money back."

"I'm sorry you are having problems with the horse, Colonel McCormick, but I assure you he was in perfect health when I delivered him to you. Your wife even rode him around the paddock and he had no problems."

"I don't know how you did it, Baltazzi, but you covered up his injury and I want my money back."

"I'm sorry, but a deal is a deal. I delivered a sound horse to you and I will not take an injured horse back." He hung up the phone. McCormick stopped payment on the check. Two days later, a man drove through the large, white brick, columns of the "Whitehall" driveway and knocked on the door. A few seconds later, a servant answered the knock.

"Good morning. My name is George Croft. Is Mr. McCormick in?"

"Just a minute, please, I'll get him for you," the man said as he was determining if the person standing there was worthy of calling his master to the door. He decided that he was. A few minutes later the sound of padded feet echoed down the hall.

"What can I do for you Mr. Croft?" Colonel McCormick asked.

"My firm has been retained by Mr. S. Charles Baltazzi to represent him in a claim against you for failure to fulfill a contract for the purchase of the horse Bacchus II for the sum of $3,500. Here is your summons to appear in the court of common pleas in two weeks."

"You can't be serious," McCormick sputtered. "Baltazzi sold me a bill of goods. That horse was lame from the minute we got him and I'll prove it. You'd better prepare yourself for a fight, sir. Baltazzi has now made this a matter of personal honor. Good day, Mr. Croft." The door slammed shut in George Croft's face. A short while later the phone at Henderson and Salley rang.

"Good afternoon, Henderson and Salley," the secretary said, "how may I help you?"

"I'd like to speak to Mr. Julian Salley please," the caller said.

"May I say who is calling?"

"This is Colonel Richard McCormick."

"Just a minute, Mr. McCormick, I'll get Mr. Salley for you."

"How are you Mr. McCormick?" Julian said, in his perfect southern drawl. "I can't tell you how much Eulalie and I enjoyed the open house you and Amy had when you moved into "Whitehall." Willis certainly did a magnificent job."

"Thank you, Julian, I appreciate that, but that's not why I called. I need your legal help."

"Why, certainly, how can I help you?"

"A few weeks ago I bought a jumper for Amy from Warner Baltazzi. Do you know him?"

"I've run into him a few times around town. I believe he lives just down the street from you."

"That's right. That was one of the reasons that Amy and I went to him for help in finding the best jumper possible for her. When he delivered the horse, everything seemed fine. I gave him a check for $3,500, and I thought that was the end of it. Well, lo and behold, Amy took the horse out for a hunt and it came up lame. When I confronted Baltazzi with this information, he claimed the horse was in perfect health when he turned it over to me, therefore, something must have happened to it on the hunt. Amy says nothing happened. I've checked with the other riders, and they said he was not injured during the hunt. Baltazzi refused to give me my money back, so I put a hold on the check. An hour or so ago a Mr. Croft showed up at my door with a summons to appear in court in two weeks. It seems Baltazzi is suing me for breach of contract. He didn't have the decency to come and talk to me to see if we could work something out. Now I'm taking this personally. It's not about the money, it's about my honor and integrity. Will you represent me Julian?"

"I'll be glad to, Mr. McCormick. Why don't you come by my office tomorrow morning and we can get started. I'd like you to bring all the documents you have that relate to the case so that I can start to build a defense."

Two weeks later, Julian stood before Judge S.W.G. Shipp from Florence, S. C., the presiding judge at the evidentiary hearing and laid out his case for the defense. His cousin, and best friend, George Croft, did the same for Mr. Baltazzi. When both lawyers had finished Julian rose to address Judge Shipp again.

"Your honor, I believe we have conclusively proven that the horse sold to my client was damaged goods. Therefore Mr. McCormick was perfectly within his rights to withhold payment. I beg the court to provide a summary judgment that Mr. Baltazzi's case is without merit."

"Julian, I'll grant you that there is much evidence to support your client's position. There is also much evidence to support the plaintiff's, so we'll let a jury decide which of you has the preponderance of evidence on your side." With that the judge rang down the gavel and said, "Next case."

The long awaited trial started on a Friday and went through Saturday afternoon. Once again the courtroom was filled with Winter Colony residents. Feelings were running high on both sides of the question. In particular, Thomas Hitchcock was adamant that his friend Warner Baltazzi would never have delivered a lame horse to Amy McCormick. The McCormicks had their partisans as well. Whatever the jury might decide, there was bound to be a rupture in the body politic as well as the social fabric of Aiken.

"Ladies and gentlemen of the jury," George Croft pleaded, "If you believe that Mrs. Amy McCormick, being the able and experienced horsewoman she is, would ride off to a hunt with a lame horse, then you would be right to find for her. But, we all know that she wouldn't do that. You must therefore conclude that the horse was injured in one of the jumps during the hunt. My client, Mr. Baltazzi, can in no way be held responsible for that, therefore, he is rightly entitled to full payment for the healthy animal he delivered."

"My learned opponent has said that my client was in receipt of a healthy animal," Julian countered, "and therefore, any subsequent damage to the horse had to be caused by an accident on the hunt. I submit to you that you must strongly consider the affidavit I offered in evidence from Monsieur LePechines in Paris. He categorically stated that Bacchus II had a knot on his right rear stifle joint before he left Paris. Such a knot might not be apparent to a lay person, such as any of you, or even to my client, but it was obvious to any trained horseman. I contend that this injury was present when the horse was delivered, and the plaintiff chose to ignore it, hoping that it would go away. Well, it didn't go away. Instead it became inflamed and aggravated on the hunt, resulting in chronic lameness. Therefore, I beseech you to look at all the evidence presented, and find in favor of my client."

Though it's reasonably certain that many of the jurors were sympathetic to Julian and the McCormicks, the opposing forces supporting Warner Baltazzi were able to bring more pressure to bear. The Hitchcocks, Whitneys, Milburns, Iselins and their allies, all long time winter visitors and property owners, held sway over most dealings affecting the Colony. The McCormicks on the other hand, though powerful in their Chicago environs, were no match for the entrenched interests of the moneyed easterners. The jury found in favor of Baltazzi. Enraged, McCormick appealed to the South Carolina Supreme Court. That court upheld the original verdict, and Amy McCormick was required to pay the $3,500 for a lame Bacchus II. Adding insult to injury, she was also required to pay an additional $100 in court costs.

Colonel Robert McCormick may have suffered a major setback, but he was far from defeated. He responded to the affront dealt him by challenging the tax assessments on

"Whitehall." Armed with lower assessments on comparable adjacent properties, he waged war with the city and county tax assessor's offices. Again he lost. He had crossed that narrow, imaginary, line that separated the "ins" from the "outs" in Aiken, and he would never regain access to the inner sanctums of the Colony. In the parlance of the Colony, he had been "frosted." However, he could not refuse the gauntlet that was thrown down by the local power structure. Coming from Chicago, he knew a thing or two about dirty politics. He walked into the tax offices and declared, "I'll be damned if I'll ever pay another dollar in taxes to the city or county of Aiken." With that he marched over to Julian Salley's office.

"Julian, I want you to draw up the proper papers to deed "Whitehall" to General Charles Summerall, Commandant of the Citadel, as his permanent retirement home."

McCormick had served under Summerall in the army and held the general in high esteem. Since the Citadel was the property of the South Carolina government, it paid no taxes on any of its properties, which would now include "Whitehall." The general occupied the home following his retirement from the Citadel. The Colonel had his pyrrhic victory.

Allegiances in the Winter Colony were like a two-edged sword. They could cut both ways. Eulalie and Julian learned to walk that fine line in order to minimize the effects on their livelihoods.

18

Grand Piano

Those who came to Aiken during the winter, and brought their horses, provided most of their own entertainment. Between polo matches, fox hunts, trail riding and carriage driving, there was plenty to occupy the Colony, but for many, when the sun went down it was time to party. Money was no object for these captains of industry and barons of Wall Street—or for their wives. One *grande dame* hosted a party for her little terrier dog. She set the dog on a satin pillow so that everyone could admire its $15,000 diamond necklace. Another woman gave a luncheon where everyone was served while seated on horseback. A third served oysters in their shells, which, when opened, each revealed a rare black pearl inside. Still another party in the garden of a posh Hayne Avenue property supplied garters to all the women guests. And, not just any garters, these were diamond encrusted. The men were encouraged to flounce the women's skirts up so that the garters were visible to the other guests. Local townsfolk, gawking through the fence while ignoring their own impropriety, were mortified that such bawdy behavior was occurring right under their noses. Forceful letters to the paper decrying the affair went unpublished. In the name of comity with Aiken's rich and powerful visitors, the publisher declined to print them.

It was not unheard of that entire orchestras and troupes of performers were brought in from New York by private Pullman cars for just a few hours of entertainment. A frequent guest at Joye Cottage was the famous actress Lillian Russell. It was common knowledge that she carried on a long, but platonic, affair with "Diamond Jim" Brady. Brady came often to "York House" the cottage that his sister Mabel Brady Garvan leased at 253 York Street, SE. Brady was a self-made man of tremendous appetites, especially for food and diamonds, and he had the girth and the jewelry to prove it. George Rector, a famous New York restaurateur of the time said, "Jim is the best twenty-five customers I ever had." Less known was the unsubstantiated rumor that Bill Whitney shared Miss Russell's favors as well. Eulalie Salley was happy that Miss Russell came to Aiken, for she was a staunch ally of the suffrage movement in New York.

William Whitney attended a piano concert at Carnegie Hall shortly after the turn of the century. He was mesmerized by the artistry of the performer, concert pianist Jozef Hoffman. Hoffman, born Jozef Kazamierz Hoffmann in Krakow, Poland, was a child prodigy. He performed before an audience at the age of five and was on tour at the age of twelve. Many of his contemporaries claimed he was the greatest concert pianist of the twentieth century. In 1882, the great Anton Rubenstein took Hoffman as his only student. In 1911, Hoffman gave a series of 21 concerts in which he played 255 different classical musical compositions, never repeating a single one, and never needing sheet music. His ear was so keen that he could hear a piano concert and then reproduce it perfectly. He possessed a perfect mechanical mastery of the piano. Had it stopped there his star would not have burned as brightly as it did, for he also had a great spiritual feeling for the music. He once remarked to a student.

"In the framework of the composer's structure you must be faithful, and you have no leeway at all. You must never tamper with the composer's intentions. But in all details that are incidental to the composer's structural framework you have great leeway, and what you do with these details makes you an artist."

Hoffman was of very small stature and had small hands.

Despite this seeming handicap, he still became a surpassingly gifted artist. He was heard to make an offhand comment backstage following one of his concerts that he found the standard piano keys to be too wide for his hands. This information was passed on to the Steinway Corporation. When he sat down at his next performance, he was presented with a brand new Steinway concert grand piano—one with keys that were one-eighth inch narrower than standard piano keys.

Whitney was so impressed with Hoffman that he invited him to Aiken to entertain his guests at Joye Cottage. Among the guests that night was Marie Eustis, niece of Celestine Eustis. Marie was married to her first cousin, George Eustis, Louise's brother. They had one child, George, and they had separated after thirteen years of marriage. The entire Eustis family pressured Marie to reconcile with George, who had moved back to New York. He came to Aiken often and took George and Marie for picnics in Hitchcock Woods. She was sorely tempted by all the attention, but fate conspired to prevent reconciliation.

Marie arrived late to the concert at Joye Cottage. She stood briefly in the doorway, silhouetted by the bright entry lights. Her dark hair was piled high on her head. She wore a deep pink dress with a short train, embroidered in pale green leaves and sweetheart roses. Hoffman saw her and was immediately captivated by the vision. He tore into a piece by Mozart, hammering the keys with animal ferocity. The act got her attention. She came to sit by the new Steinway and began to talk to Jozef.

"Until I came down those steps, I didn't realize who you are," she said.

"And who am I?"

"You are the twelve-year old boy I saw perform in Newport, Rhode Island many years ago. I remember that you couldn't reach the pedals, and they had attached metal stilts to your shoes," Marie said.

"I must confess I don't remember you, my dear. What is your name?"

"Marie Eustis."

"Are you related to Miss Celestine Eustis?"

"She's my aunt, and Lulie Hitchcock is my cousin. I was married to her brother George."

"Were married?"

"Well, we are still married, but separated."

"I see," Jozef said. "I love your aunt. She's an absolute delight. Do you think she would allow me to call on you at her home?"

"Certainly, just ring her up and make a date. I look forward to seeing you again."

Arriving home after the concert, Marie burst into her aunt's room at *Mon Repos. "Tante*, you'll never guess who Mr. Whitney invited to entertain for his Christmas party, Jozef Hoffman. You remember. We heard him perform at the Metropolitan Opera last year. He must have played for over three hours tonight. The guests wouldn't let him stop. I've never heard anything like it."

"My goodness, Marie, I haven't heard you this excited since George left," her aunt said.

"Oh, it was so thrilling. He's staying for a week, and he asked if he could call on me here at *Mon Repos.* Without thinking, I said, 'Of course you can.' I hope you don't mind."

"Of course not my dear, I'm just happy to see a flush back in your cheeks again."

Marie and Jozef saw each other daily for the rest of his stay in Aiken. They continued to correspond after his return to New York. News of the liaison reached George who came immediately to Aiken and redoubled his efforts to mend the marriage. Despite his entreaties Marie was adamant that the marriage was over.

In the dark of night, George took his son back to New York with him. Marie quickly followed, trying to retrieve her child. George was alerted that she was coming and booked passage to Europe. Undaunted, Marie followed on the next liner to France. She finally tracked George to Berlin, where she cornered him and demanded the return of her son. George treated it as a big joke.

"Of course you can have him back. I had no intention of

keeping him from you."

Marie took her son and his governess, Martha Tuck, to a small seaside resort on the north coast of Germany, the small island of Rugen. She needed time to think and to arrange for the divorce. This last escapade had ruptured any possibility of reconciliation. She took long walks along the beach with George. One sunny, windswept, day on the beach she saw a small man at his easel, painting a shore scene. She walked over to admire the work. The artist looked up from his painting.

"Marie! Is that really you?"

Her accidental artist was Jozef Hoffman.

"Jozef, what are you doing here?"

"I could ask you the same."

"I came to Berlin to get my son back from his father," Marie said. "He took him away without permission. We're here to recuperate from the ordeal before going back home."

"I'm sorry you had to make such a grueling journey. As to your inquiry, I'm taking a few days off from my European tour for the same reason. I needed a rest. Nothing relaxes me like the ocean and painting. But, enough of that. Now that you are here, I'd like to take you and George to dinner this evening."

Jozef and Marie saw each other every day for two weeks. When he left for London she went with him. He proposed to her there, before her return to America.

"Marie, I cannot forbid you to marry Mr. Hoffman, but I must object in the most strenuous of terms," Celestine Eustis admonished her niece. "You have no idea the life you'll lead, following him all over the world. It won't be like your vacations to Italy or your romps through France. You'll be staying in second rate hotels and grabbing meals on the go. And what of George? That's no life for a small boy."

Other members of the family tried equally as hard to discourage her, and with the same result. It was no use. Marie was in love and she was going to marry Jozef Hoffman. She obtained her divorce and headed back to London where she and Jozef were married.

For the next few years, Marie traveled with Jozef on his concert tours. She visited all the capitals of Europe, where she basked in his reflected glory and was entertained by royalty; however, one tradition became sacrosanct. No matter where his concerts took him, the Hoffmans always returned to Aiken for the Christmas holidays. They built a home on the west side of South Laurens, between the railroad cut and South Boundary Avenue. Jozef named the cottage "Fermata" which means a pause, or stop, in a musical composition. The 34 room cottage backed up to the Hitchcock Woods. Another house, located on the adjacent lot, was bought and annexed to the Hoffman home. The Eugene Grace cottage "Rosecroft," with its majestic gardens, sat just across Laurens from the Hoffmans.

Ultimately, Marie tired of the constant travel. She now had not only her son George but Anton and Jozefa from her new marriage to consider. Her tours with Jozef became less frequent. She settled into a routine in Aiken.

In 1916, her cousin Louise Hitchcock founded the Aiken Preparatory School for Boys. Many of the sons of privilege were spending more school months in Aiken than in their hometowns up north. Louise felt they needed a first class educational institution to match those back home. She provided the seed money for the school and soon it had grown from five to fifty students. Over the years, names like Whitney, Milburn, McLean, Hitchcock, Grace, Vanderbilt, Bohlen, Colt, Astaire, and von Stade, would grace the rolls of Aiken Prep. Marie Hoffman enrolled her young son Anton there, but she also saw a need beyond this school for boys. She wasn't happy with the second-class treatment the daughters of the privileged received in Aiken. In Europe she had seen how carefully prepared the daughters were for introduction into society. She wanted that same preparation for her Jozefa. In 1919, she and Jozef founded the Fermata School for girls. There were five girls in the initial class. The four teachers conducted classes in rooms on the third floor of "Fermata."

When he was in residence, Jozef Hoffman practiced in his salon at the rear of his home. On warm summer nights he threw open the windows and presented magnificent concerts for the forest creatures of Hitchcock Woods—and for the residents across the fairways of the Highland Park Golf Club, including Eulalie Salley. Eulalie's mother had sold her home on Laurens and moved with the Salleys to their new bungalow on Highland Park Avenue.

"I remember with great fondness sitting on my back steps in the evenings and listening to him play," Eulalie said. "He was the most amazing musician I ever heard. It broke my heart when he left Aiken. We lost a real treasure."

After two years, it was obvious that a permanent home was required to house the growing enrollment of Fermata. Hope Goddard Iselin shared Marie's conviction that young girls deserved the same opportunities as their male counterparts. She threw her support and her fortune into the cause of Fermata. Together the two women purchased eleven acres on Whiskey Road from a Colonel Kuser, turning his columned mansion into a school building and adding tennis courts and a pool. The new facility opened its doors in 1921 to 90 young girls. Palmetto Golf Club abutted the property and was visible from the upper rear windows of the main house. Legend has it that Jaqueline Bouvier was in residence for one year, but there is no conclusive evidence to support that notion. It is a fact, however, that her half-brother Hugh Auchincloss attended Aiken Prep. Diana Barrymore, of the famed acting family—Ethel, John, Lionel—was also a student at Fermata. A film biography based on her life is titled, *Too Much, Too Soon*. Ethel Barrymore was her grandmother. Ethel's son, Sam Colt, was enrolled at Aiken Prep at the same time. One of his antecedents invented the Colt 45 pistol.

The strain of the long separations while Hoffman was on tour became difficult for the marriage. Jozef began to see other women. When Marie confronted him with the rumors of his infidelity, he wrote her a lengthy letter trying to explain it away. After three crimped pages of extraneous news, he wrote this.

"There is no doubt that I am different from other people. But

how else could this be? First I was born a different animal from others; second, I was brought up differently than others; third, I've lived a different life than others. Why wonder then and accuse me of certain lacks, when I have so many other qualities which average people do not possess? One cannot be perfect in every respect. One quality usually develops at the expense of another."

One of Hoffman's *lacks* was not an ego. Nor did he lack a temper. His tantrums and explosions when dissatisfied with his tour preparations were legendary.

Finally, the tension was just too much. His performances were suffering, and he asked for a divorce. Marie finally consented to it in 1925. In 1926 Jozef accepted the directorship of the Curtis School of Music in Philadelphia. Shortly thereafter, he married his mistress, Elizabeth Short. Marie continued to run Fermata for a number of years, eventually selling it to the headmaster, Mr. F. A. Tabor. Tabor at that time was also the headmaster at Aiken Prep. He ran Fermata until the 1940's when the main building was consumed by a fire. The Hoffman home "Fermata" at 325 Laurens was severely undermined by a flood in 1960 and had to be demolished. A compound of gray townhomes occupies that spot today.

Marie moved to Vevey, Switzerland, on the shores of Lake Geneva. When the children were grown, and away, she returned to Aiken where she wrote an advice column for the Aiken paper under the *nom de plume,* "Marquita". Both she and Jozef passed away in the 1950's.

19

The New Generation

Eulalie doggedly continued to pursue her dream that suffrage would eventually come to pass in America. From 1913, when she helped to form the suffrage chapter in Aiken, until July 1920, when twenty-four year old representative Harry Burns of Tennessee cast the final and deciding vote for that state's approval of the nineteenth amendment, she crisscrossed the country making speeches, lobbying politicians, and raising funds for the cause of women's rights. Even after national approval was in hand, she pressed on for ratification in South Carolina. Senator Gilbert McMillan continued to present the legislation to the House, and the majority still stubbornly refused to pass it, ignoring the fact that the amendment's passage had given their state's women the legal right to vote in national elections. Most also voted in local and state elections, with the powers-that-be turning a blind eye. Eulalie was elected vice president of the third region of the Equal Suffrage League which included South Carolina. During the pivotal years leading up to ratification she traveled to 41 states addressing thousands of women, urging their support.

In the run-up to voting on the nineteenth amendment, Eulalie went to Washington to lobby the South Carolina delegation for its support. While there she joined in the street protests and parades. She had set up her soap box on a corner near the capitol building and was urging all passers-by to help them win passage of the amendment. A policeman addressed her.

"Lady, you're not allowed to speak from a soapbox."

"I came here to make a speech and I'm going to make it," she said politely.

"You go right ahead, but I'm going to have to arrest you," he replied. With that Eulalie mounted her soapbox and began her address. The policeman stopped her.

"You're such a pretty little thing. If you won't finish it, I won't arrest you. You're too pretty to go to that dirty old jail."

"I want you to arrest me," she said. "When my newspapers at home hear that I have been arrested, it will help the cause tremendously."

The policeman walked away mumbling to himself.

In 1924, Eulalie attended the Democratic convention as an alternate delegate. She was seated next to William Jennings Bryan when Al Smith's name was placed in nomination. She saw Bryan many times in the coming years at state conventions, and they became close friends.

The latter half of the nineteenth century witnessed a vast accumulation of wealth as the American frontier moved further west. Railroads, steel, coal, and oil were the four major industries that began to dominate the financial landscape. Names such as Morgan, Vanderbilt, Astor, Mellon, and Carnegie filled the newspapers as they manipulated the financial landscape for their own economic gain. The concentration of wealth among these industrial titans gave rise to a political movement that urged the courts and congress to rein in the tactics of the rich and powerful. The "Progressive" movement helped to elect Republican Theodore Roosevelt in 1900. His platform promised to disassemble the most egregious of the trusts and combines that were running roughshod over the economy. Through several laws passed in that era, he was able to dismantle the most flagrant trusts, earning him the nickname, "The Trust Buster." He succeeded in breaking-up the Standard Oil Trust of John D. Rockefeller and the Northern Securities Railroad Trust of J. Pierpont Morgan. His actions created many enemies among the movers and shakers of industry. Thereafter, T.R. was never again a welcome visitor to Aiken.

William Howard Taft succeeded Roosevelt in the election of 1908. He continued his predecessor's efforts to dismantle the worst of the more than 2,000 trust mergers that had occurred in the late 1800's. Taft ran again in 1912, but was challenged by Roosevelt. Roosevelt was not happy with the direction in which Taft was taking the Republican Party. T.R., when he decided to challenge Taft, said, "I am throwing my hat in the ring", the first known usage of that phrase. Roosevelt's "Bullmoose" party succeeded in splitting the Progressive/Republican vote, allowing the Democrat, Thomas Woodrow Wilson, to become the 28th president of the United States.

Theodore Roosevelt and Family

Eulalie Salley was ecstatic that Wilson, a Democrat and an avowed pacifist, was in the White House.

"Mother! Mother!" she called to Martha Chafee as she vaulted up the stairs, "He won! He won!"

It was well after midnight and the final returns had just come in on the Atwater-Kent radio sitting on the kitchen counter. The entire family had worked hard to elect Wilson, not only because he was a Democrat, and they liked his politics, but because he was an old friend of the family.

"Why, I can remember when he used to come running down the street with his fiends playing kick-the-can," her mother said. "The Reverend Wilson's house was only a few blocks from ours on Greene Street. He was pastor of the Presbyterian Church. They moved away just a few years before you were born. Tommy was such a nice boy."

Wilson was in office just over a year when a 19-year old Serbian, Gavrilo Princip, put a bullet through the head of Archduke Franz Ferdinand, heir apparent to the Austro-Hungarian Empire. The assassination in Sarajevo was the first domino to fall. When the last had fallen, all of Europe and much of Asia Minor was at war. Before it was finished, 32 nations would become involved in the First World War. However, the major combatants were the French and English on one side and Germany, Austro-Hungary, Italy, and Turkey on the other.

The Germans and Austrians invaded France, Belgium, and the Netherlands from the north, while Great Britain poured troops across the channel to support the French. For three long years, battles surged back and forth, all across northern France and the Low Countries. Trench warfare, chemical warfare, and tank and aerial battles took a terrible toll on both sides. Some positions around Verdun and the Somme changed hands multiple times, with each exchange bringing more suffering and incredible carnage.

Wilson struggled to honor his promise to stay out of the war, but T.R. and others urged him to get America involved. They argued that it was part of America's manifest destiny and that the U.S needed to be at the table when all the dust settled. Wilson resisted until a German U-Boat sank the British passenger liner *Lusitania,* with hundreds of American lives lost. On April 6, 1917, almost three years after hostilities began, the United States declared war on Germany and its allies. Within weeks the draft boards began calling up registrants to serve in the army. On June 16, the first 14,000 U.S. troops landed at St. Nazaire on the French coast. When the last shot of the war was fired, and an armistice declared on November 11, 1918, over 2,000,000 Americans had served in the "War to End All Wars," as Wilson had characterized it in his justification speech.

Among those who served were several prominent Winter Colony members. William Corcoran Eustis, Celestine Eustis' brother, was secretary to General John J. "Blackjack" Pershing, commander of all American forces. Tommy Hitchcock was also involved.

Eulalie Salley knocked softly at the door of *Mon Repos.* She waited as she heard footfalls crossing the parlor floor.

"Miss Salley," Mr. Hitchcock's valet George said, "Please come in, I'll get Mrs. Hitchcock for you."

A few minutes later, Lulie Hitchcock came down the stairs from her upper floor sitting room. She dabbed at her eyes with a handkerchief.

"Eulalie, how kind of you to come," she said.

"It was the least I could do," Eulalie said. "I just heard on the radio this morning. This awful war is touching us all I'm afraid. Have you heard any more from Tommy?"

"No. The only thing they know for sure is that he was shot down behind the German lines. One of the other pilots saw him go down. He thinks Tommy survived the landing. He saw him get out of his plane. He appeared to be injured. We don't know how severely. If he's alive, he's in German hands now."

"I'm so sorry," Eulalie said. "If there's anything I can do for you, please call me. The whole community is praying for Tommy, and for you."

"Thank you, that's so very kind. Tell everyone how much I appreciate their prayers."

Tommy Hitchcock was only seventeen in 1917. He was a senior at the Aiken Preparatory School for Boys and at St. Paul's in Concord, New Hampshire. The United States hadn't yet entered the war. Like most red-blooded youth of the time, he was anxious to enlist right away. The army said he would have to wait. Unbeknownst to his mother, Tommy Sr. pulled strings in Washington. He called Teddy Roosevelt and asked if he could help. Roosevelt couldn't get Tommy into the army right away, but he had friends in the Foreign Service who could help. Within weeks young Tommy was training with the famous French Air Service group known as the *Lafayette Escadrille.* The squadron was organized mainly to accommodate Americans and Canadians who wanted to get into the fight prior to America entering the war. The name was chosen to honor the Marquis de Lafayette, who fought with Washington in the Revolutionary War. On July 4, a contingent of newly arrived American doughboys celebrated by marching to the Paris grave of General Lafayette. Colonel Charles E. Stanton saluted and uttered the now iconic phrase, *"Lafayette, nous voilá"* (Lafayette, we are here).

Tommy arrived in Paris and stayed with family friends, before being assigned to the Escadrille flight training school. Upon completion of training, Hitchcock was approved to fly combat missions and was brevetted (commissioned) an officer. He moved to the forward base at Pau, France and began immediately to sortie over the lines in his Sopwith Camel. Within a few weeks, he had two confirmed kills, one a German Albatross with its two-man crew, a pilot and a gunner.

A month after his eighteenth birthday, Tommy was shot down in a dogfight with three Albatrosses. He mistakenly thought his two wingmen were with him when in truth they had turned back to base. He was in a perfect position to attack. He was above and behind two of the planes. What he didn't know was, there was a third Albatross behind and above him. He eluded the first run by the German, but the second sent a bullet through his seat and into his buttock. It exited through his thigh, fortunately missing the bone. He crash landed in a field behind German lines and the last thing he saw before passing out was German soldiers advancing on the plane.

Tommy awoke in the hospital surgery of a prisoner-of-war camp. He was in agony from the wound and the surgery to repair it. Weeks later, after bouts of fever and infection, he was moved to another camp. Over the next six months he was moved several times. At each camp there were groups of prisoners actively planning their escape. Hitchcock was successful in escaping once but was recaptured and returned. Before his last move, he succeeded in stealing maps from a German atlas. When his train slowed to cross a Danube bridge, Tommy broke free and jumped into the darkened woods alongside the track. With his map and meager food supplies he traveled by night and hid in woods and barns by day. After eight long, arduous, days he crossed the Danube into Switzerland. He was safe at last.

Tommy Sr. and Louise finally received the jubilant news that their son was well and free. He went by train back to Paris where he once again stayed with family friends. By the time his status was sorted out, the war was over and he returned home a hero.

Gloria Vanderbilt Whitney, granddaughter of William C. Whitney, could not serve in the military, but she did serve in other ways. She took a sizable portion of her inheritance and founded a hospital near Paris to treat wounded American troops. After the war she produced several sculptures commemorating the war, including one at St. Nazaire, France, where the first troops landed. In 1929, she established one of the finest art museums in the world, "The Whitney," whose current home is at Madison and 76th in Manhattan.

The "War to End All Wars" had cost the lives of 15,000,000 people and 10,000,000 horses. Another 20,000,000 people were wounded. An entire generation of French and German youth was wiped out. The grim statistics were:

Germany – 2,000,000 dead – 4,300,000 wounded

France – 1,900,000 dead – 4,300,000 wounded

Italy – 1,200,000 dead

Great Britain – 900,000 dead – 1,700,000 wounded

United States – 117,000 dead – 205,000 wounded

In addition to the 35,000,000 directly affected by the war, another 75,000,000 people around the world died during that period from the devastating outbreak of the "Spanish Flu." It is estimated that more casualties of the war were flu victims than war victims.

The Treaty of Versailles, formally ending the war, was signed in 1919. Some of its provisions were so onerous that they ultimately caused the collapse of the German Weimar Republic that emerged after the war and led to the rise of Adolph Hitler and WWII. The "peace" following WWI lasted just twenty years.

That would not be the last word on Tommy Hitchcock. He was schooled by both his mother and father in the finer points of polo. He enrolled in Harvard and led his teams to several championships. His exploits on the polo field became legendary. His nickname was "Ten-Goal Tommy." He was recognized as the greatest to ever play the sport in the United States. He excelled in other sports as well: football, rowing, golf, tennis, sailing, and any other endeavor he chose to undertake. His blond good looks and athleticism caught the eye of women and men alike—one man in particular.

F. Scott Fitzgerald based two of his most famous literary characters on the real-life adventures of Tommy Hitchcock—Tom Buchanan in *The Great Gatsby*, in 1925, and Tommy Barban in *Tender is the Night* in 1934. Although Fitzgerald didn't meet Hitchcock until two years after the publication of "Gatsby", he was well aware of his reputation for derring-do. Unlike many young men of his position and wealth, Hitchcock did not shirk the duties and responsibilities that accrued to his status. Not only did he volunteer for military service at the age of seventeen, when he was too young, he volunteered for military service after Pearl Harbor, when he was too old. Not content to sit out the war, he took an advisory position with the U. S. Army Air Corps and was instrumental in the development of the P-51 dive bomber, the plane that turned the tide in the air war over Europe. When several P-51s failed to pull out of their diving runs and crashed, Hitchcock led a team to find out why. The suspected cause was faulty aerodynamics created by extra fuel tanks slung under the wings. Hitchcock volunteered to test a proposed solution. He put his plane into a steep dive and was unable to pull out. Despite impending death, he continued to radio to the ground exactly what he was experiencing. Tommy Hitchcock did not survive the fiery crash that ensued, but his skill and knowledge contributed to the solution for the P-51. He died as he had lived: reckless, patriotic, flamboyant and faithful to the ideals instilled in him by his parents, Thomas and Louise Hitchcock.

Neither of Tommy Hitchcock's parents was alive when he perished, but the communities of Aiken, S.C., Westbury, New York, and Cambridge, Massachusetts were in deep mourning for the loss of their golden son.

Tommy Hitchcock Jr. – Equestrian and Soldier

20

The Rich and the Famous

John Jacob Astor came to the United States from Germany—by way of London—in the late 1700's and began a fur trade that reached across the continent to Oregon, where the city of Astoria bears his name. He also became involved in the opium trade, shuttling vast shipments of the addictive drug from Turkey to the opium dens of China. He then took much of his accumulated fortune and began buying real estate in Manhattan. He rightfully predicted that New York would grow to be a world trade and financial center. Upon his death in 1848, he was considered the richest man in America—maybe the world.

John Jacob Astor IV, the great-grandson, came to Aiken in the early 1900's. He bought a home at 325 Colleton Avenue, diagonally across the street from William K. Vanderbilt's home "Elm Court." When both were resident in Aiken, two of the wealthiest families in the world faced each other diagonally across the tree-shaded promenade of Colleton Avenue at Union Street.

In 1911, Astor divorced his first wife, Ava. Divorce was frowned upon by high society. Keeping a mistress, discreetly, was tolerated, but not divorce. Despite his wealth and position, he was viciously ostracized. The couple escaped to Europe for an extended honeymoon to avoid the unceasingly bad press in the New York papers. They were in Egypt when Madeleine discovered she was pregnant.

"John, I want to go home. I want our baby to be born in New York," Madeleine said.

"Very well, my dear, I'll make the arrangements."

John Jacob Astor IV and Madeleine

The RMS "Titanic" sailed from Cherbourg, France on April 10, 1913. After stops at Southampton, England and Queenstown (Cobh), Ireland, the world's newest and largest luxury liner set sail for New York with John Jacob Astor IV and his five-month pregnant wife Madeleine aboard. As the ship left the harbor, the radio operator delivered an ominous message to the bridge—the "Caronia" had reported that several large icebergs were drifting into the sea lanes en route to New York. As the ship steamed westward, urgent and more ominous sightings of pack ice and large icebergs poured into the ship's radio room. Neither J. Bruce Ismay, President of the White Star Line (owned by one of J. Pierpont Morgan's many trusts), nor Captain E. J. Smith seemed particularly concerned. After all, the "Titanic" was the newest and most modern of ships. The designers and builders of the giant cruiser thought they had made it impervious to the sea-going hazards of the past. They argued that its steel reinforced hull and water tight integrity could withstand any peril. That belief was severely tested at 11:40 p.m. that night. A near frozen lookout shouted down from the crow's nest that an iceberg lay dead ahead. Captain Davis ordered the helmsman to come hard to port while he telegraphed the engine room to reverse the engines. Too late. The starboard side of the "Titanic" plowed into the massive iceberg, peeling back the hull below the water line like a can opener. She had suffered a mortal wound. Too many of its watertight compartments had been compromised—the ship could not survive.

Eulalie listened to the brassy rings coming from her telephone earpiece. She was about to hang up when she heard the click of a receiver going off-hook at the C. Oliver Iselin home off Whiskey Road.

"Hello, this is Mrs. Hope Iselin."

"Mrs. Iselin, this is Eulalie Salley. I'm sorry to disturb you so early in the morning, but I just heard such terrible news on the radio. If you haven't already heard, I thought you would want to be told. I know how close you are to Mr. Astor."

""What is it Eulalie? Has something happened to John? I just came back in from a ride with the Hitchcocks. I haven't heard anything."

"The report says that the ocean liner "Titanic" hit an iceberg last night and sank east of Nova Scotia. The announcer said that Mr. and Mrs. John Jacob Astor were on board. He didn't say anything about survivors."

"Oh my God!" Hope Iselin gasped. "Thank you, Eulalie. I'll get Oliver to contact his New York office to see if he can get any further word. I'll phone you if we hear anything new."

The morning headlines in newspapers from coast to coast trumpeted the news–

Titanic Sinks after Hitting Iceberg

Hundreds lost at sea - 866 passengers rescued - 1250 perish
John Jacob Astor IV reported among the missing

News of the catastrophe was on the lips of everyone in Aiken but especially those of the Winter Colony, who counted the Astors among their own. Details of the disaster trickled in over the next few days. Amazing tales of individual heroics were recounted. One in particular heartened the Colony and in some small measure eased the pain of Mr. Astor's loss.

RMS Titanic

It was obvious to the passengers and crew aboard the "Titanic" that there were not enough usable lifeboats for everyone aboard. The message went out that women and children would be loaded first. A sailor grabbed Astor's arm as he accompanied Madeleine to lifeboat number four.

"Sir, we must get all the women and children aboard first," he said.

"I understand," Astor said, "but my wife is in a delicate condition, and I must see her safely to her seat."

He was allowed to pass. When everyone was seated, he stood, saluted, and went back to his station. Two immigrant Italian children, who spoke no English, stood near him on deck, dazed and confused.

"Come with me," Astor said. He took the boy and girl by the hand, led them to a life boat, and saw them safely seated. Years later the young boy verified that it was Mr. Astor that saved his life. That was only one of many reported acts of heroism aboard the doomed vessel. However, there were others aboard whose actions were less than heroic.

Eulalie related the story of one man who had gained access to a lifeboat by disguising himself as a woman. The man, when discovered, was excoriated and banished from society. Previously, he had been a prominent figure in all the gossip columns. Now, no self-respecting reporter of the social scene would go near the pariah. He showed up in Aiken and tried to buy a home. He was so rejected by the community that he soon packed his bags and left town. Rumors had it that shortly thereafter he committed suicide. Joseph Bruce Ismay earned eternal condemnation by escaping in collapsible lifeboat C, while Captain E. J. Smith heroically watched from his position on the bridge as he went down with his ship.

Following a period of mourning, Madeleine Astor resumed her social life. She returned to Aiken where she had been a visitor before her marriage to Astor. She was received with open arms by the Winter Colony community. It was there that she renewed her acquaintance with childhood sweetheart William K. Dick, heir to a sugar fortune. They were soon married. Thereafter, they vacationed often in Aiken and were frequent guests of the Iselins. As a couple, they won the Iselin Cup at the Palmetto Golf Club.

William Kassam Vanderbilt

In 1852, William Gregg, son of the founder of Graniteville, built a splendid mansion at 306 Colleton Avenue. Twenty years later, in 1872, the home was converted into the first county courthouse and jail. The county commission paid $15,000 for the house, which was significantly higher than the original asking price. Several of the commissioners were convicted of graft and sentenced to jail, ironically serving their sentences in the newly purchased building.

The courtyard of the house bore witness to the hanging of the four men convicted of murdering two German immigrants to Aiken. The purchase of the house followed closely on the heels of the formation of Aiken County, which was carved from the existing counties of Edgefield, Barnwell, Lexington and Orangeburg. Looking at a modern map of South Carolina, two parallel, arrow-straight, lines, roughly thirty miles apart, run from the Savannah River on the west to the Edisto River on the east. These artificial, non-geographical, purely political, boundaries were created with the singular purpose of isolating the Savannah river area rabble-rousers. These four counties were a major breeding ground of discontent in the run-up to secession. They also figured prominently in the resistance to Reconstruction after the war and were hotbeds of insurrection against the carpetbagger government in Columbia. Placing a new, politically friendly, jurisdiction in the middle of the four counties was seen as a solution to the unending conflicts in the area. It didn't work.

When the sixty men arrested for the riot in Hamburg were arraigned in the new Aiken courthouse, the galleries filled with the prominent citizens of Aiken, all dressed in red shirts. The carpetbagger Republican government understood the not-so-subtle hint and abandoned the prosecution. Aiken County joined the rebellion and took part in the subsequent insurrections, which ultimately led to the disbanding of the Reconstruction government in 1877.

In 1881, a new and more functional courthouse was constructed at the intersection of Park Avenue and Chesterfield Street. The Gregg mansion reverted to a residential property. Otis Chafee, Eulalie's paternal grandfather, bought it. Subsequently, Edwin Harriman, President of the Baltimore and Ohio Railroad, briefly owned it.

William Kassam Vanderbilt, grandson of Cornelius Vanderbilt, founder of the Vanderbilt family dynasty, came to Aiken looking for a winter home in 1914. His younger brother George, who built the baronial estate known as "Biltmore" in the mountains near Asheville, had died that same year. His niece, Gertrude, was in Aiken with her husband, Harry Payne Whitney, who had inherited Joye Cottage in 1904 after his father died. There were many associations and ties drawing W.K. Vanderbilt to Aiken.

"Miss Salley," W. K. Vanderbilt said, as he cornered Eulalie at a social function, "I have it on good authority that you are the most knowledgeable person in Aiken when it comes to real estate." The two were together at one of Joye Cottage's nonstop parties. Today's event was a carriage ride through Hitchcock Woods, followed by a lawn party under the maturing oaks that Harry's father had planted.

"I certainly appreciate the compliment, Mr. Vanderbilt, but I can't make any such claim."

"Now don't be modest, Eulalie. May I call you Eulalie?"

"Please do, we don't stand much on formality down here."

"Then call me Bill. Now, about that real estate?"

"Well, I have been dabbling in it a bit. I've made some suggestions to friends of the Iselin's that seem to have been well received."

"See, you are an authority. Have you thought of going into the business?"

"I must say I have given it some thought. But I'm so involved in the Suffrage League I don't know when I would do it. The money would certainly come in handy. There are so many expenses…" she let the sentence trail off.

"I'm looking to buy some property. I don't really need a big estate like Harry has here. Just a place to get away from the winter and do a little entertaining. I have my horses in New York and Paris, so I'll only need a small stable and paddock area. Have you heard of anything like that that might be available?'

"Let me think. Oh yes! My husband just did the closing for a property on Colleton Avenue. The agent remarked that the house across the street was going on the market soon. If you'd like I can get the particulars for you."

"I would surely appreciate that, Eulalie."

The property in question was the former house built by William Gregg, and most recently owned by the Harriman family. Julian knew the house was going up for sale. A week later, Vanderbilt bought the property and turned it into a winter playground for his family and friends. What had been referred to as "The Walpole Place" was renamed by Vanderbilt as "Elm Court." That was the same name as an aunt's property in Massachusetts that Vanderbilt visited often. At the same time, he inspired Eulalie Salley to enter the real estate business. Vanderbilt was reported to have made a significant contribution to the League in her name for her efforts.

Vanderbilt's wife was Alva smith of Mobile, Alabama. She was the daughter of a successful merchant and small plantation owner—not the typical background for a bride marrying someone in the New York social register. Alva's friend, Consuelo Yznaga, introduced the couple and she later became the godmother to their child, and her namesake, Consuelo. The young woman became one of the most beautiful and most desirable young women in high society. Sir James Barrie, author of Peter Pan once remarked, "I would wait all night in the rain to see Consuelo get into her carriage."

Alva was determined that Consuelo should marry into royalty. Marriages between threadbare but titled Europeans, and American heiresses of great wealth, was in vogue during the Edwardian era. Consuelo's godmother, Madame Yznaga, had forced her own daughter into such a loveless combination. Now Alva wanted a title for her own Consuelo, notwithstanding what Consuelo herself may want. Alva paraded a series of titled and foppish candidates past Consuelo, but none were to her liking, primarily because she was already secretly engaged to Winthrop Rutherfurd, whose father had accumulated an enormous fortune speculating in real estate in Manhattan. Consuelo and Winthrop were able to keep their engagement secret for a while, but when Alva discovered the affair, she ordered Consuelo to call off the engagement.

Consuelo Vanderbilt

Consuelo threatened to elope, at which point Alva threatened to kill Winthrop. Consuelo relented and Alva carted the headstrong young girl off to Europe for more title shopping. She finally settled on Charles Spencer-Churchill, Ninth Duke of Marlborough. All-in-all, the duke carried a very impressive pedigree and all the proper credentials of European nobility. He was first cousin to Winston Churchill and related to the Earl of Spencer whose granddaughter, Diana, would marry Prince Charles of Great Britain. The Duke had everything he needed—except money to replenish the coffers at Blenheim Palace. The Vanderbilts took care of that. After the wedding, the duke received a $2.5 million dollar marriage dowry ($75M when adjusted for inflation). As she made her obligatory vows, tears flowed down Consuelo's cheeks, under her veil. Their son, John Albert William Spencer-Churchill, became the tenth Duke of Marlborough, so the Vanderbilt bloodline still courses through British royal veins.

The fallout from Alva's high-handed treatment of their daughter, and Consuelo's forced marriage to the Duke of

Marlborough caused a major rift in the family. Shortly after Consuelo's wedding, Vanderbilt sued Alva for a divorce. Seven years later he married Anne Harriman, a daughter of the famous banking and railroad family. Ironically she was the widow of Winthrop Rutherfurd's brother, Lewis. The Harriman family owned homes in Aiken for over twenty years. The Harriman Polo Field off Sumter Street is part of their legacy to Aiken. Averell Harriman, Governor of New York and adviser to presidents, spent many winters in Aiken. Together with his brother Roland, he founded the private investment bank, Harriman Brothers. They merged their bank with Brown Brothers in 1931, forming the largest privately owned banking company in the world. It remains so today. Among its many notable partners were Prescott Bush and his father-in-law George Herbert Walker, both antecedents to two American presidents. The biennial Walker Cup amateur golf tournament between The United States and Great Britain is named for Mr. Walker.

Following her divorce from Vanderbilt, Alva married Oliver Hazard Perry Belmont of horse racing fame (Belmont Stakes and Belmont Park). In another strange quirk of fate, Alva Belmont became a major proponent of women's suffrage. She attended the international suffrage conference in London in 1909 as an alternate delegate. She was so favorably impressed with the passion and dedication of the women at the conference that she returned to New York and began to support their efforts, enthusiastically. She provided office space for the National Association for Women's Suffrage (NAWSA) on Fifth Avenue and persuaded the group to move its headquarters there from Washington.

Anna Shaw, an immigrant from England, and the first female Methodist minister in America, was influential in Alva Belmont's decision to back the league. She was president of NAWSA. It was she who traveled to Aiken and went to a small rural black Baptist church with Eulalie Salley to solicit signatures for the suffrage petition. It was her inability to overcome her stage fright that required Eulalie to speak in her place that day. When Shaw returned to New York, the organization received a large contribution from Alma Belmont, a portion of which was directed to South Carolina's chapters.

Consuelo and the Duke of Marlborough separated in 1906 and were divorced in 1921. The marriage was annulled in 1926, at the Duke's request. The Catholic Church justified the annulment by declaring that Consuelo had really loved Winthrop Rutherfurd and was coerced into the marriage by her mother. Consuelo continued to maintain a close relationship with certain members of the Duke's family, especially Winston Churchill.

Tommy Leiter

Tommy Leiter, another moneyed playboy of the gilded age, was the son of Joseph Leiter and grandson of Levi Leiter, a co-founder of Marshall Field Department Sores and Silver's Five and Dime stores.

Joseph Leiter bought 8000 acres near DuQuoin, Illinois and started a coal mining operation there. He created the town of Ziegler in honor of his mother's family and designed it to resemble Washington, D.C., with the company headquarters at the center. Deadly and protracted strikes led him to lease the mines to other operators.

Joseph Leiter is most famously remembered for attempting to corner the wheat market in 1897-98. He amassed 22 million bushels of wheat futures and drove the price up from 64 cents to $1.86 per bushel. The market ultimately collapsed and Leiter lost $10,000,000. His father, Levi covered his losses.

Joseph Leiter, was killed in a hunting accident in Louisiana, leaving Tommy as the only male heir to a huge fortune. Tommy later moved to Aiken with his wife Marion, who was from Alabama. They divorced and Tommy stayed on to throw his wild parties—beef stew dinners every Sunday night—in the large dining room he added to the rear of his house, "One Acre Farm," at 405 Colleton Avenue.

Joseph Leiter and his wife Juliette had come to Aiken in 1924 where they saw York House, located at York and Colleton.

Eulalie Salley had recently bought it, together with her mother and sister. Leiter told Eulalie that if she would decorate the house to his wife's specifications he would lease it for five years at a sum of $6,000 per year. Eulalie did as she was asked, even venturing north to buy furniture for the house. Juliette insisted on red shades throughout the house to provide "oomph."

When Eulalie was finished, Leiter refused to sign a lease. Eulalie was crestfallen and in danger of losing the house. Her friend, and Winter Colony resident, Frederick Snow was incensed at Leiter's actions. He told Eulalie not to worry. Snow prevailed on Francis Garvan, a friend from Westbury, Long Island, to lease the house. Garvan signed a five year lease. Garvan's wife, Mabel, was the sister of Diamond Jim Brady. The $30,000 for the lease more than offset the $10,000 purchase price and the cost of decorating the house.

Tommy Leiter bought "One Acre Farm" from his aunt, Mrs. Huston Rawls. The house was built in 1895 by Herman Hahn and sold to Joseph Harriman before it was completed. Mrs. Huston Rawls, sister to Juliette Leiter, later acquired the property. She in turn sold it to Tommy Leiter. Tommy's aunt, Bertha Munsell, lived in Columbia, S.C. She was a major player in the suffragist movement and hosted Eulalie Salley and other prominent members of the movement in her home there.

After Tommy Leiter divorced, he continued his weekly dinners and began to drink heavily. He liked to spice up his parties. On one occasion he had the local fire department pick up his guests with sirens blaring. The party was a huge success, but the firemen nearly lost their jobs. Eulalie cautioned Tommy that his premature aging and health problems were a result of his drinking.

"Yes, what you say is true," he told Eulalie, "but I had a hell of a good time getting to look like I do now."

Tommy Leiter lived life to the hilt and was a prominent fixture in the social whirl of Aiken for many years. He was famous for drinking only the first serving from a bottle of champagne. He said only the first taste was any good. There were dozens of partially filled champagne bottles on his back porch when he died in 1958. He was only 46, and he left behind a daughter. He is buried in Rock Creek Cemetery in Washington, D.C.

"One Acre Farm" was sold by the Leiter executor, Middleton Train, to Colgate Whitehead Darden for $40,500 on December 19, 1958. The property was inherited by Elizabeth J. Darden on October 28, 1967.

21

Friends in High Places

Spurred on by the encouragement she received from members of the Colony, Eulalie aggressively entered the Aiken real estate market. She achieved modest initial success, scoring small sales while building her reputation and her client base. One day she was sitting at her desk upstairs in the bank building when a couple walked in. The man crossed to her desk and extended his hand.

"My name is Charles Taylor. This is my wife Virginia. Some of my friends have recommended you as a knowledgeable real estate agent. My wife and I are interested in buying a winter home here. Can you show us what's available?"

"Of course, Mr. Taylor, please have a seat while I pull together some offerings that may appeal to you."

Eulalie prided herself on being able to determine what kind of property her clients would like, but she was having difficulty doing that with the Taylors. She knew they had money; Mrs. Taylor was dripping in diamonds. The Taylor family fortune was derived from an ice manufacturing business. He was trustee of a \$2.5 million dollar inheritance in addition to other holdings.

Some of Eulalie's clients were interested in horse properties while others only wanted a quiet cottage off the beaten path. Some were athletic and outgoing. Others were reclusive and private. "What were the Taylors?" she wondered. She decided to take a chance and follow her instincts. After a few minutes of searching through her files, she handed a sheaf of papers to Mr. Taylor.

"This is a home I think you might like," she said. The property had been part of a plantation going back many years. The farm had been called "Rye Patch," and the name stuck for the house, built on the property at the corner of Whiskey Road and Berrie Avenue. The asking price was $60,000, a noteworthy amount of money when one considers that the average house in Aiken probably was built for less than a thousand dollars.

Eulalie led the couple through the house and gave them an extensive tour of the grounds and outbuildings. There were formal gardens on the ten acre estate with ample room to add stables and paddocks. Easy access to the trails of Hitchcock Woods made the property a potential equestrian paradise. It turned out the Taylors were not as strongly into equestrian pursuits as their neighbors on Berrie Road, the Dolans and the Rutherfurds.

The property was surrounded by high walls constructed of bricks salvaged from a famous home in Savannah. Eulalie was fond of telling the story of several locals she had taken on a tour of the house. The Italianate brick wall featured arched gateways and occasional decorative piercings along its Whiskey Road façade.

"Why do these Yankees build those high brick walls?" a curious guest asked.

"For privacy," Eulalie said.

"Then why do they leave those big holes in the walls?"

"Oh, they left those so we could see their privacy."

"There's no reason to look further…" Mr. Taylor said at the end of their tour. Eulalie almost choked. She was afraid that she had misjudged her client and had showed him a property not to his liking. She hoped she hadn't committed a major *faux pas* that would drive him away. "I rather like this don't you, Virginia?"

He turned to Eulalie. "We'll take it," he said.

Eulalie's despondency turned to elation.

"We'd like you to get it ready for us when we come down," he said, and then jokingly added, "We like lamb chops and roses."

Eulalie didn't know whether to take him seriously or not, but she wasn't taking any chances. She had learned that the wealthy visitors expected to be handled with kid gloves and to have their every wish fulfilled. When the Taylors arrived for the season, Eulalie had the house furnished and decorated to perfection, their servants trained, and a scrumptious lamb chop luncheon laid out on the long, antique Duncan Phyfe dining table. There were roses everywhere. Mr. Taylor circled the table in amazement, finally turning to his wife and exclaiming,

"Pinch me, Virginia—I don't believe it. I just don't believe it."

Eulalie had learned the key to success with these coddled millionaires, and she would profit from it handsomely. She developed a motto to describe her services—"*We do everything but brush your teeth.*"

Edmund Pendleton Rogers purchased "Rye Patch" from the Taylors in 1931, shortly after his marriage to Dorothy Knox Goodyear, sister of Seymour Knox (The Balcony). Dorothy Goodyear was widowed in October of 1930 at the age of thirty-four when the Rolls-Royce driven by her husband Frank slammed into a tree. She and the other occupants were only slightly injured. Frank had a broken neck. She was left a widow with four children under the age of fourteen. The Goodyear family was prominent in Buffalo, having amassed a fortune in coal, iron, lumber and railroads—not tires. Edmund Roger's father was a wealthy banker and confidante of Franklin Roosevelt. The Rogers and the Roosevelts owned neighboring estates in Hyde Park, New York.

Edmund also owned a cottage at the exclusive Jekyll Island Club on the Georgia coast as well as a large mansion in Westbury, New York, near the Thomas Hitchcocks. When at Jekyll, the Goodyears stayed at the R. H. Macy cottage which was next door to the Rogers' cottage. Edmund and Dorothy met, fell in love, and were married eleven months after Goodyear's death.

The Rogers began immediately to improve their new winter home in Aiken. They expanded the house to accommodate their combined six children then added a guest house and two large stables with adjoining paddocks; Dorothy was an accomplished horsewoman. The tennis court, added by the Taylors, was removed and replaced with an elaborate rose garden. Additional formal gardens were also installed. However, the most astonishing addition to the house would not occur until 1938. The project began that summer when Edmund received a call from his brother Herman.

"Ed, I have a very special request of you and Dorothy," Herman began. "I will understand if you choose not to honor it, but it would be a great favor to Katherine and me if you did."

"What is it Herman? You sound so serious?"

"The Duke and Duchess of Windsor are planning their first visit to the United States since his abdication. They've asked if I can locate a place for them that is temperate in the winter and has the right social climate—and they do not wish to go to Florida. I immediately thought of Aiken. Do you think you could host them along with Katherine and me for a few weeks?" Edmund Rogers had to recover his wits before he could answer.

"I don't know what to say. I'm utterly flabbergasted. I know I'd like to accommodate you, but I'll have to speak to Dorothy before I commit. She's out riding with the Iselins at the moment. As soon as she comes in I'll talk to her and call you right back."

"Dorothy, come into the library," Edmund said when he heard the back door slam.

"Just let me clean up a bit first, it was very mucky in the paddock," she responded.

"No! Come right now!" he shouted.

She ran across the hall, fearing that he was ill.

"What's the matter, are you ill? I thought you were having a heart attack or something"

"No, nothing like that, but it's a wonder I didn't. You're not going to believe this. You'd better have a seat."

She prepared herself for the worst.

"I received a call from Herman this afternoon. He has a very unbelievable request of us. The Duke and Duchess of Windsor are coming to the states, and Herman wants us to host them for a few weeks."

It was Dorothy's term to be dumbstruck. She started to respond but couldn't form the words. Finally she became coherent.

"Oh my God! What an honor that would be. But, I don't know if we have room for them and your brother; along with all the others who'll be in and out. When are they coming?"

"Sometime after October I think. Why?" He could see the wheels turning in his wife's head as she counted off the months.

"That's five months. I'll do it if we can put an addition on the house for the Windsors by then."

"Done!" Edmund said. "I'll call Herman and tell him."

The Duchess and Herman's wife Katherine were old friends. They first met in San Diego where both their naval officer husbands were stationed. Katherine's husband was killed in WWI. Wallis stayed behind in San Diego when her husband was posted to a ship stationed in Shanghai. She was carrying on a relationship with an Argentine diplomat. When the affair ended, she sailed for China to join her husband, Earl Winfield Spencer. The reunion was short lived. Mrs. Spencer fell ill and left for medical treatment in Hong Kong. According to a Chinese diplomat's wife, the only Chinese Wallis learned while she was there was, "Boy, pass me the Champagne."

On a trip to Peking (Beijing), Wallis ran into her old friend Katherine who in the meantime, had married Herman Rogers, the wealthy scion of a New York banking family. Herman was in China to write a book. He had a small retreat outside Peking and invited Wallis to stay with them. During her stay in Peking with the Rogers, Mrs. Simpson had an affair with Galeazzo Ciano, future son-in-law of Italian dictator Benito Mussolini. Wallis Spencer returned to America after a year's sojourn in China. In 1927, she divorced the alcoholic Spencer after 11 years of an abusive, tempestuous, marriage.

Wallis met British shipping executive Ernest Simpson the next year. Like most men upon first meeting Wallis, Simpson was smitten with her feminine wiles. He returned to England and divorced his wife in order to marry Wallis. Wallis accepted Simpson's telegraphed proposal while staying at the Villa Lou Viei in Cannes, France, another home of Mr. and Mrs. Herman Rogers. She married Simpson and moved into a luxurious London flat full of servants. Luckily, Ernest was well heeled. Wallis and her widowed mother lost all their money in the Wall Street crash of 1929.

Wallis quickly made friends with those well connected in the royal social orbit, eventually meeting Prince Edward VIII, heir-apparent to the British crown. Edward was rumored to have at least three mistresses at the time. Wallis soon made him forget them all. He was besotted with his twice divorced, well travelled, well loved, paramour.

King George V died on January 20, 1936 and Edward ascended to the throne. The newly crowned king explored every option that would allow him to marry Wallis Warfield Spencer Simpson—and still keep the crown. If he married her without the blessings of the church—or the commonwealth governments—it would create a constitutional and religious crisis. The firestorm erupting around her forced Wallis to flee to the Roger's home in France. She just wanted to escape the embarrassment and ridicule of the London press. There were even threats on her life. The threats were so virulent that Rogers slept in an adjoining bedroom with a pistol under his pillow. Wallis was being pressured from all sides to give up the king. After an onslaught of petitions she was finally persuaded to do so. A royal emissary drew up a letter of renunciation. She reluctantly agreed to sign it, but Edward would not hear of it. He would give up the throne before he would give up Wallis. On December 10, 1936, King Edward VIII abdicated the British throne, handing the crown to his brother Albert, who became King George VI.

Edward fled to the Eugene de Rothschild estate, Schloss Enzesfeld, in Austria. He waited there until Wallis' divorce from Simpson was finalized. Several venues were suggested for their marriage. For varying reasons each was rejected. Wallis turned once more to Herman Rogers, who in turn contacted a French-born American friend who owned a chateau near Monts, France. Would his friend, Charles Bedaux, host the wedding of the Duke of Windsor to Wallis Simpson at his Chateau Candé? Yes, he would. Wallis went there immediately upon receiving word that the divorce from Simpson was final. Edward joined her straightaway.

Mary, the Queen Mother, through her son King George VI, forbade any of her subjects to attend the wedding. A crisis arose over finding an Anglican cleric to marry them. A brave priest, the Reverend Robert Jardine, Vicar of St. Paul's in Darlington, County Durham, risked ex-communication from the Anglican Church in order to perform the ceremony. Happily, he was not ex-communicated.

By all accounts the Duke and Duchess of Windsor enjoyed their stay in Aiken immensely. They were seen at several venues around town: Palmetto Golf Club, Willcox Hotel, Hitchcock Woods, Whitney Field, as well as many private homes. One place they were not seen was at "Rye Patch," for the Rogers had bricked up the archways and the pierced openings in their wall. Plain folks could no longer see their privacy. The closed arches are still visible from Whiskey Road.

The Duke loved to play cards. It is doubtful that the former Prince of Wales had enjoyed many opportunities for casual games of poker or bridge in his former royal circumstance. He was now able to indulge himself in the friendly confines of this small oasis of rich, famous, and friendly people. Nancy Potter Bourne McKim, a former Pond's Cold Cream model, commented on the Duke's card skills.

"The Duke loved to play cards, but he was not very good at it. We would have to teach him everything, and then we would take his money."

Robert and Nancy McKim entertained the Duke of Windsor in their elegant home "Box Stall" at 621 Colleton Avenue. The

McKims had three children, including Lily Pulitzer of fashion fame.

Robert McKim's first wife was Lillian Stokes Bostwick, granddaughter of Jabez Bostwick, a partner in the Standard Oil Trust. Miss Bostwick was an alumna of the Fermata School. Lillian's brothers George, Dunbar and Albert were all famous for their polo skills and were all prominent members of the Aiken Winter Colony.

After her divorce from McKim, Lillian married Henry Ogden Phipps whose grandfather was the second largest shareholder in Carnegie Steel. Phipps became a partner at the Smith, Barney investment firm and later became managing director of the Bessemer Trust which was formed to manage the Carnegie Steel assets of the Phipps' family heirs. The trust expanded in later years to serve other client fortunes which had been amassed during the "Golden Age." Today, Bessemer Trust manages $65,000,000,000 for 2100 families.

Lillian's "career" with Phipps included the building and decorating of their fifteen homes and establishing the Phipps Museum in Palm Beach, Florida. Her daughter, Lillian McKim, founded the Lilly Pulitzer fashion design house.

Ogden Phipps also became famous in horse racing circles. He inherited "Bold Ruler," a Preakness winner, and mated him to the Chenery family's mare, "Something Royal." Phipp's amazing good fortune in the business world deserted him on this occasion. The two families agreed to let a coin toss decide who would own the foal. Penny Chenery called heads, and the coin came up heads. She had won. The foal's name—"Secretariat."

When Louise Hitchcock discovered that Eulalie had sold "Rye Patch" to the Taylors she stormed into Eulalie's office, mad as a wet hen.

"I understand you have sold "Rye Patch" to the Charles Taylors," she said menacingly. "You know I am very particular about who is in Aiken's Colony, and I *don't* find them in the social register."

Un-intimidated by Mrs. Hitchcock's daunting presence,

Eulalie replied, "If you don't find them in the social register, then there is something wrong with your register. They are lovely people. I am certain you will like them."

"I'll call on them tomorrow," Louise said huffily as she turned on her heel and stormed out.

True to her word, Louise Hitchcock did call on the Taylors, and she invited them to lunch. It was well understood that if a new resident of the Colony was not invited to the Hitchcocks for lunch soon after arriving in Aiken they would receive the Aiken "frost" and be cast into the outer darkness.

Celestine Eustis was tacitly recognized as the Queen of Aiken's Winter Colony, from her arrival in 1873 until her death in February, 1921 after she had suffered a fainting spell while participating in a foxhunt. She was 84 years old at the time. Her niece, Louise Hitchcock, was the heir-apparent to the throne. In truth, Louise Eustis Hitchcock had already assumed the role of regent to her aging aunt and was well prepared to accept the crown. Her *Tante* Celestine had left an enduring legacy for her adopted city—one that continues to the present day. Her gifts to Aiken, both tangible and spiritual, served to mold a unique community, one that *Lulie* Hitchcock embraced and built upon.

In 1878, five years after Celestine's move to Aiken, a tornado demolished the historic wooden chapel which was built in 1867 at the corner of Park Avenue and York Street. Celestine Eustis, a devout Catholic, immediately contacted friends in New York.

"Who is the best church architect in America," she asked.

"James Renwick" was the answer.

Renwick was world renowned for designing grand cathedrals and public buildings. Among his most famous projects were St. Patrick's Cathedral in New York and the Smithsonian Castle in Washington, D.C. It didn't hurt Celestine's chances of commissioning Renwick that he had been chosen by Louise Hitchcock's maternal grandfather, W.W. Corcoran, to design and build the Corcoran Gallery in Washington.

Less than two years later, the new Chapel of Ste. Clare of the Holy Cross was dedicated. The Gothic revival chapel features stained glass windows commissioned by Miss Eustis. They were designed by Nicolas Lorin of Chartres, France. Lorin had also designed the Founder's Windows for St. Patrick's Cathedral in New York.

The growing influx of winter residents—heavily Catholic—soon outgrew the capacity of St. Clare's quaint chapel. A larger sanctuary was necessary to accommodate the swelling congregation. In 1905, with major assistance from Celestine Eustis and her friends, a new cathedral, also in the Gothic Revival convention, was completed. A life size, bronze, statue of Madonna and Child by Gustave Doré stands in the vestibule of the elaborate church. It was the gift of Beatrice Kennedy Lamontagne, another winter resident. The statue was damaged in a fire on March 7, 1966. Most of the damage was confined to the statue's base, sparing the painted figures of Mother and Child.

St. Mary's Help of Christians

Miss Eustis was also very interested in the natural beauty of Aiken. She contributed much time, money and effort to the beautification of her beloved village. She donated 200 acres on the western side of town to the city in 1897 for Eustis Park. The city sold forty of those acres to the developers of the Park in the Pines Hotel on Richland Avenue. The hotel, a clubhouse, and a squash court were built on the property. Fifteen years to the day, after the Highland Park Hotel was consumed by flames in 1898, the Park in the Pines went up in smoke. Only the dining room wing was spared destruction. The loss of this grand hotel together with the Highland Park was devastating to the economy of Aiken. Accommodations for hundreds of winter visitors had vanished.

Park in the Pines

Highland Park Hotel – Pre 1898 Fire

Highland Park Hotel - 1914

22
The Willcox

Frederick Willcox emigrated to Aiken from the English Midland city of Cheshire in 1891 along with his Swedish-born wife, Elise Wellborn. Fred worked as a chef at the Highland Park Hotel until it burned. He then bought a large one-and-one-half story Victorian house at the northwest corner of Colleton and Chesterfield and opened a catering service. Large verandahs ran along the full length of the house on the east and west sides. Willcox later enclosed both verandahs in glass, converting them into formal dining rooms. Kitchens and prep rooms occupied the center and rear of the house. The family's living quarters were located upstairs. Their business was successful from the outset. There was a huge demand for their upscale catering services. The two sons, Albert and Frederick, worked in the Willcox kitchens.

A famous chef, Ernest Wiehl, was brought in from Europe to assist Elise. He expanded the kitchen and recruited assistants to supplement his own superlative culinary skills. He purchased a house across from the Willcox at Colleton and Newberry. His wife fell in love with the pale yellow color of the siding on the house and called it her "Jasmine Cottage." Each room had its own fireplace. The original house still stands and has been lovingly restored by a couple from France who have adopted Aiken as their home.

Much of the social life of Aiken had previously revolved

around the Highland Park Hotel, and when it burned in 1898 there was a gaping hole in the social fabric of the colony. Days after the smoke cleared, Louise Hitchcock called on Frederick Willcox.

"Fred, I know you are already busy with engagements throughout Aiken, but I have a favor to ask of you anyway."

"Mrs. Hitchcock," he answered in his heavily accented Midlands brogue, "you know that I will always help you in any way that I can."

"The fire at the Highland Park Hotel has forced many people to seek accommodations in rooming houses, hotels and private homes," Louise said. "That has placed a heavy burden on all the existing facilities to try to fill the void. I know that you have taken in some of the displaced roomers, as have several other members of the community, and I appreciate that. However, I would like for you to go beyond that and consider expanding your operation permanently to provide dining facilities and guest rooms."

"I have already considered that, Mrs. Hitchcock, but it will be very expensive, and I haven't really accumulated an adequate amount of savings yet."

"Don't you worry about that Fred? You just go down and talk to Henry Dibble. I'm sure he will provide all the funds you need." She smiled and winked. Fred suspected that she had been to see the banker before she came to see him, and the financial skids had been greased. He never knew if she underwrote the expansion or not. It didn't really matter. The Winter Colony continued to burst at the seams and Fred Willcox prospered along with it.

The Willcox – circa 1905

In 1900, with that push from Mrs. Hitchcock, Fred constructed a three-story rectangular addition in the French Mansard style to the west of the original Willcox house. The two buildings were connected by a *port cochere* and an entrance to the hotel. The demand was so great for rooms that a second guest building was added in 1906 when an existing two-and-one-half story home at Colleton and Newberry was purchased, redesigned and converted into guest rooms. The new wing was connected to the original hotel by an enclosed walkway.

The influx of colonists continued unabated and by 1910 Fred Willcox expanded once more. He demolished the enclosed walkway between the two hotel wings and replaced it with an elliptical ballroom. Mr. Willcox died suddenly in 1924 and his son Albert took over the management of the hotel. Albert brought the hotel to its present configuration in 1928 when the ballroom was razed and replaced with a three floor structure that bridged the original two hotel wings. This final addition, in Colonial Revival style with a columned portico, featured a large receiving room/lounge with fireplaces at both ends and a restaurant to the rear.

Albert completed the addition just in time for the collapse of Wall Street in 1929. The ensuing depression devastated mainstream America but hardly created a ripple among the super-rich. A few families curtailed their Aiken visits, but they were quickly supplanted by new generations from the wealthy dynasties created in the preceding "Golden Age."

The guest lists at the Willcox through the early decades of the twentieth-century read like a "Who's-Who" of the social, political, sports and celebrity worlds: Roosevelt, Astor, Baruch, Churchill, Windsor, Vanderbilt, Astaire, Grace, Harriman, Crosby, Mountbatten, Carnegie, Eisenhower, Arden, Duke, McLean, etc. The list is as long as it is impressive. That such a small hostelry, tucked away in a remote corner of South Carolina, attracted so many of the world's elites boggles the imagination. When the Duke of Windsor returned later to attend the Masters Tournament at Augusta National, he requested a room at the Willcox. The hotel was solidly booked, and his request was denied.

Local lore credits the bellman of the Willcox with devising a most ingenious method of determining which unannounced guests should be accepted at the hotel—most visitors were either known to the staff or recommended by residents of the colony. The bellman would greet the unknown newcomer at the hotel entrance while surreptitiously examining his footwear. If the shoes did not originate from Peel or Maxwell in London he would shake his head as a signal to Mr. Willcox that the guest did not meet the hotel's lofty standards.

The Willcox remained the hub of social activity until the 1940's when the attention of the nation turned to war. Many still came to Aiken, but its preeminence as the home of the Winter Colony began to decline. Albert continued to run the hotel until his retirement in 1957 when he sold the hotel to Joseph Eways, an Oriental rug dealer from Palestine. Attempts to bring the hotel in line with other modern inns met with mixed results, and Eways sought to convert the property to other uses. There was even a petition to have the structure demolished. That petition was defeated by a single vote of the head of Aiken's engineering department. Finally a major renovation was carried out in 1987, restoring the hotel to its original glory. The Willcox was purchased by the Garrett Hotel Group in 2000, and they embarked on further renovations and modernization.

In September of 2009, Shannon and Geoff Ellis, who were married in Aiken at the Green Boundary Club in 2002, returned from their sojourn in New Zealand to open a restaurant at the historic inn. When it became apparent that the then current owners were planning to cease operations, the couple jumped at the opportunity to purchase the property. In the succeeding years the Willcox has regained its prominent role in Aiken's social life. It has attracted an international clientele while still maintaining its appeal to locals from all levels of society. Accolades and honors have poured in from several major magazines and hotel rating agencies. Once again the Willcox has become, as it was for the Winter Colony, "The Living Room of Aiken."

23

Lucy Mercer Rutherford

For a span of twenty years, the Willcox is reputed to have played host to a frequent yet clandestine visitor. His arrivals and departures were always shrouded in mystery. Few outside his closely guarded entourage were even aware of the visits, and there are no public records of how often he came. Those who knew were either sworn to secrecy or chose to remain silent out of respect for the man and his position. This historical figure, the one man most responsible for defeating Hitler and preserving western democracy, came and went with barely a trace. There were no press reports bearing an Aiken byline that announced his arrivals and departures as there were for other noteworthy visitors. Unlike his trips to Yalta and Tehran, where he met with Churchill and Stalin, Franklin Delano Roosevelt's visits to Aiken dealt not with the affairs of the world but with the affairs of the heart.

Lucy Page Mercer was the daughter of Carroll and Minnie Mercer, both descended from prominent and wealthy Maryland and Virginia families. By the 1880's Carroll's father had blown through most of the family inheritance and Minnie Tunis, in the fashion of the day, had married Percy Norcorp, a foppish British swell whom she believed would expand her social influence on the Washington scene. As it turned out, Percy Norcorp's main talent was in finding ways to squander Minnie's inheritance.

Drinking, gambling and philandering were his major pursuits. Three years and a sizable fortune later, Minnie defied societal taboos and divorced Percy Norcorp.

At twenty-three, the statuesque, dark-eyed, beauty was acclaimed the most beautiful woman in the nation's capitol, a fact not lost on Carroll Mercer. Having seen his fortunes and life-style diminished, Mercer, in 1880, followed in the footsteps of other impoverished gentry and joined the military, using family connections to gain a commission in the Marine Corps. While serving aboard the *USS Richmond,* Mercer found himself temporarily in Washington and immediately fell back into the social whirl of the city. He met Minnie Tunis Norcorp at a party and immediately embarked on a crusade to woo her. The combination of her wealth and beauty were irresistible. He was no slouch in the looks department either. Carroll Mercer stood over six feet in his socks with blond hair and gray eyes.

Mercer wangled a temporary two month assignment in the D.C. area where he wooed and won Minnie's affections before he was shipped off to the Isthmus of Panama where the construction of a canal was underway. His tempestuous nature landed him in the brig and he was sent back for a court martial in New York where he was given a two-year suspension and stripped of half his pay. He served out the suspension and was shipped off to London.

The relationship with Minnie was a haphazard affair. When her divorce from Percy was finalized, she followed Carroll to London. They were married in June of 1888 at St. Martin in the Fields by Queen Victoria's chaplain. She followed her new husband to assignments in Turkey and Egypt, where she became pregnant. After giving birth to a daughter, Violetta, in 1890, it was not hard to convince Mercer to resign his commission and return to the States.

The couple settled into a grand house on Rhode Island Avenue in Washington. Minnie had the three prerequisites necessary for overcoming the stigma of her divorce: breeding, money and good looks. Within weeks they had resumed their former position in Washington society. They were seen at every major affair and belonged to all the best clubs. Spectators were in awe when Minnie passed in her large brougham pulled by a pair of matched black stallions and driven by a liveried coachman, as well as being attended by an equally bespangled footman. It was into this milieu that Lucy Mercer was born on April 26, 1891.

The glittering life the Mercers were living carried a high price tag. Their lavish spending, when combined with the "Panic of 1893" and the subsequent stock market crash, severely diminished Minnie's fortune. Recriminations and quarreling ensued. Minnie blamed Carroll for their dwindling fortune and Carroll escaped into drink. This was the acrimonious environment in which Violetta and Lucy were raised.

Fast approaching financial ruin, Carroll jumped at the chance to re-enlist. In April, 1898, when the Spanish-American war broke out, he was commissioned a major and joined the troops in Cuba as a supply officer. Despite his and Minnie's best efforts to extend his military service at the end of the war, Carroll was discharged. The drinking and quarreling recommenced and by 1903 their money was depleted. The couple separated and Minnie faced the embarrassing prospect of having to get a job to support her two girls. She took them to New York, thinking she would be able to find a position as a decorator for the wealthy families there. Through her contacts she was able to secure several male patrons to her business. Wagging tongues suggested that the gentlemen were paying Minnie for more than her design services.

Minnie, recognizing her own diminished role in the Society Blue Book, was determined that her daughters would not suffer the same fate. Through means not fully understood, she was able to secure one-year appointments for both Violetta and Lucy in a prestigious London finishing school. Now eighteen and twenty, the girls reunited with Minnie as she returned to Washington and a reunion with Carroll Mercer. Despite society columns announcing the reconciliation, none ever really occurred.

While Carroll bounced from pillar-to-post in his downward alcoholic spiral, Minnie resumed her career in home decoration.

She started receiving a small monthly stipend from an anonymous Mercer relative which allowed the three women to live in relative comfort. Violetta pursued a career in nursing while Lucy worked with her mother in the fashionable interior decorating firm of Elsie Cobb Wilson. Wilson was a decorator famous for satisfying the eccentric whims of the Washington elite.

Among those familiar with the Wilson shop was Anna Roosevelt, sister to the former president Theodore Roosevelt and to Eleanor Roosevelt's late father Elliot. Auntie Bye, as she was affectionately known in the family, saw her niece Eleanor drowning in the social minutiae that was the lot of the wives of senior government officials. Eleanor, as the wife of the Assistant Secretary of the Navy, Franklin Roosevelt, was attempting to fulfill these overwhelming social obligations while simultaneously trying to settle into a new home with three rambunctious children. Eleanor had been orphaned at ten and then parceled out to various relatives for rearing. She suffered from a debilitating lack of self-image. She did not inherit the good looks of her parents and was constantly reminded of that by her grandmother. Her chaotic childhood, together with her extreme lack of confidence, denied her the social skills expected of someone in her position. Auntie Bye recognized in Lucy Mercer all the character, breeding and organizational skills that were sorely lacking in her niece. She called on Eleanor and suggested that Lucy Mercer might be the answer to her prayers.

Where Eleanor might be described as homely, Lucy was a radiant beauty. Jonathan Daniels, an assistant and press secretary to Roosevelt—and later biographer to Lucy Mercer—said, "Every man who ever knew her, fell in love with her."

Thus began the unlikely pairing of two women who would play such dramatic roles in the life and career of Franklin Delano Roosevelt—and in the resulting arc of world history.

Franklin D. Roosevelt

Eleanor Roosevelt

Lucy Mercer

In the winter of 1914, Lucy was welcomed with open arms by Mrs. Roosevelt and her three children. Eleanor was to bear two more sons during Lucy's tenure as her social secretary. While her employer was unprepared for the demands of social life in Washington's political jungle, Lucy had been schooled in all the graces required to do battle with the arbiters of social correctness in the city. She quickly organized Eleanor's engagements and responded to her voluminous correspondence. The children loved her and she became an extension of the family. Within days she conquered the mountain of mail lying in the middle of the living room floor and brought order to her employer's social calendar. Her duties ranged far and wide, from minding the children, to walking the dog, to running errands. All this activity did not escape the eye of the master of the household.

It is not known precisely when FDR took more than a fatherly interest in his wife's young aide—he was almost ten years her senior. From documents released over the years it is evident that the affair persisted for a long time, maybe as much as three years. The affair may have gone undiscovered forever had Eleanor not chanced upon a small packet of letters neatly tied in a red bow. Even then she may have respected her husband's privacy, had not the letters been addressed in a most familiar hand. The letters were in her husband's luggage as she unpacked after his WWI trip to the battlefront in 1918. FDR contracted influenza while on the trip and was rushed home. Millions of people around the world were dying in the worldwide epidemic of the Spanish Flu. Roosevelt very nearly became one of its casualties. Eleanor met his ship at the dock in New York with an ambulance, a doctor and two aides. They whisked the nearly delirious Roosevelt off to the family estate in Hyde Park where he could be ministered to properly. There is little doubt that had he been in full control of his faculties, Eleanor would never have gained access to his luggage and the incriminating letters. Roosevelt was too intelligent and politically astute for that to happen under normal circumstances, but happen it did.

It is probable that Eleanor had got wind of the affair long before the letters emerged. Franklin had found excuse after excuse to avoid joining his family in the summers at their Campobello retreat off the coast of Maine. Eleanor also knew that Lucy was attending social events and cruising on the Chesapeake with FDR on his Navy yacht, "Sylph." When she returned from Campobello in the fall of 1917, Eleanor peremptorily dismissed Lucy. She had not discussed it with Franklin. He was taken by complete surprise.

Five days later, Lucy was at the Navy Yard receiving her physical examination to become a Yeoman 3rd Class in the United States Navy. She was assigned to the Office of the Assistant Secretary of the Navy and occupied the same building as FDR, adjacent to the White House. With Mrs. Roosevelt back in town Franklin needed to be more circumspect in his rendezvous with

Lucy. He knew from his wife's tone and demeanor that she suspected what was going on.

Former Vice-President Levi Morton owned an estate, "Ellerslie," grander even than Hyde Park and just up the Hudson in Rheinbeck, New York. Franklin had been there many times to visit the Morton children. Edith Morton, Levi's daughter, was married to William Eustis, who would become General "Black Jack" Pershing's personal secretary in the war. Eustis was also the brother of Celestine Eustis of Aiken. William Eustis bought an old plantation in Leesburg, Virginia, just outside Washington, and restored it to its ante-bellum glory. "Oatlands" was famous for the many influential people entertained there.

None would prove more influential than the dashing young man that brought the beautiful Lucy Mercer to their home. Little did Edith know that her childhood friend would one day become leader of the free world and the most powerful president of the twentieth-century. She was just doing a favor for an old friend and turning a blind eye to his indiscretions. Lucy attended many lavish dinners at "Oatlands" and met many important people there. One such person was Winthrop Rutherfurd. He had married Alice Morton, Edith's sister. Alice died on June 19, 1917 during the period when FDR and Lucy were frequent visitors to "Oatlands." Rutherfurd was bereaved and in mourning, but he certainly must have noticed the beautiful and vivacious young woman on Franklin's arm.

Whether through sheer bravado or a feeling of invincibility, Roosevelt became ever more careless in his trysts with Lucy. His activities were the fodder for cocktail party gossip. His cousin, Alice Roosevelt Longworth, called to tell FDR she had seen him dashing about the Virginia countryside with a woman who was not Eleanor. Alice, who was a free-spirit, took to inviting Franklin and Lucy to her parties—without Eleanor. Alice had a love/hate relationship with her first cousin, Eleanor. They were on opposite sides of the political spectrum. Alice, daughter of TR, was a staunch Republican. The "heart-on-her-sleeve" Eleanor was a liberal Democrat to the core. Alice was famous for imitating Eleanor's high-pitched voice and serious demeanor. When she was chastised for making fun of Eleanor and abetting Franklin's infidelity, she said, "Franklin deserved a good time. He was married to Eleanor." Ironically, both Eleanor and Alice spent much of their childhood with Auntie Bye, the solid rock to which the entire family clung. Alice's mother died in childbirth, a calamity for which TR never forgave his daughter. After her birth in February, 1884, Teddy turned Alice over to Bye's care and headed west.

Alice Roosevelt married Nicholas Longworth, a congressman from Ohio who would become Speaker of the House of Representatives and have a congressional office building named for him. They were married in the White House in 1906. Six years later, when he threw his support behind the Republican nominee, William Howard Taft, Longworth became *persona non grata* to the Oyster Bay Roosevelts. TR, who ran against Taft on the third-party Bullmoose ticket, never forgave him. The Longworth marriage was tempestuous to say the least. His drinking, gambling and philandering led Alice to seek a divorce, which the family steadfastly refused to permit. Her reaction was to become even more fractious and undisciplined. She was rumored to have had several affairs. The couple's only child was widely thought to actually be that of Senator William E. Borah, facetiously known as the "Stallion of Idaho." That resulted in Alice being referred to as "Aurora Borah Alice."

Alice Roosevelt Longworth

Eleanor's immediate response to finding Lucy's letters was total shock and disbelief. When Franklin was sufficiently recovered, she decided to confront him with the letters and then to offer him a divorce. When Sara Delano Roosevelt, the president's strong willed mother, was told of her son's indiscretion and of Eleanor's offer of a divorce, she would have none of it. She had worked too long and too hard to advance her son's political career to see it founder on the rocks of a silly, extramarital, affair. She forbade a divorce and commanded Franklin to end the dalliance at once and to apologize to Eleanor. Roosevelt acquiesced. The two women elicited a promise from FDR that he would end the relationship and there would be no more affairs. Eleanor accepted him at his word, but she never forgave him. From that day forward, the two lived as political helpmeets but not as husband and wife. Lucy slipped from sight. There were none of the scandalous stories that would have filled the airwaves in modern times. The press and FDR's staff respected his privacy.

Lucy Mercer re-emerged into the social spotlight in 1920 when she became the second wife of Winthrop Rutherfurd, the scion of a New York real estate fortune. His father, Lewis Rutherfurd, besides being a very astute real estate investor, was a world renowned amateur astronomer. He was the first to take telescopic photographs of the moon. The Rutherford crater on the moon is named in his honor.

Winthrop Rutherfurd had been secretly engaged to Consuelo Vanderbilt before her mother ended the affair. The scars from that romance left him altar shy. It was not until 1901 at the age of thirty-eight, and after becoming the most eligible bachelor in all of the New York society columns, that Rutherfurd married his first wife, Alice Morton. She was the daughter of former Vice President Levi Morton. Winthrop built an 18,000 square foot mansion for his new bride and named it "Allamuchy," taken from the nearby village of that name—which in turn was derived from an old Indian settlement. The property was adjacent to his father's equally impressive estate, "Tranquility."

Both are located in the rolling hills of New Jersey near the Delaware Water Gap. Alice died in 1917 of a ruptured appendix at the age of 38. She left Winthrop a widower with four sons and a daughter.

Rutherfurd first met Lucy Mercer while on a visit to "Oatlands", his sister's estate in Leesburg, Virginia. It is not known how well they got to know each other then. Winthrop was still in mourning and concerned about rearing his five children alone, but he must have taken note of the striking beauty on Franklin Roosevelt's arm. Their next meeting would occur in Aiken, South Carolina where they both visited in the winter months. Winthrop had many friends in the sporting world who lived in Aiken. Lucy loved the little village and its warm, southern hospitality. It appealed to something in her own gentle nature.

There were so many mutual attractions to Aiken that the Rutherfurds were thrown together at multiple social events. She was inevitably the most beautiful woman present, and he was the most attractive and distinctive unattached man. He remembered Lucy from "Oatlands." He immediately fell in love with the charismatic beauty. Someone described Lucy's smile as the most beguiling in the world—rivaling the *Mona Lisa.* Another remarked, "I think she was the most beautiful woman I ever saw. It was a beauty the artist and the photographer didn't catch. Her beauty was in her expression and her graceful manner."

Despite the nearly thirty-year age difference, the couple married in February of 1920, less than two years after the discovery of the "scarlet letters" and less than two years after Alice's death. Lucy was approaching thirty years of age, which in those days was considered borderline spinsterhood. No doubt the shaky family financial situation and her mother's influence figured into her decision to accept the aristocratic and dapper Rutherfurd's proposal of marriage.

By all accounts the Rutherford/Mercer marriage was loving and reciprocal. He adored her, and she doted on him. That is not to say that their relationship bore the same degree of passion nor the intense immediacy of hers with Roosevelt, but it was obvious that they cared deeply for each other and there was nothing Lucy might want that Winthrop would not provide. He provided a secure port from the storm she had passed through, and she provided a warm and loving household for his children, all of whom came to accept Lucy as their surrogate mother.

The Rutherfurd's only child, Barbara, was born on June 14, 1922. With young Barbara in tow, they returned to Aiken. Winthrop was bent on extending his fox terrier breeding operation to Aiken—the Rutherfurd terriers won best in show three consecutive years at the Westminster Kennel Club. He also had an abiding interest in horses, and he needed sufficient property to indulge that passion as well.

The Rutherfurds were introduced to Eulalie Salley shortly after their marriage, by Bertha Munsell and her sister, Mrs. Thomas Leiter. Bertha and Eulalie had toiled together in the quest for women's suffrage. Bertha was visiting her sister in the Leiter's new Aiken home and the two invited Eulalie to lunch. During the meal the subject of Eulalie's real estate business arose. Bertha insisted that Eulalie allow her to introduce some of her friends as potential clients. Eulalie demurred.

"Thank you, Bertha. I appreciate the offer, but I feel more comfortable just dealing with the local Aiken folks."

"Don't be silly," Bertha said. "These people are going to buy from somebody and it might as well be you. After all, who knows more about the comings and goings of this town than you?"

That afternoon, Eulalie Salley was introduced to Mr. and Mrs. Winthrop Rutherfurd, and a lifelong friendship was born. Lucy and Eulalie became intimate friends and entertained each other often. It is possible that no other person, apart from her husband—and FDR—was as close to Lucy as Eulalie Salley. Mr. Rutherfurd held Eulalie in the same high esteem and turned to her for advice about real estate as well as personal matters. Her charm and discretion were contagious.

The Rutherfords purchased a large estate on Berrie Road, near Rye Patch and across from the Palmetto Golf Club. It consisted of several acres and had access to Hitchcock Woods.

It was an ideal spot for breeding hunting dogs and raising horses. The Rutherfurds, with his brood of five and their own daughter Barbara, spent much of the year in Aiken at the house on Berrie Road.

Unfortunately, the original wood structure burned. Winthrop decided to replace it with a three-story, French Mansard, design constructed of Flemish-bond brick that was essentially indestructible. He engaged Julian Peabody, son-in-law of Thomas Hitchcock, to design the house. In 1928, the construction cost was $100,000. It was the largest sum ever paid for a house in Aiken. When the family moved into the baronial home it was christened "Ridgeley Hall." It was one of the few homes in Aiken equipped with an elevator. No one can be certain, but some believe this addition was made at the behest of Lucy. On August 25, 1921, Franklin Roosevelt had been diagnosed as having poliomyelitis—he would never walk unaided again. Lucy certainly was apprised of the president's condition by some of his closest aides and friends. Someday, the only man she had truly loved with all her heart would surely visit Ridgeley Hall.

Ridgeley Hall

Several times during the years after the onset of his polio, letters to Lucy from FDR concerning his schedule and whereabouts seem to indicate they could have met on numerous occasions. Most historians disagree on the number of times Lucy and Franklin saw each other between 1918 and Roosevelt's inauguration as president in 1933. On that occasion she stayed with her sister Violetta at 2238 Q Street in Washington. Violetta had married Dr. William Marbury and was living a comfortable, if not extravagant, life. A limousine, dispatched from the White House, picked Lucy up and drove her through the throngs to the East Portico. The driver handed Lucy a ticket to the event, and she proceeded to a spot discreetly removed from the ceremonies. She watched with a breaking heart as the formerly vibrant and physically robust man she had known and loved, struggled with such difficulty to stand in his metal braces. She saw him rest his hand on the 1686 Roosevelt family bible and repeat the words of Chief Justice Charles Evans Hughes that made him the 32nd president of the United States. Eleanor and Sara, the two women who had ended FDR's affair with Lucy, flanked the new president while his son Jimmy offered a steadying arm. For the fifteen years of his presidency Franklin Roosevelt always kept Lucy close in spirit—as well as in person—whenever possible.

Sara, Franklin and Eleanor Roosevelt - 1920

There is ample evidence that they spoke on the phone and exchanged correspondence hundreds of times. There are also numerous entries in White House logs marking the arrival and departure of a "Mrs. Paul Johnson." This lady's calls were always put through without question by the White House switchboard, and no one doubted that the name was a pseudonym for Lucy Mercer Rutherfurd.

On March 19, 1944, Winthrop Rutherfurd died in Aiken after a long and debilitating illness. He was 82. Lucy took him home to Allamuchy for burial next to Alice, his first wife. Lucy's 24 years of devotion to her husband were at an end. She had received condolences from the president, along with a request that she come to Hyde Park. Eleanor was away, and it would be an opportune time to visit.

Ignoring the prospective impropriety of allowing such a short span of time between Winty's death and the invitation, she accepted. Daisy Suckley, a cousin as well as longtime friend and confidante of FDR, said his spirits were visibly lifted, and he was noticeably more energized upon hearing that Lucy was coming to see him. Daisy first met Lucy shortly after Roosevelt contracted polio. He sent her to Aiken to give a full account of his illness to Lucy. That is indicative of how staunchly devoted he was to keeping the relationship alive and to his utter faith in Daisy's discretion.

Immediately upon her arrival, in a government car from the Poughkeepsie station, Roosevelt insisted that Lucy accompany him around the estate in his specially equipped Ford. No sooner had Lucy alighted from the government limousine than Franklin ushered her into his Ford. He took her for an extensive tour of the Hyde Park property. He showed her "Top Cottage" explaining his plans to retire there. There are no records of their conversations that day, but it is certain that they caught up on the intimate details of each other's lives since their last meeting. So much had happened: Winthrop's death, the War, his illness and the million other diversions that occupied his every waking moment.

At 6:30 on Sunday evening, Lucy was back at the station in Poughkeepsie, readying to return to Allamuchy. She was leaving behind the idyllic setting that might have been her own, had cruel fate not intervened.

Almost immediately following his trip to Hyde Park, FDR went for a thorough physical examination at Bethesda Naval hospital. His new doctor, Howard Bruenn, recommended a period of complete rest. It was thought the president would return to Hyde Park where the entire family was gathering for the holidays. Instead, he had his aides contact his old friend and counselor Bernard Baruch to see if he could "hole up" for a few days at "Hobcaw," Baruch's baronial estate near Georgetown, South Carolina. "Of course you can," came back the answer, and FDR was off for what became a four-week respite from the rigors of the war and governing. It was not entirely coincidental that Lucy Rutherfurd lived only a few hours up the road in Aiken from the "Hobcaw Barony." The 23,000 acre estate offered all the privacy any king or potentate could desire. It was tailor-made for FDR and Lucy. He was able to re-charge for what would become the final year of his presidency—and his life. Mr. Baruch graciously sacrificed enough of his priceless gas ration stamps for Lucy to make the 140-mile trip. Earlier that year, Lucy had moved from Ridgeley Hall to a more manageable house at 516 Marion Street. That cottage, "Tip Top Too," was built in 1926 by Allan Pinkerton, founder of the famous detective agency.

That summer—shortly after FDR decided to accept his party's nomination for a fourth term—he longed to get back to Hyde Park for a period of relaxation and restoration. Over Labor Day weekend he scheduled a private train to take him home. Reporters traveling with the president were told to prepare for a nineteen-hour journey. They didn't understand how it could take that long to cover the 300 miles from D.C. to Hyde Park. Assumptions were that it had something to do with presidential security. They were awakened before dawn as the train clattered to a stop. The rising sun revealed a dingy little railroad station on the Lehigh and Hudson line, not the Penn

Central track on which they had left Washington. The fading sign dangling from the small ticket office said "Allamuchy." The president's armored and bulletproof Ford rolled up to the special elevator on his private car and whisked him off. He waved to the reporters and explained that he was going to visit an old friend whose husband had just passed away.

FDR's visit to "Allamuchy" was as emotionally fraught as Lucy's visit to Hyde Park had been. The president was once again chipper and upbeat. Lucy had gathered her entire clan to meet the head of the free world and to enjoy a sumptuous lunch. FDR sat at Lucy's side, ignoring the protocol that always placed him at the head of the table. Daisy accompanied the president on this trip and remarked at how lively and energetic Lucy seemed in comparison to their first meeting in Aiken, over twenty years prior.

Promptly at 3:30, FDR said his good-byes and returned to the train, reinvigorated. He was due at the Highland, N.Y. station by 6:45 to meet Eleanor. She was preparing a special dinner party for his return. Curious as to the change of route and its termination at Highland, Franklin explained to Eleanor that it was for security purposes. The Secret Service didn't want foreign spies to become accustomed to a habitual route to Hyde Park.

Hobcaw Barony

After Roosevelt bought Warm Springs and established it as his Southern White House, he often managed to redirect his private train through Aiken on its route south. Rumors abound of the train stopping behind the Willcox Hotel and the president being carried by secret service agents up the backstairs to his room. A more likely scenario is that the train stopped at the small station in Warrenville, just four miles away, where a waiting car took him back to the hotel. There are no definitive accounts of how many times he visited Aiken, but unsubstantiated stories would indicate several. There were reports that FDR was seen in the company of Lucy Rutherfurd and Eulalie Salley on the verandah of "Edgewood." During the war, Lucy kept a "victory garden" on her small farm in the Boylston community, east of Aiken. She was often seen there, gathering vegetables to distribute to her friends and the needy in Aiken. One of her neighbors reported seeing a large, black, limousine parked in front of the small cabin on the farm. Two burly men in suits lounged near the car, while a man in a wheel chair was seen seated on the porch with Mrs. Rutherfurd. One can draw his own conclusion as to the identity of the man in the wheelchair.

It is known that Lucy visited FDR at Warm Springs on several occasions. Following FDR's recuperation at "Hobcaw," and the winning of his fourth term as president, he was itching to get back to Warm Springs. Eleanor declined to go, but Daisy and FDR's cousin, Polly Delano, would go with him instead. Both women were well aware of FDR's many secret trysts with Lucy and rightly figured she would join them in Warm Springs. The president's train left Washington on November 27, 1944.

Franklin developed a severe toothache on the trip down. A dentist was summoned to Warm Springs from Fort Benning, in nearby Columbus, Georgia, to extract the infected tooth. The president was in high spirits despite the pain and he continued to talk around the wad of gauze clenched between his teeth. He spent the day signing papers and attending to other business. When Lucy arrived that afternoon with her daughter Barbara, Polly and Daisy were unceremoniously banished to another cabin so that Lucy could be closer to the president. Barbara was now 22 and a very lovely girl in her own right. She had been invited to the White House on several occasions. Mother and daughter made for a stunning couple. Daisy was again struck by how beautiful and poised Lucy was. There are biographies that hint at the possibility that Barbara could have been Roosevelt's daughter. Most serious historians give little credence to those claims. It is unlikely that the newly married Lucy would have encountered FDR in 1922, so soon after the onset of his polio.

The next day dawned bright and crisp, and despite the cold, FDR insisted on piling everyone into his specially equipped Ford for a picnic at Dowdell's Knob. It was one of his favorite spots in all the world. The vista from the overlook extended for miles across the pine covered hills at the foot of the Appalachian Slope. He came here often with Lucy. In an exchange with Anna, Roosevelt's daughter and co-conspirator in his secret meetings with Lucy, she related a conversation she had with Lucy on that November morning in 1944.

"I had the most fascinating hour I've ever had. He just sat there and told me some of what he regarded as the real problems facing the world now. I just couldn't get over thinking that I was really listening."

Roosevelt confided to Lucy that he was trying to arrange another Tri-Partite meeting with Churchill and Stalin with the intent of bringing Russia into the war against Japan. Anna listened to Lucy and said of that conversation,

"...Lucy didn't know she was telling me something that was very revealing to me. I realized that no secrets were kept from this woman. As Lucy spoke of being entranced by the president's words, I realized that Mother was not capable of giving him this–just listening."

Roosevelt insisted on accompanying Lucy as far as Talbotton, on her return to Aiken. They rode in FDR's limousine with the top down, despite the 17 degree temperature. The little jaunt went smoothly until one of the Secret Service cars ran over and killed a pig. Roosevelt insisted that the owner be found and compensated for his loss. The owner, a black farmer, stood dumbfounded on the roadside, with a five-dollar bill in his hand, as the president of the United States drove away. At Talbotton, Lucy left him and returned to her own car. FDR sat there wistfully, watching the Rutherfurd car recede into the distance.

The president returned to Washington on December 17th. It had been over two weeks since he saw Lucy off in Talbotton. He missed her terribly. He asked Daisy to call her to see if she would meet the train in Atlanta and accompany him back to Washington. Willingly and dutifully, Lucy agreed and was standing on the platform at Union station in downtown Atlanta when the presidential train rolled in. She joined the president in the parlor car as Daisy and Canadian Ambassador Leighton McCarthy discreetly left so that the two could be alone.

The next time Lucy would see FDR was at his fourth and final inaugural on January 20, 1945. Lucy did not share in the post-inaugural festivities but returned to her sister's home on "Q" Street. Daisy dropped by that evening to fill Lucy in on the events that occurred inside the White House after she had left.

Three days later, despite his obviously failing health, President Roosevelt boarded the "USS Quincy," a heavy cruiser, for the voyage to Yalta and that Tri-Partite meeting which he had divulged to Lucy at Warm Springs. It would be his last meeting with his war-time partners. As he sat on deck with Anna, watching the Virginia countryside glide past, he pointed to a spit of land and said, "Over there is where Lucy's family used to live, that's where they had their plantation." It was the property of John Tunis, Minna Mercer's father. Thoughts of Lucy were never far from Franklin Roosevelt's mind.

On March 12th, Eleanor was on a trip to North Carolina for several days, and Lucy was staying with Violetta. She saw FDR three times in the span of three days, once at "Q" Street and twice at the White House. The last evening she spent three hours alone with the president, leaving the next day before Eleanor's return. Anna saw nothing underhanded in arranging the FDR/Lucy meetings. She saw them as islands of serenity for her father in a sea awash with unimaginable turmoil and overwhelming responsibility.

Roosevelt returned to Warm Springs at the end of March.

He needed the warm southern sun and the refreshing swims in the hot springs. He also wanted to prepare for the upcoming convention in San Francisco which would give birth to the United Nations. His telephone log for the first ten days in Warm Springs showed eight calls from Aiken.

On April 9th, he was joined in Warm Springs by Lucy Rutherfurd and Madame Elizabeth Shoumatoff. Shoumatoff was a portrait artist who had been commissioned by the Rutherfurds to do numerous family portraits. In 1943 Lucy had convinced FDR to sit for Madame Shoumatoff. He squeezed in two sittings and then a third when she could not finish in two. She presented the finished portrait to the president later that year. He ordered copies to present as gifts. Whether FDR truly liked the painting is immaterial—it represented another link to his beloved Lucy.

The president was so eager to see Lucy that he had his chauffeur drive him to Macon, Georgia to intercept Shoumatoff's Cadillac limousine. After eighty-five miles of fruitlessly imagining that every approaching car was Lucy, the president gave up and headed back toward Warm Springs. As the Shoumatoff Cadillac entered Manchester, Georgia, Lucy saw a crowd gathered around a car parked at a gas station. In the back seat was the president sipping a Coca-Cola. His face lit-up at the sight of Lucy. FDR invited Lucy and Madame Shoumatoff into his car, while the portrait photographer accompanying them, Nicolas Robbins, was relegated to driving the Cadillac on to Warm Springs.

Lucy and the artist were assigned to the guest cottage. Nicolas Robbins, the photographer, was put up at a local hotel. Madame Shoumatoff wanted several photos to use after the formal sittings were complete. Robbins, like most men, was smitten with Lucy and could hardly keep his eyes off her. He was heard to remark, "I have seen two smiles like that in my life. One was on da Vinci's *Mona Lisa*, and the other was Mrs. Rutherfurds."

The scene on the evening of Monday April 9, 1945 in the president's cabin was joyful and animated as everyone enjoyed the vodka and caviar that FDR had received as a gift from Stalin at Yalta. The president regaled his guests with tales from the meeting, many at the expense of Stalin.

Tuesday the 10th welcomed warm temperatures and a cloudless sky. Roosevelt was wheeled into his living room where there was better light. Robbins began shooting photos at various angles and in different poses. The president stopped him in mid-stride and asked him to take a photograph of Lucy. Robbins complied. The resultant print, with Lucy's hands demurely clasped in her lap and with a faint smile on her face, became a final memento of her last days with the man she loved so dearly. Robbins said that he also took a photo of the president and Lucy together, but no print has ever surfaced. If it exists, it is the only picture ever taken of the two together.

The Unfinished Portrait of FDR

Exhausted from the afternoon sitting, Roosevelt insisted on driving Lucy to Dowdell's Knob. Just the two of them, with Fala, his beloved Scottie. With the security detail at a discreet distance, Franklin and Lucy watched the sun descend behind the distant hills. Daisy Suckley remarked that FDR returned with more color in his cheeks than before he left. The Lucy *tonic* had worked its magic once again

Most of Wednesday was consumed by the president's official duties. Lucy and Daisy stayed in their cabin, talking and crocheting. Late in the afternoon, FDR announced he would like to go for a drive. This time he asked Daisy to join him with Lucy and Fala. Daisy was struck by how attentive and sweet Lucy was to the president, noting in her diary that evening,

"Lucy is so sweet with Franklin—no wonder he loves to have her around—Toward the end of the drive it began to be chilly and she put her sweater over his knees—I can imagine just how she took care of her husband—She would think of little things which make so much difference to a semi-invalid, or even a person who is just tired like Franklin."

On April 12, the president awoke at 8:30. He seemed rested but complained of a headache and a stiff neck. He waded through several newspapers and various communications from Washington before working on his stamp collection. He called the White House to remind them to obtain the first stamp commemorating the United Nations. Madame Shoumatoff arrived at noon and recognizing the president's drawn look offered to return later. "Oh no," he said, "I'll be through in a few minutes and I'll be ready for you,"

Between snatches of a quick lunch the president notified the artist that she had only fifteen more minutes. She quickened her pace. At that moment, Daisy looked up to see the president's head slump forward and his hands thrash by his side.

"He looked at me with his forehead furrowed in pain and tried to smile. He put his left hand up to the back of his head & said, 'I have a terrible pain in the back of my head!' He spoke so faintly that I don't think anyone else heard it."

Pandemonium erupted in the room as calls went out for

help. Daisy, Madame Shoumatoff and the two attendants struggled to carry the inert form of the dying president to his bed. The president thrashed around and then lapsed into unconsciousness. Lucy rushed in with smelling salts. She was followed immediately by Dr. Breunn.

Lucy realized that her presence at Warm Springs would prove very awkward if the president were to die. She grabbed Madame Shoumatoff and told her that they must leave immediately. With gas pirated from one of the security cars, the three set off for Aiken at 2:30. Lucy insisted they stop at a hotel so that she could phone Warm Springs. It was impossible to get through to the Little White House. Lucy received the answer she desperately wanted not to receive when she looked into the swollen, teary, eyes of the switchboard operator—the President was dead.

There are differing opinions as to whether Lucy and Franklin had resumed an intimate relationship after Roosevelt became president. Eulalie Salley was adamant that Lucy was faithful to her husband and that no further physical relationship occurred between FDR and Lucy after 1918. That she was able to love both men in such strong and disparate ways is testament to her character and her nurturing temperament. In later years Eulalie described one of Lucy's biographers as a "stinky fellow" upon reading some of his scandalous allegations. That accounted for the large collection of ceramic skunks that Eulalie had at the time of her death. She received the little mementoes from Lucy's dedicated friends from all over the world.

While sorting through FDR's effects after the funeral, Eleanor came across the small portrait of her husband painted by Madame Shoumatoff in 1943. Recognizing then the significance of the artist's relationship to Lucy Mercer, Eleanor knew the painting should be given to Lucy. However, the pain was too fresh to allow her to send it personally. She gave it to Margaret (Daisy) who forwarded it to Lucy. After receiving the watercolor from Margaret, Lucy was moved to write to Eleanor for the first time since she left her employ in 1918.

"Margaret has written to me that you gave her the little

watercolor of Franklin by Mme. Shoumatoff. Thank you so much. You must know that it will be treasured always. I had wanted to write you for a long time to tell you that I had seen Franklin and his great kindness about my husband when he was desperately ill in Washington . . . and that I hoped so I might see you. . . The whole universe finds it difficult to adjust itself to a world without Franklin, and to you and his family. The emptiness must be appalling. I send you—as I find it impossible not to, my love and deep sympathy as always, affectionately, Lucy Rutherfurd." Years later, Lucy offered the portrait to the Roosevelt library in Hyde Park. Eleanor refused it. When asked if the refusal was out of resentment, her answer was, "Yes."

The unfinished portrait for which the president was sitting when he died remained with Mme. Shoumatoff for many years. Before her death she donated it to the Little White House museum in Warm Springs where it remains on display to the public.

Upon receiving the small portrait, Lucy called Anna Roosevelt. Despite all the injury to Anna's relationship with her mother caused by her facilitation of the meetings between Lucy and FDR, Lucy and Anna maintained a warm and lasting bond. Lucy followed the call with a revealing letter to Anna, one that Anna kept under lock and key for the rest of her life, showing it to only a few friends and family members.

> *May 9, 1945*
>
> *Anna dear,*
>
> *I did not know that it was in me just now to be so glad to hear the sound of any voice and to hear you laugh was beyond any words wonderful. I know that you meant more to your father than anyone. I love to think of his very great pride in you. He told me so often with such feeling of all you meant of joy and comfort on the trip to Yalta. He said you had been so extraordinary & what a difference it made to have you. He told me of your charm & your tact & how everyone loved you. He told me how capable you were & and how you forgot nothing. . . . I hope he told*

you these things, but sometimes one forgets. . . .The world has lost one of the greatest men that ever lived, to me the greatest. He towers above them all effortlessly.
Lucy Rutherfurd

In response to the letter, Anna sent Lucy one of her favorite parables, The Traveler, written by Dorothy Dumbrille following FDR's death.

The Traveler stood at the Gate, his face lined with fatigue, his shoulders drooped.

"I had hoped I would not have to come so soon," he said.

But the Angel answered him: "You are weary My Son and your work on Earth is finished."

"Only a few months more," he pleaded, "then I would have laid down my work gladly.

"Your work will be carried on My Son."

To end the parable the Traveler said

"I would enter the Portal, Sir, but . . . I have been many years a cripple, unable to walk alone."

"Let fall your staff My Son," said the Angel. "Come."

And the Traveler let his stick fall to the ground and stood upright, alone, and walked through the Portal.

Lucy revealed to Mme. Shoumatoff in a meeting two months after FDR's death that she had burned all of his letters. A few she missed have survived to fill in many of the voids of history. Lucy also kept copious notes and diaries chronicling events in FDR's life. Those too have been invaluable in piecing together one of the most intriguing love affairs of the twentieth century.

Anna's relationship with the Rutherfurd's continued, even past Lucy's death in 1947, when she sent a pair of FDR's cuff links to Barbara. They were likely a gift from Lucy to FDR. Barbara married Robert Knowles, in 1946. He was great-grandson to the poet Henry Wadsworth Longfellow, and a prominent amateur golfer. As the official scorer at the Masters golf tournament, Bobby devised the red/green scoring protocol that is still used.

The Knowles daughters, Alice and Lucy, still reside on Berrie Road in Aiken. Mr. and Mrs. Bobby Knowles built their home on the foundation of the original cottage owned by C. W. Dolan of Rosemont, Pennsylvania, which burned. It is just down the street from Ridgeley Hall. The Dolan's home was called "Calico Cottage." C.W.'s brother, Yale Dolan, had a cottage on South Boundary called "Cocktail Corner."

Eulalie Salley brokered the sale of Ridgeley Hall to the Elbert family of Long Island, New York, after Lucy moved. They sold it to the Sisters of Mercy Catholic order. A classroom building for the order's St. Angela's Academy High School was built on the 11 acre property. St. Angela's was founded in 1900 by the Ursuline Order and occupied a corner at Richland and Pendleton. Ridgeley Hall itself became a convent for the nuns who taught at the academy. The school was shuttered in 1988 due to declining enrollments. The high school merged with the St. Mary Help of Christian's school on York Street in downtown Aiken.

Joel Conte, owner of a retail jewelry business, bought the Ridgeley Hall property in the early 1990s. He converted the classroom building into stables and the gymnasium into a storage barn for hay.

Lucy Mercer Rutherfurd died of leukemia at "Tip Top Too" on July 1, 1947 shortly after her sister Violetta had committed suicide there. With both Winthrop and Franklin gone, and with her sister's death, Lucy wrote that it was difficult to adjust to life without them. Of Franklin, she wrote, in French, the language of intimacy they shared in their private moments—"*On aurait voulu de voir achiever cette tache de geant qu'il affrontai avec tant de souriante grandeur*"—One would have wished to see this gigantic task finished which he met with such smiling grace.

24
Let's Pretend

Gouverneur Morris, great-grandson and namesake of one of the framers of the United States Constitution, came to Aiken as an already accomplished man of letters. His works were acclaimed far and wide and would become the screen plays for over twenty movies. One in particular, The Man Who Played God, was responsible for reviving the sagging early career of Bette Davis.

In 1910, Morris bought a rambling, white, clapboard, house at 312 Horry Street which he would expand many times. He loved Aiken and came each winter. Many times while here he hosted the pre-eminent writer and journalist of the time, Richard Harding White. The two men were great companions and enjoyed their times together in Aiken. Their escapades led Morris to name his cottage "Let's Pretend" as in fairy tale stories. When, in 1916, at the age of 54, White died suddenly, Gouverneur Morris and nine other famous men were asked to write tributes to his memory. Such was White's acclaim that Theodore Roosevelt and Winston Churchill were among those asked to pen encomiums to the celebrated writer.

Following the loss of his dear friend, Morris' fortunes went into decline and his marriage fell apart. When his wife Elsa took their two children and left, Morris' life went into a tailspin.

His despondency led him to shutter "Let's Pretend" in 1916 and leave Aiken, abandoning his home and all the haunting memories it conjured in his mind.

Let's Pretend

Four years later, the still furnished home was on the list of properties for the Master's sale at the courthouse—properties that carried tax liens to the county. It was Eulalie Salley's custom to comb through the listed properties looking for diamonds in the rough for her real estate business. The listing for the quirky cottage on Horry Street caught her eye. She was encouraged by a friend to bid on the house—a house that she had never visited. She knew of its historical significance as the former home of Gouverneur Morris, so she plunged into the bidding. When the gavel fell, she had purchased "Let's Pretend" for $10,000, a considerable sum in 1920. Suddenly, she realized what she had done and she became panicky. What would she tell Julian? After all, she had just begun her real estate career and was still heavily involved in the struggle for women's suffrage. Much of the money she had made on commissions had gone to her New York adventure and to support the cause. She didn't have $10,000, and she knew Julian would be furious. She turned to the friend who had encouraged her to buy the house.

"What do I do now? I don't have $10,000."

"Go on, talk to Mr. Croft. You can make arrangements."

Mr. Croft, the Master and a personal friend, knew that Julian was out of town.

"It's all right, Eulalie. We can take care of it when Julian returns."

She left the courthouse and drove directly to "Let's Pretend" at the corner of Colleton and Horry. The house was nearly obscured by an ivy covered, brick wall and a row of large camellias. She was trembling so, that her driver had to undo the lock on the front gate. A four-year growth of weeds and peeling paint greeted her in the courtyard. She was already regretting her impetuous purchase. Like many of her clients, she was suffering "buyer's remorse."

She pushed the door open and her senses were immediately assaulted by four years of accumulated mustiness. Her nostrils burned as she proceeded down the darkened hallway. Dust motes rose behind her, dancing in the few shafts of sunlight that penetrated the gloom. Overgrown shrubbery covered the windows and cloaked the interior in a shroud of darkness. Cobwebs hung from the cut glass chandeliers. Layers of peeling wallpaper unfurled from the walls. She could hear the scurrying of rats as they rustled through the newspapers strewn across the floor. She shuddered.

Eulalie took a deep breath, composed herself, and continued her exploration. The many additions made by Morris led to strange angles in passageways and to many steps where floor levels changed. Her alarm at the condition of the house was lightened by an amazing discovery. As she ran her fingers across the dust covered surfaces of the furniture, she recognized them as extremely rare and valuable antiques. It seems that Gouverneur Morris was a student of fine furniture, a fact born of his privileged childhood in New England. Many of the prized pieces had been imported from Boston, New York, Charleston and Europe. Among the pieces abandoned by Morris were six chairs inlaid with pearl and silver eagles that were made for Napoleon. There was also a museum quality Queen Anne highboy and an original Duncan Phyfe game table. Audubon bird prints and valuable wood-block etchings from the seventeenth century decorated the walls. Dishes and silverware rested on the shelves and in the drawers. Except for the dust and debris, the home looked as if its tenants had just gone out for a Sunday stroll. Objects in the daughter's bedroom remained undisturbed from the last time she played with them.

On her way home, Eulalie's anxiety over facing Julian was softened by the potential she saw in "Let's Pretend," especially in the treasure trove of antiques that came with the house. Inexplicably, Morris had abandoned them in his hurried departure from Aiken and its harsh memories.

"Tell Croft to put it on sale again," bellowed Julian upon hearing of the purchase. "We're not about to keep that house."

"But, why?" Eulalie countered.

"I don't like the neighborhood—it's low ground and unhealthy," he responded.

"It's not low! It's just flat!" Eulalie responded.

Julian picked up his paper as if to dismiss the subject. "I will never live there! Get rid of it! I won't live in that rat's nest!"

Eulalie decided to let the sleeping dog lie overnight. She was in Henry Dibble's office as soon as the doors opened the next morning.

"Henry, can I take over the mortgage on "Let's Pretend" in my name only?" she asked. If he had said no she had an ace up her ruffled sleeve. If all else failed, and Julian refused to buy it, her mother had committed to do so.

"My dear Eulalie, don't fret. I'll fix it with Julian," Henry said.

She never knew whether Dibble actually spoke to Julian or not. She charged ahead as if there was no controversy and began the renovation of the house. Her efforts were cloaked in secrecy; for she wasn't sure Julian realized they still owned the property. She lived in fear that he would make her sell it. She arranged the furniture in great, covered, heaps in a few rooms while repairs were made to others. She instructed the workmen to take extreme care in moving things about. They had no idea of the value of the house's furnishings. She reconnected the utilities and began to wash and launder all the fine linens that were left behind. She carefully removed the grime covered damask drapes and oriental carpets for cleaning. Within four stealthy months, she and her mother transformed "Let's Pretend" into the idyllic hideaway that Morris had envisioned when he purchased it. Clandestinely, over the last few weeks of renovation, Eulalie moved select items from the Highland Park home to the new house. She planned a supper menu of all Julian's favorite foods and sent the maid to Hahn's to procure the ingredients. When Julian returned to work that afternoon, Eulalie pinned a note to the front door of their Highland Park home and moved her mother, son, and daughter to their new home. The note read, "We have moved to "Let's Pretend." Won't you join us for dinner?"

Shortly after five, there was a knock on the door of the Horry Street house. Though still annoyed by the entire episode, Julian was appreciative of the work the women had put into the renovation. The results were dazzling.

"I'm glad to see you," she said, oozing feminine charm as she opened the door. "Come in. The dining room is this way."

Tapers in the ornate, silver, candelabras cast their shimmering light across the polished mahogany of the period dining table. The Lowestoft porcelain, imported by Morris from Suffolk, England, rested on the delicate lace table mats. Gleaming, six-piece, place settings of fine British silverware flanked each plate. Eulalie was aware that the roughhewn Julian was seldom aware of such refinements, but that night she had him in her thrall. After dinner, which Julian appeared to enjoy immensely, Eulalie offered him a tour of the house.

"And this is mother's room . . . and this is my room."

Julian looked around approvingly then surprised her by asking, "And where is my room?"

"You said you wouldn't live here." She paused for effect. "However, if you would like to, there's a very nice room right here that you could have. The bed is already made." After dinner, Julian went back to his office. At 10:30 he returned, suitcase in hand, to join his family at "Let's Pretend."

While poking around among the many boxes she found piled high in the attic, Eulalie stumbled onto a secret door to a hidden room. Several trunks inside the room contained piles of clothing and small boxes of long forgotten Morris memorabilia. She spent hours poring through the letters and mementoes, enjoying vicariously the memories of the famous man who had accumulated the treasures. One particular letter sent Eulalie flying down the stairs in search of her mother. Mrs. Chafee was engrossed in one of the many books they had discovered in the house. She looked up as the giddy Eulalie plopped down beside her on the sofa.

"Mama, Mama, look what I have found!" Eulalie pressed back the folds of a letter and began to read.

Dear Mr. Morris,

When a man walks in Eden it is an impertinence to offer him congratulations: All the same I rejoice at the kind thought that prompted you to tell me of your great happiness. But, O my son, remember that matrimony is not a state as the church falsely asserts, but an art, a craft, a profession which the man and the woman must diligently practice and pursue from the altar to the coffin. Law is a fool to it. Physic mere bungling; Divinity the alphabet; Finance the multiplication table; and war, child's play. Study it humbly, prayerfully and incessantly and when in doubt (this advice is above all rubies) throw up your hands!

"Please convey my best to Miss Waterbury. I like her given name because I have an Elsie of my own who is precisely 33-1/3rd of my world to me. She is only nine, but already I foresee the day when some ruffian of a young man will propose to abduct her. And she'll say 'yes'. That's the sting of it...

Be very, very, tender to Elsie.

Yours with thirteen years of experience (but I am sure you feel you know it all—same as I did)."

Rudyard Kipling

The letter was penned in 1905, upon the engagement of Elsa Waterbury and Gouverneur Morris. It found its way into the trunk sometime between 1910 and 1916, when Morris abandoned "Let's Pretend," and after his marriage to Elsa fell apart. Eulalie reflected on the sentiments expressed by Kipling.

"Practice and pursue," she thought. "It would be a waste. As long as I am married to Julian, things will remain the same."

She accepted the loss of romance and tenderness between herself and Julian, but she cherished their compatible and harmonious relationship. Their careers took them in opposite directions, but she was always happiest when she crossed the threshold of "Let's Pretend." Eulalie would own two more homes after she moved from 312 Horry Street. Neither would ever offer the level of peace and contentment she felt there.

25

Paradise Lost

The ensuing six years, following the purchase of "Let's Pretend," were among the happiest of Eulalie's long and tumultuous life. The real estate business thrived with the support of Winter Colony friends such as the Vanderbilts, the Rutherfurds and the Hitchcocks. It was also during this period that she saw the successful conclusion of her crusade to win the franchise for women. Through her efforts and those of thousands of others, the nineteenth amendment to the U.S. Constitution was passed in 1920. It was not a complete victory for her, since South Carolina did not ratify. However, she could be certain that her efforts, along with those of thousands of others, had been pivotal in educating and energizing women all across the country.

Eulalie took from the "Let's Pretend" experience a newfound confidence in her abilities. She discovered that she had a discerning eye for furniture and fashion as well as for landscape gardening. She opened an antique furniture shop adjacent to her offices on Park Avenue. It became a popular hangout for the winter visitors who grew tired of their own pretentious cliques or became bored with dawn to dusk equestrian and sports activities. It became known as "The Club" for a select few of her friends. She took to serving tea in the afternoon for those who dropped by. They found the surroundings every bit as elegant as those of their Long Island drawing rooms and felt at ease in discussing the events and worries of the day. Not a little local gossip was shared. Through these ad hoc *soirees,* Eulalie was able to gather invaluable intelligence for her businesses.

One very auspicious client obtained in this manner—a woman whose daily earnings from the Singer Sewing Machine Company came to $3,000—was a frequent visitor to the antique store. Marian Elbert, wife of Robert G. Elbert, bought Ridgeley Hall from Lucy Rutherfurd. She would pop in to Eulalie's shop often and announce, "I can only spend about $2,000 today." Needless to say, she was one of Eulalie's favorite customers. When the lady would grow tired of a piece, or when her 12,000 square-foot mansion became overcrowded, she would bring items in for resale. The revolving twenty-percent commissions earned on the items added appreciably to the shop's success. The lady would often sit discreetly behind a screen to eavesdrop on what other customers had to say about pieces they had seen in her house that were now on sale. A 1946 ledger of Eulalie's contains 29 pages of consignments to the shop from Mrs. Elbert. The rich could afford to be eccentric.

The Albert Bissells were also frequent visitors. As heirs to a portion of the DuPont fortune, and executors of the DuPont Winterthur Museum at Brandywine, Delaware, they were authorities on antiques and came to admire Eulalie's latest selections for the shop. The Bissells owned "Louviers" a cottage at 1376 Dibble Road that was built in 1905 by her parents James and Julia DuPont Andrews.

The Bissells played host for many years to one of the most fascinating men ever to grace Aiken with his presence, John Seabrook. Seabrook was a scion of the family whose 45,000 acres of farmland in New Jersey gave birth to a product taken for granted in modern society—frozen vegetables. The family also introduced the ubiquitous frozen TV dinner to American dining tables—and dens. John grew up on the farm and worked there as a boy. He began working with his father as the business grew by leaps and bounds. When the business was sold, Jack, as his friends called him, moved to Philadelphia where he was successful in several industries, including shipping. He served as CEO of Gotaas-Larsen, the large Swedish shipping consortium which founded Royal Caribbean Cruise Lines.

Jack was divorced at 30 and remarried to Elizabeth Toomey of Philadelphia at 36. In April 1956, Elizabeth Toomey, 32, was a reporter for United Press and won an assignment to cover Grace Kelly's wedding to Prince Rainier in Monaco. Jack was one of 60 in the wedding party—all ensconced on the first class level of the "SS Constitution." The Kellys had reserved the entire first class deck to avoid the bothersome press circus down below. Elizabeth wangled an invitation to dinner in first class where she met Jack Seabrook, and as they say, the rest is history. They were married in October. John Seabrook, Jr., who like his mother is a writer, has written a fascinating article about the voyage and the royal wedding. *Marriage of the Century* was published by *Vogue* in 2004.

Each year, Seabrook would load his Oldenburg and Hanoverian warmblood horses and his carriages onto specially prepared rail cars and head to Aiken. He would spend ten days to two weeks with the Bissells, careening around Aiken in one of his 30-odd carriages. His most famous carriage, Nimrod, was built in England in 1906. He found the carriage in great disrepair, languishing in an old barn in California. Seabrook brought the carriage to his home in Pennsylvania where he had it faithfully restored to its original condition. The two-ton behemoth was pulled by a team of four matched horses that Jack could control with the reins in one hand, or "four-in-hand" as the practice was called. He was often seen, reins in one hand and champagne flute in the other, extolling the virtues of driving in Aiken. He once told Eulalie Salley, "If I were looking for a house, this is the way I would do it. You can look over the walls and into the gardens."

After twenty-five years, Elizabeth told Jack that it was about time they bought a place of their own in Aiken. They acquired "Green Shingles" on Berrie Road in 1989. "Green Shingles" was the former home of Monsignor George Lewis Smith, Pastor Emeritus of St, Mary's Catholic Church. Monsignor Smith died in 1987. The Seabrooks renamed the cottage "Nimrod South."

John Seabrook gave up competitive coaching at 81, after performing one last service to his adopted community. When the beloved city manager, Roland Windham, retired in1991, Jack was waiting outside his offices with Nimrod and four beautiful, matched, white, horses to drive him home for the last time.

John Seabrook died in Aiken in August of 2005. Among his last public appearances was at a tribute for Bobby Knowles, Lucy Mercer Rutherfurd's son-in-law, on the lawn of the Palmetto Golf Club. Knowles, who had devoted himself to the club and was revered by its members and the community, died in 2003 at the age of 88.

"The world has far too few genuine characters, and Bobby was certainly one of them. He will be sorely missed," said Mr. Seabrook.

Margaret Behrend, widow of a Westinghouse executive, came to Aiken and established a winter home. She was very lonely and just to have someone to talk with she came to Eulalie's shop every day and bought one piece of silverware. By the end of her first year she had quite an extensive collection of fine silver. Her husband, Bernard Behrend, had been very strict and reclusive, so they had few friends. Once, Mrs. Behrend asked Eulalie to breakfast. When Mrs. Behrend momentarily left the room, the maid confided to Eulalie that, "You are the only visitor who has ever had a meal in this house." Mrs. Behrend, like many local Aikenites and several in the Winter Colony, was drawn to Eulalie's warmth, integrity and passion for life.

The Massachusetts Institute of Technology offered Mrs. Behrend a large sum of money for her husband's machine tool collection. MIT wanted it for their museum because of its historic scientific significance, but Eulalie had other ideas. For the same historic reasons she wanted to retain the collection for South Carolina. She persuaded a political friend from Barnwell to get the state legislature to appropriate $500,000 to purchase the collection for Clemson University. Because of Eulalie, the Clemson offer was accepted. It was a selfless act on her friend's part—and one that Eulalie never forgot. Margaret Behrend later donated her husband's papers and over 3,000 books, mostly scientific and many rare, to the university.

In 1926, Mrs. Austin Niblack, (nee Helen Cudahy) of the Chicago meatpacking fortune, wanted to buy a home in Aiken. She remembered "Let's Pretend" from visits to Gouverneur Morris. She had never visited the house during the Salley's time there, but she was assured that Eulalie would not sell it. Julian had other ideas. He did not share the same sentimental attachment to the house that his wife did.

Helen Niblack asked an Aiken friend, Ira Coward, if he would advance a proposal to the Salley's about a possible sale of the house. Julian approached the crestfallen Eulalie with the offer and urged her to sell the house. Besides his lack of sentimentality, Julian always liked to turn a profit. Coward's proxy offer was for $35.000—three-and-one-half times what they had paid for the house just six years before—and the profits from the sale of the antiques had added thousands more. Eulalie was still reluctant to part with her dream house.

"If you will sell it, you can get any house in Aiken, within reason," Julian pleaded.

"Would you let me have the Goss house on Hayne Avenue that my mother owns?"

"Yes!"

Eulalie thought about it overnight. In the morning she reluctantly agreed. Nostalgia set in immediately. The summer sun was setting as Julian left for his office. They had just finished their last supper at "Let's Pretend." Tomorrow morning the movers would descend and begin to pack six years of precious memories for the move across town to Hayne Avenue.

Eulalie walked slowly down the hallways, moving from room to room in the fading light. She caressed the staircase. Tears welled in her eyes as she tried to imprint every detail of the house to her memory, just as she had done so long ago at her debut party just up the street. The tears began to roll down her cheeks. She walked into her bedroom and fell across the bed, sobbing.

"I don't want to leave," she cried. Suddenly she felt a presence in the room. A voice spoke to her.

"Why do you weep?"

She recognized the voice. It was her father.

"Don't you know that the things you have in this life are only loaned to you for a little while?"

Those words would return often to comfort Eulalie during the remainder of her life.

26

Rags to Riches

The Twenties were a period of national convulsion. Europe was coming out of the World War that America had been drawn into. Louise Hitchcock had almost lost her son Tommy in a plane crash over German territory and waited six long months to discover he was still alive. Other sons of Aiken and their winter visitors were not so fortunate. Stricken mothers grieved and hung gold stars in their windows. The wealthy were not immune. Several sons of Aiken's Winter Colony made the ultimate sacrifice for their country. It was during this period that Eulalie met one of the most interesting characters ever to come to Aiken.

Evalyn Walsh was born in a tumbledown, wooden, shack on the side of a barren hill near Leadville, Colorado on August 1, 1886. Her father, Thomas, had emigrated from his native Ireland to seek his fortune in the gold rush then unfolding in the American West. In 1870 he transformed his lucrative skills as a carpenter into a $100,000 grubstake with which he acquired Camp Bird Mines in Ouray, Colorado. Walsh discovered a fabulously rich vein of gold ore in 1896 and turned his grubstake into $20,000,000. He was able to keep his mine going in the midst of great labor strife by treating his workers humanely. He required them to work only eight hours per day and provided them with room and board of high quality. He built schools and hospitals for their families while he quietly amassed his fortune.

Walsh married a stunningly beautiful school teacher named Carrie Bell Reed in 1879. In 1902 he sold the mines, moved his family to Washington, D.C., and built a lavish home on Massachusetts Avenue. It seems that every newly minted millionaire in America was moving to Washington to join the social and political whirl. Walsh was soon consorting with senators, diplomats and presidents as well as the other *nouveau riche* denizens of the nation's capital.

Walsh-McLean House - Washington

Like a duck takes to water, Evalyn Walsh took to Washington. As an only child after her brother's death in 1905, her father lavished all his attention on the beautiful Evalyn. Whatever Evalyn wanted, Evalyn got. Her circle included, among others, T.R.'s son Elliott Roosevelt, Warren Harding's wife Florence, and T.R.'s daughter Alice Roosevelt Longworth. Their combined appearances at three or more parties in one evening were not uncommon.

In 1908, Evalyn eloped with Edward "Ned" Beale McLean, son of the publisher of the Washington Post and the Cincinnati Enquirer. With a $200,000 dollar stake from the two families, the couple was off to a lavishly expensive honeymoon in Paris. Even at that they overspent their allowance, and when they couldn't pay the hotel bill they had to be bailed out by her father.

In 1911 the Ned McLeans, continuing their profligate ways, bought the renowned Hope diamond from Pierre Cartier for a rumored $300,000. The original 115 carat stone that was spirited out of India by Jean-Baptiste Tavernier in 1653, was re-cut over the years until its final rendition of 45 carats.

The Hope Diamond

Rumors of a curse attached to the stone arose from the legend that Tavernier had pried the stone from the eye of a Hindu idol. The fact that no one ever saw or heard of the matching 115 carat stone from the other eye didn't deter those who maintained there was a curse placed on the incredibly valuable gem by the Hindu gods. The tragedy and violence that dogged many of the subsequent owners only served to keep the legend alive. The gem passed through the hands of numerous members of nobility and wealthy gentry over the years, including Louis XIV, Louis XV and Louis XVI of France. Louis XVI and his last wife Marie Antoinette lost their heads during the French Revolution. Some attribute their misfortune to the Hope curse. The diamond disappeared during the ensuing revolutionary turmoil but later turned up in London in the royal jewel collection of King George IV. The royal family sold it to the wealthy Hope family, and the stone remained in their possession for decades. It was during this period that it became known as the "Hope" diamond.

Evalyn disliked the setting of the stone and had it redesigned by Cartier into a necklace pendant with a circle of diamonds. She wore it often to balls and society events, occasionally hanging it around the neck of her Great Dane for a touch of sensationalism. She would often feign loss of the "Hope" at parties and send all the guests scurrying in search of it. Miraculously, it always turned up safely. It was still in her possession when Evalyn McLean filed for divorce in 1931. Edward "Ned" McLean was a raging alcoholic and Evalyn had developed a dependency on opiates. The divorce proceedings were dropped when "Ned" was declared incompetent and placed in a sanitarium. They were finally granted a divorce in Lithuania in 1929. That divorce was later declared invalid. "Ned" died in a Maryland sanitarium in 1941 at the age of 52. Allegedly, he danced there with Zelda Fitzgerald, another infamous patient. Evalyn died in 1947 at the age of 60. Before her death she stood disconsolately in the rain, in her fur coat, to watch their beloved POST newspaper auctioned off following bankruptcy proceedings. The Meyer/Graham family that bought the paper ran it for almost seventy years until its recent sale to Jeff Bezos, founder of Amazon.com.

The one million dollars she spent on her dog's birthday party, where the Great Dane wore the Hope diamond, landed her a line in Cole Porter's musical Anything Goes.

When Missus Ned McLean (God bless her)
Can get Russian reds to bless her.
Then I suppose
Anything Goes.

Evalyn Walsh McLean

The McLeans were familiar with Aiken. Evalyn had enrolled her sons in the Aiken Preparatory School. She rented a house on Hayne Avenue from Eulalie to be near her children. It was widely known that she kept the Hope diamond at that home when in residence. Most people assumed she had it well guarded and in a safe place. Eulalie was a frequent visitor to the McLean home.

"Eulalie, would you like to see the diamond?" Evalyn said one day. Eulalie was as curious as anyone about the fabulous stone.

"I surely would, Evalyn."

She was led upstairs to Evalyn McLean's bedroom. She glanced around, expecting to see a large safe or strongbox of some sort. To her surprise Evalyn walked over to a dresser and opened the top drawer. She reached in beneath some of her lingerie and pulled out a silk stocking. There, tied neatly in the toe of the stocking, was the most famous piece of jewelry in the world. There was speculation that Mrs. McLean had copies made of the stone and that the original was locked away securely somewhere in Washington. Eulalie swore that the stone she saw in the silk stocking was the original.

When Eulalie moved to "Edgewood" Evalyn leased the Goss house. That house was later destroyed by fire, and only the stone fence adjacent to the Hahn house on Hayne remains.

Evalyn McLean continued to divide her time between Washington and Aiken. She was in residence in Aiken in 1932 when the terrible news came of the kidnapping of the Charles Lindbergh baby. The child was taken in the night from his second floor nursery at the Lindbergh home in New Jersey. Lindbergh was arguably the most famous person in America, and the response to the kidnapping was swift and intense. Nearly every law enforcement agency in the country became involved in the investigation. As could also be expected, many unscrupulous people sought to benefit from the tragedy. The investigation dragged on for weeks and there were several reported sightings and several ransom attempts. Many rumors connected the *Cosa Nostra* or Mafia to the crime. All the leads turned into dead ends and there was still no baby found. Aiken figured in one of the more bizarre incidents associated with what newspapers called "The Crime of the Century."

Evalyn McLean was a good friend of the Lindberghs. She offered her condolences and her aid to the family. She thought that the McLean family's ownership of the Washington Post could help to ferret out the criminals responsible for the heinous crime. Through social contacts, she knew of a private detective in Washington—Gaston Means. She employed his services, asking him to be a go-between with the Mafia or whoever else might be implicated in the kidnapping. If she had been just a little more diligent in checking out Means history, she would have discovered his criminal record consisting of several swindles and con games. Means immediately booked passage to Aiken, where Evalyn was in residence. He assured her that he could help to find Charles Lindbergh, Jr. He said he had contacts in Brooklyn who knew where the child was being held.

"I know where the baby is," he told Mrs. Mclean. "If you will give me $150,000 and keep the baby in hiding for three weeks after he is handed over to you, allowing the kidnappers time to escape, I will arrange for the baby to be returned to you."

She did not hesitate to write the huckster a check. After his departure she had the Hayne Avenue house's upper floors remodeled and fitted with a nursery for the baby. She hired a nurse and, per Gaston Mean's instructions, boarded a train for Mexico and a rendezvous to receive the child. Upon arrival, she arranged to send a wire every hour to a friend back home with instructions that if the friend didn't hear from Evalyn he was to go to the police immediately. Alas, when she arrived in Mexico there was no Means—and no Lindbergh baby. It was all a hoax. The baby was later found murdered, near the Lindbergh home in New Jersey. Means then had the audacity to ask Evalyn for more money. That's when she finally called in the authorities. Means was arrested, tried, and convicted of grand larceny. He died in Leavenworth Prison in 1938.

Bruno Richard Hauptmann, an illegal immigrant from Germany, with a criminal record there, was eventually apprehended, tried, and found guilty of the kidnapping and murder of the twenty-month old Charles Lindbergh, Jr. Despite no direct incriminating physical evidence of Hauptmann's guilt, the circumstantial evidence was overwhelming. He was electrocuted on April 3, 1936. Over the years, many conspiracy theories arose denying Hauptmann's guilt. Most of those centered on evidence that was supposedly fabricated by the police. The fact that Hauptmann was caught trying to spend some of the ransom money was sufficient for most people to conclude that he was guilty of the "Crime of the Century."

Prior to the Lindbergh kidnapping, such cases were matters for local and state jurisdictions. However, the sensational nature of this case prompted Congress to pass a law making kidnapping a federal crime. The case also gave a major boost to the career of J. Edgar Hoover. Even though the State of New Jersey was the putative chief investigative body, it was the advanced resources of Hoover's agency that uncovered the most incriminating evidence. Thereafter, the government's Bureau of Investigation became the Federal Bureau of Investigation and elevated Hoover's stature in government circles.

Evalyn Walsh McLean was witness to even more tragedy from her home on Hayne. Alice Roosevelt Longworth was one of her intimate circle of friends until Evalyn formed a close relationship with President (1921-23) Warren Harding's wife, Frances. The Hardings and the Roosevelts were at opposite ends of the political spectrum at the time. Alice resented the relationship and drew back from Evalyn. She was also estranged from her husband, Nicholas Longworth IV. Alice had served as the unofficial "first lady" for her widowed father Teddy (1901-09) during his White House years. Even then she proved to be an ungovernable handful. T.R., when asked about the tempestuous antics of his and Alice Bulloch's only child said, "I can be president of the United States–or–I can attend to Alice. I can't do both."

Both Alice and Nicholas were known for their biting humor which bridged with equal acerbity, both sides of the political divide. Alice was once heard to say, "If you don't have anything nice to say about anyone, come sit by me, dear." She was firmly in the Republican camp but had her own views about social ills. Her black chauffeur was driving her to an engagement once when he pulled out in front of a taxi. The cab driver jumped out of his car and confronted her driver, Turner.

"What do you think you are doing you black bastard?"

Turner ignored the irate cabbie, but Alice did not.

"He's taking me to my destination you white son-of-a-bitch," she shot back.

While lounging around the capitol during a recess, a fellow legislator rubbed his hand across Nick Longworth's bald pate and remarked, "Nice and smooth. Feels just like my wife's bottom." Longworth reached up, felt his head, and responded, "Yes, it sure does."

Longworth went to the house in 1902 and spent years honing his legislative skills, becoming Republican majority leader in 1923 and Speaker of the House in 1925. By all accounts he was one of the most effective speakers in American history. The Longworth House Office building in Washington honors his memory.

Longworth, whose family was a political power in Cincinnati, Ohio, may have pursued a career in classical music had he not entered the political arena. Eminent contemporary musicians such as Leopold Stokowski and Efrem Zimbalist thought that Longworth's accomplishments with the violin were comparable to other great artists of that era. One prominent rumor had Alice throwing Longworth's Stradivarius violin into the fire in a fit of rage when she discovered one of his peccadilloes. The burnt violin was valuable, but it was not the Stradivarius. Both Alice and Nicholas were frequent visitors to Aiken, though not usually in each other's company. There were occasional embarrassing moments when both showed up at the same affair. It was especially embarrassing if they were not each other's escort.

In October of 1931, Longworth was visibly fatigued from his congressional duties and in need of a rest. He was being actively considered as a presidential candidate in the election of 1932. The sitting president, Herbert Hoover (1929-33), was unlikely to be re-nominated. He had been stigmatized by the collapse of Wall Street and the subsequent Great Depression. As he had often done before, Longworth chose the relaxing and invigorating environment of Aiken, South Carolina for his recuperation. He said on this occasion that Aiken was "the perfect spot for me" to rest and recover. He stayed with James Freeman Curtis, an old friend and fellow Harvard alumnus who owned a home at the corner of Hayne Avenue and Waterloo Street. The Shellhouse Funeral Home occupies that property today. Curtis was an Assistant Secretary of the Treasury in the administration of William Howard Taft (1909-13) and a prominent New York lawyer. His daughter Laura later married G.H. "Pete" Bostwick, in October 1933. Pete Bostwick and his family were—and are still—luminaries in the Aiken Winter Colony equestrian firmament. His exploits in polo, flat racing and steeplechase are extensively chronicled in an exhibit at the Aiken Thorougbred Hall of Fame in Hopeland Gardens.

Longworth was a gregarious *raconteur* and *bon vivant*, admired by most and hated by many. His social orbits included politicians, celebrities, wealthy financiers and ordinary citizens. His infidelities and partying life style seemingly didn't lessen his attractiveness as a politician— a characteristic some would note in many subsequent choices for president.

Among those accompanying Longworth to Aiken that March of 1931 was Dwight Filley Davis. Davis was Secretary of War under President Calvin Coolidge (1923-29) and Governor of the Philippines under President Herbert Hoover (1929-33). Despite his lofty government positions, Davis is more often remembered for lending his name to the silver trophy that represents the tennis championship of the world, "The Davis Cup."

Longworth arrived in Aiken still fatigued and with a definite pallor. He played several rounds of golf at Palmetto, but the nagging cough persisted. On Wednesday April 8, he took a decided turn for the worse. His wife was summoned from her home in Washington as a team of doctors and four nurses attended her husband around the clock. News of the gravity of his illness spread and soon a throng of reporters assembled in front of the Hayne Avenue home of James Curtis.

Alice arrived in time to be at his bedside before Nicholas

Longworth died. He was 62 years old. On a pre-arranged signal, one of the doctors raised and then lowered the blinds of the second floor room where he died. The reporters scattered for the nearest phones to file the biggest story in Aiken's political history.

Alice's half-brothers, Archibald and Kermit, caught the next flight from New York to Charleston where they chartered a Southern Airways plane to fly to Augusta. The next morning, Longworth's funeral cortege wended its way down Hayne and Park Avenues to the Union Street train depot where a private car awaited to bear his remains away to Cincinnati for burial. Mayor W.H. Weatherford declared a day of mourning and all businesses closed in honor of Mr. Longworth. Citizens of Aiken lined the streets in silence as the procession passed slowly by. Among them was Congressman James F. Byrnes of Aiken, who would become a U.S. Senator, a Supreme Court Justice and a Secretary of State under Franklin Roosevelt.

Eleanor (Cissy) Medill Patterson was another wealthy dilettante of the "Gilded Age" whose encounter with Aiken was tinged with tragedy. Cissy Patterson was born to the Medill family of Chicago, founders of the Chicago Tribune and its newspaper empire. She was groomed by her mother, who became the grandest *grande dame* in Washington society, to be a socialite. She was sent to the finest girl's schools in the Northeast to prepare her to follow in her mother's footsteps. When Patterson was nineteen, her uncle Robert Sanderson McCormick was named ambassador to Austria-Hungary. While visiting him in Vienna she met and married a polish count, Joseph Gizycki. She was 22 to his 35.

The marriage was doomed from the start. Gizycki was an inveterate gambler and womanizer. He abused his servants and ultimately Cissy. She sued for divorce. The count then kidnapped their daughter, Felicia. It took the intervention of President Taft to finally obtain her release. This only occurred after Cissy's family endowed the count with a small fortune. Following that, Cissy reverted to her wayward socialite ways, traveling around the country in a private railroad car. She bought a large ranch in

Jackson Hole, Wyoming where she had torrid affairs with both a cowboy and a former cattle rustler.

In April, 1925, she married Elmer Schlesinger, a prominent New York lawyer. During that period, she wrote two novels. Glass Houses was a thinly disguised exposé on the glitzy and decadent Washington social scene. Fall Flight was a *roman-a-clef* based on her life with Gizycki.

Cissy Patterson and Alice Longworth were the best of friends until Alice found Nick and Cissy, *in flagrante,* on the floor of the Longworth's bathroom during one of their parties—the lights were on and the door was unlocked.

Cissy and Elmer were estranged when, in 1928, he died in the Palmetto clubhouse following a round of golf with his Aiken host, C. Oliver Iselin. Cissy brought her private car Ranger to Aiken to retrieve Schlesinger's body, which was lying in state at "Whitehall," the home of her first cousin, Robert McCormick. She took Elmer back to Washington for a magnificent funeral service at the family's DuPont Circle mansion.

The death of her husband and the feud with Alice prompted Cissy to abandon her frivolous lifestyle. The printer's ink running through her veins finally rose to the surface. Her brother Joseph was running the New York Daily News and her cousin Robert was publisher of the family flagship, the Chicago Tribune. She asked both of them to hire her and they both refused. They saw her as a spoiled dilettante with no newspaper acumen. She tried to buy the Washington Times-Herald from William Randolph Hearst, but he wouldn't sell. Reluctantly however, he did agree to take her on as a managing editor in exchange for her financial support of the paper. Cissy turned out to be an extraordinary newspaper woman. Within a few short years she had the Times-Herald earning over $1,000,000 per year. She could now look across town and thumb her nose at Miss McLean and her Post.

Cissy's brand of publishing was slash and burn, and take no prisoners. She was right at home in the bare-knuckled arena of Washington politics. She once said to her staff, "If my grandmother is raped, put it on the front page." At the height of her power, Colliers magazine called her "The most powerful woman in America." Henry Luce's Time wrote, "She is the most hated woman in America." Whichever was true, and maybe both were, she was a force to be reckoned with in a publishing and political world dominated by men. When Cissy and Joe Patterson, Evalyn McLean and Robert McCormick were in residence together in Aiken, the control of the news that was printed in Chicago, New York and Washington resided there with them.

27

The Roaring Twenties

There are those who might attribute *"karmic"* or "*cosmic"* significance to the fact that both the eighteenth and nineteenth amendments to the U.S. Constitution became law in the same year. The Volstead Act, better known as "Prohibition," was effective on January 17, 1920 when the first 1,000 federal agents fanned out across the nation in a government campaign against the manufacturing, importing or distributing of alcoholic beverages in the United States. The Women's Rights Act was ratified on August 18, 1920. The nineteenth amendment gave women the right to vote; the eighteenth amendment took away their right to drink. Both constitutional amendments would have far-reaching effects on the country during the years between the Wars. Their legacy and its effects still reverberate throughout American society.

The First World War was over, the Spanish Flu epidemic was past, and the flapper era was in full swing. The privations brought on by war and pestilence gave way to a period of exuberant and near unfettered decadence. For the first time the number of people living in cities in America surpassed the rural population. The wealth accumulated in the turn-of-the-century "gilded age" was itching to be spent, and Warren G. Harding wasn't going to stand in the way. He promised a return to normalcy and preached an "America First" policy. His presidency (1921-23) loosened the "progressivism" clamp on Wall Street and its financial tycoons that had begun in Teddy Roosevelt's administration and was then continued by Taft and Wilson. Harding's administration ushered in a new wave of capitalistic excess. The president himself became enmeshed in one of the largest corruption scandals of all time. While he escaped charges directly, several in his administration went to jail for their collusion in "Teapot Dome," the Wyoming oil field bribery and fraud scandal. Harding was spared further embarrassment, and possible criminal charges, with his sudden death in California while returning from a trip to Alaska.

Harding was succeeded by his vice president, Calvin Coolidge, a staunchly Calvinistic member of the Congregationalist Church. "Silent Cal" extended the *laissez faire* policies of his predecessor and also embarked on a crusade to reduce the national government's role in its citizen's lives. Unlike his gregarious wife, Coolidge was introverted and a man of few words. At one party he was seated next to Dorothy Parker, popular author, writer and co-founder of the famous literary group known as the Algonquin Roundtable.

"Mr. Coolidge," she said. "I've made a bet against a fellow who said it was impossible to get more than two words out of you."

"You lose," Coolidge said wryly.

Years later, upon being notified that President Coolidge had died Parker quipped, "How can you tell?"

The alcohol drinking habits of the country in the twentieth century were markedly different from those in modern times. Drinking and alcoholism among adult men was rampant, far exceeding current levels. The rosters of temperance societies and suffragist movements were replete with many of the same names. Along with Carrie Nation, Susan B. Anthony, who would later found the most well known suffragist group, was an early convert to the temperance movement. She formed the Women's State Temperance Society in New York long before she became a suffragette. It was at a meeting of that organization that she first met Elizabeth Cady Stanton, the woman who would become her staunchest ally in the fight for women's rights.

"The reign of tears is over. The slums will soon be a memory. We will turn our prisons into factories and our jails into storehouses and corn cribs. Men will walk upright. Women will smile and children will laugh. Hell will be forever for rent."

That was the famous Chicago evangelist Billy Sunday's prediction in a sermon following the passage of the prohibition amendment. Sunday was the most celebrated evangelist of his time. What he got instead may have been history's most egregious example of "the law of unintended consequences." Between 1920 and 1933, when the twenty-first amendment repealed the eighteenth, crime exploded in America.

Arrests for drunken and disorderly conduct increased 41%
Arrests for drunken drivers increased 81%
The number of federal convicts increased 561%
The federal prison population increased 1000%

Almost every category of crime exploded during prohibition. Most of that growth was directly attributable to the rise of organized crime. In Billy Sunday's own Chicago, there were more than 400 gang-related murders, and most of those could be laid at the feet of Chicago's Mafia boss Al Capone. Capone, along with his counterparts in New York, Detroit, Miami and other major cities, turned prohibition into a criminal enterprise that rivaled the largest corporations. From his fifth-floor suite in Chicago's Lexington Hotel, Al Capone reigned over a vast criminal empire. At the height of prohibition it is estimated that more than $4,000,000,000 was made on bootleg whisky each year.

Al Capone – Mug Shot

Capone and his cronies were

responsible for importing, distributing and selling millions of gallons of liquor. The dirty little (not so) secret was that they were aided and abetted by many so-called "upstanding" members of polite society. Chicago politicians of every stripe were on Capone's payroll—while their city was running a $300,000,000 deficit. The graft and corruption extended to Springfield where several governors and members of their administrations were implicated. The stigma and sordid legacy of that corruption has persisted into modern times. Chicago politics and corruption are considered by many to be essentially synonymous.

There is little question that the Joseph P. Kennedy family fortune stemmed in large part from prohibition. Rumors abound of the senior Kennedy's association with the New York (Luciano) and Miami (Lansky) crime families. Allegations were that he smuggled in most of the Scotch whisky that was consumed during the 1920s. When it became apparent that prohibition was coming to an end, following Franklin Roosevelt's election in 1932, Kennedy amassed a huge inventory of whisky and gin in England. After prohibition was repealed, with the ratification of the twenty-first amendment, James Roosevelt, the president's son, helped Kennedy form Somerset Importers. Both men realized immense profits from the vast cache of liquor Kennedy had stashed away in London warehouses.

Later, Joe Kennedy was named to head the Securities and Exchange Commission. When someone asked FDR why he had hired such a crook to head the SEC, he jauntily replied, "It takes one to catch one." In what many considered a *quid pro quo,* Kennedy was subsequently appointed ambassador to Great Britain's Court of St. James, a job he summarily lost when he declared England doomed following the "Battle of Britain."

F. Scott Fitzgerald's literary triumph, *The Great Gatsby*, published in 1925, painted a vivid picture of the decadence and criminality that was unleashed across the nation by prohibition. The disasters that befell Fitzgerald's fictional characters Jay Gatsby and Tom Buchanan (Tommy Hitchcock's alter ego) were directly attributable to debauchery and bootlegging.

The desire for temperance was even stronger in the South's "bible belt". As early as 1884 there was a drive to outlaw the sale of liquor in Aiken. It was already banned in the unincorporated areas of the county but remained legal in several municipalities. The campaign for a statewide ban on alcohol got as far as the state legislature, where it failed. The legislators argued that the issue should be resolved at the city and county level.

From 1892 until 1907, complete prohibition in South Carolina was avoided by the adoption of the South Carolina Dispensary System which ruled that all liquor sold in South Carolina must be manufactured, distilled and sold within the boundaries and under the auspices of the state. That was Governor Benjamin "Pitchfork Ben" Tillman's scheme to avoid the threat of almost certain total prohibition. It didn't hurt that the plan added untold millions to the state treasury—much of which found its way into corrupt politician's pockets. In 1907, the longsuffering public had had enough and voted the "dispensary system" out. The legislature ruled however, that individual counties could elect to continue the dispensary system by authorizing a single provider with a single outlet in each county. Those counties that adopted their own dispensary system got rich, to the chagrin of the dry counties. Finally, the entire house of cards collapsed and de facto prohibition reigned in South Carolina from 1915 until the passage of the nineteenth amendment in 1920 made it federal law. Bootlegging and illegal stills thrived. Every backwoods farmer with a crib full of corn and access to sugar and yeast became an independent businessman. Tunnels were rumored to run from some Winter Colony homes to the Union Street depot to facilitate the underground transport of bootleg liquor.

With or without legal constraints, the residents of Aiken and the Winter Colony never lacked for access to booze. The loophole allowing pharmacists to dispense medicinal alcohol made a farce of prohibition. Druggists brought up on charges pleaded innocent under the law and juries agreed, without ever leaving their seats. Newspapers of the era are replete with hundreds of cases brought for various violations of the law.

Most defendants pleaded guilty and were given small fines and/or prison sentences, many of which were summarily suspended by the judge for the promise of good behavior. The nation wasn't in the mood to punish these petty offenders while the Capones and Kennedys went Scot free.

Thus, by 1932, there was a public hue and cry for the repeal of prohibition and a return to a system of legal alcohol with strict government controls—anything to curb the rampant crime wave sweeping across the country. The *Charleston News and Courier*, a former bastion of support for prohibition, openly advocated for repeal. So, in 1933, with Franklin D. Roosevelt ascendant in Washington, Congress officially enacted the twenty-first amendment. They bowed to the changing attitudes of the American populace, sending the document out to the states for ratification or defeat. Still, there were so many state legislatures that were afraid to touch the "third rail" of "Prohibition" that Congress decreed the twenty-first amendment be acted on by state conventions, instead of the state legislatures. It became the only amendment ever ratified through that process, thus removing the politically fraught onus from the legislators and placing it on the shoulders of unelected convention delegates. On December 10, 1933, Utah became the 36th state to ratify the amendment. It became effective on December 15. Prohibition was over.

28

An Aiken Dynasty

Marie Lillian Stokes Bostwick Gilbert

The beautiful couple emerged into the brilliant sunlight streaming down on the Park Avenue esplanade of St. Bartholomew's Episcopal Church in New York. The throng of rice throwers they faced was liberally sprinkled with names from the pages of the New York Social Register: Rockefeller, Flagler, Mellon, Stokes, Astor, Vanderbilt.... The date for the glitzy wedding of Albert Carlton Bostwick and Marie Lillian Stokes had been marked in red on their social engagement calendars for many months.

Albert Carlton Bostwick was the son of Jabez Bostwick, a partner in the Standard Oil Trust and a major owner of the New York Railroad. Among Jabez Bostwick's partners in Standard Oil were John D. and William Rockefeller and Henry Flagler, giants of industry whose many business ventures stretched from New York to San Francisco and Chicago to Miami. The bride, Marie Lillian Stokes, was from a prominent New York banking family.

The Bostwick-Stokes wedding would play a defining role in the development of Aiken's Winter Colony. Albert Bostwick was heir to a large fortune from his father Jabez Bostwick. Jabez, like his partners Henry Flagler and John D. Rockefeller, was a self-made man who had amassed a fortune in Standard

Oil and the New York Railroad. He died of tragic circumstances in 1892 when a fire broke out in the stables at his Mamaroneck Long Island estate, "Friedhelm." Mr. Bostwick was awakened by a clamor at midnight and saw through his bedroom window that the stables were afire. He dressed hurriedly and ran to the barn. While giving orders to his stable hands, he suddenly grabbed his chest and collapsed. He suffered a massive heart attack and died soon thereafter. Jabez and Helen Bostwick had two children, Albert Carlton and Fanny Evelyn. When Jabez Bostwick's widow Helen died in 1920, the will named her daughter Fanny Voronoff and her son Albert's children as heirs to the $30,000,000 inheritance, thereby making each of the grandchildren independently wealthy.

Albert had been a first rank sportsman, winning trophies in polo and auto racing. On November 16, 1901, he set the first land speed record in excess of sixty miles per hour. Albert and Marie had visited Aiken in their short life together. Those memories would draw Marie back in later years. In 1911, at the young age of 35, Albert died, leaving Marie widowed with five children: Dorothy – 12, Albert – 10, Lillian – 7, Dunbar – 4, and George Herbert – 3.

In the meantime, their mother Marie remarried. She wed Mr. Fitch Gilbert, a prominent lawyer and farmer from Gilbertsville, New York. When Marie and Fitch Gilbert decided to establish a winter home in Aiken, they unwittingly founded the Bostwick/Von Stade dynasty that remains prominent in the community's equestrian society.

Fitch Gilbert and his new bride came to Aiken in 1927 hoping to find a winter horse property that would satisfy their varied interests. Marie had a soft spot for all animals, not just horses. Fitch loved horses, hunting and fishing. He also loved "gentleman farming." Marie asked friends from her New York circle to suggest a realtor for them. The same response came back from everyone they asked—Eulalie Salley.

"Welcome to Aiken," Eulalie said as the Gilberts stepped down from their coach at the Aiken depot on Union Street. "I'm so happy that you have chosen me to help you find the perfect home here. Your friends in New York have already contacted me and said that I should take extra good care of you. It's obvious that you are highly respected there. It's always a pleasure to welcome such nice people to our little community."

"Thank you for your kind words Mrs. Salley," Mr. Gilbert said. "I must say that you are held in the highest regard by our friends who come here for the winter. I've never heard such praise. Marie and I look forward to exploring Aiken and finding that perfect residence for our family to spend the winter months."

"That's very flattering, and I will do my best to live up to the trust placed in me. And please call me Eulalie. I have asked the porters to gather your bags. As soon as they arrive we're off to the Highland Park Hotel. When you've had a chance to freshen up we can begin looking at property. I have several that I think will interest you."

"Eulalie," Mr. Gilbert said as he started for the elevator, "I didn't get a chance to tell you before, but I'm also interested in a small farm, with enough acreage for a hunting preserve."

This last request caught Eulalie off guard. She called her office and asked an agent to start pulling together properties that fit Fitch Gilbert's description and to rush them over to the hotel. Thirty minutes later, when the Gilberts came back downstairs, Eulalie had five property files arrayed on a table.

"How did you do that?" Mr. Gilbert asked.

"You might have heard that my company does everything in Aiken real estate but "brush your teeth." We pride ourselves on being ready to meet any of our client's needs. It's all in a day's work."

"Well, I am certainly impressed," he said.

By five o'clock the Gilberts had driven past five properties and inspected two of them. None were quite right.

"Eulalie, we have three younger children and two who are already married. They all love horses, so we need a large place near the riding trails. I'd also like to have a place to house a trainer for my horses?"

Eulalie wrinkled her brow. "Let me make a few calls this evening. I know a couple of families who are considering building new homes nearer the polo fields. Hopefully, I'll have better news in the morning. I'll also show you some of the farm properties we looked at earlier. Now, I'll get you back to your hotel. I understand you have some old friends dropping by for dinner."

"Yes, the Posts are joining us. It should be a fun evening." Fred Post had moved his polo pony business to Aiken in 1911 and still counted Fitch Gilbert among his clients.

Long shadows from the early morning sun stretched across Hayne Avenue as Eulalie made her way to her realty office on Park Avenue. The new home on Hayne Avenue, bought from the Goss family a year earlier when she sold "Let's Pretend", was only a few blocks away. The two towers of the Highland Park hotel loomed above her as she rounded the curve onto Park. One of the residents she had called the night before had agreed to meet her at eight o'clock. Eulalie crossed her fingers and said a little prayer. If everything worked out, she might get two sales today, one for this client's property to the Gilberts and one for a five acre plot on Barnard that backed up to the Whitney polo field.

"Good morning Mr. Hunniwell, it was so gracious of you to meet me this early in the morning."

"Think nothing of it, Eulalie, and please call me Hollis. I've already been on a hunt in Hitchcock Woods and played three chukkers of polo at Whitney Field this morning." He cleared his throat, straightened his tie, and sat upright in the easy chair. "I don't mind telling you that what you suggested last night really intrigued me. By the way, how did you know I was considering building a new place?"

"A little birdie told me, Hollis." she said with a chuckle. "You know how gossip flies around our little town. It's impossible to keep a secret."

"Yeah, ain't that the truth? Now tell me about this proposition of yours."

"I believe you are familiar with the Fitch Gilberts from

upstate New York. Well, they are in town and looking for a horse property near the woods with room for a bunch of kids, horses and stable hands. As soon as he told me that, and since I had heard that you might be looking for a new home, I thought of your place. I was also aware of a beautiful five-acre parcel coming on the market that backs up to the Whitney polo field and I just felt it would be ideal for you. So, I put two-and-two together and gave you a call."

"What do you think I can get for my place?" Hunniwell was a savvy businessman who didn't mince words. He wanted to get right to the point. Eulalie wrote a number on a slip of paper and slid it across the desk. She sat back to observe the reaction. He smiled. "Eulalie, if you can get Mr. and Mrs. Gilbert to accept that, you've got a deal." Now all Eulalie had to do was convince the Gilberts that the property was worth that amount.

Eulalie drove under the portico of the hotel. The Gilberts were waiting. She completed the circular drive onto Highland Park and headed east on Park Avenue. She turned right at the courthouse and continued down Chesterfield, bearing left in front of the Aiken Institute where Whiskey road began and the pavement ended. Her new, black, Chrysler limousine bumped along as she dodged fresh deposits of horse manure. She passed Bill Whitney's "Joye Cottage" then "Rond Point' at the intersection with Coker Springs. She slowed to make the turn onto Dupree Place. The Iselin estate "Hopelands" was on the left. She turned into the first driveway on the right. The mailbox read 120 Dupree Place. A small caretaker's cottage sat to the left and several stables were visible in the distance. To the right, facing Whiskey Road, was the home of Mr. Hollis Hunniwell. The roof of the rambling two story house, like the other buildings, was covered with red tiles, giving the property its unique name, "Red Top." Eulalie watched in the rear view mirror for the reaction from Fitch and Marie. The smile that lit up Marie's face told Eulalie that she had made the sale. It was now just a matter of tying up the loose ends.

"It's a wonderful property and perfectly located," Mr. Gilbert said. "How much is the owner asking for it?"

"He wants $27,000 for it, but I think he might come down a little from that," she said, quoting a slightly higher number than she had written on that slip of paper.

"That's a little steep considering how much we'll need to spend on renovations and improvements."

"Oh, Fitch, it's worth every penny of it," Marie Gilbert said. "You couldn't find a better location, and the children will love it."

"I tell you what, Eulalie," he said. "If you can get the price down to $25,000, we'll take it."

Fitch Gilbert's counter offer was $2,000 more than the price quoted to Mr. Hunniwell. Eulalie was going to make both parties very happy and earn a nice commission in the process; maybe two, if she could close the deal on the Whitney Field property as well. She would add a third commission later when the Gilberts bought one of the farm properties that Eulalie had showed them. The 300 acre farm was near Jackson on SC 125. Over the following year, the Gilberts made nearly sixty more land transactions, expanding their plantation to 10,000 acres. One of Mr. Gilbert's hunting preserve partners was Albert Willcox, son of the founder of the Willcox hotel and its owner/manager. In 1952, the entire property, along with the city of Ellenton and hundreds of other farms and villages, fell victim to eminent domain. Uncle Sam aggregated nearly 310 square miles (200,000 acres) of Aiken and Barnwell counties along the Savannah River to construct the Savannah River Site for the production of weapons grade tritium and plutonium, the key fissionable components of hydrogen bombs.

Of more lasting significance to Eulalie than the commissions, was the abiding friendship she developed with Marie Gilbert and all the wonderful memories they shared. For thirty-five winters, Marie Gilbert was a prominent, if somewhat eccentric, figure in Aiken. Her love of animals led to some strange encounters with the local populace. Some time following the purchase of the farm, Marie had Fitch plant fifty acres of carrots to feed to the rabbit population of Aiken. No details remain of how she herded the rabbits onto her ranch at feeding time.

On another occasion the Salleys took a ride out into the country to check on a farm property they had bought. They were surprised to find that a Negro family was living in one of the tumbledown shacks on the property. Julian, being of a kind heart, told them they could remain on the property. Several days later, he went back to check on the family and discovered them packing up to move.

"Where are you going? Have you found another farm to work?" he asked.

No. It turned out that Marie Gilbert had heard of the plight of the family from Eulalie and went out to check on them. When Marie arrived at their house they were in the yard rubbing liniment on the leg of their ailing mule. Marie took one look at the lame, spavined, creature and offered the man five dollars for the horse, which he gratefully accepted. Then Marie got her gun from the car and shot the suffering animal, putting it out of its obvious misery.

"What's that got to do with your moving?" Julian asked the old Negro woman.

"Well," she said, looking around carefully, "the old man ain't feeling so good. So we figger we better move befo' Miss Gilbert come back." The Salleys got quite a laugh from that story.

Marie Gilbert was not one to let grass grow under her feet. As soon as the moving vans were gone, she was calling all her old friends. She was appalled at the numbers of wild animals and stray cats and dogs that were wandering Aiken's streets. Within the first year she had established an Aiken chapter of the Society for the Prevention of Cruelty to Animals—and recruited most of her friends to join. She worked tirelessly to improve the state of animal welfare in the community. Each week, almost without fail, her personal ads appeared in the local newspaper, describing lost animals that were in her care. The lane leading to the woods behind "Red Top" was lined with kennels for the strays she collected, or that were dumped on her property.

Marie established three annual events to support the SPCA.

They were must attends for everyone who was anyone in the Colony. The first was the rummage sale. Every self-respecting wife of every self-respecting household in Aiken was expected to empty her closets of fashionable clothes that were no longer in use. Local women from miles around would crowd into Aiken for the event. When the bell rang opening the doors, a tide of humanity surged through to begin fighting over the fabulous bargains. Not a few upstanding ladies appeared in church the next morning with bruises and fingernail scratches, to go along with the stylish outfits they had managed to wrest away from a fellow parishioner. Eulalie Salley described it as the world's greatest "cat fight."

The Aiken Dog Show, inaugurated in 1930 by Marie to support the SPCA, was held at the Fermata School athletic field. That is, if it didn't rain, as it did for the second show in 1931. As the heavens opened, everyone retreated to the shelter of the stables at the Whitney track. Prestigious judges were brought in from Atlanta to inspect the 100+ entries. Their able assistants included Mrs. Fitch Gilbert and Mrs. Claudia Phelps (Rose Hill). Winners that year included entries by G.H. Mead (Mead Paper-The Pillars), William Ziegler (Royal Baking Powder-Sunshine Cottage), A.H. Niblack (Cudahy-Let's Pretend), Lucy Mercer Rutherfurd (Ridgeley Hall). Support for the dog show grew year-by-year, and the increasing contributions helped to expand the reach of the SPCA's efforts.

The Horse and Mule show was introduced in the early 1930's to coincide with the annual Aiken horse show. It might not have had the elitist appeal of the two other fund raising events, but the hilarity and hi-jinks it provided delighted all classes of Aiken society, from the colony's matriarchs to the black tenant farmers. The show was held at Dunbar Bostwick's training track, built in 1936. The track, located at 620 Banks Mill Road, is now known as McGhee's mile.The trotting track drew the best sulky drivers from across the country to train their horses for the upcoming harness races in the northeast. Bostwick later added a cross-country training facility in the track's infield.

The mule show prizes were based on the general condition

of the mules, and each had to be shown by its owner. First prize for white farmers was ten dollars. For white tenant farmers, the prize was five dollars. For black tenant farmers, first prize was also ten dollars. Single entrant categories received a dollar. All the shows were segregated by race.

In 1937, after ten years of cajoling and fundraising, Marie Gilbert and Hope Iselin, together with many colony volunteers, led a campaign to create a permanent home for the SPCA in Aiken. Major donations from the organizers, together with community contributions, permitted the purchase of a two and one-half acre tract of land on Banks Mill Road, across from the Arthur Young plantation, "Crossways." A facility consisting of three buildings was erected over the next few months. The SPCA occupied that facility until 1981 when the organization relocated to its present site on Wire Road. Arthur Young, founder of one of the world's largest public accounting firms, bought "Crossways" in 1927 for $40,000 and spent $35,000 renovating it. Mr. Young died at "Crossways" in 1948 and is buried in Bethany Cemetery.

29

Aiken Dynasty—Second Generation

Marie Stokes Bostwick Gilbert left her strong imprint on her adopted winter home of Aiken, South Carolina in many ways, but none more indelible than through the exploits of the five Bostwick children she brought with her. The lives of all five would intertwine with the development of the colony, and all would leave their mark on Aiken. But it was two of the boys, Dunbar and George, who would create the grandest legacies. Legacies that continue into the 21st century.

Dorothy

1899 - 2001

Dorothy, the oldest, was 28 when the Fitch Gilberts bought "Red Top" in 1927. She had been given in marriage by her step-father five years earlier, at the family estate, Village Farms, in Gilbertsville, N.Y. She married Sampson Smith, grandson of the renowned navy admiral, William Sampson, for whom he was named. Admiral Sampson's naval career spanned over forty years. He lost his ironclad ship Patapsco in a sea battle near Charleston in 1865, during America's Civil War. In 1898, during the Spanish-American War, he was credited with destroying the Spanish Fleet in Cuba.

Lillian Bostwick acted as maid-of honor for her sister. Albert Bostwick was one of the ushers. William McKim was best man. Dorothy and Sampson made their home at Leatherstocking Farm in Cooperstown, New York and in Short Hills, New Jersey. Mr. Smith designed and built racing yachts. He and Dorothy were prominent in racing circles. Smith also developed an "auto-gyro," precursor to the helicopter. Dorothy was the first woman to hold a license to pilot helicopters. The couple divorced in 1942.

In 1950, Dorothy married Joseph Campbell, Vice President and Treasurer of Columbia University. President Eisenhower named Campbell Comptroller General of the United States in 1954, and the couple moved to Washington. Dorothy took advantage of her years in Washington to develop her considerable talent for painting. Her works are exhibited in many national galleries and museums and in the Cooperstown Art Museum, which she founded. Dorothy passed away in 2001, in Sarasota, Florida, at the advanced age of 102. Notably, she left behind a multitude of family members, including 41 great-grandchildren. Of her four siblings, only Dunbar survived Dorothy.

Albert

1901 - 1980

In addition to the large sum Albert Carlton Bostwick received when his mother died, he was already enjoying a large inheritance from his father. The Standard Oil fortune provided the means for Albert to pursue his major passion—thoroughbred horse racing. He was born to race, and pursued flat, steeplechase and polo all his life. With a six-goal rating he was the premier polo player in the family until he was unseated by his younger brother, George "Pete" Bostwick, who attained eight goal status—among the highest ratings in the world.

Both "Brother," as Albert was known to his siblings, and "Pete," owed much of their riding prowess to their uncle, F. Ambrose Clark. Clark was heir to much of the Singer Sewing Machine fortune and was married to Marie's sister, Florence Stokes. Florence was a stellar horsewoman in her own right. Her horse, Kellsboro Jack, won the 1933 English Grand National steeplechase at Aintree, considered the most grueling and prestigious race in the world. The triangular course consisted of thirty-two jumps over a 7.4 mile route. Most mounts never finished. The crowd, estimated at 250,000, caught their collective breath as Pete Bostwick, aboard Jock Whitney's entry, Dusty Foot, went down in a double somersault. Pete survived with a lacerated face.

Upon his death in 1964, Ambrose Clark left Habersham House, his Aiken estate at 726 Grace Avenue, to his nephew "Pete" Bostwick. Habersham House had been renamed "Kellsboro Cottage" after its namesake won the Grand National. Mr. Bostwick later gave the property to the Aiken Day School, which later merged with Mead Hall.

The Clarks also owned the 5,000 acre property known as Iroquois Farms, near Cooperstown, New York as well as their principal 500 acre residence in Old Westbury, Long Island. That estate was given as a campus for the State University of New York. Mr. Clark also owned an apartment in the famous Dakota building on Central Park West in Manhattan, which was built by his grandfather—John Lennon of Beatle's fame lived there and was shot on the street just outside. Finally, Mrs. Clark owned a 10,000 acre plantation north of Tallahassee, Florida. Ambrose Clark's only child predeceased him, and the bulk of his estate went into a family trust.

Ambrose Clark also owned the 10,000 acre Creek Plantation on SR-125 south of the Savannah River Site. It was left as a hunting preserve for F. Skiddy von Stade and his son John. When the von Stades no longer used the plantation, it was sold. One-third of the proceeds were left to St. Thaddeus Episcopal Church. The church established the St. Thaddeus Permanent Endowment Trust with the proceeds from the sale of Creek Plantation, forming the bulk of its original endowment.

It was Ambrose Clark who first brought the Bostwick boys to Aiken in 1913, and introduced them to polo and racing in the South. All three boys were enrolled in the Aiken Preparatory School. As time passed, Albert devoted more of his time to breeding and training thoroughbreds. Together with Dunbar, Pete and Lillian, Albert bought 25 acres in Old Westbury to build a polo facility to be enjoyed by the entire community.

They referred to it as "Polo for the People." That field is still in use.

Albert's signal racing accomplishment was a victory in the Preakness in 1933 with his horse Mate. In that fortieth running of the Preakness, Mate tied the track speed record of one minute and thirty-nine seconds. At one time, Albert had over twenty horses in training. Another of his finest mounts, Yarn, was shipped to England to run in several prominent stakes races there.

In 1936, Albert married Eleanor Purviance Sage, a divorcee, at the St. Regis Hotel in New York. Those in attendance were the Ambrose Clarks, the Fitch Gilberts, the Pete Bostwicks, and Mrs. Robert V. McKim (nee Lillian Bostwick.) The couple had one son, Albert C. Bostwick III, in 1932. Albert remained a prominent figure in the racing world until his death on September 26, 1980. Eleanor passed away in Old Westbury at the age of 100 in 2004.

Lillian

1906 - 1987

Lillian Bostwick married Robert V. McKim in 1928, at the Church of the Transfiguration, in New York City. McKim was from a wealthy New Jersey family that made Aiken their winter home early on. Like her brothers, Lillian attended school in Aiken during the winter. She spent several semesters at the Fermata School. How and when she met McKim is unknown, but it probably occurred when both were students in Aiken.

The McKims had three daughters, including Lilly, who founded the Lily Pulitzer fashion design business. The McKim/Bostwick marriage ended in divorce. In 1937, Lillian then married Ogden Phipps in the sanctuary of St. Bartholomew's, the same church in which her parents were married almost forty years earlier. Phipps was divorced from his first wife, Ruth Pruyn.

Henry Ogden Phipps' grandfather was the second largest shareholder in Carnegie Steel. His father, Henry Carnegie Phipps, was a high-scoring polo player in the Aiken of 1910-

1920. He, Devereux Milburn and Thomas Hitchcock were often teamed together. Ogden inherited his father's athleticism and was seven times court tennis champion of the United States and once of Great Britain. Following service in the navy during WWII, he joined the Smith-Barney investment house and then ran the high-powered Bessemer Trust, managing his own and the inheritances of his cohort of second generation aristocrats. All that money and power didn't necessarily shield the wealthy couple from life's tragedies. In 1962, Henry Ogden Phipps, his son with Ruth Pruyn, took his own life.

Ogden and Lillian formed one of the largest steeple-chasing combines in the world. Two of her horses were inducted into the U.S. Hall of Fame and won eight Grand National Steeplechase titles. Ogden's horse "Easygoer" won the Belmont in 1989 after finishing second in the Kentucky Derby and the Preakness

Unlike most of the dynastic horse racing families such as the Whitneys and the Vanderbilts, the Phipps bloodline continues into modern times. Ogden Mills "Dinny" Phipps headed the Bessemer Trust after his father's retirement and then retired himself in 1994 at the age of fifty-four, to devote more time to horse racing. He has entered horses in the Breeder's Cup 17 times with three winners and eight finishes in the money, claiming purses totaling $3,600,000. He also bred one of his horses to Storm Song whose dam was Summer Squall, both owned by Aiken's Cott Campbell of Dogwood Stables. Summer Squall's nephew, Storm Cat, fetched one of the highest prices ever paid for an untried horse—$6,800,000. Both Summer Squall and Storm Song are enshrined in the Aiken Thoroughbred Racing Hall of Fame, located in the former stables of the Iselin estate, Hopeland Gardens. Ironically, the hall of fame is just across the street from Lillian Phipps' childhood home, "Red Top."

Lillian Stokes Bostwick McKim Phipps died at her estate in Summerville, South Carolina in 1987 at the age of 81. Her second husband, Henry Ogden Phipps, died in West Palm Beach Florida in 2002, at the age of 93.

Dunbar

1908 – 2006

Dunbar Wright Bostwick, like his siblings, had deep ties to Aiken through his mother, Marie Bostwick Gilbert, and his uncle, Ambrose Clark. He was indoctrinated early-on into the polo and racing culture of his winter home. He became a six-goal star on the polo fields of the U.S. and around the world, teaming with his brothers Pete and Albert as well as other local polo stars such as Devereux Milburn and Seymour Knox. He attended school at Aiken Prep and at St. Paul's in Concord, New Hampshire. He enrolled at Yale in 1928 and led their hockey team to a national championship in 1932.

Dunbar continued his pursuit of polo until it was interrupted by World War II. As a U. S. Army Air Force Lieutenant Colonel he earned a Bronze Star and the Belgian Croix de Guerre as a prominent member of General Eisenhower's planning team for the D-Day invasion of Normandy. Upon his return home, he established a horse training facility at his Vermont farm on the shores of Lake Champlain where he concentrated on breeding and training harness racers. He christened the farm "Shelburne." Simultaneously, he acquired the "Powder House Stables" in Aiken, South Carolina and established the Aiken Mile racetrack for trotters. That track is now known as McGhee's Mile.

Dunbar Bostwick

Dunbar and Electra built a cottage in Aiken adjacent to Whitney Polo Field in 1938. Dunbar spent his summers breeding trotters in Vermont and his winters training them in Aiken. It was at Shelburne that he introduced a training protocol that would change the face of the sport of harness racing. One of his most famous thoroughbreds, "Chris Spencer," became lame at the end of his second racing season. Dunbar, not wanting to subject the injured horse to the rigors of track racing, would exercise him in the shallow waters along the shores of Lake Champlain. Twice a day, tethered to a small outboard boat, "Chris Spencer" would "trot" along the sandy bottom of the lake, thereby lessening the strain on his legs while simultaneously strengthening his muscles. Within a year, "Chris Spencer" was back on the harness racing circuit, winning events all across the country. He continued to collect blue ribbons for eight more years before being retired to stud at Shelburne. He was the first horse to fly on an airplane when he was taken to race in, and win, the California Stakes in 1952. The pioneering water exercise created by Dunbar Bostwick is still practiced wherever horses train and race. Most breeding and training facilities now include swimming pools for their very valuable livestock.

Dunbar was the founding director of the Saratoga Harness Racing Association, and he holds several patents related to starting devices for harness racing gates. He was also an owner of the Aviation Instrument Manufacturing Corporation on Long Island where he was instrumental in the development of radio navigation and instrument landing devices during WW II.

Dunbar Bostwick married Electra Webb, a Vanderbilt heiress, at the Cathedral of the Incarnation in Garden City, Long Island on June 29, 1932. Their nuptials were celebrated by over 600 guests and family members. The list of attendants to the bride and groom was liberally sprinkled with Webbs, Vanderbilts, McKims, Bostwicks, Gilberts and Phipps. The home they retired to in Shelburne, Vermont after the wedding was a gift from the bride's father. 500 of the guests were entertained at a post-wedding reception on the lawn of the Bostwick mansion in

Old Westbury. The couple had three children; Electra, Lily and Dundeen. There were no sons to carry on the Dunbar Bostwick name. The family almost lost their lives in November 1950 when the Shelburne home burned to the ground.

Both Dunbar and Electra returned each year to their beloved Bostwick Farms in Shelburne, and both died there: Electra in 1981 and Dunbar in 2006. After Electra's death, Dunbar married Jean Wright Burden, who also passed away at Shelburne, in 1995.

George – (Pete)

1909 – 1982

Of all the Bostwick siblings, George Herbert "Pete" Bostwick, fifth child of Albert and Marie, unarguably left the most vivid and indelible impression on Aiken, South Carolina, his adopted home. He was born in Bisby Lake, (Mamaroneck, Long island) New York on August 14, 1909. "Pete" was a diminutive figure at five feet-three inches tall and 110 pounds, but he loomed large in the world of horse racing. As a jockey his small stature was ideal for flat racing and his powerful build allowed him to excel in the steeplechase. However, it was the combination of his size, physique and fearless riding style that made him the *enfant terrible* on the polo fields of Aiken, Old Westbury and many other venues around the world. He singlehandedly developed the practice of riding his pony directly at the opponent who had the ball, then veering off at the last instant. More often than not the opponent would lose his nerve and swerve to avoid a collision. Occasionally neither rider "blinked" and there was a violent collision. The resultant carnage to horses and riders led the United States Polo Association to ban such tactics. That may have removed one weapon from Bostwick's polo arsenal, but he retained many more. "Pete" Bostwick was player of the year in 1939 when he became an eight goal player in the sport.

Bostwick practically grew up in Aiken and attended Aiken Prep, graduating in 1928. He tried college but it was not for him. He daydreamed in class and failed to study at home. The deans at Yale finally sent him back to his mother. His response when Marie Gilbert scolded him was, "There is no use sitting in school when you can sit on a horse and go somewhere."

And go somewhere he did. Uncle Ambrose took Pete under his wing and practically raised him after he left school. Pete had begun his polo lessons at the age of seven. He was schooled by his aunt, Louise Hitchcock, who was known as the "mother of polo" in the United States. Along with Pete, she taught her son Tommy, his friend Devereux Milburn, and dozens of other boys and girls. Both Tommy and Devereux became ten goal players. Ten of the *students* on her "Meadow Lark" polo team are enshrined in the National Polo Hall of Fame—G.H. Bostwick, Seymour Knox, Alan Corey, Tommy Hitchcock, Stewart Iglehart, Devereux Milburn, Cecil Smith, Louis Stoddard and Harry Payne Whitney. The "Lulie" trained cohort of Aiken players dominated the sport in the 1920's and 1930's. Aiken became the polo capital of the South during those years. Sportsmen moving from Florida to New York in the spring and from New York to Florida in the fall, stopped in Aiken to enjoy the highest level of competition anywhere.

Pete Bostwick played in his first sanctioned polo match in 1928 at the tender age of 18. He went on to compete in polo, steeplechase, and flat racing for 50 years as both rider and trainer. His first win came when he was 18 on his own horse "Beaupre" in the 1928 running of the Whitemarsh Hunt. In addition to training his own horses, he was employed by his sister, Lillian Phipps, to train and ride hers as well. She owned two of the most famous steeplechasers of all time. "Oedipus" was named horse of the year for 1950, 1951 and 1952. That success was followed by "Neji" in 1955, 1957 and 1958. Pete had his own champion in "Barnaby's Bluff" in 1962. He adopted and registered his own racing colors, a pale blue tunic and cap with a pink sash stripe across the front.

Pete spent much of his career working with Tommy Hitchcock, Sr. and actually moved into one of the bachelor pads at "*Mon Repos*." He was the first steeplechase rider to win over a million dollars in one year, while working with Hitchcock. When he went to England, where he was the first American to win at Aintree, he had to modify his colors so they would not conflict with Lord Astor's. He added pink stripes to his sleeves.

It is a little known truth that Negro jockeys played an important role in the early racing history of this country. In 1942, a groom and trainer for Pete Bostwick, Robert Wakefield, introduced his boss to his father, Jimmy Wakefield.

"Are you the Jimmy Wakefield who won the Kentucky Derby?" Pete asked.

"Yes sir, that's me," the small, slender man responded. When Pete Bostwick returned to Aiken that fall, Jimmy Wakefield came with him and continued to work for the Bostwick stables for the rest of his life.

Jimmy had just returned from France, where he fled from the German invasion. He went to France from Russia where he trained and rode horses for the Romanoff court of Czar Nicholas II and for other royalty. He was the champion jockey of Russia in 1904. When the Bolshevik revolution broke out in 1917, Jimmy led his staff and 200 horses on a thousand mile journey to Odessa in the Crimea and saved them from the revolutionaries. It was from there that he escaped to Paris. Jimmy Wakefield won the Kentucky Derby on "Eminence" in 1901 and on "Alan-A-Dale" in 1902. He won 220 races in that year alone. When he retired as a jockey in 1950, Wakefield had won over 2500 races.

Pete, together with his siblings, bought and renovated a polo field in Old Westbury, Long Island. Up until that time, polo was seen as a sport for the elite. The Bostwicks and Gilberts wanted to change that perception, so they installed bleachers at Bostwick field and invited the public to enjoy "the sport of kings." Admission was set at fifty-cents and as many as 2500 patrons would show up for the matches.

Pete's introduction to high goal polo came when Tommy Hitchcock needed a rider for an inconsequential match at an early season tournament at Sands Point, Long Island. He grabbed Pete and told him to take the field. Pete Bostwick so impressed Hitchcock and the others present, that he immediately became a team member. By mid-season he had attained six-goal status. Pete Bostwick was a trailblazer in many ways. In 1930 he became the first jockey to ride a winner in both a steeplechase and a flat race in the same day. He brought home both winners at Belmont Park race track on Long Island. On a typical day he would start by schooling horses for Tommy Hitchcock and Ambrose Clark, before hurrying over to Belmont to ride a mount in an afternoon race. As soon as he was out of his silks, he would head to Old Westbury for eight periods of polo. His stamina and fitness were unequalled in the upper reaches of the equine sporting world.

Pete Bostwick married Laura Elizabeth Curtis in 1933 when they were both 23 years old. Laura's family owned a home on Hayne Avenue and she attended the Fermata School while Pete was attending Aiken Preparatory School. They grew up together on the athletic fields and riding trails of Aiken. Among the 500 guests at their wedding in Roslyn, Long Island were all the usual suspects from the society blue book. Pete was attended by his brothers and in-laws while Laura's entourage included her sisters. Sadly the marriage ended in a Reno divorce court in April of 1949. Laura was awarded a property settlement and custody of their three children, George, James and Laura.

Pete Bostwick

Two weeks later, Pete Bostwick married Dolly von Stade, daughter of F. Skiddy and Kathryn von Stade. Mr. von Stade was a famous horseman and polo player in his own right. He teamed with the luminaries of the sport from 1910 through the 1930's, and was a member of Lulie Hitchcock's "Meadow Larks." She was honored by Time Magazine with a cover portrait in 1930 as the "Matriarch of American Polo." Von Stade was a member of the Jockey Club and a president of the Saratoga Racing Association. In business, he was an extremely successful importer of bristles. In 1914, he commissioned the famous architectural firm of Cross and Cross to design and build a baronial estate in Old Westbury, Long island. Upon his passing in 1967 the estate was bought by the Entenmann family of bakery fame. Inexplicably, the magnificent structure was later abandoned to the elements. It was razed in 2011 to make room for another ubiquitous McMansion development for the *nouveau riche* of Wall Street. F. Skiddy von Stade Sr., patriarch of the family, was prominent in horse racing and polo. He was president of the Saratoga Racing Association during the '40s and '50s and is credited with steering the old course through its desperate times. He died in 1967 at the age of 84.

Time Magazine
August 30, 1930

Pete and Dolly continued to reign over the Aiken horse world. They bought *"Mon Repos*" the former Hitchcock property on Laurens Street. They built their home there in the 1950's, where they raised four children. Their descendants continue to live there. The old squash court, once occupied by a young Pete Bostwick, Sr. is the only original building remaining on the property. It is still used as a guest house by the Bostwick family.

Pete and Dolly loved Aiken and all it represented to their world of horses. They especially loved Hitchcock Woods and its enormous contribution to the community. In the 1980's, when 230 acres between the Devil's Backbone and the railroad cut became available, Dolly, together with Margaret Mellon Hitchcock, purchased the property and donated it to the Woods. She served as a co-chairman of the 1997 "Campaign to Save the Woods" which was successful in purchasing 197 acres from the Aiken Preparatory School. She bequeathed an additional 57 acres in her will. That parcel contains the original cottage in the woods at the foot of South Boundary that serves as the Hitchcock Foundation offices.

Dolly Bostwick served as Master of the Aiken Hounds for many years and was later succeeded in that position by her daughter Lellie Ward. The Bostwick son Charlie is often seen riding in the woods with his daughter Tara Gail.

Dolly's brother, Charles, was killed in 1945, late in the Second World War, when his jeep ran over a land mine near Aachen, Germany. Lieutenant von Stade wouldn't live to witness the brilliant success of his yet unborn daughter, Fredericka. "Flicka", as she was affectionately known, was born just six weeks after her father's death. She went on to captivate the world of grand opera with her magnificent mezzo-soprano voice. Miss von Stade returns often to Aiken to visit and perform.

Another brother, F. Skiddy von Stade, graduated from Harvard and returned there after WWII to become Dean of Freshmen, a position that he would hold until his retirement to New Hampshire. He was 79 when he passed away.

Pete Bostwick died as he lived—astride a horse, playing

polo. He was between chukkers during a match in West Palm Beach, Florida. He had just mounted a fresh steed and was preparing to re-enter the fray when he slumped forward and fell from the saddle. In 1982, at the age of 72, polo lost one of its most enduring champions. Dolly continued to carry on the Bostwick name and tradition until her death in 1998.

Pete Bostwick's many exploits could not be fully contained in the numerous books and articles that recounted his life. It took a large room in the Aiken Thoroughbred Museum to house the awards, artifacts and history that represent the life of Aiken's most famous equestrian. One can only imagine Lulie Hitchcock standing at the rail watching as Pete, Tommy, Devereux, Dunbar, Skiddy and their Meadow Lark teammates gallop across that great polo field in the sky.

30

The Black Eye Patch

One of the most interesting, unconventional and outrageous characters to inhabit Aiken in the colony's heyday was Schuyler Livingston Parsons. Schuyler, who grew up in Islip, Long Island, New York was from a wealthy family that also had a home in Manhattan. Their Long Island home was known as "Whileaway" and was very near the Vanderbilt estate. Schuyler recalled as a young boy going with his father to check on the estate when Mr. Vanderbilt was out of town. His father would compile a meticulous report which he would forward to the Vanderbilts. On other occasions, when the Vanderbilts were home, the family would be invited in to spend an afternoon and perhaps have dinner. The Vanderbilt box at the Metropolitan Opera was made available to the Parsons when not used by the Vanderbilt family. Young Schuyler became a great fan of opera and hobnobbed with many of the biggest stars, including Enrico Caruso and Lily Pons. This was the environment that Schuyler Parsons knew as a child. By birthright and association, a bright future awaited the young man—had fate not intervened to dramatically alter the direction of his life.

Schuyler attended all the right schools, met all the right people, and lived the life of a *bon vivant.* He was lured by the romance of war and joined the privately financed ambulance corps in support of the French during WWI. When America entered the war, Schuyler was summarily dismissed from the corps for bad eyesight. He was taken in by the Vanderbilts in their Paris home. It was there he learned of his father's untimely death. He returned home, collected his $2,000,000 inheritance, and returned to the adrenaline filled streets of Paris.

While walking through the Tuileries near the Louvre, a German plane buzzed the area, spraying bullets as it went. The plane struck a building and then broke apart, scattering debris for blocks, some of which fell on Schuyler. He witnessed one body falling from the plane, while he ran to drag the pilot to safety. With the aid of other passersby, the wounded men were taken to the famous Hotel Crillon on the Rue de Rivoli. Crowds gathered and soon French officials began arriving, including the French president, Raymond Poincaré, and the prime minister, Georges Clemenceau. Parsons was hailed as a hero and lionized upon his return to the states.

In 1920, Mrs. Vincent Astor invited Schuyler to join her for a cruise to Bermuda in her husband's new yacht. Unbeknownst to him she had also invited an old friend from her college days, Betty Pierson. Mrs. Astor was in full matchmaking mode, and Betty and Schuyler were married May 19, 1920. The marriage ended in France three years later when Betty discovered that Schuyler was an abusive alcoholic, a latent homosexual, and that she herself was, if not a lesbian, then certainly bi-sexual.

Schuyler returned to the states but continued to support Betty in her French lifestyle. For the next ten years, she consorted with Gertrude Stein, Alice B. Toklas and the rest of the expatriate lesbian community in Paris. For much of that time she lived with Adge Baker, the famous English painter. When the depression hit, Parsons lost much of his fortune and stopped his financial support. Betty returned home and moved to Santa Barbara, California where she mingled with the Hollywood set. She was rumored to have had an affair with Greta Garbo, among other unnamed celebrities.

Seeking to further her artistic career, Betty moved back to New York and began to cultivate the emerging modern art community. She ultimately founded her own gallery where she helped to launch the careers of Jackson Pollock, Mark Rothko,

Robert Rauschenberg and many other *avant-garde* artists of that era.

After her return to New York, Betty Parsons scaled back her openly gay lifestyle. The threat from Senator Joseph McCarthy's communist witch hunts among the artistic community drove her and many others underground and back into the closet.

In the meantime, Schuyler was sinking deeper into alcohol and his dissolute lifestyle. He traveled extensively and gambled heavily, depleting much of his fortune. In 1928, after a night of carousing, he fell down a cellar stairs and landed on his head. He was diagnosed with two skull fractures and wavered between life and death for nearly a year. His vision was severely affected and he nearly lost his right eye completely. He developed multiple vision, where each eye would focus separately. The only solution was to wear an eye patch so that his brain could receive a single image. Because of continuing respiratory problems, his doctors recommended a warmer climate, and he was shipped off to Charleston, where he bought the Charles Pinckney house on King Street. He gradually recuperated while steeping himself in Charleston culture. The knowledge he developed of Charleston and the Gullah society landed a consultancy with George Gershwin and DuBose Heyward on their *Porgy and Bess* opera collaboration.

Old friends from New York, who were in Aiken for the winters, began to visit Parsons in Charleston. The city was preparing to celebrate a major anniversary and Parsons heard that Nicholas Longworth, Speaker of the House, and an old friend, was in Aiken. He rang up Longworth and invited him to speak at the celebration. Longworth agreed. At the appointed hour there was no Longworth, forcing Parsons to hurriedly find a new speaker. Longworth finally arrived and confessed that he and his entourage were so blasted from the previous night's proceedings that they pulled off the road and napped under a tree. Parsons was livid. To mollify him, Longworth agreed to speak anyway. He enthralled the crowd for over an hour, turning the potential fiasco into a huge success. The party from the night before reignited in Charleston. It included Camilla Beach who was visiting at that time. Camilla had not returned to Aiken since her husband's infamous trial on charges of slashing her throat. Schuyler was intrigued by the conversations he heard about Aiken from Longworth, Beach and the others that came down to Charleston.

"Camilla, will you take me to Aiken?" Schuyler asked, out of the blue.

"I don't know, Schuy," she said after hesitating. "I have some pretty bad memories from there. I don't know if I'm ready to face them again." It had been more than twenty years. She finally agreed.

Parsons realized he needed an income. His talents in decorating and the exquisite tastes he had developed through his social contacts, led him to open shops in Newport, Charleston and Palm Beach. His visit to Aiken convinced him that he needed to have a business there as well. That fall of 1933 he redid a cottage across Colleton from the Aiken Institute, turning it into a *luxe* antiques shop which he called "Norwood." The results turned him into the most sought after decorator in town. He hired Mrs. Belmont Tiffany to run the shop while he flitted about the country, fulfilling five-figure decorating contracts. That year alone he did seven large homes in Aiken.

Mrs. Tiffany was not available in his second year, so Parsons lured Camilla Beach back to Aiken to help him. The reputations and contacts of Parsons and Beach kept the customers coming and the cash register humming.

Schuyler divided his time between his various shop locations. On one trip north from Palm Beach he happened to sit across from a man who was very fidgety and who was pacing up and down the aisle of the train. Finally, the man drew up his courage and sat down by Schuyler.

"Sir, I was a patient at a sanitarium in Sarasota," the man said nervously. "I have just been released after years of treatment. I fear I have relapsed and must return."

"Why do you think that?" Schuyler asked.

"Well sir, when I sat down here your eye patch was on the right eye. When I came back from the dining car, it was on the left. Now it is back on the right. It is obvious that I have become delusional again." Schuyler laughed and clapped the man on the shoulder.

"Sir, you are not delusional. You see I have double vision and I must keep one eye covered in order to see. Therefore, it makes no difference which eye is covered. I move the patch from time to time to lessen the strain." The man broke into a big grin and thanked Schuyler profusely. He continued to correspond with Parsons for the rest of his life.

On its journey south, that train to Palm Beach regularly made a fifteen minute refueling stop in Charleston. The phone rang in Schuyler's Charleston office.

"Mr. Parsons," the voice on the other end said, "I am leaving New York for Palm Beach tonight. I am told that you have an extensive collection of antique tables in your shop there. Is that true?"

"Yes sir. I believe it to be one of the finest collections in the country."

"Good. We'll be stopping for fifteen minutes at the station in Charleston tomorrow. Do you think you could bring some of them to the platform for my inspection?" Schuyler didn't hesitate.

"Yes sir! They'll be there."

The train arrived to find a complete antiques display in place on the station platform. Schuyler had rented a truck and brought not only the tables but many other choice items from his collection. The prospective buyer was duly impressed. When his private railroad car left the station it had every table and most of the other pieces secured inside. It was one of the largest single sales that Schuyler Parsons ever made. The truck returned to the shop empty.

Parsons arrival in Aiken didn't escape the attention of Eulalie Salley. The competition he brought put a sizable dent in the sales from her shop. She too noticed and commented on the fickle eye patch. Though not directly involved in his business dealings, she was indirectly affected by the friends he brought to town.

Parsons was an intimate of Irene Castle. Vernon and Irene Castle were famous ballroom dancers and dance teachers, commanding as much as $1,000 an hour for lessons. They toured the world to great acclaim and opened several dance studios. Fred Astaire and Ginger Rogers portrayed the couple in a biographical film.

Irene came to Aiken on a visit and decided she would return the following winter. She asked Eulalie to find a suitable rental property for her and to draw up a lease. There were two elderly women who owned a house that fit the Castle's criteria. Eulalie knew the women could use the rental income. The Castles signed the lease and gave Eulalie a check. That summer, Irene Castle called to say she would not be coming after all. Eulalie knew the women were depending on the income and refused to refund the lease money. Irene Castle complained that she was pregnant and therefore the reason for her cancellation was an act of God, and the money should be returned and the lease cancelled.

"You may consider it an act of God, but in my opinion, the day of miracles has passed, and you must pay," Eulalie replied.

Irene Castle was on her third husband. Vernon Castle was killed in a plane crash in WWI and she had divorced her second husband, Robert Treman. She fell on hard financial times and married wealthy Frederick McLaughlin, who was sixteen years her senior. McLaughlin's father had established the very successful McLaughlin Coffee Company. Frederick used $100,000 of his inheritance to buy the Portland Rosebuds professional ice hockey team and move them to Chicago. His wife Irene helped to design the uniforms for the new team which became known as the Chicago "Blackhawks". McLaughlin had served in the "Black Hawk" division in WWI, rising to the rank of Major.

"Mrs. Salley, my wife is nervous and very upset," Mr. McLaughlin said. "If you will return the check to her, I will send you a replacement, but you must promise not to tell her." The ladies got their money. The McLaughlin Coffee Company was absorbed into Kraft Foods in 1967, during the merger mania of that era.

Parsons added a dress shop to his antiques and design store. He hired Mrs. Michael Ivanenko—a member of Russian royalty prior to the revolution in 1917—to run it for him. It was her husband and Warner Baltazzi who procured the horse that precipitated the McCormick lawsuit. A prominent Newport couple was scheduled to visit the shop. The wife called Schuyler prior to the visit.

"Mr. Parsons, my husband hates to shop and never wants me to buy anything. When we come in tomorrow, take note of the items I touch. Those are the ones I will buy. My husband mustn't know."

When they were leaving the shop the husband said, "Mr. Parsons, it has been a lovely visit. We'll come again. This is the first time I've ever gotten my wife out of a shop without buying anything."

The bill came to $4,360. On a later visit by Parsons to the couples Newport home, the husband pointed out several pieces he said they had recently bought in Paris. They were the same ones that his wife had bought from Schuyler. The wife winked and Schuyler acted properly impressed.

On another occasion, Schuyler was at a dinner attended by Mr. and Mrs. James Simpson. Mr. Simpson was head of the Marshall Field department stores.

"You know, Schuyler, I am really sore at the design group at our Chicago store. I want to build an addition to my son's house near Chicago so that we can entertain properly there, and the staff is unable to come up with a decent design for it. I need a room that can comfortably seat fifty for dinner. I don't understand why they can't handle it."

Parsons saw an opportunity and leaped at it. He went back to his studio and worked all night on sketches for the addition. At eight in the morning he called Mr. Simpson and explained that he had done a few sketches for his son's house and could he come over to show them to him."

"Sure. You must have been up all night. Why don't you grab a shower and come on over. You can have some breakfast while

I look at the sketches." Schuyler was nibbling on the last piece of bacon when Simpson came back into the room.

"The job is yours. Wait until I tell that damned decorating department of mine."

After several near calamities, the Wadsworth, Illinois project was finished and ready for the inaugural dinner that coincided with an annual hunt. Simpson walked up to Parsons with a wad of bills in his hand.

"This is yours if not a single chair is moved a foot. Half is yours if not more than six chairs are moved. And, I don't want to see you going around and putting them back in their place." When everyone was seated, Simpson walked up to Schuyler and handed him the roll of bills. "You win," he said. The job netted Schuyler Parsons over $50,000.

Evalyn Walsh McLean hired Schuyler to redecorate her Washington mansion on DuPont Circle. When the job was finished, and payment was due, the check disappeared. It had mysteriously been sent to Gaston Means to pay for the Lindbergh ransom. The error was quickly corrected with Mean's arrest, and Parsons got his $50,000 commission.

Schuyler became a fixture on the Aiken social scene. Louise Hitchcock persuaded him to hire her cousin Ellen "Chee" Bohlen. Ellen was the daughter of Charles "Chip" Bohlen, ambassador to Russia during WWII and another polo student of "Lulie." This age old custom of having "one hand wash the other" led to more business for Schuyler's burgeoning empire.

Louise asked Schuyler to join her as a judge for the 1935 Horse and Mule Show, on the occasion of Aiken's 100th anniversary. He arrived with fellow judge Chee Bohlen in a gaily festooned cart pulled by a non-descript mule. He could always be depended on to liven up any occasion.

One of Schuyler Parson's gifts to Aiken was the annual art show held at the Fermata School. It was at one of these shows that he introduced Athos Menaboni's gifted bird paintings to the world. Menaboni became one of only a few artists whose paintings stood comparison to John Charles Audubon.

Schuyler Parsons continued his peripatetic adventures in the world of art and decorating for many years, but eventually the excesses of his life, both public and private, caught up with him. He lost his fortune and wound up in Palm Beach, living on the support of relatives and the kindness of strangers.

31
Hope

If there was another woman in the pantheon of Aiken's Winter Colony elite whose impact on the community rivaled that of Louise Hitchcock, it would have to be Hope Goddard Iselin. Hope was the daughter of William Goddard, a wealthy banker from Providence, Rhode Island and Chancellor of Brown University. She was born in 1868, shortly after the Civil War, and she died in 1970 at the ripe old age of 102. In between, she contributed greatly to her adopted home of Aiken.

Hope's grandfather was Moses Goddard. He amassed a fortune in manufacturing, railroads and utilities after the Civil War. Much of his wealth stemmed from a large tract of land that had been ceded to Brown University by the federal government after the war. Mr. Goddard bought the land, and in 1894, when his granddaughter Hope married Charles Oliver Iselin, it was valued at $30,000,000, a staggering fortune at that time. Hope was one of four grandchildren in line to inherit Moses' vast wealth.

Charles Oliver Iselin was the son of Adrian Iselin, founder of a successful Wall Street bank. The family owned a large home resembling a majestic castle that overlooked Long Island Sound in New Rochelle, New York. C. Oliver, as he was familiarly known, was an inveterate sportsman and belonged to every yachting and country club within hailing distance of New Rochelle. He was heavily into ocean racing and had a 70-foot steel sloop built to race in the Americas Cup. When his first wife died, he mothballed the sloop and didn't race again until after his marriage to Hope Goddard. She was an ardent fan of sailing as well and joined her husband in his effort to win the Americas Cup.

Hope Iselin became the first woman to sail on a boat that was challenging for the Americas Cup. She served as timekeeper on three of her husband's successful defenses of the premier prize in ocean sailing. She was aboard Defender in 1895, Columbia in 1899, and Reliance in 1903. The racing sloops were much longer in those days and a decision as to when to make a turn was extremely critical. Hope performed her timing calls with great skill. Only two other women have participated in an Americas Cup race. One of those can also be claimed by Aiken—Gertrude Vanderbilt, who married Harry Payne Whitney and thus became mistress of Joye Cottage.

Hope and Oliver had many friends in common before their marriage, and several of them came to Aiken for the winter. The Iselins were quick to follow. They built their lavish home on fourteen acres off Whiskey Road, fronting DuPree Place. "Hopelands" was directly across the street from the Fitch Gilbert's home "Red Top." The rear of the Iselin property abutted "Rye Patch."

The house sat well back from the street, flanked by reflecting pools with fountains across the rear. There was a long, gravel-covered path leading from the Dupree gate to the main entrance to the house. Two brick pedestals topped with cherubim flanked the path. Stables were constructed northwest of the house. The main structure of the stable consisted of two floors with groomsmen's quarters in the five small rooms across the back of the upper floor. The occupants reached their rooms from a balcony across the rear since the front of the second floor served as a hayloft. The groomsmen shared a washroom and bath, also off the balcony, and took their meals with the servants in the main house. Tack rooms and carriages filled the first floor. Two wings extended eastward around a courtyard, with four stalls in each wing.

A caretaker's house was built west of the main building and a playhouse was added for the Iselin children. In those days one could order a kit from Sears, Roebuck to build a house for as little as $1,500. Hope ordered one for her children and had it erected between the main house and the caretaker's cottage. The "Dollhouse," as it came to be known, serves as the home of the Aiken Garden Club.

Not only was Hope Iselin a talented yachtswoman, she was just as accomplished in other sports. She excelled in golf, tennis and equestrian events. She once defeated the Russian Grand Duke Michael in a golf tournament. Her foursome included Edward, Prince of Wales. She was close to the British royal family and was often invited to share their box at Ascot. The British press was all agog on one occasion when Hope arrived at a race wearing the same ensemble as the queen mother. Hope maintained stables in both the United States and England.

Hope Iselin loved to play poker and was very adept at it. She won large sums of money from her wealthy guests. She offered her winnings as charity to St. Thaddeus Episcopal Church, but the vestry considered the money to be tainted by the sin of gambling and declined the offer. She was not deterred, and together with Oliver and her friends she underwrote the building of Aiken's first hospital in 1917. The Aiken Hospital and Relief Society was a white rambling wood structure built on land along Richland Avenue near the park that Celestine Eustis had given to Aiken. It was located at the corner of Richland Avenue and Fauburg Street, near the Inn in the Pines hotel. Hope continued to support the hospital until it was replaced by a brick structure in 1937. That facility was later expanded by architect Willis Irvin and continued to serve Aiken until a new hospital was built on University Parkway in 1976. Since then, the building has served as Aiken County's government offices. The county is scheduled to construct a new office building in 2013. When it is occupied, the old hospital structure will be demolished. However, that will not sever Hope Iselin's continuing links to Aiken.

St. Thaddeus may have exhibited qualms about accepting

"tainted" gambling winnings from Hope Iselin, but they had no such qualms when it came to her generous offer to underwrite the renovation of the main sanctuary in 1926. When St. Thaddeus was built in 1842, it was designed to accommodate worship for the house slaves of prominent plantation owners. Galleries for the slaves, supported by ornate columns, flanked the lower sanctuary. When the new design was under consideration, the galleries were considered unnecessary and perhaps somewhat intrusive. They no longer served their original purpose of segregating the white parishioners on the main level from their black servants. The decision was made to remove the galleries and expand the sanctuary. Since she had contributed so generously to the renovation, Hope Iselin was awarded the supporting columns from the galleries which she generously gave to several of her Winter Colony friends. It's not known which "cottages" incorporated the columns in their own design, but it is reasonably certain that some of them still remain hidden away in those treasured structures.

One parishioner recalled that one of his favorite memories was seeing the Iselin's Silver Cloud Rolls Royce drive up to the front of St. Thaddeus and watching as the chauffeur walked around to open the door for Hope. He would then remove her lap robe, fold it, and place it across the seat back, before assisting the impeccably dressed lady from the car and up the steps to the sanctuary. This observer said that to him, Hope Iselin represented the personification of *elegance.*

Hope Goddard Iselin

St. Thaddeus Episcopal Church

Hope Iselin was devoted to St. Thaddeus and was extremely generous to its pastors. Every new priest was immediately invited to a luncheon at "Hopelands." The sumptuous menus often included eggs Benedict, roast beef, Yorkshire pudding and Bavarian cream, all served on Italian pottery among great bouquets of flowers. One parishioner that was privy to the fetes said, "The clergy come here and they are just fine until they are invited to lunch at Mrs. Iselin's. Then they think they are God's gift to society."

Mrs. Iselin, like many of the early residents of the Winter Colony, was very sympathetic toward the efforts of Martha Schofield as she tried to provide educational opportunities to the black children of freed slaves. She and Louise Hitchcock, in particular, lent their financial and moral support to Miss Schofield and lobbied their friends for their support as well. Hope took her role a step further and served on the Schofield board for many years.

When Marie Eustis Hoffman established the Fermata School for Girls, Hope Iselin was one of the first wealthy Colonists to step forward with funding and support. When the school outgrew its third floor quarters at "Fermata," the Hoffman house on Laurens, Hope was instrumental in acquiring "Tall Pines," the 15 acre Kuser property on Whiskey Road. The three-story, ionic columned, mansion welcomed its first class in 1921. That structure was destroyed by fire in the early 1940s. The property later became home to the Fermata Swim and Tennis Club. One of the surviving original buildings, the gymnasium, continues to serve as offices and function rooms for the club. Another is the home of Linda Knox McLean on Berrie Road.

Hope and Oliver were also active members of the Palmetto Golf Club and the Aiken Tennis Club. They established the Iselin Cup which was contested each year at Palmetto. The winners were awarded an impressive silver trophy. That tournament has survived its founders and is still held each October as a member-member event. Once, when President William Howard Taft (1909 – 1913) was visiting Augusta, someone told him of the wonderful little golf course across the river in Aiken. He asked if arrangements could be made for him to play there. One of his hosts contacted Mayor Julian Salley to see if he could pave the way for the president. Julian's first thought was to call Oliver Iselin.

"Mr. Iselin, this is Julian Salley. I have a favor to ask of you."

"Certainly, Julian, how can I help you?" Iselin said.

"A friend of mine, who is in Augusta with the president, asked if I could arrange for Mr. Taft to play at Palmetto. Would you mind inviting him?"

"I'm sorry Julian, I don't know him," came the cool reply.

Oliver died in 1932. Hope continued to make Aiken her permanent home. When she died in 1970, she willed "Hopelands" to the city of Aiken to be maintained in perpetuity as a city park. The city decided that the "Hopelands" mansion was too expensive to maintain and had it demolished. In hindsight, many regret that decision. The foundations and reflecting pools, together with a sculpture of Hope Iselin, remain as integral parts of the gardens and as reminders of the great lady's role in the development and perpetuation of the Aiken spirit. The stables were preserved and house the Aiken Thoroughbred Racing Hall of Fame and Museum. The "Doll House" remains and is maintained by the Aiken Garden Club. The caretaker's cottage is used for offices and as a maintenance facility.

Hopelands Gardens is a living reminder of how much Aiken meant to Hope Iselin and how much Hope Iselin meant to Aiken. A proscenium stage, built on a lake at the back of the property, serves as the venue for summer concerts. Numerous weddings and other events are held in the gardens and the adjacent "Rye Patch" each year. Each holiday season, volunteers transform the gardens into a winter wonderland as they string thousands of lights across the fourteen acre expanse of the park and serve cider and chocolate to visitors in the museum courtyard. In addition to their vast contributions to Aiken, the Iselins placed their baronial estate in New York into a trust that maintains it as a wonderful park for the citizens of New Rochelle.

Generations to come may not know who Hope Iselin was or what impact she had on their community, but they will continue to enjoy the living legacy she left behind for her beloved Aiken.

32

Mead Hall – In Memoriam

The establishment of the Aiken Preparatory School by Louise Hitchcock provided an institution that offered a privileged education for the sons of the wealthy northern visitors to Aiken in the early twentieth century. The Hitchcocks, and many of their friends who supported the school, were devout Roman Catholics, and Aiken Prep had a decidedly Catholic bias to its teaching. Many colonists, whose dedication to their children's education overrode their religious concerns, sent their sons to Aiken Prep.

That included the George Mead family that joined the Aiken winter community in 1926. Their 43 room mansion, "The Pillars," with a magnificent row of columns across the front, was on Coker Springs Road, ideally situated in the midst of other great horse properties and with direct access to the Hitchcock Woods. It was within a stone's throw of the Coker Springs itself. The "Pillars" was built in 1898 by Mr. C. M. Hinkle, a publisher from Cincinnati, for $15,000. The property boasted ample stables, paddocks, two playhouses for the girls and a large indoor tennis facility. The tennis building also featured a large recessed area built around a great fireplace that could accommodate six-foot logs. Privileged Aiken tennis players enjoyed the magnificent facility as much for its gatherings around the fire on blustery winter days as for its excellent tennis.

In 1905 George Mead was called in to rescue the paper

company his father had founded in Dayton, Ohio. When the senior Mead died, he left a thriving company with several hundred employees to his sons. George left to seek his fortune in Pennsylvania. Within months his two brothers were driving the company into insolvency through mismanagement and profligate spending. When the creditors began to call in the company's notes, George was summoned to rescue the faltering enterprise. And rescue it he did. Mead Paper Company, through its iterations and acquisitions, became a multi-billion dollar corporation with operations throughout the world and one that continues to serve the needs of many industries.

In 1929, Mrs. George Mead and Mrs. F. Skiddy von Stade, along with other like-minded members of the community, founded the Aiken Day School for Girls, as an alternative to the Fermata School. The school began life at Kellsboro Hall (Habersham House), the former home of Ambrose Clark that had been left to Pete Bostwick, Mrs. Von Stade's future son-in-law.

The three Mead sons, George, Talbott and Nelson, continued to attend Aiken Prep where they excelled both academically and athletically. George, in particular, was an exemplary student and one of Louise Hitchcock's prize pupils in her polo school. At Yale he earned honors in football and was captain of the polo team.

George Mead Jr. Leading the Hitchcock Hounds

After graduation from Yale, George enlisted in the army. As a freshly minted lieutenant, he led his infantry platoon ashore in the first wave to hit the beaches of Guadalcanal. He became the first casualty in that long and bloody campaign to wrest control of the island and its strategic airfield from the 30,000 fanatical Japanese soldiers defending it. The character that had been instilled in George by his parents, and then nurtured by his community and his teachers, was evident to all those who served with the young Marine lieutenant. His heroic actions in the battle, before he was cut down, led to the posthumous awarding of the Silver Star for valor. The Silver Star is the third highest honor that can be bestowed by the military.

George Mead, Sr. received word of his son's death in Washington, where he was serving in the war effort under President Roosevelt. Secretary of the Navy, Frank Knox, a friend of the Mead family, read the citation in a meeting attended by the young lieutenant's father. In the process of reading the tribute, Knox was overcome with grief, and the meeting was temporarily adjourned,

The citation described how George, with courageous disregard for his own safety, plowed into the thick jungle looking for the sniper that had his platoon pinned down. He found the sniper and killed him with a shot to the head with his Colt-45 pistol. George lost his own life in the process when he was shot by another Japanese soldier. Due to his heroic efforts his platoon was able to complete its mission that day, and without further loss of life.

The news of the death of their first-born son was devastating to the Meads. However, after a brief period of mourning, they resolved to turn this wrenching family tragedy into an inspiration to other young men who were struggling to find their way in a world in upheaval.

Elsie Talbott Mead, George's mother, described her family's response to the devastating news in a long letter to her friends and family. She first expressed how grief stricken the family was and how saddened they were that such a promising young life had been extinguished in its prime. Then she told them how they were determined that George would not have died in vain.

"We have faith that whatever happens must be for the best," she said, "whether we understand it or not. We must think only how lucky we are to have had George for twenty-five years and not think of what he or we are going to miss. We cannot let ourselves think things that can do no good. We can choose which way we are going to think, and which way we think will help others." A family friend, observing the stoic response of the parents to their son's untimely death, was prompted to write to the Meads.

"George couldn't help but do the things he did when he had a father, who in his hour of sorrow sees only the great good that must come from his son's death. I bow in admiration to you."

The impact of George Mead's death was immediate and profound among the constellation of friends he had made in such a short life. Letters of sympathy and condolence poured in to the family. Many of those written tributes were compiled in a book by his nephew, Nelson Mead, titled *An Intimate Tribute*. One letter in particular stands out for its historic association with another hero of that fateful battle. An old friend wrote to the Meads upon hearing of George's death.

"I think you know how we all felt about George. He inspired a tremendous respect that was unusual in as young a fellow as he was. Though I know it was a terrible thing for him to die—yet I think it can be truthfully said that George had a fuller life in his relatively short one than most people have in a much longer time.

"That last weekend down in Aiken, when we came home, he seemed happy in what he was doing–and he took a tremendous pride in his job. He was doing the job which he really believed in and wanted to do, and he did it with the same sincerity that characterized everything he said or did.

"Went over the other day and visited George's grave, he is buried in the very first row, down near the beach where they landed. On his grave, carved into an aluminum plate, is 'Lt. George Mead August 20, 1942. A great leader of men. God

bless him.' It was really moving to see his grave there, when the last time I saw him was down in Aiken.

Signed . . . Jack Kennedy"

In one of Kennedy's biographies he is quoted as saying, "The whole thing was about the saddest experience I've ever had and enough to make you cry."

In 1955 the Meads donated their mansion on Coker Springs Road, to St. Thaddeus Episcopal Church. The 43-room structure was transformed into the school so long dreamed of by the congregation of St. Thaddeus. Fittingly, the school was named Mead Hall in honor of the fallen hero.

The school would remain at "The Pillars" for only a few years. St. Thaddeus asked for and received permission from the family to sell the property. The proceeds were used to construct the red brick building, located behind the Cornish Chapel of St. Thaddeus that, along with later additions, still serves as the home of Mead Hall.

The land surrounding the old property that was home to the Meads was subdivided and developed. Burkwood Place, a quiet cul-de-sac community of modest, well maintained homes off Coker Springs Road, occupies the site that was once witness to the childhoods of so many happy, boisterous Mead children and their many friends. All that remains to remind one of that glorious past, is the red brick wall surrounding a garden and a small workshop. The tennis court, which was at the extreme northern edge of the property, on Third Street, still stands and sees occasional use as a tennis venue. Gone are the halcyon days of joyful gatherings around the fire pit.

The Aiken Day School for girls merged with Aiken Preparatory School for boys in 1989 creating a co-educational institution for the first time. Now, seventy-five years later, the fortunes of those two schools and that of Mead Hall have come full circle. In a time of escalating costs, declining enrollments, and increased competition, Mead Hall and Aiken Prep have recognized the need for a larger private school, one offering grades K-12 and one that will allow its students to complete their education in one institution. The recently announced merger of the two schools achieves that goal. The 350 students of the combined schools provide the critical mass necessary to compete on an even footing with other private schools, both locally and nationally. Perhaps the current generation of Winter Colony descendants, remembering the legacy of their ancestors, will look anew at Mead Hall for their children, as a place to provide the new leaders of the future, as their predecessor namesakes did. One would be hard pressed to imagine a finer tribute to George and Elsie Mead and their heroic son.

33

A Riddle Wrapped in an Enigma

One of the strangest episodes in Eulalie's realty career occurred when Mrs. Aage Anke appeared in her office. Aage Anke was a cousin of the king of Denmark. She and her husband were ensconced in the Highland Park Hotel for the winter and had become the social focus for the season.

"Mrs. Salley, I want to purchase a home in Aiken for my mother," Mrs. Anke announced. "She is in retirement and is looking for a secluded house where she can be secure and have peace and privacy."

It was 1925 and Eulalie knew there was a property for sale just across the golf course from her former house on Highland Park. It was near the old railroad cut in Hitchcock Woods, known as the "Devil's Backbone." The house was originally built as a wedding present for the Edwin Smiths. It was an exact replica of Henry Wadsworth Longfellow's house in New England. It was called "Boxwood."

"I think I have just the property for you," Eulalie said.

"I will take the house if you will agree to a few conditions," Mrs. Anke said. "You will be placed on a retainer. All her bills will be sent to you and you will have access to her account. The account will never run short of money. Also, she is never, under any circumstances to be introduced to anyone. She is to know no one except you. She will come to your office once a week and you are to go to her home for luncheon each Thursday."

A few weeks later the woman arrived in Aiken with a retinue that included a German butler, a French maid and a Swedish cook. The mysterious woman was named Adele von Loesecke. Eulalie gave strict instructions to her staff that when Mrs. von Loesecke arrived at her office each Monday she was to be escorted in immediately, and she was not to be called by name. Eulalie did all the shopping for the reclusive resident of "Boxwood."

Mrs. Anke called Eulalie on Mrs. Von Loesecke's birthday and said, "I think mother needs a new car. Will you please see that she has a new Cadillac?"

On occasion the Cadillac, driven by the butler, Costal, would pull in front of Eulalie's office. Mrs. von Loesecke wanted Eulalie to go for a ride with her. When the Thursday luncheons took place, the topics of conversation ranged from politics to the operas by Strauss and Wagner that she had attended in Germany. The elegant silver place settings carried a distinctive coat of arms and she wore very expensive jewelry. Eulalie began to suspect that Madame von Loesecke had enjoyed an intimate connection to Kaiser Wilhelm and his family. By extension, Germany's defeat in WWI may have placed certain people close to the Kaiser in great danger. The intricate charade continued for several months until one day Eulalie received a frantic call from Madam von Loesecke.

"Please come and help me, Costal has locked me in my room and he says he is going to kill me. Please help me!"

Eulalie called Julian immediately and the two of them rushed to "Boxwood." Julian rang the bell insistently and finally Costal opened the door.

"I would like to see Madam von Loesecke," Julian said.

"Madam is indisposed," came the reply from Costal.

"Costal, I'm going to insist," Julian said.

The butler left the Salleys standing at the door and went upstairs. In a few minutes he returned and led them up to the bedroom. After they entered she asked Julian to lock the door.

"He's going to kill me," Madam von Loesecke said.

"Tell me about it," Eulalie said.

"I cannot, but I am terrified," she said.

Julian fired the butler and asked the sheriff to keep a watch on the house. A few days later Eulalie received a call from Madam von Loesecke saying that she was leaving Aiken. She was moving to New York. Not long after the baroness arrived in New York there was a brief article in the paper saying she had died as the result of a hit-and-run accident on a street in New York. Eulalie immediately suspected foul play.

"All you had to do was to know Madame von Loesecke to know that there was a mystery."

Much later in life, shortly before her death, Eulalie wrote to the author Faith Baldwin. She knew that Faith and the baroness had been intimates. Mrs. Baldwin replied:

Dear Mrs. Salley,

I can't tell you much about Aunt Adele, as I call her. She was born a baroness Von Loesecke. She married a Baron von Klein. They later went to Canada, and later, were divorced. She took back her maiden name. Her crests were genuine, though not royal. My mother met her when she (Adele) came to Brooklyn to live and they became best friends. Later she returned to Germany to live. She had relatives in New Jersey (now dead) and the adopted daughter Mabel, whose second marriage was to Aage Anke (this also ended in divorce). Auntie died many years ago in a Brooklyn hospital. She gave me some of her silver before this (and I bought some things when her Jersey relatives had them). The rest of her silver went back to relatives in Germany. What else I knew about her I cannot tell you. Suffice it to say that I was sent to Germany to live with her, which I did from the Spring of 1914 to the Spring of 1916, when we returned. We were to have traveled extensively but could not because of the war. Auntie was an American citizen. It was after our return that Mabel married her first husband (also a Dane). Anyway, it's long ago, so far away, and they're all gone now. Auntie was a wonderful woman, extremely talented. I loved her very much.

Sincerely yours,
Faith Baldwin

The enigmatic Baroness von Loesecke was caught up in geo-political events beyond her control and may have died as a result. No one ever unraveled the tangled web that brought her to Aiken and that ultimately killed her on that New York street.

34
Banksia

Aiken - Past, Present, Future

Shortly after the end of the Civil War, a prominent Charleston cotton merchant, Adam Gibson, came to Aiken to escape the hot, humid, mosquito infested, summers on the coast. He became so enthralled with the small village and its wholesome climate that in 1860 he decided to build a summer home in Aiken. The lot he chose was on the southeast corner of present day Newberry Street and New Lane, overlooking the forests that would become Hitchcock Woods. He bought the lot for $100 from William Perroneau Finley, a prominent Aiken attorney with extensive property holdings in and around Aiken. Gibson built a 3,500 square foot, frame house at the apex of the hill. Two years later, Gibson purchased two more lots, expanding his property to include most of the city block. Before his death in 1871, he sold the property to William Hutson Townsend, a local attorney and insurance agent, for $3,000. Townsend then purchased the remaining lots that now constitute the block bounded by Newberry, New Lane, South Boundary and Laurens.

The Aiken Winter Colony, inaugurated by Celestine Eustis and her niece Louise Hitchcock in the late 1880s, took off in earnest in the succeeding decade. In 1894, Charles Carroll Harrington, a Providence, Rhode Island banker, bought the estate from Townsend's widow. The Harringtons continued to winter in Aiken and may have been instrumental in luring Oliver and Hope Iselin to their newfound, southern, winter paradise. The Harringtons sold their property to Richard Flint Howe of New York City on April 14, 1931 for $50,000.

Following a successful career in manufacturing in Wisconsin, Howe married Amy Deering, heiress to the Deering Harvester farm implement company fortune. The Deering Company later merged with International Harvester, and Howe became an executive of the combined companies. He retired in 1911, devoting his time to public service during WWI and later to other prominent causes. For most of this time he was a regular winter visitor to Aiken.

Howe, then in his sixties, decided to remodel the old Gibson house on the estate he had just purchased. He selected prominent Aiken/Augusta architect Willis Irvin to develop plans to not only renovate the 3,500 square foot house, but to relocate it northeastward toward the intersection of South Boundary and Newberry. That move allowed Irvin to take advantage of the sloping property for the "small" addition Howe had in mind. Money was of little concern to the wealthy Howe as he instructed Irvin to expand the house by 14,000 square feet, creating one of the largest and most palatial estates in a town known for ostentatious excess. Irvin received a contract for $85,000 to deliver the new, brick, three-level, colonial revival, mansion together with its odd appendage of the remodeled Adams structure, by December 31, 1931, just as the nation was entering the dark years of the Great Depression. Surprisingly, Irvin and his general contractor C. B. Holley delivered the house, together with its surrounding serpentine brick wall, to Mr. Howe in less than six months, a feat that would be impossible in today's highly regulated building environment. Further evidence that the project was delivered on time comes from an article on the society pages of the New York Times.

"On February 26, 1932, Mrs. William Deering Howe of New York entertained in the newly completed, palatial, "Banksia" cottage of her father-in-law Richard Howe in Aiken, South Carolina."

Banksia

Howe chose the name "Banksia" in honor of the small, yellow, cluster roses that grew in abundance on the slopes of his estate.

Curiosity abounded as to why Howe chose to move and renovate the old Gibson house and then overpower it with the grand addition. Since money didn't seem to be an object, why didn't he just raze the old structure and begin anew? Robert McCreary, an architect with the Irvin firm furnished an answer to the *Aiken Standard* during an interview in 1973.

"Richard F. Howe was in his sixties then. He had a superstition that an older person should not build a new home. There was a two-story frame house on the city block he bought and he instructed Mr. Irvin to add to it. ...The house was moved from the crest of the hill to the east and the entire brick mansion and connected frame wing were added to it."

It is debatable whether Howe's superstition contributed to the prolongation of his life or the precipitation of his death. He never recovered from the broken hip he suffered in a fall at "Banksia." He died in January, 1943 at the age of 79. The following excerpt from his obituary appeared in the Aiken paper.

"Mr. Howe had been a member of the Aiken winter colony for more than a quarter of a century and with members of the Vanderbilt, Whitney, Iselin and Hitchcock families was among the early residents and settlers of the Aiken winter colony. His winter cottage here is one of the show places of Aiken and is located across the street from the home of the late William C. Whitney. Each winter with members of the colony he brought his string of horses south, where he was one of the most enthusiastic supporters of the racing and other equestrian events."

"Banksia" remained in the Howe family for several years after his death. It was sold in 1952 to a Kingsport, Tennessee businessman, S.M. Ollie, for $58,000. Ollie recognized the vast potential for profit in real estate that would come to Aiken with the announcement of the Savannah River Project (SRP). President Harry Truman's decision to locate the "Bomb Plant" for the enrichment of uranium on the Savannah River would forever change the face of Aiken. The DuPont Corporation signed a contract to acquire the hundreds of thousands of acres required and to build the facility—all for one-dollar per year over costs.

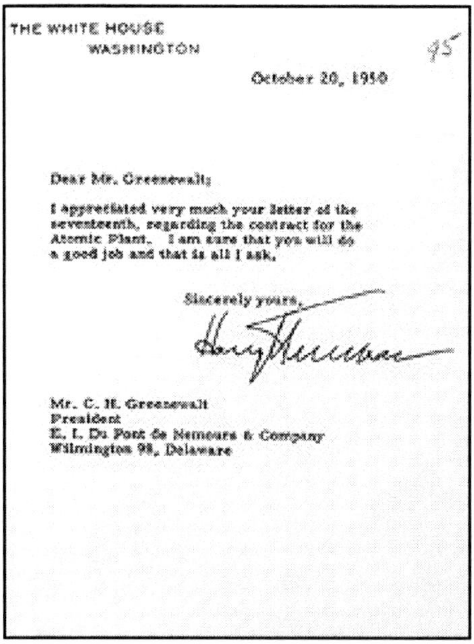
THE WHITE HOUSE
WASHINGTON

95

October 20, 1950

Dear Mr. Greenewalt:

I appreciated very much your letter of the seventeenth, regarding the contract for the Atomic Plant. I am sure that you will do a good job and that is all I ask.

Sincerely yours,

Harry Truman

Mr. C. H. Greenewalt
President
E. I. Du Pont de Nemours & Company
Wilmington 98, Delaware

"Banksia" was converted into a boarding house, and for fifteen years, it served as home to hundreds of construction workers at the SRP site. In 1957, when most of the temporary construction jobs had dried up, the Southern Methodist Church bought the property for $64,000. It was turned over to the educational arm of the church to establish the Southern Methodist School in Aiken. After four years, the Methodists decided to pull out of Aiken and sold "Banksia" to the Aiken County Commission for Higher Education. "Banksia" became the first campus for the nascent University of South Carolina at Aiken.

For eleven years the enrollment at USCA grew. The rolls swelled from the original 139 students until the building could no longer accommodate the crush of students. A new campus for USCA was opened west of town on property once owned by William Gregg. On October 22, 1973, "Banksia" was acquired by the Aiken County Public Library Commission for one dollar. The county removed the minimal changes that the home had undergone as a boarding house and college and returned it to its original condition. "Banksia" served the people of Aiken as a public library until 1984 when the library was moved to the old Aiken Institute building at Whiskey and Colleton.

The Aiken County Historical Commission moved into the old Gibson house portion of the building in 1984 and by 1988 the museum had expanded to occupy the entire Banksia building. It now houses exhibits and archives that contain the rich history and heritage of Aiken County. The museum has continued its expansion under the direction of its energetic director Elliott Levy with capable assistant directors Mary White and Brenda Baratto and a host of enthusiastic volunteers. Among the historic additions moved to the site are a one-room schoolhouse, an early settler's cabin, the Transit of Venus observatory and the William Gregg buttery (spring house/root cellar).

35

"Edgewood"

Eulalie never completely forgave Julian for forcing her to sell "Let's Pretend." She always recalled the home with the fondest memories. Whether puttering in the gardens, or wandering through the myriad corridors created by Gouverner Morris' haphazard design, it was always her dream home. It was not that Eulalie minded living on Hayne Avenue in the Goss house. It just was not "Let's Pretend." She had lived in the Goss house only a few years when she received and invitation that would change her life dramatically.

The return address on the invitation read, "Alva C. DePass, Columbia, South Carolina." Alva DePass was an attorney for the Tillman estate. Eulalie knew him from the dark days of Lucy Tillman's fight to regain her children, which lasted from 1908 until 1911. The invitation was to a house party for Eulalie and twenty others to be held in Edgefield—not only in Edgefield, but at "Edgewood", the ancestral home of Lucy Dugas Tillman. It had been nearly twenty years since the case had been finally decided in Lucy's favor, and her two daughters were returned to her. And it was subsequent to Lucy's death.

As she drove up the cedar and tea olive scented lane to the magnificent plantation house, Eulalie was lost in the events of that long ago time when two young girl's lives were filled with such torment and uncertainty. Her reverie was jarred as the house came into view. The paint on the magnificent columns and wide verandas was peeling. Large swaths of the fading clapboard siding were rotted or missing entirely. Her heart sank and she cried as her driver pulled up to the embracing arms of the front steps. The once immaculate hedge rows of azaleas and camellias were an unkempt riot of random growth. She had no idea that such depredation had come to the storied home. Lucy and Ben Tillman had lived in the house for a time before moving to Washington. The following years saw a succession of Negro families, then finally nothing. She was heartsick as she mounted the steps.

Edgewood – Prior to Restoration

A makeshift table was erected in the drawing room and spread with the contents of a large wicker basket. A fire roared in the fireplace and a festive mood washed over the crowd. After dinner, everyone gathered before the fire and told tales they had heard of ghosts and strange noises in the old house—of Lucy Pickens parading around in rustling skirts, and of old Uncle Holcombe clumping along on his peg leg. The colonel had lost the leg in "The War." Finally, sleep overcame the party, and the guests took their pillows and blankets to their assigned rooms to bed down for the evening. All save Eulalie and Mrs. De Pass. They decided to go for a moonlight walk along the old garden paths. They returned to find the front door bolted and decided to become the ghosts everyone had been talking about. Recognizing the momentary fright inside the house Eulalie decided to play a prank on the party.

"This is the ghost of Mrs. Pickens. Why have you locked me out?"

After the brief fright, they were allowed back inside. Eulalie turned in with visions of the former grandeur of the old house and all the history captured within its walls. This had been the home of a governor, a Russian ambassador, a godchild of the Czar and the wife of a senator's son. It was not possible that it would be allowed to decay and fade from memory. As her eyes fluttered to sleep a plan was fermenting in her head. When Eulalie returned to Aiken, she picked up the phone and on an impulse she called a realtor friend in Edgefield.

"Minnie, this is Eulalie Salley from Aiken. Are you sitting down? I don't want you to faint. I want to buy "Edgewood."

Like the dog that finally caught the car it was chasing, now that she owned it, she didn't know what to do with it. She first offered it to the Edgefield Daughters of the Confederacy, but they didn't have the wherewithal to maintain it. What was she to do with this grand, dilapidated, historic, White Elephant? Suddenly, she experienced an epiphany. She remembered the 15 acre plot of ground that she had kept for herself on Kalmia Hill. It was near the spot where her grandfather had first built his house in Aiken and across the way from William Gregg's property. She now knew what she must do. She would move "Edgewood" to Kalmia Hill.

It was 1929. Eulalie asked several contractors to take on the task of dismantling "Edgewood" and moving it to Aiken. There were no takers. It was considered to be an impossible job. Finally, she convinced Byron Hair to take on the project. He turned out to be a wonderful choice and did a remarkable job of disassembling and then reassembling the magnificent house. He meticulously marked each piece with a coded number so that the house would be exactly as it was in Edgefield. Eulalie tried to recover various elements of the house that had been sold off or vandalized, but to little effect. Mantels and chandeliers had to be replaced from old drawings or from fading memories. Then came the stock-market crash of September, 1929, followed by the Great Depression. Julian lost much of his money in a failed bank and Eulalie's income plummeted along with the economy. The restoration was half-finished.

"We'll just have to stop," Julian said. "We've lost everything we've had."

"Everything we've had, we have made," Eulalie reminded him, "and now we have experience. Now let's start over."

"Start over with what?'

"Experience."

Julian had five dollars and Eulalie a dollar and a half. She went to bed with a prayer on her lips. "Something has to happen," she told herself. The next morning there was a check waiting at her office for several thousand dollars. It was from one of her clients. The accompanying note read, "I know what has happened. You may consider this a gift or a loan." There are those who believe Lucy Mercer Rutherford was the benefactor. Eulalie plowed ahead, not knowing from week-to-week if she would be able to meet her payroll. Each week she did. Many other strong men just gave up in the face of unprecedented adversity. One desperate man took his team of six beautiful horses out into the field and shot them. He could not afford their feed. But, Eulalie soldiered on. She continued to restore "Edgewood" in bits and pieces as funds became available. Irreplaceable hand carved moldings and wainscotings that she had bought years earlier and stored, were a perfect fit for her drawing room. Two elaborate chandeliers which had been given to Lucy Pickens by the Czar of Russia were stolen before Eulalie could remove them. Mrs. Eugene Grace discovered them in an antique shop. She bought the chandeliers and offered to sell them to Eulalie. Eulalie couldn't afford them. Thirty years later, when Mrs. Grace died, she willed the still un-hung chandeliers to Eulalie.

In 1932 the Salley family made the final move in their marriage, to "Edgewood." They had gone from Laurens Street to Highland Park, then to "Let's Pretend" on Horry.

Following her heartrending departure from "Let's Pretend" in 1926, there was the six year stay on Hayne Avenue in the Goss house. Finally, Eulalie felt at home again. It was not "Let's Pretend," but it was a grand home in which to entertain and to enjoy her children and grandchildren. It also helped to promote her real estate business. Eulalie remained in the house on the hill for the rest of her life—another forty years—twenty-four as a widow.

Following a glowing review of the renovated and decorated house in the March 31, 1969 issue of the *Aiken Standard*, Eulalie was persuaded to open "Edgewood" to the public for a tour of homes. The tour was a great success as throngs traipsed through the house examining every nook and cranny of its beautiful restoration. A visitor with a decidedly northern accent saw Eulalie in the hallway and remarked, "It's very nice, but isn't it a little shabby."

"This is an old house," Eulalie replied, "and everything in it is old, but in the south, we do not use the word *old*. We say things are mellow."

"Oh, are you the owner?"

"Yes, and in the South we don't use the term old, we say it's mellow."Eulalie vowed never to subject herself to that kind of rudeness again. In addition to moving all the trees she wanted for "Edgewood," Eulalie was able to defray some of her enormous restoration costs by selling others to some Winter Colony residents. She moved a 100-year-old Red Camellia to "Live Oak", the home of Mrs. Everett Crawford. That task took three long nights to traverse the twenty miles to Aiken, and Eulalie was along for the entire journey.

William Ziegler, of the Royal Baking Powder family, asked Eulalie to move a giant tea olive from "Edgewood" to "Sunshine," his cottage on Whiskey Road. After it had been excavated, it took a team of twenty mules to pull the enormous plant from the ground. That tree, purchased for $1,500, can still be admired on the grounds of the Willis Irvin designed house—now the Green Boundary Club.

The Salleys continued to live in the grand plantation house known as "Edgewood" for the rest of their lives. Julian passed away in 1951 and Eulalie in 1975. Her daughter, Eulalie Rutledge, remained in the house after Eulalie's death. The structure, now known as the "Pickens-Salley" house, was sold in 1985 to Ronnie Bolton, local real estate developer. Bolton, recognizing the historical value of the house, generously donated it to the University of South Carolina Aiken. Once again "Edgewood" was on the move. In 1986 it was separated into three sections and trucked to the USCA campus, a scant mile away. There it remains to this day, where it serves as offices for the chancellor of the university. In memory of his beloved mother, Eulalie, Julian Salley, through a land donation, established the Pickens-Salley House Fund to provide income for the perpetual maintenance of the house.

Edgewood on USC Aiken Campus

36
The Woods

No account of Aiken and its rich history as a winter resort for wealthy Yankees would be complete without telling the story of "The Woods." No one who has lived in Aiken for any period of time would fail to understand the meaning of that phrase. To an Aikenite "The Woods" can have only one meaning—Hitchcock Woods. The 2,000 acres comprising Hitchcock Woods has evolved over the years from the original 8,000 acres owned by the Hitchcocks and Whitneys.

Early on, both Thomas Hitchcock and Bill Whitney realized the significance of the pristine tract of virgin forests through which they "rode to hounds." The Hitchcock Woods foundation was established and dedicated to the perpetual maintenance of that property for the people of Aiken. Though the final boundaries of Hitchcock Woods have moved and shifted over the years, its ultimate limits were decided when the final 230 acres, which had been given to Aiken Prep for their stables and riding club by Louise Hitchcock, were deeded back to the Woods in 1985.

"*Mon Repos,*" the Aiken home to which the Hitchcocks returned each winter, was on the eastern edge of the woods, facing Laurens Street. The original home (Legare) and its replacement both burned. When the third manifestation of "*Mon Repos*" was dedicated, Lulie insisted that the Monsignor from St. Mary's bless the new house.

Hundreds, if not thousands, of guests were entertained in the grand dining room of that beautiful home where Louise sat with her back to one fireplace and Thomas' to another. Countless young men and women who comprised her polo school traipsed through the home before and after the matches. She always insisted that each rider groom his or her own perspiring horse when the games were over. She did not allow them to hand the horse off to one of the grooms. It was her way of teaching them responsibility.

Over the years, many amenities were added to the woods by Hitchcock and Whitney: show rings, jumping trails, a tea house, a race track, bridges, lakes . . . and all for the enjoyment of Aiken's equestrian community. An annual event in the Woods is the "Blessing of the Hounds" which inaugurates the Aiken Hunt season. This event, which occurs at the Memorial Gate in the Woods dedicated to Tommy Hitchcock's brother, Francis, was first held in 1913. Hundreds of Aikenites and visitors trek down the mile-long path off South Boundary to witness the event each year. For many it marks the official beginning of the holiday season.

Hunters at the Blessing of the Hounds - 2012

The 99th anniversary ceremony was presided over by Linda Knox McLean, Master of the Hounds. Ms. McLean is the daughter of Northrup (Norty) Knox and great-granddaughter of Seymour Knox who built the large estate next door to the Green Boundary Club on Whiskey Road known as "The Balcony."

The Knox family is from Buffalo, New York. Seymour Knox made his fortune as a dime store merchant. In 1911 he merged his company, S. F. Knox, with the F. W. Woolworth chain, for which he received $12,000,000. Three generations of the Knox sons were Chairmen of the Marine Midland banking empire, now a part of HSBC. Ms. McLean's father and uncle owned the Buffalo Sabres hockey team. Norty Knox excelled at polo, earning an eight-goal rating, the only amateur to do so since WWII.

The great Norty Knox on the superb Ragamuffin

As each new visitor discovered the delights of Aiken, most sought to buy or build where they could have easy access to Hitchcock Woods. To that end, many of the most recognizable names owned properties close to or abutting the woods: Gilbert, Iselin, Rodgers, Bostwick, Ziegler, Knox, Seabrook, Rutherfurd, Howe, Whitney, Mead, Grace, Dolan . . .

Celestine Eustis died in Aiken in 1921, and was laid to rest at "*Mon Repos*." Her niece, Louise, whom she had brought to Aiken with her in 1868, died on Easter Sunday, 1934. Lulie had suffered a fatal injury on the day after Christmas, doing what she loved to do, riding in Hitchcock Woods with the young people. Her eyesight had deteriorated to the degree that the children would warn her of the next impending jump by shouting, "Jump Gran." She fell following a jump and never recovered from her injuries. As pallbearers, she was attended by six of her grieving black servants. Eulalie Salley spoke reverently of Mrs. Hitchcock following her funeral.

"All Aiken is a monument to her. She was a real faithful friend, a wonderful person. More than once she came to me with a list of names from the delinquent tax rolls and gave me the money to pay them. They never knew who had paid their taxes."

Will Rogers, who had been invited to Aiken by the Hitchcocks, was quoted by a New York paper as saying,

"Courage, horsemanship, sportsmanship, and great maternal love was all embodied in one frail white-haired woman, 67 years old. Mrs. Thomas Hitchcock, godmother and patron saint of American polo and lover of a horse."

Though Louise Eustis Hitchcock was taken from her home and friends in a tragic manner, her untimely death spared her having to endure two other major family tragedies.

Tommy and Louise Hitchcock's daughter, Celestine, married the noted New York architect Julian L. Peabody. Julian was well known and admired in Aiken for his outstanding architectural skills. He was responsible for the design of many of the Winter Colony homes, including Ridgeley Hall (Lucy Mercer Rutherfurd), The Balcony (Seymour Knox II) and Black Stables (Bayard Warren), among others.

On January 24, 1935, the 387 foot tramp steamer "S. S. Mohawk" left New York harbor on its weekly run to Havana, Cuba. New York was recovering from a late January snowstorm and a nor'easter that left heavy seas in its wake. For reasons now shrouded in history, the steamer veered off course and was struck by the Norwegian freighter, "Talisman." Seventy minutes later, the stricken ship lay in pieces on the bottom of the ocean off New Jersey. It took with it to a watery grave Julian and Celestine Peabody. The couple left behind two children, Julian and Daphne, a grieving family, and stunned communities in Aiken and Long Island. Julian, an accomplished artist as well as architect, was en route to Guatemala where he planned to sketch historic buildings for future designs and paintings.

Tommy Hitchcock, Jr., having survived the rigors of World War I, was killed in 1943 while testing a P-51 dive-bomber in England. He had been instrumental in the original design of the plane and was determined to work on the modifications it needed to prevent crashes. Hitchcock had been judged too old for active service in WWII, but he insisted on doing his part for the war effort. He died a hero.

Thomas Hitchcock, Sr. passed away on September 29, 1941, just before the war that would take the life of his son. He was 81. He was laid to rest alongside his beloved Louise at "*Mon Repos*," near the grave of *Tante* Celestine. The graves remain on the property that is now owned by the Bostwick family.

"The Woods" remain as a testament to the love and generosity of a very special family, the Hitchcocks. The people of Aiken shall forever be in their debt.

37
The Entertainers

Aiken was not only a magnet for wealthy northerners during the heyday of the Winter Colony, but it also attracted its share of entertainers and celebrities. Lillian Russell, a noted actress and singer at the turn of the century, spent many winters there in the company of the flamboyant Diamond Jim Brady. Vernon and Irene Castle, the celebrated ballroom dancers, came to Aiken to unwind from their strenuous schedules and to enjoy the company of those of *noblesse oblige* who wintered here. Jozef Hoffman, world renowned concert pianist, came and stayed for many years.

Others came for the general sporting ambience that was provided by the surrounding area. It was not only the famous golfers and politicians who flocked to the Palmetto Club, the Aiken Golf Club and nearby Augusta National or who enjoyed the many private tennis facilities in the area. Most winter seasons found the likes of Bing Crosby, Phil Harris, Will Rogers and Andy Williams hobnobbing with the wealthy Aiken winter cottage owners.

Andy Williams was so taken with Aiken—and a certain attractive young woman resident— that he decided to buy a cottage of his own. He purchased "Two Trees," the former estate of W. R. Grace on Magnolia Street. The rear of the huge tract backs up to Whiskey Road across from Hopelands Gardens and "Red Top," the former Fitch Gilbert property, and is hidden from view by a brick wall and trees. The original structure was built in 1929 on former plantation farmland. Grace chose the name for his cottage to honor the two lonely trees on the property at that time. Andy Williams bought the property in 1980 and sold it in 1985. He loved to come to Aiken, but the demands of his touring schedule made it difficult for him to come often. The original house, built by W.R. Grace and bought by Williams, burned in 1988 and was replaced by a more modern structure. It is still one of the largest properties in Aiken's horse district.

Joanne Woodward, widow of Paul Newman and an Oscar winning actress in her own right, came to Aiken often to visit her mother, Mrs. Robert Carter. Miss Woodward's paternal grandfather was from the Vale of Montmorenci, just outside Aiken. Joanne began her stage career in little theater in Greenville, S. C. Joanne's mother later married Robert Carter and moved to the large white house at 602 Barnwell Avenue in Aiken. Joanne became a frequent visitor. The house is directly across the street from the Aiken Preparatory School. When Mr. Carter passed away, the Newmans purchased a home for Mrs. Carter adjacent to their estate in Westport, Connecticut.

Of all the celebrities that came to Aiken, none cut a more colorful and dashing figure than Fred Astaire. Born Fred Austerlitz in Omaha, Nebraska, he and his older sister Adele were thrust onto the vaudeville stage by their mother. Her aspirations to escape small town life in Nebraska were fueled by the early success of the dancing duo. In 1905, Mrs. Austerlitz changed their name to Astaire, believing it to be more palatable to American audiences. Whether attributable to the name change or their innate talents, the Astaires became overnight sensations. They were recognized as the most famous child stars in vaudeville. Hollywood soon beckoned. By 1933, Fred had starred in several movies and signed a contract with RKO Studios to do a series of nine ultra-successful pictures with Ginger Rogers. She famously said that she could do everything Fred Astaire could do, and she could do it in high-heels and backwards.

Fred and Adele Astaire – Vaudeville Days

Around the same time that Astaire signed the RKO contract, he was courting a young socialite from New York named Phyllis Livingston Baker. She was the daughter of a prominent physician in Boston. Fred and Phyllis were soon married and came to visit Phyllis' aunt, Mrs. Bull. Mrs. H. W. Bull owned a Winter Colony home on Easy Street in Aiken, just across from Joye Cottage. Their cottage was called "Prickley Pear." The Astaires became frequent visitors to the Bull home, especially in the winters and during breaks between his movie commitments. The house burned in 1946.

The Astaires had two children, a boy, Fred, and a girl, Ava. Phyllis and the children spent long periods in Aiken while Fred was busy in Hollywood. He would come every chance he had. Fred, Jr. enrolled at Aiken Prep. His father often attended sporting events in which Fred participated.

Other luminaries from Hollywood came to visit the Astaires when they were in Aiken. On one such occasion, in November 1937, several local teenage girls camped out on Easy Street hoping to catch a glimpse of the famous dancer. Among those in the group were Rosamond Durban (McDuffie) and the Willcox sisters. They had rehearsed the current dance craze, *The Big*

Apple, and were anxious to impress Astaire with their moves. One of the girls, Edith Hahn (Anderson), was chosen to ring the doorbell. The Bull's butler answered.

"May I help you?" he asked.

"We're here to see Mr. Astaire. Would you ask him to come out so we can dance "*The Big Apple*" for him."

"I'll see if he's available," the butler said. Minutes later Astaire appeared to the delighted squeals of the gaggle of girls.

"I understand you want to demonstrate some dance moves for me." He said. "Let's see what you've got."

The girls began to gyrate to the dance's steps and were soon joined by Astaire. A few minutes later his wife Phyllis stepped out to say, "Come Freddie, We must get going." Obediently, he got into the car and they drove off. However, all the excitement was not over. Another car pulled out of the driveway to follow the Astaires. The driver was Randolph Scott. They were going to Palmetto for a round of golf. Scott's latest film High, Wide and Handsome was appearing at the Patricia Theater in downtown Aiken. Scott and his wife, noted horsewoman Marion DuPont, owned a home in Camden, S.C.

Mr. Astaire assiduously kept his personal and private lives separate. He seldom sat for interviews and avoided the press at all costs. He broke that pattern on one of his visits to Aiken when he granted an interview to George Karger of Life Magazine. He consented to several photographs as well. One showed him onstage at the Patricia Theater in Aiken recreating scenes from his latest film Second Chance, as the movie unfolded on the screen behind him. In another scene, Karger had Astaire do a routine with Fred, Jr. who was five at the time.

Astaire also displayed his talents on the grounds of Palmetto Golf Club where he had arranged several paper squares on the tenth hole marking his practice dance steps. He had not yet seen the issue of Life with Karger's pictures and he asked if anyone in the crowd had. An anonymous face pushed forward to show it to him—and ask for his autograph.

Fred Astaire and Ginger Rogers

Mrs. Astaires's aunt had retained Eulalie Salley's landscaping company to maintain her gardens at "Prickley Pear." Eulalie was working on the design one morning when a tall, slender man walked down from the house to meet her.

"Do you mind if I talk to you about the garden?" he asked her, without introducing himself.

Eulalie took that as a clue that she shouldn't introduce herself either. She later remarked that he had the biggest feet she had ever seen and that he seemed a little clumsy coming down the steps. However, the visitor was polite and charming and seemed to enjoy chatting with her. He appeared again the next two mornings to resume the conversation, still without introducing himself. The fourth morning he appeared again, this time in the company of Mrs. Bull.

"Mrs. Salley, do you know to whom you have been talking each morning?" Mrs. Bull asked.

"Well, I suppose he is Fred Astaire, but I don't know," Eulalie said.

"Yes," Mrs. Bull replied. "He said at breakfast this morning, 'Do you know that lady has never introduced herself and she has never asked me for my autograph?'"

The Astaires continued their visits to Aiken until 1946 when "Prickley Pear" burned. It was never rebuilt. Phyllis Astaire died of lung cancer in 1954 leaving a devastated Fred. He was filming Daddy Long Legs at the time and felt he couldn't complete the movie. He offered to pay for the costs of canceling the film. The producers declined his offer but left the door open. Astaire finally realized that he couldn't give up both his wife and his career and came back to finish the film.

Fred Astaire remained single until 1980 when he married Robyn Smith, a jockey 45 years his junior. Robyn had ridden for the Alfred Vanderbilt stables. Fred maintained his interest in horses and racing during his single years. His horse "Triplicate" won the Hollywood Gold Cup and the San Juan Capistrano Stakes. Despite their age difference, the couple was devoted to each other. Fred Astaire died of pneumonia in 1980. Throughout his career he had refused to have a movie made of his life. He stipulated in his will that one should never be done. He said the clause was there, "because he didn't want his life to be misinterpreted, and it surely would be."

38
The Years Between

The Salleys settled into their new home at "Edgewood" on Kalmia Hill during the middle of the Depression. The devastating effects of that economic calamity, coupled with the costs of moving and renovating "Edgewood," had left the couple in dire financial straits. Undaunted and with the help of her secret benefactor, Eulalie forged ahead to rebuild her real estate business. Julian's fortunes recovered as well. His legal work for the county, the railroads, and his wealthy Winter Colony clients, helped him to restore his own solvency. However, it soon became apparent that Eulalie's income from real estate, antiques, landscaping and insurance was far outstripping her husband's. Not to be outdone, Julian used his knowledge of the mushrooming number of distressed property sales created by the Depression, together with Eulalie's money, to amass land holdings throughout the area. Searches of real estate transactions and property transfers during that period are replete with the names of Julian and Eulalie Salley. Many properties bought for as little as ten dollars were later sold for thousands. The names of many Winter Colony residents also appear in the tax records during that period, indicating that the Salley's maintained their close relationships in that community by spreading the wealth around. Several transactions were joint acquisitions with other names on the deeds such as Louise Hitchcock, Hope Iselin and Marie Gilbert.

It was during this period that Eulalie formed a company with her sister Mattie Hall and Dr. George McMurphy of Charleston to develop Kalmia Hill. The Kalmia Company systematically accumulated properties from Hayne Avenue to the top of the hill overlooking the Horse Creek Valley. From her "Edgewood" vantage point at the summit of Kalmia Hill, to the red brick hospital building in the eastern distance, Eulalie and her partners accumulated vast amounts of acreage. Among the tracts they bought were the original estates of William Gregg as well as their paternal grandfather, Otis Chafee. They began to subdivide the property into parcels of an acre or larger. Despite criticism that such large lots were a waste of valuable land, they plowed ahead, creating a much sought after neighborhood for the growing, upper middle class of Aiken.

An earlier developer had wanted to establish a racetrack in the area. Facetiously, Eulalie named two of the streets Saratoga and Belmont. The Kalmia Company dissolved in the late 1930's when Dr. McMurphy moved to North Carolina, and the contentious relationship that had always existed between the two sisters led to a parting of their ways shortly thereafter.

Mattie had married Dudley Hall of Boston in 1907, when she was 18. Upon his death in 1922, after fifteen years of marriage, Mattie returned to Aiken—she never liked life in Boston and had come back to live with Eulalie and her mother every winter. With her inheritance she was now independently wealthy. She dabbled in real estate with Eulalie and later formed her own company. She died childless in 1961, leaving her million dollar estate to care for the indigent of Aiken.

The social life of Aiken in the late 1930's still revolved around the comings and goings of the Winter Colony. There were still hunts and rides and carriage parades, and grand parties. The younger generation eschewed the more Spartan ways of their parents. Each new entrant vied to build a bigger and more ostentatious cottage. Cottages were still being bought, and sold, and built. But there was an almost imperceptible shift in the character of the times. There was an undercurrent of inevitable change in the air. Many of the second and third generation colonists were no longer making Aiken their priority. With modern trains and reliable air travel, a world of choices had opened up to the moneyed set. Resorts in Florida and California began to lure the affluent away. Palm Springs and Palm Beach were as easily accessible as Aiken. Homes on the Costa del Sol and the Cote d'Azur were an easy plane ride away. Aiken was changing, and it would never again regain the luster and prestige it had once held.

The Depression had already slowed the migration of wealth to Aiken, but the single catastrophic event that signaled the end of the golden era was Pearl Harbor. The nation was now on a war footing, and the fun and frivolity associated with the Winter Colony seemed awkward and inappropriate to a nation whose young men were going off to fight and die. The sons of Aiken from all walks of life were going to join them. George Mead would make the supreme sacrifice on a sandy spit of land in the Solomon Islands called Guadalcanal. Tommy Hitchcock would die in the fiery crash of a P-51, trying to make the plane safe for other airmen. A landmine in Aachen, Germany killed Charles von Stade. Other names on the war memorial in downtown Aiken, from David Alexander to John Zielinski, may have been less notable but were no less mourned by the loved ones they left behind to grieve and to imagine what might have been. Among those who served and then returned to take his place in the life of Aiken was Julian Salley, Jr.

Julian was born in 1912 and followed in the footsteps of his father. He graduated from The Citadel and then went on to the University of South Carolina for his law degree. With his Phi Beta Kappa key proudly affixed to his tie-clasp, Julian joined his father in practice at the Aiken law firm of Henderson and Salley.

His life as a small town barrister was rudely interrupted on December 7, 1941. His Uncle Sam needed him. Julian's training as a cadet at the Citadel landed him an officer's commission and, as a tank commander, he was soon following General George Patton's Third Army Division across Europe.

The war years were a time of great anxiety for Julian and Eulalie. Their only son was caught up in the great crusade raging across Europe. Letters flowed back and forth between mother and son. Between the lines each fully understood the peril Julian was facing and yet they managed, through the artifice of deflection, to lift each other's spirits. In the midst of unspeakable battlefield carnage, Julian was hungry for news of the events at home as a reminder of the normalcy he had left behind and to which he hoped to return. Eulalie longed to know that her son was safe and well. Their letters became a lifeline sustaining both of them until the seemingly eternal nightmare finally ended.

One of the most poignant letters Eulalie wrote to Julian was dated June 6, 1944, when she presumed that her son was being swept up in the great invasion of Fortress Europe.

June 6, 1944
Darling,

So this is D-Day. After Roosevelt's speech last night, tho he did not say anything about it, I felt the zero hour was at hand. Early this morning when I turned on my radio, there was the news. It certainly gave me a very strange and dreadful feeling – mingled with one of relief. I don't believe that anything has ever happened that creates as many conflicting emotions. I am proud to have you in the front lines, for surely you must be there. My thoughts and my prayers will be with you every moment. The whole nation seems to be on its knees tonight. Early in the morning Ronald Colman read beautifully a prayer by some woman whose name I did not get. This was followed by one written and delivered by the President. All radio programs have been thrown to the winds and war news comes in every five minutes. If they would only tell me where you are and that you are safe! May God

keep and protect you. May he give you the ability to give the greatest aid to this noble cause and above all, may he carry you through this ordeal by fire and bring you back a better and finer man to a mother who loves you so dearly.
Affectionately,
Mother

Eulalie could not know that Julian's tank unit would not cross the channel for a week after the invasion. Her prayers were answered. Julian was part of the great liberating force that rolled across Germany to free Europe from the clutch of the mad man, Hitler.

When the war was over, Julian retired as a Lieutenant Colonel and returned to Aiken where he resumed his position with Henderson and Salley and where he would remain for 50 years. For 22 of those years he served as Aiken County attorney. He was also prominent in many service organizations as well as a member of the Hitchcock and Whitney Foundation boards.

The strain of the Depression years and the oppressive burdens of war wore heavily on Julian Sr. Taciturn by nature; he often internalized the things that Eulalie was able to express more openly. His health began to wane. He died of cancer in 1951.

Eulalie continued to run her businesses even though the vagaries of advancing age began to slow her to an extent. Life now afforded her more opportunity to enjoy her children and grandchildren. Her daughter Eulalie had married Thomas Pinckney Rutledge, descendant of three of South Carolina's most storied families, the Rutledges, the Pinckneys and the Laurens. They had a daughter, Salley (Carr).

Julian Salley married Helen Hoblett of Bloomington, Illinois. They had one daughter, Sarah (Wood). Helen died in 1989. Julian then married Johnatha Todd who died in 1999. Julian died in 2005 at the age of 93. Between his father's death in 1951 and Eulalie's in 1975, Julian was an ever present and stabilizing force in his mother's life.

39

The Cold War and the Bomb

On November 28, 1950, leading members of the cities of Aiken and Ellenton, South Carolina were called to a meeting in Aiken. The subject of the meeting wasn't revealed in the invitation. Upon their eleven o'clock arrival at the meeting hall they were introduced to several members of the Atomic Energy Commission and E. I. DuPont de Nemours Company of Wilmington, Delaware. There was a puzzled look on the faces of the local participants. The puzzle was soon solved.

President Harry Truman had received an appropriation of $260,000,000 from congress to establish a facility in the United States to produce fissionable materials for a hydrogen bomb. The task of deciding where to build the plant was given to the DuPont Company. DuPont had been the prime contractor in the highly classified Manhattan Project which was housed under the football stands of the University of Chicago's Stagg Field. That project led to the development of the atomic bombs that were dropped on Hiroshima and Nagasaki, Japan, ending WWII. The bombs had been assembled at a remote plant in Hanford, Washington under the aegis of DuPont, following their successful tests in the Nevada desert.

J. Robert Oppenheimer, frequently called the father of the atomic bomb, is reputed to have quoted from the Bhagavad Gita, a Hindu scripture, upon witnessing the destructive power of the first test, "*Now I am become death, the destroyer of worlds.*"

The urgency of the program that created the Savannah River Project had its roots in the escalating cold war that was developing between Russia and the United States.

Klaus Fuchs, a refugee German scientist and communist sympathizer who had fled from Germany to England before the war, was sent to work on the Manhattan Project at Los Alamos, New Mexico. While Fuchs, secretly a communist sympathizer, was contributing significantly to the development of the atomic bomb, he was simultaneously scheming to funnel to Russia all the information necessary for them to build an atomic weapon.

Through Harry Gold and Julius and Ethel Rosenberg, Fuchs was able to smuggle all the documents the Kremlin would need to build a nuclear bomb. Undetected, Fuchs returned to England where he worked for their atomic energy agency until his treasonous activities were discovered. The extent of his treachery was not fully comprehended until 1949 when his secret messages were finally decoded. Fuchs then confessed to MI-5, the British Intelligence agency. The genie was out of the bottle. Russia exploded its first atomic weapon on the remote steppes of Kazhakstan in August of 1949. The USSR had become a nuclear power. Fuchs served nine years in an English prison before being traded to East Germany in a spy swap. Harry Gold served half of a thirty-year sentence and was released in 1965. Julius and Ethel Rosenberg were executed for treason.

In a letter to President Greenwalt of DuPont on October 20, 1950, President Truman very succinctly stated his reliance on Du Pont to get the job done.

"Dear Mr. Greenwalt: *October, 20, 1950*

I appreciated very much your letter of the seventeenth, regarding the contract for the Atomic Plant. I am sure you will do a good job, and that is all that I ask.

Sincerely yours,
Harry Truman"

When Du Pont was given the green light it took only four months for them to select a site for the Nuclear Development Facility. They looked all over the country for a location that was similar to the three previous facilities developed by the AEC: Hanford, Oak Ridge and Los Alamos. The AEC and Du Pont relied heavily on extensive studies that had been conducted by the Army Corps of Engineers.

The determinant criteria were:

1. Vulnerability to attack
2. Various operating requirements (which were classified)
3. Accessibility to population centers
4. Public health and safety
5. Availability of suitable land
6. Availability of large quantities of water
7. Navigable river for transport of heavy reactor components

The 310 square miles in South Carolina, containing the towns of Ellenton, Hawthorne, Meyers Mill, Dunbarton, Leigh, Robbins and Snelling, came closest to meeting all the criteria. The land lay in parts of three counties; Aiken, Barnwell and Allendale.

Ellenton - 1950

There were approximately 5,000 residents in the identified territory of 200,000 acres or about one human being for every 40 acres. That population was almost exclusively dependent on agriculture for its livelihood. Many of the residents were black sharecroppers and tenant farmers who received very little compensation for the disruption of their lives.

170,000 acres would be preserved as primary forest, providing a buffer around the central reactor building sites. 16,000 acres would be devoted to the industrial complex that would house the five planned reactors. 14,000 acres would be devoted to research facilities.

Two of the prominent local members at that fateful meeting were H. M. Cassells, a merchant in Ellenton, and Odell Weeks, mayor of Aiken. Upon hearing what was about to transpire, Mr. Cassells immediately pledged the full cooperation and support of the town of Ellenton to the project.

"We will cooperate with you to the fullest and we heartily welcome this project to this area. I sincerely believe that the people in and around Ellenton will cooperate also."

Mayor Weeks echoed the comments of Mr. Cassell. He assured the representatives that Aiken would cooperate and do its part to welcome the "Bomb Plant."

Had both men known the calamitous disruption that SRP would bring to their communities they might not have been so eager to welcome it to the area. 5,000 people were about to have their lives turned upside down as they were forced to abandon homes that had been in their families for generations. Today only the concrete foundations of a few downtown buildings mark the spot where Ellenton was once a thriving farming town of several hundred inhabitants. As one resident described it,

First came the politicians to hold our hands.
Next came the assessors to place a value on our property.
Finally came the law to evict us.

Someone in the audience remarked that Aiken was about to become the "Oak Ridge" of the South — that person needed a lesson in geography — Oak Ridge is in Tennessee, and long considered part of the South.

The residents of the area received a total of $19,000,000 for their 200,000 acres and the improvements thereon. The timber alone was estimated by some to be worth $38,000,000. A hand printed sign along the highway in Ellenton spoke volumes about what the people were giving up,

"It is hard to understand why our town must be destroyed to make a bomb that will destroy someone else's town that they love as much as we love ours. But we feel that they picked not just the best spot in the US but the best spot in the world. We love these dear hearts and gentle people who live in our Home Town.

Someone remarked that Ellenton's epitaph should have been,

"They gave their town so that civilization could survive."

Among those forfeiting their lands were Fitch Gilbert, who gave up his 10,000 acre plantation; W.R. Grace, whose 7,000 acre preserve was absorbed; and Julian Salley, who gave up his beloved Bent Lake. One of the few indulgences he allowed himself was the weekly fishing trip to his little hideaway. He used the solitude and the peacefulness of the lake to recharge his batteries—and in all probability to gird himself for his trials with Eulalie.

In August of 1951, three supervisors and 120 interviewers arrived in Aiken to begin the process of recruiting the 8,000 men needed to construct the Savannah River Project. Over the next twelve months 73,000 men were interviewed.

Contractor John Robbins was selected by DuPont to build four mini-cities for the influx of workers. Each site was composed of several hundred trailers. The highways around Aiken were crawling with convoys of house trailers. In addition, the towns of Aiken, Augusta, Barnwell and Williston received 1000 trailers. DuPont originally charged $82.50 per month for the trailers, including utilities. This fee to the workers was later reduced to $66, with the Atomic Energy Commission picking up the difference of $22.50.

Private trailer parks sprang up all over the area to house another 18,000 people. A village of several thousand trailers lined Pine Log Road. Aiken, with a population of 7,000 people in 1950, swelled almost overnight to more than double that number. The impact on schools, hospitals, utilities, roads and the infrastructure in general, was staggering. However, the population coped and even flourished.

The local economy, so accustomed to subsisting on the largesse of the Winter Colony, had begun to decline with the onset of WWII and the diminution of visits by the colonists. The SRP infusion of money allowed the surrounding communities to mount a strong comeback. The new residents began to participate in the local affairs. They helped to start a community theater and other civic and professional organizations. At its peak, SRP employed more than 28,000, mostly engineering and research types. At one point, more PhDs were employed by SRP than in the remainder of the entire state of South Carolina.

One anecdote concerns the efforts of Eulalie Salley to make the newcomers feel at home, while offering them her real estate services. She had built a trailer park in an area off Whiskey Road, that she called Oak Hill. That area later became known as New Ellenton. One of her tenants came to Mrs. Salley's home on Kalmia Hill. The visitor was invited into the library of "Edgewood."

"What is that?" the woman asked Eulalie, pointing to the ornate fireplace.

"What?" Eulalie said, puzzled.

"That, that with the fire in it."

"My dear. Have you never seen a fireplace? Where did you grow up?"

The woman explained that she had grown up in trailers, moving from job to job with her father. She had married a construction worker and never had a real home.

"Oh, I wish everyone at Oak Hill could see your beautiful home."

"They may. Why don't you bring them for tea one day?"

"What time should we come?" the visitor asked.

"Why don't you come about four?" Eulalie responded.

"That's too late," the woman replied. "We have to be home and have supper waitin' for our men folks at five."

"What time would you suggest?" Eulalie asked.

"How about two?"

"Whatever you say."

On Tuesday, the women came dressed in their Sunday finest—some even in evening gowns—and were invited into the parlor. They sat on the fancy furniture and hardly spoke a word, they were so intimidated by the magnificent surroundings. Both Eulalie and her daughter tried in vain to engage the women in conversation but to no avail. The women refused to relax. Finally Eulalie excused herself and went into the dining room where the punch bowl was located. She proceeded to empty a bottle of Jack Daniel whiskey into the punch then came back to announce that tea would be served in the dining room. Fifteen minutes later the women were chattering like magpies. They had such a grand time that they stayed until after five.

Epilogue

In the 175 years of its existence, the small southern town of Aiken, nestled snugly in the nurturing sand hills of South Carolina, has been tempered in the crucibles of three great wars.

The flourishing agrarian society that created such wealthy planters as the Salley's and the Gamble's in the 18th and 19th centuries, was decimated by the great Civil War and the oppressive reconstruction period that followed. Out of the ashes of that conflict grew a community that attracted great wealth from the north—wealth that had been amassed during the industrial revolution of the last half of the 19th century.

The period of great wealth consolidation continued following the turn-of-the-century, but was interrupted by World War I. The failure of the Allies to create a lasting peace with Germany, together with the excesses of that era, combined to sow the seeds of its own destruction. An insignificant, little known, corporal in the Austrian army was already inciting the next world-wide conflagration. The crash of Wall Street, and the Great Depression that ensued, ushered in harsh economic times for the citizens of Aiken. The Winter Colony itself survived basically intact, but there was a perceptible shift in its influence and importance in the lives of the community. The world was changing and Aiken was not immune to the effects of that change.

World War II, when the little Austrian corporal's excesses exploded on the world stage in the person of Adolph Hitler, marked the end of the golden era of Aiken's Winter Colony—that fifty-year period, from 1890 until 1940—when over 200 "cottages" were constructed and countless multitudes came to enjoy the pleasures of Aiken. The war itself didn't destroy the Colony, but it unquestionably set in motion events that would alter it forever. Pearl Harbor signaled the end of America's innocence. The nation could no longer sit in secure isolation behind the two great oceans that safeguarded it from the rest of the world. Like it or not, the United States had emerged as the single power capable of saving the world from Hitler's fascism and Stalin's communism. There could be no turning back. The movers and shapers of the world who had called Aiken their own were now urgently needed in war rooms and on far-flung battlefields. The effects of that war were every bit as overwhelming to the long term fortunes of Aiken as the great Civil War had been. The Yankee wealth was leaving and there were not enough *summer blackberries* to sustain the community they were leaving behind.

Nonetheless, Aiken would rise again like a great Phoenix from the ashes. For the same Great War that had ended one period of her splendid history would usher in another. If it is true that, *it is an ill wind that blows no good,* then the ill winds rising from the Great Steppes of Kazakhstan blew clear across the world, depositing their good fortune on Aiken's doorstep. The Cold War manifested itself for Aiken in the form of the Savannah River Project, a development that boosted the general economy of the entire Central Savannah River Area and largely replaced the losses of a diminishing Winter Colony for Aiken.

Through it all one person was front and center, bearing witness to history, and in many instances actively working to shape that history—Eulalie Salley. The life of Eulalie Salley is a testament to the impact that a single, dedicated and courageous citizen can have on the world. Her history is inextricably interwoven with that of the little village she so dearly loved. The Aiken that she left behind, upon her death in March of 1975, would be a vastly different place had she not passed this way, and those who have followed in her footsteps would be much the poorer for it.

The End

Acknowledgements

Ms. Sarah Wood - Her contributions of time and content were of tremendous help in telling the story of her grandmother, Eulalie Salley. Her insights, memories and anecdotes were invaluable in telling the story of this remarkable woman.

It would have been impossible to write this story without the wonderful biography of *Eulalie* written by Ms. Emily Bull Cooper in 1973, while she was a member of the staff at the *Aiken Standard.* Ms. Cooper compiled the information for her book during a series of interviews with Eulalie in 1973, just two years before her passing. Ms. Cooper now resides in Columbia, S.C. and continues to write about the rich history of that period.

Ms. Constance Myers conducted interviews with numerous pioneers of the women's movement while compiling her *Oral Histories of the American South.* Her conversations with Eulalie Salley ranged across a broad spectrum of Eulalie's involvement in that movement and her enormous contribution to it. Listening to these tapes, made when the lady was 90 years old, makes one marvel at the keen intellect and saucy wit of Eulalie, undimmed by the passage of time.

Mr. Henry (Henk) Salley, Julian Salley's cousin, added many personal reminiscences of the Salley family and their interconnection to the community. To him I am very grateful.

Mr. Elliott Levy, Ms. Mary White and Ms. Brenda Barrato allowed full and complete access to the archives of the Aiken Historical Museum at Banksia. The treasure trove of books, essays, photographs and exhibits there were critical to the success of this undertaking. Thank you.

Ms. Deidre Martin, Vice-Chancellor of University Advancement at USC Aiken was very supportive. She made key documents available to me and referred me to other valuable sources of information.

The on-line archives of the *Aiken Standard* and its predecessor newspapers contributed_an abundance of articles and photographs that were critical to a fuller understanding of Eulalie Salley and her times.

To all the others who shared their memories of Eulalie and the Winter Colony with me, I thank you. Your contributions added immeasurably to the completeness of the story.

Finally, to my long-suffering wife, Sydney, I thank you for your patience, understanding and keen editorial advice.

PROSE PRESS
The origin of the word prose is Latin, prosa oratio, meaning straightforward discourse.

Prose Press is looking for stories with strong plots. An affordable, quality publishing option with guaranteed worldwide distribution.
prosencons@live.com

CPSIA information can be obtained at www.ICGtesting.com
Printed in the USA
LVOW08s1017300416

486053LV00001B/3/P